LAW AND MENTAL HEALTH

Law and Mental Health

A Case-Based Approach

ROBERT G. MEYER
CHRISTOPHER M. WEAVER

THE GUILFORD PRESS
New York   London

©2006 The Guilford Press
A Division of Guilford Publications, Inc.
72 Spring Street, New York, NY 10012
www.guilford.com

Printed in the United States of America

This book is printed on acid-free paper.

Last digit is print number: 9 8 7 6 5 4 3 2

Library of Congress Cataloging-in-Publication Data

Meyer, Robert G.
  Law and mental health : a case-based approach / Robert G. Meyer,
Christopher M. Weaver.
      p. cm.
  Includes bibliographical references and index.
  ISBN-10: 1-59385-221-5   ISBN-13: 978-1-59385-221-4 (hardcover :
  alk. paper)
  1.   Mental health laws—United States—Cases. 2.   Insanity—
Jurisprudence—United States—Cases. 3.   Forensic psychiatry—
United States—Cases.   I. Weaver, Christopher M. II. Title.
  KF480.A7M49 2006
  344.7304′4—dc22

                                                   2005022588

About the Authors

Robert G. Meyer, PhD, is a Full Professor in the Department of Psychology at the University of Louisville. He received an MA and PhD from Michigan State University, is board-certified by the American Board of Professional Psychology in both clinical and forensic psychology, and is a fellow in Divisions 12 (Clinical) and 41 (Law and Psychology) of the American Psychological Association. Dr. Meyer is the author of over 60 published articles, 23 book chapters, and 14 books, including *The Clinician's Handbook: Fifth Edition* (with Christopher M. Weaver); *The Child Clinician's Handbook, Second Edition* (with William G. Kronenberger); *Case Studies in Abnormal Behavior, Seventh Edition; Law, Behavior and Mental Health* (with Steven Smith); and *Preparation for Licensing and Board Certification Examinations in Psychology.* He is past editor of the *Bulletin of the American Academy of Forensic Psychology,* a past-president of the Kentucky Psychological Association, and former associate member of the Ethics Committee of the American Psychological Association. He received the regional Grawemeyer Award (with Steven Smith) from the University of Louisville for innovative curriculum development for their course in law and psychology, and was recently presented with the Distinguished Career in Psychology Award—the highest honor of the Kentucky Psychological Association.

Christopher M. Weaver, PhD, is currently serving as a Research Fellow at the University of California–San Francisco (funded by the National Institutes of Health), where he extends his professional service and research to include training psychiatry residents in effective risk assessment and risk communication techniques. He received an MA and PhD in Clinical Psychology from the University of Louisville, where his research focused on the assessment of psychopathy and recidivism risk in sex offenders. He also received the Grawemeyer Fellowship Award for outstanding psychology research while at the University of Louisville, where he continues collaborative research with the Kentucky Department of Corrections. Dr. Weaver is coauthor (with Robert G. Meyer) of the *The Clinician's Handbook, Fifth Edition,* and has also published in the areas of sexual addiction, execution of offenders with mental retardation, and professional issues in forensic psychology. He has served as assistant editor of the *Bulletin of the American Academy of Forensic Psychology,* and has authored or coauthored over a dozen presentations at professional conferences.

Acknowledgments

We first acknowledge the many undergraduate and graduate students who had a hand in helping put this book together, and we extend special thanks to Luciano Tristan for his work in the initial development of the text. We also thank Julie Nelson, Chelsea Rothchild, and Eric Annala for their assistance in researching and drafting the material, and Corey Pallatto for her editorial assistance and development of the teacher resources for the text. We next thank the following for their significant work on respective chapters: Gina Arnett (child abuse), Scott Forbes (jury selection and process), Mary Hundley (civil commitment and dangerousness), Sonia Mills (juvenile law; personal injury), Julie Oliver (competency), and Michelle Duling (addiction and drug abuse). Last, but not least, we thank Jim Nageotte, Senior Editor at The Guilford Press, for helping mold the book into its current form—with which we are most pleased.

Contents

Chapter 21 Child Abuse   334

Chapter 22 Child Custody   349

LAW AND MENTAL HEALTH

Introduction
Law and Mental Health

This book is written for advanced students and professionals in the mental health fields. Our focus is a broadly defined region of interface between the legal system and mental health issues. Our concentration is not specifically "forensic mental health," nor is it "mental health law." The former suggests instances when mental health professionals intentionally do work related to the legal system, while the latter seems inclusive only of law that dictates the general practice of mental health services. In addition to these areas, we have included topics (i.e., capital punishment) in which the relationship is less readily apparent, but in which the legal and mental health fields have much to learn from each other.

DEFINING MENTAL HEALTH

We define *mental health* broadly to include clinical practice areas (e.g., duty to warn, confidentiality) and more purely "forensic" topics (e.g., criminal responsibility, personal injury). More research-oriented (as opposed to "clinical") areas are also discussed (e.g., the admission of expert testimony on eyewitnesses). As many mental health practitioners can attest, most of these areas can have an impact upon virtually any mental health client. Children are often subject to psychological testing in schools; adult clients may be the subject (on either side) of a personal

1

injury suit, and so forth. Understanding topics such as "mental compe-tency" and "jury selection" can serve to round out one's knowledge base, thus increasing efficacy as a practitioner, not to mention readiness for the ever-looming possibility of legal involvement.

Social science research forms the foundation from which all ethical and well-informed clinical mental health pursuits emanate. The two are (or should be) inextricably linked. Research drives practice, which in turn creates questions and necessities for more research. Thus, there is commonality among all those involved in mental health–related endeav-ors, from basic behavioral animal research to the treatment of attach-ment problems in child survivors of physical abuse.

That having been said, mental health–related disciplines are clearly not the *same*. There are differences among mental health subspecialties in terms of both population focus and philosophical underpinnings. Psy-chiatry *is* especially partial to the medical model. Psychology *does* place more emphasis on psychometric testing, and marriage and family coun-selors *do not* tend to focus on treating the individual. However, they are *all* concerned with mental health.

WHY STUDY LAW AND MENTAL HEALTH?

Issues of law and mental health significantly affect each other. Laws relating to mental health licensure, malpractice, and limitations on human experimentations are a few examples of the ways in which the law directly affects mental health practice. At the same time, the law is increasingly dependent on the mental health professions and the behav-ioral sciences. Mental health professionals commonly participate in a wide range of judicial and administrative proceedings. Examples in-clude cases concerning emotional injuries, involuntary civil commit-ment, and child custody, to name but a few. It is also likely that social sci-ence research will continue to inform the development of the law. Professional organizations, such as the American Psychiatric Association and the American Psychological Association, are frequently called upon by courts to express their opinions on various topics.

A second reason for the study of law and the mental health profes-sions is that they seek to solve common problems. Practitioners in these fields often serve the same clients and patients, and their research inter-ests are often closely related. Dealing with child abuse and violent behavior and detecting deception are examples. In seeking solutions to social problems, the disciplines of law and mental health can and do inform each other both in practice and in research.

These common concerns of the two professions suggest a third reason for studying them together: Both raise similar fundamental philosophical questions concerning the nature of human behavior. For example, the free will–determinism debate is of great importance to the mental health professions and to many aspects of the law. Do people really *choose* what actions they take? Clearly, some people with severe mental illness cannot. Yet a fundamental assumption of the law is that people are punished for acts they *chose* to commit. At what point do people cease to have a choice in their actions? Interdisciplinary consideration of these and other, similar debates often provides a special perspective that differs from that provided by a single discipline. It also produces an interesting opportunity to challenge the commonly accepted principles (and sacred cows) of both disciplines.

ROLES MENTAL HEALTH PROFESSIONALS PLAY IN THE LEGAL SYSTEM

[An expert] is somebody who is more than 50 miles
from home, has no responsibility for implementing
the advice he gives, and shows slides.
　　　　　—Former Attorney General Ed Meese

Today, the mental health professional may in fact assume a number of roles within the legal system. Those who purposely involve themselves in the legal arena may be referred to as forensic mental health professionals. Psychiatrists and psychologists first developed board certification procedures in the forensic practice of their respective professions only in 1978, quite late relative to other specialty areas. Mental health professionals' participation in the legal system has since increased exponentially, and it appears that the effects of that growth will not abate any time in the future.

Expert Witnesses

Only recently have most mental health professionals been allowed to testify as experts. Traditionally, physicians were the only "qualified" experts in the area of mental health issues. Any physician was considered qualified to testify in any area of medicine, including psychiatry. This practice could be taken to the extreme, because even an obstetrician or proctologist could be qualified to discuss a mental health issue, while a psychologist or social worker would not be allowed to testify.

This era has passed, and psychologists, social workers, and other mental health professionals now regularly testify. The current position generally accepted by courts reflects recognition of the level of training and knowledge of nonphysician mental health professionals. Rules of evidence concerning the minimum qualification of expert witnesses have been modified accordingly. The weight that should be given to testimony by experts varies depending on the jury (or judge) and on the nature of the testimony presented. For instance, psychologists are not typically called upon to testify about the administration of drugs.[1] Psychiatrists are similarly seldom expert in the evaluation of psychological test data.

The role of an expert witness is to assist the jury (or sometimes the judge) with special knowledge or understanding that the jury does not have. In fact, the inability of laypeople (i.e., jurors) to understand the relevant topic is typically a prerequisite to the admission of the expert into the courtroom. Given their mastery of the field in which the testimony will be offered, expert witnesses may express opinions, as well as present facts, that might not be observable by the layperson. For instance, an expert forensic clinician may determine that someone who appears completely insane is actually faking or malingering psychological disorder (Boyd, McLearen, Meyer, & Denney, 2006). While an expert witness may be hired by either side in a legal dispute, or directly by the judge, the expert's task is to be unbiased.[2]

Forensic Consultant

The role of consultant in forensic cases is also a common one. Mental health professionals often provide legal participants with information in jury selection, preparation of direct and cross-examination questions, review of treatment records, procurement of appropriate expert witnesses, recommendations for packaging and sequencing of evidence,

---

[1]This specific example will most likely change, subsequent to the passage of a 2002 bill in New Mexico that allows psychologists to prescribe certain medications, although it may only have an impact upon testimony in jurisdictions that pass similar legislation. Louisiana has now passed a similar bill.

[2] By *unbiased* we mean that the job of experts is to perform the duties expected of them without consideration for which legal party (prosecution, defense, or even judge) hired them. For example, an assessment of a defendant's sanity should yield the same results whether the prosecution (who is arguing against insanity) or the defense (who is arguing for insanity) did the hiring. As one might well imagine, this is an aspirational goal and not always seen in practice.

and courtroom jury monitoring. Other consultant functions may also be performed.

RESEARCH AND DECISION MAKING
IN LAW AND MENTAL HEALTH

As will become evident throughout this text, there are difficult unresolved problems involving the very natures of the legal and mental health fields (English & Sales, 2005). At the heart of these difficulties lie differences in how the two respective fields acquire basic knowledge and reach decisions. Is cognitive-behavioral therapy (CBT) more effective than drug treatment in treating depression? Are anti-sodomy laws constitutional? Can one rely on the testimony of eyewitnesses? Either or both fields may be interested in these questions, but the information-gathering and decision-making processes used by each field are different. There are three broad approaches available to resolve such questions: the analytical, the empirical, and the philosophical.

The Philosophical Method

Philosophical research is similar to analytical research, with the exception that the analyses and arguments are filtered through some position or philosophy (e.g., morality, republicanism). Philosophical studies involving law and the behavioral sciences have received too little attention but are an essential part of progress in both fields. Ultimately, philosophical positions define what the law will be and the direction it will take.

The Analytical Method

An analytical method applies logic and reasoning to sometimes contradictory evidence to determine what has happened (as in the case of a trial). Those employing analytical research methods may also evaluate existing law and propose reform based on the logical application of existing social policy. It is through analytical research that reforms can be formulated and proposed. Analytical research has been the traditional form of research in law.

The Empirical Method

Empirical research, which employs various types of scientific experiment and measurement, has been a mainstay of behavioral science for

BOX I.1. How the Three Research and Decision-Making Methods May Address the Question "Is Cognitive-Behavioral Therapy (CBT) More Effective Than Drug Treatment in Treating Depression?"

Method	Research approach	Decision-making approach
Philosophical	May rely on preexisting philosophical opinions, or may include a review of relevant arguments before adopting a new philosophical standpoint.	Based on the belief that behavior should not be treated with mind-altering drugs, CBT is preferable to drug treatment.
Analytical	Two opposing sides call experts to offer opinions and call people who have firsthand knowledge of the treatments to testify.	An expert testified in favor of CBT and seemed more qualified than another expert who favored drug treatment. Witnesses testified about the efficacy of both treatments, but those who had received drug treatment described some negative reactions. Taking all of this into account, CBT is favorable.
Empirical	Depressed people were randomly assigned to receive either CBT or drug treatment. Depressive symptoms were measured before and after the treatment.	Those receiving CBT showed a significantly larger decrease in depressive symptoms than those who received drug treatment. CBT is better at reducing depressive symptoms in this population.

decades but has also gathered considerable momentum in recent years within the realm of legal scholarship; much of the focus of empirical research has been on examining how legal and social services systems work, with some other efforts directed toward experimental studies designed to test basic assumptions and tenets of the legal system and any proposed reforms. See Box I.1 for a description about how each of the three methods addresses one of the questions posed earlier.

Controversy and Complementarity among Methods

The legal and mental health fields were founded on different views as to which research and decision-making method is best. Indeed, this may be a function of the types of tasks with which each profession deals. An empirical approach may provide a more accurate answer to a particular question as applied to the specific individuals who were studied, but the results may apply only to that or a similar group (Grisso & Vincent, 2005). The legal profession cannot afford the luxury of conducting empirical research that would apply to each individual who comes through a courtroom.

It is the mental health professions' almost exclusive reliance on empirical knowledge that is the source of much turmoil between the legal and mental health fields. By its very nature, empirical research rarely (if ever) resolves an issue with absolute certainty. There are always caveats and confounds when one tries to apply the results of empirical research to real life. A skilled attorney may be able to get a mental health clinician to focus on these uncertainties, thereby undermining the clinician's credibility with the judge and/or jury. Yet, in the views of the mental health profession, a clinician who acknowledges the limitations of his or her knowledge is actually *more* credible than one who makes absolute claims in the absence of data.

Our disciplines will undoubtedly be strengthened by a continued reliance on all three of these approaches to research and decision making. Such interreliance is fostered and enhanced by the interdisciplinary efforts that have characterized some of the research in law and the behavioral sciences in recent years. The size and importance of the questions with which these disciplines must deal require legal research and reasoning, empirical research with sound statistical analyses, solid philosophical footings and direction, and the creative interaction of *all* disciplines involved (i.e., law, psychology, sociology, etc.).

However, it is from the differences in these approaches that the legal and mental health fields (indeed, the legal and many other fields) can seem so at odds with each other at times. There are legal decisions that seem to make no sense from the standpoint of a social psychologist (i.e., unwavering reliance upon eyewitness testimony), and courts can often be frustrated with what they perceive to be wavering testimony by a mental health practitioner who is merely appropriately explaining the limits of certainty of his or her testimony. We also see this phenomenon on a smaller scale when students (or practitioners) of law and mental health participate in joint training. Law students struggle with questions that seem to have no concrete answer (commonplace to the mental health practitioner or student), while students in mental health programs have relative difficulty distilling facts to arrive at a clear ultimate decision on a matter (a task at which law students excel). While frustrating at times, these different perspectives are also the source of rich discourse and ingenious compromises, the synergy of which is often much better than either field could have accomplished alone.

We have now defined the scope of this text: to look at the case law in areas of interplay between the fields of mental health (as broadly defined earlier) and law. But before we can begin to look at case law, we need to understand the legal system as a whole.

AN OVERVIEW OF THE LEGAL SYSTEM

Courtroom: A place where Jesus Christ and Judas Iscariot would be equals, with the betting odds in favor of Judas.
—H. L. Mencken, American essayist

Central to the U.S. legal system is the division of powers among the legislative, judicial, and executive branches of government that the framers wisely embedded in the Constitution. Most states also follow this general schema, and the most common label of a law relates its branch of origin. *Statutory laws* are written by state legislatures or by the Congress. *Case law* is made as courts interpret statutory laws. Court decisions clarify the statutes and so effectively become part of the law. For example, a particular state-licensing statute may fail to mention whether licenses from other states will be honored (known as reciprocity). If a court in that state interprets the statute as disallowing reciprocity, then that decision has the same effect as if the legislature had explicitly disallowed it in the original statute. Nonreciprocity becomes a part of the state's case law. Of course, the legislature could then choose to modify the law to allow reciprocity, or the original court's decision could be appealed to a higher court. Courts strongly value the concept of "precedent" of relevant past court decisions. Changing a legal standard by overturning a precedent can have adverse effects. To minimize this, courts try to rely on the reasoning of earlier decisions when possible and to leave well-settled ideas undisturbed, a doctrine known by the Latin term *stare decisis* (to stand by a decision).

Jurisdiction and the Appellate Process

Jurisdiction is an essential component of both federal and state law. The term *jurisdiction* describes a court's power to hear and decide a case, and is defined by statute or constitutional provision. There are several types of jurisdiction, the most important of which include original, appellate, and subject matter jurisdiction. Original jurisdiction implies that a court has authority to hear and decide a case, usually when first filed. Appellate jurisdiction means that a court has authority to review, and possibly overturn, a case already decided in a lower court. Appellate courts generally review cases at their discretion; while people have the right to appeal lower court decisions, the appellate court may refuse to review the case. Subject matter jurisdiction means that the court is qualified by statute or the Constitution to hear a particular type of case. State courts have jurisdiction for cases concerning state laws. Federal courts have jurisdiction concerning federal laws.

Trial courts are a state's general court of original jurisdiction. Most serious matters are heard here. Many states find it useful to have specialized trial courts to hear only civil or only criminal matters. Some states further establish subject matter jurisdiction for courts that will serve other highly specialized roles (e.g., family courts, to handle divorce and custody proceedings).

State criminal courts deal with the prosecution of persons accused of violations of the criminal law. Criminal laws pertain to those behaviors that are specifically prohibited, and in general, behavior that is not specifically mentioned in criminal code is not prohibited. Criminal law includes both misdemeanors (generally less serious offenses) and felonies, and can be conceptualized as prohibiting acts that are so problematic they represent an affront or threat to society. In contrast, civil law deals with private rights and remedies. It attempts to resolve wrongs between citizens, including civic groups. Some significant areas of civil law include torts (civil liability), contract law, and family law. Many issues in the arena of law and mental health come under state law, but, unfortunately, one mark of state laws is their lack of uniformity between different states. Some areas of law are a crazy quilt of incompatible legislation, while others, influenced by broader, nationwide trends, may be quite consistent.

In the federal system, the general courts of original jurisdiction are district courts. Each state may have one or more districts, and large districts may even have more than one division. Each district is administered by a federal magistrate and a federal district court judge. Appeals from federal courts are handled by 14 circuit courts of appeal, plus one for the District of Columbia. These courts may review decisions by district courts within their jurisdiction, review orders of many administrative agencies, and issue some original writs in appropriate cases. The U.S. Supreme Court has limited original jurisdiction and may exercise appellate jurisdiction over district and circuit courts, and the highest courts in each state; that is, the course of appeal from a state supreme court would be directly to the U.S. Supreme Court. Figure I.1 portrays the hierarchical direction of legal appeals typical in the United States.

The appeals process may seem straightforward; if one is dissatisfied with a lower court ruling, he or she can appeal to a higher court. In practice, the legal maneuvering is much more complicated. Often appeals merely lead to orders that a court of original jurisdiction hold a new trial, reconsider some matter under new guidelines, or refrain from some action. Also, when appeals under one rationale no longer seem likely to succeed, it is at times possible to start back with new appeals at a lower level, with a new rationale. For example, a criminal defendant could assert that new evidence had come to light that was not available in an earlier trial. Thus, many cases traverse a torturous process of appeals before they are resolved or settled. Very important, precedent-setting cases often have a rich history all their own.

Standard of Proof

A *standard of proof*, as required by the due process clause of the Fourteenth Amendment, is the degree of confidence society thinks the fact finder should have in the correctness of factual conclusions for a particular type of adjudication. The three most common standards of proof, in increasing degree of the necessary definitiveness of the evidence, are (1) *preponderance of evidence*, which applies to most civil cases; (2) *clear and convincing evidence*, which demands more cogent evidence to be produced; and (3) *beyond a reasonable doubt*, which is the required standard of proof in criminal cases.

In addition to the standard of proof, the U.S. legal system operates on a foundation of rules and regulations that is unparalleled by any other working legal system. The most fascinating and dynamic means by which these rules evolve are through case law.

CASES AND CASE LAW

In the context of this book, the word *case* carries with it a dual meaning. A *case study* in mental health terms means a particular example of a client presented for the purpose of explaining or representing a broader phenomenon. In legal terms, a *case* is a particular legal proceeding. The rulings contained in legal cases constitute *case law*, which is used to define legislative and constitutional law, as well as to refine (or redefine)

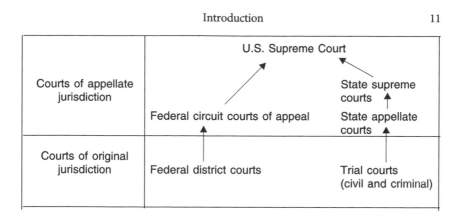

FIGURE I.1. The hierarchy of legal appeals.

previous case law. Thus, in such a manner, the law as a whole takes its shape and is put into practice. Therefore, for the purposes of our text, *case* refers both to the specific examples presented (i.e., case studies) and to the legal proceedings (i.e., legal cases) that provide precedent within their respective topic areas. Before we delve into these cases in detail, we must first start with the basics.

Case Law: What's in a Name?

Much can be learned about a legal case merely by examining its name. To begin with, in most instances, the court case represents an adversarial undertaking in which one side is pitted against another side. Each side can have one or more parties involved. A *party* in this sense may be an individual, a group of individuals (as in a class-action suit), a company or other organization, a state, or even a country. Thus, we are provided with the general format for the labeling of most court cases: *Party 1 versus Party 2*, or as typically abbreviated, *Party 1 v. Party 2*, an extension of which could easily be *Parties 1–7 v. Parties 8–14*. In the latter instance, the case would probably be referred to merely as *Party 1 v. Party 8* for the sake of simplicity.

An examination of the parties in a case name offers more information. First of all, the party names indicate whether a case has been undertaken in criminal court (when a crime has been committed) or in civil court (when a wrong has been committed by one party toward the other party). In criminal cases, typically, one of the parties is the government that originally made the act illegal. Thus, a murder committed in violation of state law by a Mr. Meyer could take on the name *West Virginia v. Meyer*, or *Commonwealth*[3] *v. Meyer*, or even *People v. Meyer*. These labels mean essentially the same thing: that the state and Mr. Meyer are opposing parties in the case. The logic here is that the offense was committed against the people of the state, and their representatives: the state government. Notice that the government (the party that was allegedly wronged) is named first. Depending on the jurisdiction and the nature of any appeal, subsequent court proceedings stemming from this initial case may have the parties transposed (i.e., *Meyer v. State*). Should a criminal case be appealed all the way to the U.S. Supreme Court, the actual name of the state would take the place of the generic term *State*. Since such cases typically involve the allegation that the state infringed upon the constitutional rights of the other party, the case name typically takes a form such as *Meyer v. Kentucky*, implying that the wrong was committed against Mr. Meyer by the Commonwealth of Kentucky. If a federal criminal charge were brought against Mr. Meyer, the case might be initially labeled *U.S. v. Meyer*, with the party that was allegedly wronged being the United States of America as representative of all of her citizens.

Civil court cases employ a similar naming structure, except that there may not be any government involved as a party to the case. For instance, in a case where Mr. Meyer alleges that Mr. Weaver committed some wrong against him, the name of the case would be *Meyer v. Weaver*. If Mr. Weaver then wanted to countersue for damages resulting from a frivolous lawsuit, the new case would be known as *Weaver v. Meyer*. An interesting phenomenon may take place when an individual wants to sue a government body for perceived wrongdoings, because that government may actually be immune from such a lawsuit. In these instances (or perhaps when an attorney merely feels he or she will be more successful in this manner), a case may be brought against a government official (i.e., Governor or Attorney General) instead of the actual state. Such was the case in the long string of Texas legal proceedings known collectively as *Penry v. Lynaugh* (1988), in which Lynaugh was the State Attorney General, and Penry was a man appealing his death

---

[3] Some of the 50 states (i.e., Kentucky and Pennsylvania) continue to refer to themselves as Commonwealths rather than States. While there are undoubtedly some subtle legal distinctions between the two, they are considered synonymous for the purposes of this text. As in another of the examples, some states include *The People of the State*, commonly abbreviated as *People*, as a party in a criminal act to reflect that the alleged crime was committed against the people of the jurisdiction themselves.

sentence. Thus, there may be several unrelated cases from Texas in which Lynaugh was a party, not because the Lynaughs are particularly litigious people, but merely because of the governmental status of one particular Lynaugh. The most recent case in this particular example, *Penry v. Johnson* (2001), reflects a change in the Texas Attorney General's office. A similar example is seen in the Pennsylvania cases of *Halderman v. Pennhurst* (1977) and *Romeo v. Youngberg* (1980), in which Youngberg was the superintendent of the Pennhurst institution, and Halderman and Romeo were individuals alleging that the institution had infringed upon their rights. As such, both Pennhurst and Youngberg represented essentially the same party. Because several iterations of any case may take place, individual proceedings are sometimes only distinguishable by the year in which they were decided (i.e., *Meyer v. Weaver* [1990] and *Meyer v. Weaver* [1993]); thus, we attempt throughout this text to delimit specifically this aspect of each case.

An interesting variation on the naming of a case takes place within the realm of juvenile law. In cases of particularly heinous acts committed by someone under the age of 18, the individual may be transferred to adult court. Once there, the standard rules of adult court (including the naming) apply. However, when a case remains in juvenile court, a fundamental assumption changes in that the proceedings are no longer considered adversarial in nature. Thus, a juvenile case may involve no "versus," because it is assumed instead that all parties involved are seeking a common goal: a result in the best interests of the juvenile. An example of this labeling system is seen in the landmark Supreme Court case *In re Gault* (1967), with *In re* being Latin for "in the matter of" or "concerning." Thus, *In re Gault* was a legal proceeding "concerning" a young person by the name of Gault. Another form of label that may signify that a case involves a juvenile is the use of initials, meant to maintain the anonymity of the juvenile to the extent possible. An example of this type of label is seen in the juvenile law case *Parham v. J. R. and J. L.* (1979). Other attempts at maintaining juveniles' anonymity have included briefly summarizing the case rather than using any form of the juvenile's name. Such an attempt resulted in our last and most amusing example, the 1966 case of *Two Brothers and a Case of Liquor* (as cited in *In re Gault*, 1967).

The Importance of Historical Case Law

The field of forensic mental health and, more broadly, the interplay between professionals in mental health and legal settings, is expanding almost daily. With increasing specificity in practice, increased complexity of knowledge, and expansion of each field into realms traditionally considered under the purview of the other, many of the underlying tenets of the two professions are being called into question, at least implicitly. Considering that the two fields frequently disagree in terms of concepts, methodology, and basis of knowledge, it is no surprise legal and mental health professionals look askance at one another.

Despite the cultural divide between the two fields, there is merit for those in mental health to study the cases that have established legal precedent that pertains to their work and interests, and that have drawn (for better or for worse) on the scientific advances made in the behavioral sciences. In most accounts of these cases, however, the fascinating and sometimes tragic details, and the impact each case had on the participants, is lost.

This book brings those details back to light, and brings them to bear on the legal and mental health issues as they exist today. As we progress through this text, we hope the reader will be able to comprehend more fully the process by which mental health and law currently interact.

About This Book

In seeking our arguably wide-sweeping approach of "law and mental health," we are necessarily limited in the amount of discussion that can be afforded to the basics of each topic area (e.g., research on jury decision making). Thus, this text assumes some familiarity on the reader's part with each of the topic areas, be it through professional knowledge or concurrent instruction. We have not attempted to provide a foundation of knowledge in forensic mental health topics. Rather, we have designed this book to complement such a foundation.

Chapters in *Law and Mental Health* are grouped into seven parts: Psychological Issues and Involvement in Basic Courtroom Proceedings, Legal Precedent in Everyday Clinical Practice, Clinical Forensic Evaluation, Civil Rights and Civil Law, Specific Mental Diagnoses in the Law, Violent Criminals and Violent Crime, and Juveniles in the Legal System. The text introduces readers to basic information needed to comprehend the development of the case law in each subject area and expands on individual cases within each area. Readers are provided with an overview of case law on each topic, as well as the details of each expanded case (typically two per chapter). The text presents both the histories of the individuals involved in each expanded case and the impact that each continues to have on the respective areas as we know them today.

Readers of *Law and Mental Health* are presented with a wide variety of legal cases. Cases range from the classic, such as the 1966 *Miranda v. Arizona*, which established the *Miranda* rights read to all suspects upon arrest (i.e., "You have the right to remain silent"), to the contemporary, such as the 2002 case of *Atkins v. Virginia*, in which it was deemed unconstitutional to execute offenders with Mental Retardation. Cases also vary in terms of their exposure in popular media, the breadth of which is exemplified in the cases of Timothy McVeigh (convicted of bombing the Murrah Federal Building in Oklahoma City) and James Batson, whose case established legal precedent regarding racial discrimination in jury selection. Topics covered range from psychological profiling to personal injury to prisoners' rights.

Upon completion of *Law and Mental Health*, readers should possess a solid fundamental knowledge of the temporal progression of case law in each area. We hope the text not only presents a comprehensive and important review of legal and mental health material but that it also does so in a manner that is both thought provoking and enjoyable to read.

The text employs a modular construction, in that chapters may be read sequentially or otherwise, depending on a reader's preference or an instructor's assignment. We provide enough information in chapters that the reader will be able to understand and make sense of the cases they comprise. Yet we also explain the interplay between topics presented in subsequent and previous chapters.

Legal and mental health scholars have written extensively about the similarities and differences between these two parent fields, most noticeably with respect to the gaining and the application of knowledge. This difference of perspective often leaves legal and mental health professionals misunderstanding each other and, in many circumstances, dismissing each other. As an example of such a circumstance, we offer the area of criminal psychological profiling. Despite its "psychological" (or sometimes "behavioral") label, it is rarely performed by any mental health professionals, and almost never by forensic psychologists. Profiling is usually undertaken by law enforcement officials, with a dabbling here and there of sociologists, criminologists, and psychiatrists. In fact, forensic psychologists do not look favorably upon the topic at all, and we acknowledge that its inclusion in this text may be seen as suspect by many in that subfield. Yet we have chosen to include it not only because of its appeal to law enforcement and related fields but also to assert that the scope of "law and mental health" is wider than some may want to admit. For the flaws in psychological profiling should not be cause for its dismissal, but rather should call it under *increased* scrutiny. Dismissing the topic of profiling, when forensic psychology as a field has the resources and the knowledge to contribute and improve upon the practice, may be every bit as egregious as law enforcement continuing to practice it in the absence of adequate research to support it.

Profiling is happening *right now*. Judges are *right now* disallowing expert testimony based on misconceptions and confusing testimony. Mental health clients are *right now* engaged in death penalty trials and personal injury lawsuits. Children are being abused and parents are engaging in heated custody battles *right now*. These are all areas in which mental health has something to say to the law, and the law has something to say to mental health professionals. This discourse takes place every day in courts of law throughout the country. If we are to hear and understand this conversation, then we must learn the language of the legal system: case law. Case law is the tie that binds this book together.

THE STUDY OF LAW AND MENTAL HEALTH: THE TIME IS NOW

Maintaining the judicial and criminal justice systems that provide the foundation for modern U.S. society is a task of almost unimaginable magnitude. Complicating the picture, the United States has one of the world's highest per-capita imprisonment rates. Unlike other systems in society, such as financial or medical systems, the legal system has no method of accountability and no way of determining whether it effectively finds the truth. Due to the power of a trial judge to dictate proceedings, there is in essence no standard procedure. A system without standard procedure is (at least) difficult to research.

> In the trial of the century, the specter of mistrial arose when it was reported that some jurors, in between recesses and sidebar conferences, might have heard some actual testimony. An angry Judge Ito sternly told them to disregard it.
>
> —Dave Barry, "Windows on the World,"
> *Miami Herald*, December 31, 1995

Any inadequacies in our legal system are exacerbated by the high incidence of mental illness among those who are typically the focus of legal proceedings. Although no one agrees on an exact percentage, our reading of the literature leads to a consensus estimate that approximately 20% of the general population suffer from some form of significant mental disorder during their lifetime (Meyer, 2006). The prevalence of mental disorder among those involved in the legal system is even higher.[4]

In contrast, mental health fields benefit by having the legal system as an external check on and guide for standard practices. We hope that this book not only delineates this process but also inspires students in the mental health field to work toward effecting positive change and growth in the legal system. We believe our readers have a lot to offer.

---

[4] Different studies in this area may arrive at widely divergent estimates of the percentages of mentally ill offenders in prison, primarily due to varying definitions of mental illness. While a review of this literature is outside the scope of the current text, all studies we have seen corroborate the increased prevalence of mental disorder in the legal system over that in the general population.

PART I

Psychological Issues and Involvement in Basic Courtroom Proceedings

Throughout this text, we discuss in detail the legal proceedings that have led to important precedent in key areas in which psychologists and other mental health professionals are likely to be involved. Each court case typically involves at least one fact finder (judge or jury) and numerous *fact* witnesses. Cases in which mental health professionals are most interested may also involve one or more *expert* witnesses. In reading through these cases, keep in mind that even the most basic proceedings of each case are dictated by a long history of *previous* cases.

In this first section, we review the procedures by which jurors and witnesses enter the courtroom, and the precedent behind these procedures. In Chapter 1 we examine the law that relates to the creation and functioning of a jury. Many mental health professionals consult with attorneys regarding the selection of jurors. Legal precedent applies to those who conduct research on jury behavior, in that studies are set up to reflect actual courtroom proceedings. And the research may in turn inform participants in the trial (i.e., mental health consultants), or inform lawmakers in reforming laws that pertain to jury functioning. In Chapter 2 we address the means by which someone may be qualified to testify in the role of an expert witness, and explore some of the special circumstances that apply to expert witnesses. We also discuss a specific type of fact witness, the eyewitness, because eyewitness testimony is itself a subject of expert opinion.

CHAPTER 1

Jury Selection and Process
Precedent Impacting Jury Consultation and Research

In all criminal prosecutions, the accused shall enjoy the right to a speedy and public trial, by an impartial jury of the state and district wherein the crime shall have been committed. . . .
                    —Sixth Amendment to the U.S. Constitution

A jury consists of twelve persons chosen to decide who has the better lawyer.
                    —Robert Frost

The right to a trial by jury has been with American citizens since the ratifying of the Bill of Rights on December 15, 1791. This most sacred of rights guarantees a buffer of peers between defendants and public officials. While most defendants may waive the right to a jury trial, opting instead for a judge to be the trier of fact, the right to a trial by jury is unwavering (see Box 1.1 for an interesting caveat). However, such was not always the case.

THE HISTORY OF THE JURY

Roman law often used a "citizen judex" system, under which a man of some standing and a few of his colleagues would accept a referral from a magistrate, informally hear the case, and render a decision. However,

---

BOX 1.1. Trial by Jury: A Right or Requirement?

The right to a trial by a jury of peers is an essential component of the American legal system. However, it is not uncommon for defendants to waive this right if they believe that a judge may see their side more favorably than would a jury. Such a waiver is particularly common in cases that involve a lot of legal technicalities. For instance, if a defense attorney believes that she can successfully challenge a confession by her client, it may not matter if the jury becomes aware of the confession at all. However, a judge may better be able to ignore the confession in rendering a verdict. Furthermore, an individual judge may simply be more predictable than an entire jury. The point is that it may well be a significant benefit to a defendant to waive a jury trial.

However, in the 2002 case of *Ring v. Arizona*, the U.S. Supreme Court ruled that only a jury may impose a death sentence on a defendant. Imposition of the death penalty requires that aggravating circumstances exist in the particular case, making the appropriate punishment beyond that of the "typical" murder. In *Ring*, the Court ruled that the Sixth Amendment to the U.S. Constitution required a *jury*, not a judge, to determine whether or not aggravating circumstances exist in a case. The Court struck down an Arizona law by which a judge could individually establish that aggravating circumstances exist and subsequently sentence a defendant to death.

---

such courtliness did not immediately catch on throughout Europe. In 12th-century England, a legal dispute could be settled by opposing parties fighting in some ordeal. A favored form of trial by ordeal in England was the "drowning pool"; if the accused sank, it was an indication of guilt. If still alive, he or she could be pulled out for further interrogation. If applicable to the particular ordeal, a wealthy or powerful individual could hire a "champion" to represent him. This tradition is an early precursor to the use of attorneys that we see today. Also in medieval England, many trials by ordeal took place during a high point of the church mass. In fact, this form of legal proceeding only faded out when the church forbade priests to participate.

THE REQUIRED NUMBER OF JURORS

Scandinavians had long used tribunals based on committees of 12. But the true trial by jury was established in England in A.D. 725 by Morgan of Glamorgan, Prince of Wales, who wrote, "For as Christ and his Twelve Apostles were finally to judge the world, so human tribunals should be composed of the king and twelve wise men." Thus was born the standard of 12 jurors. The Magna Carta of 1215 then later guaranteed jury trials as a right. The Elizabethan Act of 1562 established the concept of perjury, and the practice of jurors obtaining information from witnesses during trial rather than from other sources.

Many of the basic tenets of the jury process developed in Europe were brought to the American colonies, where they were adopted into American law. The number of jurors, while typically 12, continued to be worked out in legislation and case law into the 1970s, as the U.S. Supreme Court addressed the issue of the minimum number of jurors required to ensure a fair trial. In *Williams v. Florida* (1970), the court decided that a six-person jury was constitutional and that the Sixth Amendment did not guarantee a jury of 12 persons. What it did not do, however, was establish a minimum number of jurors. In *Ballew v. Georgia* (1978), the Supreme Court established six as the minimum number of jurors necessary. The following year, in *Burch v. Louisiana* (1979), the court rethought this decision and ruled that juries smaller than six persons are allowable. However, juries of five or fewer need to agree upon any rulings unanimously. Juries of six or more persons may disagree, at least to some degree.

JURY SELECTION: ACCEPTANCE THROUGH ATTRITION

While the phrase "jury selection" is typically applied to this process, it is fairer to say that potential jurors are excluded until the appropriate number remains. Thus, rather than selecting jurors they want, attorneys select jurors they *do not* want and try to get them excused from further consideration.

The Jury Venire

The first step in the process is the acquisition of a jury panel, or venire (Kovera, Dickinson, & Cutler, 2003). The venire consists of several individuals who have been called for jury duty. The number may vary, but a typical size is around 30 or 40. The selection process for the venire members varies by jurisdiction but may include searches through voter registration, vehicle licensing, phone listings, or other means. The venire typically gathers in the courtroom, whereupon individual venire members may ask to be excused from jury duty for hardship reasons, and so on.[1] By this time, members of the venire have typically filled out rather extensive questionnaires that catalog demographic variables, and may include questions that the attorneys have requested.

The Voir Dire

The judge and/or attorneys for either side may ask questions of the venire members. This process is known as voir dire, meaning "to say the truth."[2] Based on responses to any or all of these questions, attorneys may then seek to exclude certain venire members from further service. An increasingly common example of such a concern is the level of media exposure that a prospective juror has had to the case. Requests for exclusion are known as challenges. A challenge toward a venire member may take one of two forms: a peremptory challenge or a challenge for cause.

Challenges for cause are the most straightforward type. An attorney who is able to show (or the judge is able to discern) that any venire member holds some type of bias or prejudice toward one side or the other may argue to the judge that the juror should be stricken for cause. The ultimate ruling comes from the judge, and there are typically an unlimited number of strikes for cause allowed. Examples of reasons why someone may be stricken for cause include a venire member stating that he or she would in no circumstances be able to hand down the death penalty in a capital case, or perhaps stating that he or she is a relative, friend, or acquaintance of the defendant or victim.

Peremptory challenges or strikes may be exercised at the discretion of either side, with a few exceptions (more on the exceptions later). Attorneys rarely have to give any indication as to why they chose to use a peremptory strike on a venire member. However, given that these strikes carry with them very little accountability as to their use, the judge limits the number of peremptory strikes prior to starting voir dire. While the number of strikes varies between jurisdictions, a typical number of peremptory strikes is 10 per side. As an extra protection for the defen-

---

[1] The judge may grant excuses for hardship for circumstances, such as the presence of small children in the home or even prearranged vacation plans.

[2] Those readers knowledgeable about the French language may recognize that the literal translation of voir dire is "to see, to say." However, its use in the modern courtroom harkens back to the Old French definition of *voir* (also seen as *voire* or *voier*), which meant "truth" or "truly," itself derived from the Latin *verum*, meaning "truth." Thus, the meaning "to say the truth" illustrates the basic assumption that venire members will truthfully divulge any beliefs or preconceptions they may hold that could inappropriately hinder their participation in the trial process.

dant against community prejudice, the defense is usually offered more peremptory strikes than the prosecution. Either side may use a peremptory strike on a venire member if the judge refuses to grant a strike for cause. In fact, it is a common tactic among trial attorneys to first attempt to strike for cause, in the interest of saving precious peremptory strikes.

The voir dire process continues in this manner, until there are enough venire persons left to constitute the jury (and, in some jurisdictions, alternate or backup jurors). Should too many venire members be stricken to empanel a jury, an additional venire may be brought in from which to select the remaining jurors. Those who remain have been "selected" to make up the jury for the trial.

Scientific Jury Selection

How then do attorneys decide which venire members will be most harmful or beneficial to their side? Traditionally, attorneys trusted their experience, intuition, and legal folklore for picking members of the jury. For example, an assumption may be that someone employed in a mental health field (prototypically very liberal) would be somewhat prodefense in certain types of cases (i.e., involving the death penalty). Thus, a prosecutor may seek to exclude the juror, while a defense attorney may try to elicit an answer to some question that makes the prosecutor favor the juror. All of this and more may take place based solely on the *assumption* that a mental health worker would be prone to favor the defense. Nevertheless, many attorneys have developed belief systems based on previous experiences at trial, anecdotes and gossip, and/or logic and common sense to form a body of lore that constitutes what could be termed "prescientific jury selection." It is not a random procedure; it is just not entirely scientific either.

Social scientists began to focus on some of these assumed phenomena, since many of the assumptions could be tested empirically. For instance, an experiment could be designed to determine whether conviction or acquittal could be predicted based upon field of employment (e.g., to test whether mental health professionals refuse to give the death penalty). Through such means, an industry has sprung up in which some mental health professionals[3] offer themselves as consultants to attorneys

---

[3] While it varies by specific field, such consultation may be considered clinical practice (with the attorney as a client). Thus, for instance, a social psychologist who has researched jury selection all of his or her life may not be legally considered qualified to offer such consultation, because he or she is not eligible for clinical licensure.

for the purpose of picking out potential jurors that may be favorable (or unfavorable) to their side. This is the process referred to as *scientific jury selection.*[4]

Most agree that the advent of scientific jury selection began with the trial of the "Harrisburg Seven," a group of Vietnam-era antiwar activists indicted for conspiracy, including a plan to kidnap then presidential advisor Henry Kissinger (Kovera et al., 2003). Social scientist Jay Schulman and his colleagues commandeered an army of volunteers (seldom available for most trials) that carried out approximately 1,000 phone interviews and established that an original concern that the public would already be against the defendants was unfounded. They followed this up with 250 in-depth interviews to determine juror variables that would be favorable to their cause. The researchers established that the prototypical ideal juror for the case was a female Democrat, with no clear religious persuasion, who held a skilled blue-collar or white-collar occupation. The trial eventually ended in a mistrial and was perceived as a validation for the jury selection process, because predictions had heavily favored a guilty verdict.[5]

THE CASE OF THE MITCHELL–STANS CONSPIRACY TRIAL: THE IMPORTANCE OF CONSISTENT JURY SELECTION PROCEDURES

An early, well-known case that involved some atypical jury selection was that of John Mitchell and Maurice Stans. The two men were accused of conspiring to impede the Securities and Exchange Commission's (SEC) investigation of Robert Vesco, himself a participant in the Watergate scandal (Zeisel & Diamond, 1976). Two characteristics of this case were atypical. One was the fact that both defendants were members of President Richard Nixon's cabinet. John Mitchell had been the Attorney General, while Maurice Stans had served as the Secretary of Commerce. There had been quite a bit of publicity because of their high-profile

---

[4] Volumes have since been written on the topic. For those interested in reading about the topic in more depth, a timely review of scientific jury selection is offered by Kressel and Kressel (2002).

[5] What if the Harrisburg Seven had not been able to afford the jury selection consultants? According to predictions, they may indeed have been found guilty and sentenced. Thus, the outcome of the trial was arguably more dependent on their assets than it was on their guilt or innocence. Is this fair?

positions in the administration. Besides the public nature of their jobs, they had also testified, along with their accuser, John Dean, in front of the Congressional Watergate Committee that had investigated the whole ordeal. Because of the amount of coverage the case had received, the judge insisted that the jury be sequestered.[6]

The other atypical issue (for that time) that made this case unique was the fact that the defense counsel had employed a type of scientific jury selection, similar to that described earlier. In this case, a popular opinion survey had been employed. The results were then used to support the motion for a change of venue (when either side requests that the proceedings be moved to another jurisdiction, away from a potentially biased jury pool). When this motion was denied the defense decided the information from the survey could help to aid in selecting jurors.

The use of surveys to aid in jury selection had only emerged in the few years leading up to the *Mitchell–Stans* trial. Before then, it was more or less unheard of and had only reached the media in two other cases, the trial of Reverend Phillip Berrigan in Pennsylvania and that of Dr. Angela Davis in California. Jury selection had seemingly been helpful in these two cases, but the method used depended on an almost unlimited supply of politically motivated volunteers; hence, it was not applicable to most trials.

Any employment of scientific jury selection was somewhat of a gamble at the time because of the lack of research demonstrating its effectiveness. However, the defense consultant was able to come up with a profile of the "worst possible juror": "a liberal, Jewish Democrat, who reads the *New York Times* or the *New York Post*, listens to Walter Cronkite, is interested in politics and is well informed about Watergate" (Zeisel & Diamond, 1976, p. 167). The vast majority of people believed that this would be an open-and-shut case for conviction given the amount of evidence against the two defendants.

Mitchell–Stans Jury Selection

There were three stages of questioning (voir dire) in the *Mitchell–Stans* jury selection process. During the judge's introduction, he informed the

---

[6] Sequestration can take many forms, the most stringent of which is when jurors are bused from the courtroom to a secured hotel and allowed little to no communication with the outside world, until they are transported back to court the following day. This process continues until the trial is over. As one can imagine, it is both very expensive for taxpayers and very taxing on the jurors themselves. Thus, it is avoided at all costs and only used under extreme circumstances.

potential jurors that the trial was expected to last 5 or 6 weeks, and that they would be sequestered if selected to sit on the jury. He then called for jurors to whom this would cause undue hardship. In the second phase of questioning, the jurors were asked publicly to give personal information, including any involvement they might have had with the federal government, legal proceedings of any kind, and the nature of their record of military service if they had one. In the next phase of the selection, members of the jury pool were interviewed individually in the judge's chambers by the judge, the prosecution, and the defense. Here, they were asked about their political involvement, their knowledge of the Watergate scandal, and to what types of media they were regularly exposed (i.e., Walter Cronkite). During these three stages of questioning, 144 of the original 196 were dismissed for hardship, incapacity to serve on the jury, or prejudice toward one side or the other, leaving 52 prospective jurors in the pool.

Under the Federal Rules of Criminal Procedure, the laws that dictate procedure in federal court, the defense was allowed 10 peremptory strikes compared to the prosecution's six. However, in an effort to compensate for all the one-sided, pretrial publicity, the judge allowed the defense 23 peremptory challenges and allowed the prosecution 11. The defense used all of its challenges, while the prosecution ended up using only six. Interestingly, the demographic breakdown of the final jury did not change from that of the original venire with regard to race, sex, or age. Nor did it change regarding the jurors' political party registration. But had the jury pool been representative of the population in general, affording the defendants a "jury of their peers"?

Of concern was the lack of randomization in the selection of the jury pool. Ninety-five percent of the jury had surnames that came from the first half of the alphabet. While it is unlikely that people from any given part of the alphabet would be biased toward either side of a legal case, it demonstrated that there had been a problem in the selection. According to Zeisel and Diamond (1976), the chances of randomly selecting this ratio of names is 1 in 100 million. Under the law, an entire jury can be challenged on the grounds of violation of selection procedures. Nevertheless, no specific procedural violation could be demonstrated, and the trial proceeded as planned.

Mitchell and Stans at Trial

The judge in this trial had predicted the case would last 5 to 6 weeks, but it actually lasted for 10. The media followed the testimony very intently. During the first weeks of the trial, one of the jurors became very ill and had to be replaced. This is where the trial would take an interesting turn.

The jury's initial vote at the beginning of deliberation was 8 to 4 for conviction. However, an alternate juror by the name of Andrew Choa was yet to have his significant impact. Most interesting, Choa should never have made it past voir dire. As a man interested in politics, a *New York Times* reader, and well informed about Watergate, the defense should have seen him as undesirable according to the "profile." The fact that the defense had wanted him on the jury should have prompted the prosecution to exercise one of its remaining peremptory challenges to strike him. As it turned out, Choa was a Republican who had made a small campaign contribution to Nixon. Thinking this indicated favoritism toward the defendants (both members of Nixon's administration), the defense agreed to keep him, and the prosecution did not object. When an original juror fell ill, Mr. Choa was drawn from the list of alternates.

Andrew Choa was the Vice President of First National City Bank, and his presence during the trial and deliberation seemed to influence the entire jury. During the 10 weeks at trial, he routinely used his position at the bank to arrange for the jury to have time outside of the hotel in which they had been sequestered. He would have them come to the bank's private theater for movie screenings, and he arranged for them to view the St. Patrick's Day parade from a window of the bank (meaning they could see the parade without having to mingle among the crowd). The other jurors may have felt obliged, even unconsciously, to the man that had broken the monotony of their sequestration so many times. In deliberations, Mr. Choa personally had several pieces of evidence reread to the jury. His comments came down heavily for the defense, such as the time he referred to a memo that was particularly damning to the defense as "trash."

The high-profile nature of the scandal, the higher number of peremptory challenges and especially Mr. Choa's presence on the jury may have all pushed the case's outcome in the direction opposite to what was expected when the trial ended with an acquittal. Authors on the subject (Zeisel & Diamond, 1976) likened this conversion to that in the movie *Twelve Angry Men*, in which Henry Fonda's character succeeds in persuading the rest of the jury to acquit after an initial vote for conviction. With the help of scientific jury selection, the case is widely cited as clear evidence that jury selection may drastically alter the outcome of a trial.

INDIVIDUAL FACTORS IN JURY SELECTION

The jury process, from voir dire to deliberation and verdict, is subject to all kinds of influences, including judges' instructions, courtroom procedures, unanimity requirements, and even characteristics of individual jurors. One important characteristic is a juror's race or ethnic background.

Race and Juries

Beginning in 1880 with *Strauder v. West Virginia*, it was established that a state law allowing only Caucasian males to serve on juries was unconstitutional based on the due process clause of the Fourteenth Amendment. It was asserted that a state denies a black defendant equal protection of the laws when it puts him or her on trial before a jury chosen from a venire from which members of his race have been excluded by law. However, it did limit this decision only to those *summoned* for jury venire, not to those *selected* to serve on the final jury.

Eighty-five years after *Strauder*, toward the end of the Jim Crow era in the South, another important decision was made regarding juror race. *Swain v. Alabama* (1965) became a precursor of sorts to the next case that we review, in that *Swain* was the first U.S. Supreme Court ruling on the exclusion of jurors based on race once they had been selected for the jury venire. The defendant's counsel in *Swain* was easily able to prove a systematic exclusion of African Americans on trial juries over a period of time, because there had never been an African American on *any* civil or criminal jury in the entire history of Talladega County, Alabama. The Supreme Court overruled the Alabama courts' decisions, stating that it would be constitutionally impermissible to allow a prosecutor to employ peremptory challenges systematically and consistently to prevent African Americans from serving on juries, without any regard to the circumstances of the particular case in question. To allow this would be to allow the denial of African Americans the right and opportunity to participate in the administration of justice enjoyed by Caucasians. Yet rulings consistently protected the right of attorneys to make peremptory challenges without stating any reason. Justice Marshall offered the seemingly naive explanation, "We have no reason to believe that prosecutors will not fulfill their duty to exercise their challenges only for legitimate purposes" (*Batson v. Kentucky*, 1986, p. 14).

Clearly (and perhaps luckily) Justice Marshall's blind trust was not felt by all courts. A commonly cited ruling that challenged this naivete came over two decades later in the case of *Batson v. Kentucky*. Despite precedent in over 100 years of like-minded rulings, the case illustrates the ongoing tension surrounding the issue of race in our legal system.

THE CASE OF *BATSON V. KENTUCKY* (1986): JUROR RACE IN JURY SELECTION

In the early 1980s, a house in Louisville, Kentucky was burglarized. While the case began in a manner similar to the hundreds of other break-ins, the fallout of this particular burglary was soon to have an impact upon the civil rights and legal policies of the entire nation.

The woman whose home was burglarized reported that she had seen an African American male in the front room of her house taking several purses. Her neighbor had also noticed a man loitering around the front of the house earlier in the day, and stated that she [the neighbor] had seen the same man fleeing from the back of the victim's house shortly before the police arrived. Later that same day, James Batson was arrested after being identified by both the woman in the house and the neighbor as the man that they had seen inside and around the home. The purses, which had contained jewelry and other easily identifiable personal items, were found near Batson's residence. Batson and another man had also pawned two rings that had belonged to the burglary victim earlier in the day.

Batson at Trial

James Batson and his codefendant were brought to trial in the Circuit Court of Jefferson County. He was charged with second-degree burglary and possession of stolen property. During the jury selection, the prosecuting attorney used his peremptory challenges to strike all four African Americans from the jury pool to ensure that the jury selected would comprise Caucasians only. James's legal counsel then moved to discharge the jury. Citing the Sixth and Fourteenth Amendments, he contended that his client was being denied his right to equal protection of the laws and an impartial jury from a cross-section of the community. Without directly ruling on the defense attorney's request for a hearing on this issue, the trial court denied the motion, stating that parties could use peremptory challenges to strike anyone that they saw fit. The judge cited a previous ruling in *Swain*, which stated that the jury was not guaranteed to be a fair cross-section of the community; only venire or jury pool was. Batson was subsequently convicted. Having a previous criminal record, he was sentenced as a persistent felony offender[7] and given a 20-year prison sentence.

Batson's Appeal Process

The appeal process for this case was particularly long and drawn out, reflecting the extensive history of prior cases involving race in the legal system. The Supreme Court of Kentucky affirmed the trial court's decision and upheld the conviction on the grounds that, under *Swain*, a defendant cannot establish an equal protection violation by showing that only African American venire members were subjected to peremptory challenges in a particular trial. The Court clarified that a prosecutor *could* use those peremptory strikes based on race if he or she was concerned about a lack of sympathy for the prosecution case against the defendant of the same race. *Swain* only prevented racial exclusion if there was no other explanation.

Batson appealed his case to the U.S. Supreme Court, which eventually overturned the ruling based partially on the argument that the defendant would be denied his right to a jury of his peers. In addition, the Justices felt that this attitude about group solidarity and striking jurors for lack of understanding was particularly damaging and stigmatizing for members of the group being stricken.

The Legacy of the *Batson* Decision

In *Batson*, the U.S. Supreme Court ruled that an opposing attorney could request a race-neutral explanation for striking a juror if it was suspected that venire members were being excluded on the basis of race. Such an objection by an attorney has since become widely known as a *Batson* objection. As stated by Justice Powell, "Nor may the prosecutor rebut the defendant's case merely by denying that he had a discriminatory motive or affirming his good faith in making individual selections" (p. 17). While perhaps not immediately evident, this ruling represented a significant shift in the use of peremptory strikes. The hallmark of such a strike was that attorneys may simply make the strike without explanation, thus continuing to conceal any hints of the strategy they will use in the trial to follow.

---

[7] The Kentucky "Persistent Felony Offender" law is a type of law commonly referred to as a "Three-Strikes Law" under which sentences are significantly lengthened for someone with a prior criminal record.

BOX 1.2. "Produce the Body"

Habeas corpus is Latin for "produce the body," or "have the body." A habeas corpus proceeding is one in which a prisoner is questioning the legality of his or her imprisonment. A writ of habeas corpus is a legal document commanding the person doing the detaining (typically, the warden of the prison), to "produce the body" of the detainee in court so that he or she may be set free if the imprisonment is deemed illegal. A habeas case is a new civil suit initiated by the prisoner asserting that his or her rights are being violated. The case need not include any statement about guilt or innocence. At stake in a habeas case is the prisoner's freedom, rather than money. As such, a writ of habeas corpus is sometimes referred to as a "great writ of liberty."

It is a subtle distinction, but a habeas case is entirely different and separate from an appeal of the original case. Thus, in *Batson v. Kentucky* (1986), the U.S. Supreme Court ruled that race-based juror exclusion was appropriate grounds for a criminal appeal. In essence, the defendant was arguing that he should not have been convicted in the initial trial because the jury was defective. In *Miller-El v. Cockrell* (2003), the court ruled that such juror exclusion also constituted grounds for the prisoner to initiate a civil case, a habeas corpus case. Here, the prisoner's assertion was that he was being unlawfully detained because he was put there by a defective jury. Again, it is a subtle distinction, but one that allows a defendant two attempts at making a similar argument.

Throughout this text, references are made to the relevance of habeas corpus in specific cases. In recent decades, the U.S. Supreme Court has shown a trend of rulings denying federal habeas corpus application to specific prisoner allegations originating in state courts.

After the *Batson* decision that established that race could not be the only criterion for exercising peremptory challenges by the prosecutor in criminal trials, subsequent cases extended this application to the defense in criminal trials and to both sides in civil suits. Then, in *J.E.B. v. Alabama ex rel. T.B.* (1994), the Supreme Court extended this protection to include gender. In 2003, the U.S. Supreme Court specifically extended *Batson* to include the right of a defendant in such a case to initiate a habeas corpus hearing (*Miller-El v. Cockrell*, 2003; see Box 1.2 for a description of habeas corpus).

LEGAL REFORM IN JURY SELECTION AND PROCESS

Attention to the jury process makes it evident that the system for impanelling juries can be very inefficient, and even questionably effective. For one thing, there exists no empirical evidence that the system attains "truth." Also, there are no guidelines for juries that provide a uniform method of gathering, combining, and analyzing relevant information to arrive at the truth.

It is evident that many legal maneuvers restrict or void certain pieces of useful information from reaching the jury, thus constricting the potential for gaining any ultimate truth.[8] Also, while this is slowly changing, our legal system traditionally has very little allowance for interactive participation of jurors, a method used in other systems to maximize effectiveness. For example, jurors could themselves pose questions, and do so at a time when the information would be most useful to them.

The lack of reform is not for lack of legitimate suggestions. Throughout the years, potential reforms have been offered by numerous groups (Meyer, 2006; Sales & Shuman, 2005). These have included suggestions to help the jury (i.e., simplify the language and concepts used in the legal system, and provide uniform definitions to any vague and/or complex terms, e.g., "clear and convincing," "beyond a reasonable doubt") to obtain a more representative jury (i.e., provide effective penalties for those people that avoid or do not respond to a jury summons), and to equal out expenditures by either side, so that clients can avoid being steamrolled by the assets available to the prosecutor, and prosecutors can hope to compete with defendants who have seemingly unlimited expense accounts.

But due to the separation of power in American government, the judicial system ultimately has to answer only to itself. Justice Marshall's naive comments cited earlier demonstrate an overconfidence among legal practitioners that their fellow peers will always conduct themselves appropriately. Moreover, the system itself sends contradictory messages to its practitioners: If it is legal to exclude jurors based on race, then an attorney arguably has the *duty* to do so if it will result in better advocacy for his or her client. Perhaps these situations account for the agonizingly slow implementation of any type of jury reform. The American legal system is arguably one of the best in the world, but it is not perfect. Many of these imperfections are problems pertaining to some part of the jury process, and these problems provide a glimpse of the future of jury reform.

---

[8] For example, during the O. J. Simpson trial, 16,000 objections were raised, with approximately 9,000 overruled and 7,000 sustained. Not only was each sustained objection an instance where information was kept from the jury, but each objection was also a disruption in the flow of proceedings to which the jurors were supposedly attending.

CASE REFERENCES

Ballew v. Georgia, No. 76-761 (U.S. filed March 21, 1978).

Batson v. Kentucky, No. 84-6263 (U.S. filed April 30, 1986).

Burch v. Louisiana, 441 U.S. 130 (1979).

J.E.B. v. Alabama ex rel. T.B., 114 S. Ct. 1419 (1994).

Miller-El v. Cockrell, 2003 U.S. LEXIS 1734; 537 U.S. 322 (2003).

Ring v. Arizona, 536 U.S. 584; 122 S. Ct. 2428; 153 L. Ed. 2d 556; 2002 U.S. LEXIS 4651 (2002).

Strauder v. West Virginia, 100 U.S. 303; 1879 U.S. LEXIS 1830 (1880).

Swain v. Alabama, 380 U.S. 202; 1965 U.S. LEXIS 1668 (1965).

Williams v. Florida, 399 U.S. 78; 90 S. Ct. 1893; 26 L. Ed. 2d 446; 1970 U.S. LEXIS 98 (1970).

CHAPTER 2

Admission of Expert Testimony and the Eyewitness

> When a psychologist or psychiatrist testifies during a defendant's competency hearing, the psychologist or psychiatrist shall wear a cone-shaped hat that is not less than two feet tall. The surface of the hat shall be imprinted with stars and lightning bolts. Additionally, a psychologist or psychiatrist shall be required to don a white beard . . . and shall punctuate critical elements of his testimony by stabbing the air with a wand. [Before the expert's testimony about competency] the bailiff shall contemporaneously dim the courtroom lights and administer two strikes to a Chinese gong.
>
> —Actual wording included in New Mexico's 1995 Senate Bill 459, passed by the House and Senate, but ultimately vetoed by Governor Gary Johnson

One of the primary means by which a mental health professional may participate in legal proceedings is by testifying as an expert witness. Other witnesses, known as *fact witnesses,* can only testify to facts (i.e., something they know firsthand to be true). An *eyewitness* is a special type of fact witness brought in to testify about what he or she actually witnessed. Knowledge that is not firsthand information (i.e., the statement "Allison told me that she saw Bob steal the necklace") is known as *hearsay,* and a fact witness would not be allowed to make such a statement in court except in extremely rare circumstances (i.e., the victim and only eyewitness is a traumatized child).

In contrast, expert witnesses are allowed much more leeway. For example, an expert may offer an opinion about one of the parties in the case: "In my professional opinion, the defendant represents someone who is at serious risk to reoffend in the near future." Or the expert may testify about a body of scientific knowledge: "There have been numerous studies, including some of our research, indicating that children under age 3 may falsely report inappropriate touching." Note that neither of these statements recounts events that the expert actually witnessed first-hand. Yet such statements are not hearsay when offered by an expert witness. The potential power of the expert is that he or she may be used to tie the facts together. The use of expert witnesses in any given trial can range from useful to essential (Slovenko, 2002). Given this potential power, expert testimony is not without its constraints. The case law we discuss in this chapter explores the evolution of experts in court and the constraints on them.

As demonstrated in the quote at the beginning of this chapter, mental health experts do have their detractors. Psychiatric and psychological testimony have often been ridiculed at the stand given the inherent uncertainties and ambiguities that arise in the study of the human brain and behavior. In fact, it was not until 1962 that psychologists secured the right to offer mental health diagnoses in courts (*Jenkins v. U.S.*, 1962). Such concerns illustrate practical implications of the fundamental differences between the legal and mental health professions' definitions of *truth* and *knowledge*, as alluded to in the introductory chapter. Legal professionals (and, to a large degree, the public) want definitive answers to complicated questions such as "Did the defendant, at the time of the crime, appreciate right from wrong?" Mental health professionals should know that definitive answers to such a question may be misleading, probably unethical, and downright untruthful, which (oddly enough) makes them illegal.

Adding to these problems is a widely held public belief that mental health professionals are primarily used to get a large number of defendants acquitted by reason of insanity. John Hinckley's case drives the point home. Hinckley, President Reagan's would-be assassin, was found not guilty by reason of insanity, yet psychiatrists could not even determine whether Hinckley was psychotic. Some form of psychosis, characterized by a loss of contact with reality, is typically required (albeit not specifically) for a finding of insanity. They gave vague descriptions of his symptomatology, which met the criteria for up to three different mental illnesses. Many Americans were outraged.

A related concern is whether or not testimony by experts becomes *too* compelling, and thus overrides other relevant testimony. Cases such as O. J. Simpson, Jeffrey Dahmer, John Hinckley, and so on (see Meyer, 2006) have raised this issue. Nietzel, McCarthy, and Kern (1999) provide the best data here, and their "meta-analytic" conclusion as to the effect of an expert witness (vs. not using one) is a correlation of .15 (i.e., it directed 57.5% of the study participants in the desired verdict direction, and 42.5% the other way; note that the *complete absence* of a relationship would result in a 50%/50% split). Not compelling, but not worth ignoring either.

This chapter also includes a discussion of case law regarding the admission of eyewitness testimony (frequently focusing upon the veracity of child testimony). This issue is relevant to any mental health professional whose client may be a witness to a crime (i.e., physical or sexual assault), or to anyone being sought as an expert to testify about the social science research on eyewitness testimony. At the end of this chapter, we bring the discussion full-circle by discussing a recent case challenging the admissibility of expert testimony regarding eyewitness research. Thus, we necessarily must first understand the broad issue of expert admissibility. How does the law define *expert*, and what is and is not allowed in an expert's testimony?

THE DEVELOPMENT OF
EXPERT ADMISSIBILITY CRITERIA

On the Witness Stand (1908), by Harvard professor and experimental psychologist Hugo Munsterberg, is probably the earliest written description of a psychologist performing duties that would today be labeled "expert witness testimony" (Ewing, 2003). That seminal work earned Munsterberg the unofficial title of "Father of Forensic Psychology." (For an excellent contemporary review of work in forensic psychology, see Ewing, 2003.) While experts offering testimony dates to 1908 or earlier, the significant U.S. case law on the issue starts in 1923. It addresses an issue fundamental to expert testimony: the standard by which the opinion of an expert is considered admissible as evidence. That case, *Frye v. U.S.* (1923), remains a very influential ruling. It resulted in what would become known as the "Frye rules" for the admission of expert testimony, which assert that a technique or procedure has to have "gained general acceptance in the particular field in which it belongs" in order to be allowed into evidence.

ESTABLISHING A DEFINITION OF *EXPERTISE*: *FRYE V. U.S.* (1923)

James Frye, a young African American, was arrested in Washington, DC, for the murder of a prominent white physician. After several days of police interrogation, he confessed to the murder. Then, days before his trial, Frye repudiated his confession, claiming that he had been coerced by a promise of half the $1,000 reward should he confess. William Moulton Marston[1] administered his systolic blood pressure test to Frye and concluded that Frye was telling the truth and was innocent. Marston, a former student of Hugo Munsterberg, had claimed that his use of the systolic blood pressure measure as a lie detection method was the end of mankind's search for a test of deception.[2]

The defense petitioned for Marston to be qualified as an expert witness and for his results to be accepted as evidence. The presiding judge ruled to exclude the lie detection evidence, because it was not based upon a well-recognized and scientific principle. This ruling was eventually upheld by a Federal Court of Appeals, yielding the *Frye* standard for expert admissibility. Were an expert's opinion not based on "generally accepted" procedures, it would not be allowed as testimony.

THE LEGACY OF THE *FRYE* STANDARD

Over the years, this rather narrow standard has led to some apparent injustices. For instance, what about new technologies that have yet to permeate the practice in a field? The actor Charlie Chaplin, for example, lost a paternity suit in the 1940s, after a California court decided that a newly developed blood test eliminating him as the father was not reliable enough to be binding on the jury. Today, such a test is considered conclusive proof of paternity and would have exonerated Mr. Chaplin.

Since *Frye*, a continuing dilemma for judges has been to discern

---

[1] Marston along with his wife, also a psychologist, went on to develop the comic book character, Wonder Woman. Evildoers caught by Wonder Woman's "Lasso of Truth" were forced to look into their own hearts and tell the truth. This lie detection method worked without fail and was accepted by fans of the comic despite not being well-recognized by other superheroes.

[2] A perpetual self-publicizer, Marston also offered to test Bruno Hauptmann, the man accused of kidnapping and killing the Lindbergh baby (Bruno and company declined), and repeatedly tried to involve himself in other famous cases.

what "field" needs to "generally accept" any would-be testimony. For example, what field should judge the acceptability of the polygraph (lie detector)? Is it physiology, psychology, medicine, or specifically polygraphy? The latter may seem an obvious choice by name alone. However, letting any "field" define its own acceptance can be dangerous. How honestly can we expect practitioners who make a living performing a technique to critique their own procedures? Chapter 16 provides an illustration of a field currently experiencing just such problems.

While the *Frye* standard was widely used across a number of jurisdictions, the Federal Rules of Evidence (1987) that defined admissibility in Federal Courts emphasized a "helpfulness standard" rather than "scientific acceptance" in deciding upon the admission of expert testimony. In other words, would the testimony be helpful to the finder of fact? As we see in our next case, *Daubert v. Merrell Dow Pharmaceuticals, Inc.*, U.S. Supreme Court justices decided firmly in support of the thrust of the Federal Rules. The importance of the *Daubert* proceedings is made clear by the unusually high number of amicus briefs (22) filed by various groups.

THE CASE OF *DAUBERT V. MERRELL DOW PHARMACEUTICALS, INC.* (1993): THE EVOLUTION OF QUALIFICATIONS FOR THE ADMISSIBILITY OF EXPERT TESTIMONY

Daubert involved the question of whether the drug Bendectin, marketed by Merrell Dow, caused serious birth defects when ingested by pregnant women. The plaintiffs sought to admit expert testimony about the dangers of Bendectin to assert that the drug company should have known about the dangers and warned pregnant women against its use. However, the data upon which the experts based their opinions had not been formally published in a scientific journal (or otherwise). The original trial court therefore refused to consider the expert testimony as per the defendant's assertion that the data had not been scrutinized by others in the field and thus could not possibly be "generally accepted."

The *Daubert* Court noted that the rule requires that the information be "scientific," which "implies a grounding in the methods and procedures of science," (p. 2) and that it must be "knowledge," which means more than "subjective or unsupported speculation." It also noted that the information must "assist the trier of fact," which suggests that the testimony of the expert must "have a reliable basis in the knowledge of the discipline."

The *Daubert* Court emphasized that it is the responsibility of federal judges to review expert evidence to ensure that it rests on a reliable foundation and is relevant to the case. As part of this function, the Court suggested that the following factors be used in evaluating the reliability of any procedure that was to be the basis of an expert's opinion:

1. Whether it has been tested using some accepted scientific methodology.
2. Whether it has been subject to peer review and publication.
3. Whether the known or potential rate of error of the scientific technique justifies its use.
4. Whether it has achieved a degree of acceptance within the scientific community.

Note that these criteria are not used to directly assess the expert's *opinion*, but the *procedures* upon which the expert bases their opinion (e.g., a specific psychological test). Regarding relevance, the Court emphasized that the essential question is whether the expert testimony has scientific validity within the context of the issues presented by a particular case. Thus, while the *Daubert* decision seemingly placed additional restrictions on the *Frye* rule, the Court also recognized the criteria as a "flexible" standard. The four *Daubert* factors are therefore not mandatory but rather are advisory. Thus, courts are free to utilize one or more (or none) of them at their own discretion given the particular circumstances and nature of the case at hand.

In the ruling, the Court also acknowledged the fundamental differences in the scientific and legal fields, explaining that "there are important differences between the quest for truth in the courtroom and the quest for truth in the laboratory. Scientific conclusions are subject to perpetual revision. Law, on the other hand, must resolve disputes finally and quickly" (p. 14). The Court further expressed its view that "vigorous cross-examination, presentation of contrary evidence, and careful instruction on the burden of proof are sufficient to deal with bad scientific evidence that is presented to a judge or jury" (p. 14). In short, a court need not be as concerned about allowing questionable expert testimony when opposing counsel could merely present opposing evidence and let the jury sort it out.

Thus, this case has something in it both for those who support the expansive admission of expert testimony and for those who want to limit it. On the whole, however, the case came down on the side of the broad admission of expert opinion even when it had not achieved a large measure of acceptability within the profession of the expert. In that sense, it is the end of the *Frye* rule. At the same time, judges should be encouraged to provide some limits on the admissibility of such evidence consistent with the Court's caution to trial judges. Practitioners involved in cases in which unreliable expert opinion is being presented may be called upon to help demonstrate to the judge that the proposed testimony does not meet the four factors identified by the Court in *Daubert*.

Unfortunately, the Court did not directly consider another option for coping with questionable scientific evidence (namely, the appointment of independent experts), which is allowed by Federal Rule 506. Such an alternative response may have alleviated concerns about any questionable testimony were an independent expert, hired by the judge, to come in and educate the court about why the initial testimony was questionable.

THE LEGACY OF *DAUBERT*

In spite of the potential influence of *Daubert* on the states, many state courts have rejected it as setting a new precedent. For example, the California Supreme Court, in *People v. Leahy* (1994), held that even though California has statutory language that is easily interpreted as consistent with *Daubert*, the principle of *stare decisis* (following precedent) provides a legal basis for retaining the *Frye* standard in California state courts. In this case, based on the *Frye* test, a specific field sobriety test was disallowed, resulting in an overturning of a DUI (driving under the influence) conviction.

A fundamental flaw that has become evident in the system set forth in *Daubert* is that judges still must often make a decision between valid scientific procedures and "junk" or "fad" science. The overwhelming majority of judges is not sophisticated enough in issues of science (lacking the years of training necessary) to make these discriminations. As Judge Joseph McLaughlin eloquently stated in *McCullock v. H.B. Fuller Co.* (1995), although judges must be discrete gatekeepers of expert testimony under *Daubert*, they are not "St. Peter at the gates of heaven, performing a searching inquiry into the depths of an expert witness's soul" (p. 7). The alternative, leaving jurors to decide on issues of science, presents even more problems, because jurors would be left to rely on their own assumptions, perceptions, and misperceptions in evaluating complex phenomena.

Directly on the heels of the *Daubert* decision came a decision from the 7th Circuit Court of Appeals that called into question *Daubert's* applicability to psychological testimony (*U.S. v. Hall*, 1996). This decision drew a clear distinction between what it termed "Newtonian science," which the *Daubert* criteria were designed to evaluate, and social science evidence for which *Daubert* criteria might or might not be appropriate.

THE CASE OF *KUMHO TIRE CO. V. CARMICHAEL* (1999): CLARIFYING THE APPLICABILITY OF *DAUBERT*

Kumho, a more recent case that also has a sizable impact on all expert testimony, including psychological testimony, was a product liability case in which a tire blowout resulted in the death of one person and the injury of others. In the proceedings, a tire expert was called in to testify as to his opinion of whether the tire failed due to improper upkeep, or due to manufacturer error. He did so, basing his opinion on his own four-point test for tire failure. The opposing side argued that the expert's testimony was scientific in nature because of its "test" basis and thus subject to *Daubert* criteria. Because the expert's test clearly did not meet these criteria, the testimony was not allowed. On appeal, the 11th Circuit Court reversed this decision, stating that *Daubert* did not apply to testimony based on the expert's experience or skill.

However, the Supreme Court eventually reversed the 11th Circuit's ruling that the expert in this specific instance had offered a specific "test" to which the *Daubert* criteria could be applied. In so ruling, the Court provided some clarification as to the applicability of the *Daubert* criteria on expert testimony. First, the U.S. Supreme Court reiterated the gatekeeping ability of trial judges for both scientific and experience-based testimony. It further elaborated that such gatekeeping could be overturned only if there were clear evidence of abuse of this discretion. The Court also stated that the *Daubert* criteria might very well be applicable to nonscientific testimony.

However, we would caution that *Daubert's* applicability should be judged by deciding whether the criteria represent reasonable measures of the testimony's relevance and reliability. Shapiro (1999) gives an illustrative example of a case in which *Daubert* criteria would clearly be inapplicable. Colleagues who routinely perform child custody evaluations are quick to note that many of the scientific factors enumerated in *Daubert* are not relevant to such assessments. For example, what would be the known error rate (a complex statistical analysis) in a child custody evaluation? Nevertheless, most people who do custody evaluations follow a generally accepted methodology of interviewing not only the children but also the parents, observing parental interactions with the children, and gathering secondary sources of data and reviewing records. As long as that approach can be demonstrated to have solid support in a variety of child custody literature, then the testimony would be deemed relevant and reliable, and need not be subject to the criteria outlined in *Daubert* (pp. 20–21). Speaking to the flexible nature of the *Daubert* standard, *Kumho's* Justice Breyer dubbed the system for admissibility of expert testimony as "problematical," noting that some cases may call for the consideration of all four of *Daubert's* factors, while other cases should only consider one or two, or even a different set of factors.

One thing that *Kumho* did set out in a rather concrete fashion is that "tests" are subject to the *Daubert* criteria. Therefore, the impact of the *Kumho* case on mental health practitioners will likely be greater scrutiny of the reliability and validity of procedures (i.e., "tests") used in arriving at opinions. This may include the psychometric properties of any instruments, as well as the empirical basis for any clinical conclusions. An immediate impact on attorneys is that both sides would now be well served to officially establish the applicability of the expert testimony on the record, lest it later be deemed as having been inappropriately admitted. It is not uncommon for opposing attorneys merely to stipulate that an expert is admissible. To stipulate means that the point in question is agreed upon by both sides.[3] To continue to stipulate admissibility may prove troublesome in light of the Supreme Court's ruling in *Weisgram v. Marley* (2000) that appellate courts may completely dismiss a case (rather than remanding it back to the lower court) that was based upon inappropriately admitted expert testimony.

FRYE, DAUBERT, AND *KUMHO*: AMENDING THE RULES OF EVIDENCE

The Federal Rules of Evidence are under constant revision, with changes typically reflecting case law rulings or correcting previous ambiguities. The most recent amendments to the Federal Rules of Evidence regarding the admissibility of expert testimony were issued on December 1,

---

[3] While one advantage to stipulation is saving time, attorneys on the opposing side sometimes offer stipulation as a means to keep an expert with an extremely impressive list of credentials from discussing those credentials in front of the jury.

2000, and reflect the evolution of case law presented throughout this chapter. The relevant rule (702) now reads

> If scientific, technical, or other specialized knowledge will assist the trier of fact to understand the evidence or to determine a fact in issue, a witness qualified as expert by knowledge, skill, experience, training, or education may testify thereto in the form of an opinion or otherwise, if (1) testimony is based upon sufficient facts or data, (2) the testimony is the product of reliable principles and methods, and (3) the witness has applied the principles and methods reliably to the facts of the case.

An interesting offshoot of *Frye, Daubert,* and *Kumho* (and a manner in which to begin to analyze the fallout of the more recent rulings) is the admissibility of polygraph evidence, especially since *Frye* dealt with a "lie detection" procedure. It would appear to us that such evidence easily satisfies any "scientific" requirements of *Daubert,* especially following the wider reaching decision in *Kumho.* In *U.S. v. Galbreth* (1995), upon appeal in New Mexico, a polygraph used to support a defendant's truthfulness in a tax evasion case was allowed in a federal district court, based on *Daubert.* The court specifically discussed the expert's (Dr. David Raskin of the Psychology Department of the University of Utah) "impeccable credentials," his use of a "directed lie control technique" that had scientific backing, and the fact that there was state licensing for polygraphy. At the same time, a California appeals Court, in *U.S. v. Sherlin* (1995), also using the *Daubert* standard, nevertheless refused to admit polygraph evidence to support a criminal defendant's truthfulness. This court used Rule 403 of the Federal Rules of Evidence to assert that even relevant evidence may be excluded if in the discretion of the court its benefit is substantially outweighed by any danger of prejudice against either side. (See Honts and Perry [1992]) for an excellent discussion of *Daubert* and polygraph admissibility.)

THE ADMISSIBILITY OF THE DSM-IV

An interesting case from the 9th Circuit Court of Appeals, *U.S. v. Scholl* (1999), limited the admissibility of testimony based on the fourth edition of the *Diagnostic and Statistical Manual of Mental Disorders* (DSM-IV; American Psychiatric Association, 1994). Mental health clinicians know it well through its use for health insurance reimbursement. It is widely considered the standard text for diagnosing mental disorders, although it certainly has its flaws (Greenberg, Shuman, & Meyer, 2005). Any precedental court rulings would likely also have an impact upon subsequent versions of the publication (i.e., DSM-IV-TR).

In this case, an expert (a psychiatrist) was allowed to testify regarding Compulsive Gambling Disorder, but his testimony was limited to the essential clinical components of the disorder. The expert was attempting to use information contained in the "Associated Clinical Features" section of the DSM-IV to discuss how denial and distortions in thinking could lead to falsification of tax forms. Upon request, the expert was unable to produce any published research to support such a connection. The court ruled that the expert could only discuss the scientifically established components of the disorder but was not allowed to testify as to denial or distortions in thinking, nor was he allowed to give testimony as to his ultimate conclusion.

ACCESS TO "DISCARDED" EXPERTS

What happens when an expert arrives at an opinion that is harmful to the case of the hiring attorney? In accordance with professional ethics, experts hired to perform an assessment for court are expected to do so without bias, regardless of which side in the dispute (if either) hires them. As such, it is not uncommon for an expert to perform an assessment, only to have the hiring attorney decide not to use the testimony. If this happens with a witness initially hired by the prosecution, then the prosecution is required to turn the results over to defense counsel. However, what happens when the expert was initially hired by the defense? Even information that supports a defendant's guilt does not have to be disclosed by the defendant's attorney, because such a requirement would clearly impinge upon a defendant's ability to assist counsel. The courts have actually dealt with this issue, specifically with regard to expert testimony.

In *U.S. v. Alvarez* (1975), it was held that the defense's right to effective counsel is impaired when the state is able to use experts that the defense has discarded. Later, in *U.S. ex rel Edney v. Smith* (1976), it was held that the state has a right to a discarded expert once an issue of mental state is raised. The logic here is that once such an assertion is made, the burden of proof switches to the defense, at least with regard to the parts of the procedure that address the defendant's mental state.

The overall issue is still unsettled, but the following cases reiterated the importance of considering whether or not the defendant raises the issue of mental capacity. For instance, in *Buchanan v. Kentucky* (1987), the defendant used "extreme emotional disturbance" as a defense against a homicide charge. As rebuttal testimony, the prosecutor was allowed to examine and enter a report that the defense psychiatrist had prepared as part of an *earlier* determination of appropriateness for commitment and transfer to a hospital setting for psychiatric treatment. The defendant had never been informed that such a release to the prosecutor could occur, had never actually been formally evaluated for mental status, and had not been informed by the psychiatrist of any limits of confidentiality. Nevertheless, the U.S. Supreme Court upheld the prosecution's maneuver, in large part because the defendant had raised the issue of mental state.

In *Illinois v. Knuckles* (1995), a case in which Knuckles had allegedly murdered her mother, psychiatrist Kyle Rossiter, MD, was hired by the defense to testify as to the defendant's diminished capacity for criminal responsibility (insanity). Rossiter interviewed the defendant and took notes but did not prepare a report. When he was later called by the prosecution, the defense objected, saying that he was protected from testifying under the defense's attorney–client privilege. The Illinois Supreme Court ultimately agreed on the grounds that Dr. Rossiter did not submit a report, nor did he testify (allowing cross-examination), nor was the issue of mental status formally raised by the defendant, as it had been in *Buchanan*.

As will be seen time and again, the Court, as in *Knuckles*, failed to address the ultimate issue, opting instead to rule based on a fact very specific to the case. While such a ruling should be given limited precedent value, this practice is not always followed. As noted earlier, even if the question of mental capacity had been raised, the ruling may still vary across jurisdictions. If the relevant state law followed *Edney*, access to the mental health professional would have been available, but if it followed *U.S. v. Alvarez*, access would not be permitted.

Perhaps the information presented in this chapter up to this point serves an interesting illustration. When assessed in terms of the "whole picture," legal cases (each individually purporting to arrive at a logical end) can culminate in a state of affairs that is at least as confusing as mental health testimony. The following section on eyewitness testimony illustrates how the issue of expert admissibility and acceptance remains unresolved, despite a history of legal evolution.

EXPERT ADMISSIBILITY IN THE CONTEXT OF EYEWITNESS TESTIMONY

The accuracy of eyewitness accounts has long been the study of social scientists. Thus, it would stand to reason that social scientists could play a useful educative role in courtrooms regarding these findings. Yet the issue of eyewitness testimony instead illustrates the differences between the determination of legal "truth" and mental health "knowledge." Eyewitness descriptions continue to be seen by law enforcement officials, attorneys, judges, and juries (and probably even bailiffs and court reporters) as being the most reliable and accurate reports of any event that may be the focus of a legal proceeding. However, any forensic mental health professional worth his or her salt knows that any eyewitness testimony warrants close scrutiny to determine its veracity (Deffenbacker, Bornstein, Penrod, & McCorty, 2004). Under certain circumstances (i.e., the presence of a deadly weapon), eyewitness testimony may actually be one of the *most* fallible forms of testimony. For the purposes of this text, we stick primarily to case law on this issue, but an abundance of available sources present or summarize the research at the heart of this debate. One particularly timely review is offered by Wells and Loftus (2003), who, in their conclusion, liken eyewitness memory to trace physical evidence from a crime scene. As with physical evidence, they argue, eyewitness memory may be contaminated. Yet the legal system very frequently refuses to acknowledge this possibility. Case law on the matter illustrates the problem.

CASE LAW REGARDING EYEWITNESS TESTIMONY

Just as there are restrictions and limitations regarding expert witnesses, there are also limitations on the admissibility of testimony by fact (i.e., nonexpert) witnesses. Two limitations on fact testimony are that the witnesses themselves must be suitable (i.e., usually based on age and capability[4]), or that the veracity of eyewitness memory is challenged in an otherwise suitable witness.

Historically, the only per se[5] limitation on the admission of eyewitness accounts concerned the age at which children could be expected to give honest, reliable testimony. The case of *R. v. Love* in 1687 (as cited in Meyer, 1995) began a trend of limitations and regulations regarding the age at which eyewitness testimony would be admissible. This case held

---

[4] For instance, when giving testimony about something they saw, people's visual acuity must be commensurate with the circumstances (i.e., lighting, distance) under which they report making the observation.

[5] A per se limitation means that all people fitting into that category are excluded, no questions asked. Thus, in the first example, all children under age 14 were excluded, regardless of their individual sophistication.

that no child under the age of 14 would be allowed to testify in a court of law, regardless of personal or cultural characteristics (e.g., intelligence, race, or religion). This was based on a presumption that children under 14 did not yet comprehend the moral obligation to be truthful and had a developmental inability to distinguish between what is the truth and what is not. In 1709, the case of *Young v. Slaughterford* lowered the age for witness inadmissibility to 12, saying that by this age one could already understand the consequences of committing perjury. A ruling in *R. v. Travers* (1726) later set the boundary at age 9 but allowed unsworn testimony from younger children. The logic here was apparently that children that young could not appreciate the meaning of swearing to their truthfulness.

Over 150 years later, the legal system would officially acknowledge a fundamental flaw with per se exclusions in child testimony, namely, that there are vast individual differences among children of similar age. For instance, a particular 9-year-old may be able to provide more reliable testimony than a particular 14-year-old. The move toward recognizing individual characteristics became evident in *Wheeler v. U.S.*(1895), when the Court asserted that no witness would be disqualified by reason of age alone.

Case law on eyewitness testimony has been shaped by several classic cases from the late 1960s and 1970s. Initially, these cases established some ground rules for acceptance of eyewitness identification. For instance, some legal wording that continues to have legal precedent includes the admonition that courts should consider the "totality of the circumstances" in determining whether or not an identification procedure was suggestive (i.e., the authorities "suggested" to the eyewitness whom he should identify as the offender; *Stovall v. Denno*, 1967). *Simmons v. U.S.* (1968) later provided us with the following regarding identifications actually made in the courtroom: "Identification at trial following pretrial photo identification, will be set aside only if the procedure was so impermissibly suggestive as to give rise to a very substantial likelihood of irreparable misidentification" (p. 2). During this period, courts also ruled that eyewitness identifications could be inadmissible when there was a "substantial likelihood" of misidentification (*Foster v. California*, 1969), although identifications seemed relatively immune to challenge if they were made at the time of the actual crime (*Coleman v. Alabama*, 1970).

In perhaps the primary landmark case on eyewitness admissibility, *Neil v. Biggers* (1972), the Supreme Court listed the following five factors to be considered in determining accuracy: (1) the opportunity of the witness to view the criminal at the time of the crime; (2) the degree of attention of the witness; (3) the accuracy of the witness's prior description of the criminal; (4) the level of certainty demonstrated by the witness at the time of confrontation; and (5) the length of time between the crime and the confrontation. Since 1972, numerous lower courts have been influenced by the *Biggers* standards.

Now, having reviewed the case law relevant to eyewitness admissibility, the stage is set for a difference of opinion, because social science research directly contradicts a part of the legal precedent. It is to this discussion that we now turn our focus.

The Admission of Experts on Eyewitness Testimony

There is an incongruence between social science research and legal proceedings when it comes to eyewitness testimony. For example, a wealth of extant research seems to show a *lack* of importance to eyewitnesses' level of certainty. Yet eyewitness certainty was specifically recognized in the *Biggers* decision, a ruling that continues to hold significant precedent today.

Despite problems supported in research, judges and juries continue to place significant importance upon eyewitnesses. One reason is that it is simpler to understand and believe someone who claims to have seen something than to understand and believe the complicated process that can lead to inaccuracies in memory. Furthermore, for the legal system to fully recognize the problems with eyewitness testimony would be to admit to hundreds of years of reliance on faulty testimony in arriving at "the truth." To date, the general approach taken by courts (when they have allowed any challenge to the general veracity of eyewitness claims at all) has been to allow experts to testify about a limited component (e.g., that certainty is not directly correlated with accuracy) of the body of research supporting problems with eyewitness testimony. How then do the rules of expert witness admissibility (as in *Frye, Daubert,* and *Kumho*) apply to the research on eyewitness testimony? It just so happens that a more recent New York Supreme Court ruling addressed this issue directly. Thus, our discussion comes full circle, back to the role of expert witness.

The Case of *People v. LeGrand* (2002): General Acceptance in a Field and a Misapplication of Expert Testimony

In *People v. LeGrand* (2002), the defendant was arrested for the murder of a taxi driver after he (LeGrand) was identified by an eyewitnesses.

The rather unique spin on this identification was that it actually took place 7 years after the crime. The defense motioned the court to admit expert testimony from Dr. Roy Malpass, a Professor of Psychology at the University of Texas–El Paso, regarding research on four phenomena that can contribute to eyewitness inaccuracies. In making his ruling, the judge defined these phenomena (each with respective citations) as follows:

(1) **Confidence-accuracy correlation** refers to "the relation between the accuracy of an eyewitness's identification and the confidence that [the] eyewitness expresses in the identification" (Wells, Gary L., Small, Mark, Penrod, Steven, Malpass, Roy S., Fulero, Solomon M. & Brimacombe, C.A.E., "*Eyewitness Identification Procedures: Recommendations for Lineups and Photospreads*", Law and Human Behavior, vol. 22, no. 6, [1–39] at 14 [1998])

(2) **Postevent information** refers to the proposition that "eyewitness testimony about an event often reflects not only what [the eyewitness] actually saw but information they obtained later on" (Kassin, Saul M., Tubb, V. Anne, Hosch, Harmon M. & Memon, Amina, "*On the 'General Acceptance' of Eyewitness Testimony Research: A New Survey of the Experts*", American Psychologist [in press], [1–19] at 13 [2001]; *see also* Kassin, Saul M., Ellsworth, Phoebe C. & Smith, Vicki L., "*The 'General Acceptance' of Psychological Research on Eyewitness* [**3] *Testimony: A Survey of Experts*", American Psychologist, vol. 44, no. 8, [1089–98] at 1091 [1989])

(3) **Confidence malleability** refers to the proposition that "an eyewitness's confidence can be influenced by factors that are unrelated to identification accuracy"(Id.); and

(4) **Weapon focus** refers to "the visual attention that eyewitnesses give to a perpetrator's weapon during the course of a crime" (Steblay, Nancy Mehrkens, "*A Meta-Analytic Review of the Weapon Focus Effect*", Law and Human Behavior, vol. 16, no. 4, [413–24] at 414 [1992]). (*People v. LeGrand*, p. 2; see also Deffenbacker et al., 2004)

In this case, both attorneys agreed to use of the *Frye* criteria over the *Daubert* criteria for the admission of any experts. The judge agreed on the grounds that the general acceptance of the research within its respective field (common to *Frye* and *Daubert*) was the only questionable issue remaining, the other three *Daubert* criteria having been satisfied. The judge specifically agreed that each of the four areas of testimony above were very pertinent to the case at hand.

To address these issues, the prosecution presented testimony from psychologist Ebbe Ebbeson, PhD, who described problems with the relevant research, including how the results of some studies disagreed with others. In the end, despite some very problematic aspects of the eyewitness identifications in this case (i.e., that they were made 7 *years* after the crime), the judge ruled that the "problems" in the research, as described by Dr. Ebbeson, were enough to conclude that each of the four areas of testimony listed earlier, were not "generally accepted" in the field of psychology. While this ruling may have limited precedent value, and indeed has many potential areas for challenge, it serves to underscore the fact that the debate regarding expert admissibility rages on.

The Expert Witness and *LeGrand*: An Illustration of the Larger Issue

The judge in the *LeGrand* case was informed about some general problems in the psychological literature on eyewitness testimony. However, there are similar problems (perhaps not *quite* to the same extent) in virtually every area of psychological (or other) research. However, most anyone who could be qualified as an expert on eyewitness testimony knows (or *should* know) about these limitations and what they mean. Thus, while there are problems, we at least seek to understand them. For instance, while one article may disagree with another, it is typically possible to address why one may be more relevant to the current case, or to find flaws in one article, thus favoring the other.

The literature does suggest that there are problems with eyewitness testimony. That not all researchers agree on the operation of these problems underscores the fact that the problems with eyewitnesses are not yet fully understood. Thus, the judge opted to allow a problematic process (eyewitness testimony) to proceed, about which the problems are not even acknowledged, rather than admit the scientific testimony, about which the problems are not only acknowledged but also relatively well understood.

Criticisms have been levied (Levett & Kovera, 2002) against the judge in the *LeGrand* case for misunderstanding the nature of psychological research (i.e., that conclusions in an active research area *will* change over time). This area is an important (and we have argued, fundamental) one; it is nevertheless misunderstood even by many psychologists (although those who do not understand it should not be testifying about it in court). How then, did experts' testimony about the typical problems seen in a particular body of research lead to the conclusion that none of the research should be explained to the jury? Many possibilities exist. For instance, the experts may have sufficiently explained their testimony, only to have some of it lost on the judge, or the ability of counsel to elicit testimony may have favored one side. However, the judge's decision to exclude all testimony on eyewitness research was informed largely (if not solely) on the basis of the testimony of Drs. Malpass and Ebbeson. If the judge's decision was based on a misunderstanding (or perhaps incomplete understanding) of the implications of this testimony, some of the responsibility may in fact lie with these experts. Perhaps Dr. Malpass could have done a better job of acknowledging the limitations in the research up front. Perhaps Dr. Ebbeson could have better explained that the nature of research, which, almost by definition, dictates that the presence of such limitations is very much accepted (indeed assumed) within the field.

As it currently stands, the *LeGrand* trial represents another blemish for social science research in the eyes of the legal profession, as well as another failing of the legal system to social scientists familiar with the limitations of research. Perhaps the bottom line is that the opinions of only two experts (each potentially prone to his own agenda) should never be used in deciding the "general acceptance" in the field. This again underscores the different approaches taken by the legal and mental health fields in deciding upon an issue. Undoubtedly, many proponents of the legal approach would see no problem with the procedural methodology previously described. A basic assumption of the legal system is that when two sides present the best argument possible, the prevailing side will be the one that is the most correct. We, on the other hand, heartily agree with a suggestion by Levett and Kovera (2002) that a need exists "for panels of psychologists, chosen to reflect differing views on a particular topic, to draft position papers on psychological issues that may appear before courts, giving time for these papers to be circulated among experts in the field for comment and revision" (p. 23).

We would further recommend that any such position statements be created in a way that facilitates their endorsement by professional organizations in the respective fields (i.e., the American Psychological Association). Such publications would ensure that judges in cases such as *LeGrand* could (note that we did not say *would*) arrive at accurate conclusions regarding the general acceptance of testimony in a given field. The need for professions to develop position statements reaches far beyond the issue of eyewitness testimony. For instance, a similar debate is brewing with regard to the admission of expert testimony about false confessions. State courts are deeply divided when it comes to admitting or rejecting expert testimony on the matter, despite a decade of research on false confessions (Fulero, 2001). At least some of the research seems to demonstrate rather clearly that, in some circumstances, some people may confess to a crime they did not commit. Just like the fallibility of eyewitnesses, false confessions defy common logic—all the more reason to have an expert educate the finders of fact in legal proceedings.

Having position statement sanctioned by the major organizations in a field or, in the absence of such a document, having unbiased, court-appointed experts testify about an area of research, would significantly increase a judge's ability to make accurate judgments about "general acceptance" in a field. Such practices would also go a long way toward producing a legal system in which the decisions made by juries and courts are both legally *and* scientifically sound. After all, is that not the intended purpose of the expert witness? It should be.

CASE REFERENCES

Buchanan v. Kentucky, 483 U.S. 402 (1987).
Coleman v. Alabama, 399 U.S. 1; 1970 U.S. LEXIS 17 (1970).
Daubert v. Merrell Dow Pharmaceuticals, Inc., 509 U.S. 579; 1993 U.S. LEXIS 4408 (1993).
Foster v. California, 394 U.S. 440; 1969 U.S. LEXIS 2050 (1969).
Frye v. U.S., 295 F. 1013 (D.C. Cir. 1923).
Illinois v. Knuckles, 165 Ill. 2d 125; 1995 Ill. LEXIS 80 (1995).
Jenkins v. U.S., 307 F.2d 637 (1962).
Kumho Tire Co. v. Carmichael, 525 U.S. 959; 1999 U.S. LEXIS 6835 (1999).
McCullock v. H.B. Fuller Co., 61 F.3d 1038; 1995 U.S. App. LEXIS 20246 (1995).
Neil v. Biggers, 409 U.S. 188; 93 S. Ct. 375 (1972).
People v. Leahy, 8 Cal. 4th 587; 1994 Cal. LEXIS 5373 (1994).
People v. LeGrand, Cal. App. Unpub. LEXIS 7994 (2002).
R. v. Travers, 93 E.R. 793 (1726).
Simmons v. U.S., 390 U.S. 377; 1968 U.S. LEXIS 2167 (1968).
Stovall v. Denno, 388 U.S. 293; 1967 U.S. LEXIS 1087 (1967).
U.S. ex rel Edney v. Smith, 425 F. Supp. 1038 (E.D. N.Y. 1976).
U.S. v. Alvarez, 519 F.2d 1036 (3rd Cir. 1975).
U.S. v. Galbreth, 908 F. Supp. 877; 1995 U.S. Dist. LEXIS 20642 (1995).
U.S. v. Hall, 93 F.3d 1337; 1996 U.S. App. LEXIS 22173 (1996).
U.S. v. Scholl, 528 U.S. 873; 1999 U.S. LEXIS 5825 (1999).
U.S. v. Sherlin, 67 F.3d 1208; 1995 U.S. App. LEXIS 29047 (1995).
Weisgram v. Marley, 528 U.S. 440; 2000 U.S. LEXIS 1011 (2000).
Wheeler v. U.S., 159 U.S. 526 (1895).
Young v. Slaughterford, 88 E.R. 1007 (1709).

PART II

Legal Precedent in Everyday Clinical Practice

In Part I we laid the foundation for some of the procedures used in today's courtrooms and introduced some avenues by which mental health professionals may enter into the legal arena. Now we turn to key court cases that currently dictate everyday mental health practice.

Mental health practice is, of course, dictated by science, and by the training and experience of the clinician. But, very importantly, mental health practice is also very heavily dictated by both formal law and professional ethics. Like most professions psychology, social work, psychiatry, and other mental health fields have established ethical guidelines and rules for licensed practitioners. In many instances, law and ethics are one and the same, because state legislatures have created codes that criminalize unethical professional behavior. For instance, it may not only be unethical to breach professional confidentiality, but it may (depending upon the jurisdiction) also be illegal. Another example that brings both ethical and legal ramifications is engaging in a sexual relationship with a client. Psychologists and other clinicians may be civilly liable for such activities (*Zipkin v. Freeman*, 1968) as well as have their credentials (typically given by a state) stripped (*Morra v. State Board of Examiners of Psychologists*, 1973). Furthermore, the mental health practitioner may be *personally* liable for any money awarded to the victim, because the sexual behavior falls outside of the purview of insured "treatment functions" (*Roy v. Hartogs*, 1975, 1976).

Given that professional ethics codes, legal codes, and case law are constantly evolving, it is not surprising that procedures and protections in place today were not always the norm. The chapters in this section detail the historical development and case law in mental health practice. Chapter 3 traces the development of informed consent in both the legal and medical contexts. Chapter 4 traces the roots of confidentiality and privileged communication—basic professional protections afforded to clients. Finally, Chapter 5 presents the historical development of the duty of mental health professionals to protect the health and welfare of their clients, and at times to protect the public from their clients.

CASE REFERENCES

Morra v. State Board of Examiners of Psychologists, 212 Kan. 103; 1973 Kan. LEXIS 493 (1973).
Roy v. Hartogs, 81 Misc. 2d 350; 1975 N.Y. Misc. LEXIS 2386 (1975).
Roy v. Hartogs, 85 Misc. 2d 891; 1976 N.Y. Misc. LEXIS 2080 (1976).
Zipkin v. Freeman, 436 S.W.2d 753; 1968 Mo. LEXIS 739 (1968).

CHAPTER 3

Informed Consent

The right to *informed consent* means that a person cannot legally agree (consent) to a given course of action unless he or she has first been properly informed about the nature, risks, and benefits of that course of action. The idea of informed consent evolved through the Fourteenth Amendment of the U.S. Constitution, which deals with due process and the right to a fair trial. Thus, the right to informed consent lies deep within the roots of the constitutional freedoms afforded to all U.S. citizens.

Rules regarding informed consent apply in many professional areas, including both law and mental health. Information provided to an individual prior to trial, interrogation, treatment, or other type of legal or medical procedure must be designed to inform, as well as to protect the individual from harm or self-incrimination.

VOLUNTARINESS, DISCLOSURE, AND CAPACITY

There are three key legal elements in informed consent: voluntariness, disclosure, and capacity. The first, and most elementary component is *voluntariness*. For consent to be voluntary, it must be made of the person's own free will, and not coerced. Readers will notice the theme of voluntariness pervades this discussion, and many others throughout this book. *Disclosure* means that all information relevant to making the decision must be presented. In a health context, for instance, this may include side effects, alternative treatments, limits to confidentiality, constitutional rights, and so on. When this "disclosure" has taken place, a person is considered adequately "informed." *Capacity* refers to the person's mental ability to understand the legal or other consequences of the actions in question. Incapacity is the conclusion when someone is found not guilty of a crime due to "insanity." This specific concept is the focus of Chapter 7. Persons who are legally "insane" at the time of a crime are said to have lacked the mental "capacity" to commit the crime. Similarly, a person must be of sufficiently sound mind to provide true informed consent. The logic here is that the disclosure of information does little good if the individual lacks the ability or "capacity" to take it into account and come up with a decision.

The term *informed consent* first appeared in the court system in 1957, in *Salgo v. Leland Stanford Jr. Board of Trustees*. However, the 1914 case of *Schloendorf v. Society of New York Hospital* provided the first clear statement that a client must be apprised of the potential benefits and major risks of any proposed treatments, as well as available alternative treatments. This case provided the grounds for the disclosure component of informed consent.

The first case provided below gives a detailed explanation of the importance of informed consent and the element of disclosure within a legal context. The issues decided upon in this case may be relevant considerations in competency or related mental health assessments, bringing *Miranda v. Arizona* into immediate interest for mental health practitioners (Heilbrun, Marczyk, & DeMatteo, 2002).

The Case of *Miranda v. Arizona* (1966): The Importance of Disclosure

On the night of March 2, 1963, an 18-year-old woman had just gotten off work from her job at the refreshment stand in the Paramount Theater in downtown Phoenix, Arizona. She got on the bus that would take her closer to home. Upon exiting the bus, she began to walk toward her home. At that point, she noticed a light green, older model car parked across the street in the ballet school parking lot. The car pulled out of the lot and came so close to her she had to jump out of the way to prevent being hit. The driver, a Mexican American man of average height and build, parked across from an apartment complex on the same block. Wearing blue jeans, a white T-shirt, and dark-rimmed glasses, the driver got out of his car and walked toward the young woman. He had a distinct tattoo on his arm. He grabbed her and told her that he would not hurt her if she did not scream. With one strong hand, he held her hands behind her back, his other hand held tightly across her mouth. The attacker forced the young woman into backseat of his car. He tied her hands behind her back, and tied her ankles together. She felt something cold and sharp against her throat. "Feel this?" the man asked the young woman, commanding her to remain still.

The man then drove the car into the desert, with the young woman in the backseat crying. Twenty minutes later, he stopped the car in a desolate area, untied her hands, and directed her to remove her clothing. She refused, and he began to remove them himself. The young woman would later recount, "I was pushing against him with my hands. I kept screaming. I was trying to get away but he was a lot stronger than I was, and I couldn't do anything" (p. 2). The man raped the young woman, later justifying himself by saying that he "did not get it all the way in," because the woman continued to scream and fight him off.

The attacker then drove back to town, allowing the woman to put her clothes back on. He asked her to give him some money, and she handed him the four $1 bills she had. Before freeing her, he said to her, "Pray for me." The young woman ran home and immediately told her parents, who immediately called the police.

The victim provided a detailed description of her perpetrator and the car to the police. Based on this description, the police picked up a man by the name of Ernest Miranda that Sunday morning. Miranda was placed in a lineup; the police hoped the victim would recognize him as her attacker. The young woman was very shy and failed to recognize Miranda at that point.

One week later, when the victim and her brother-in-law were driving just a few blocks from where the abduction had occurred, they spotted a car similar to that driven by the attacker. The driver recognized the victim and sped away, but they were able to remember the license plate and report it to the police. The car was registered to a young woman who had been robbed only a few weeks before. That robbery victim had provided police with a similar physical description of her attacker as that provided by the rape victim, including the man's distinctive tattoo. The police eventually located the stolen car outside of a local restaurant. Upon further inspection, the officers noticed a rope in the backseat similar to that with which the victim had described being bound. The officers knew a particular employee of the restaurant to be none other than one Ernest Miranda. The police took Miranda into custody and organized another lineup. The victim was unsure of her decision once again, but she did say that Miranda had similar build and features.

At this point, the police took Miranda to an interrogation room, where he asked the officers how he did. "You flunked," they told him, and began to question him about the rape. Miranda eventually confessed to grabbing this woman, restraining her, driving away with her, and raping her. Official records of the confession consisted only of partly typed and partly handwritten accounts.

Little did Miranda know upon his arrest that he had the constitutional right to due process, elements of which included the right to refuse to talk to the police officers and the right to have an attorney present free of charge. In confessing to the crimes, Miranda had certainly consented to engaging in a course of action that would have significant legal ramifications for him. But given his ignorance of his constitutional rights, was this consent "informed"? Miranda's attorneys would contend that it was not.

Miranda at Trial and Initial Appeal

Ernest Miranda was brought to trial in June 1963, convicted, and sentenced to 20–30 years on each charge, to be served concurrently.[1] Miranda and his attorneys appealed to the Arizona Supreme Court on the grounds that the confession was coerced due to the fact that Miranda feared the police. They also contended that Miranda gave the confession without knowing his constitutional rights, including the Fifth Amendment's protection against self-incrimination. The Arizona Supreme Court was unimpressed with the arguments and affirmed the conviction. It held that the confession was in fact voluntary, made by the defendant by his own free will, without coercion or promise for immunity, and that despite not being explicitly informed so, he understood his statement could be used against him.

---

[1] Multiple sentences such as this can be served either concurrently (at the same time) or consecutively (one at a time). In this instance, the concurrent sentences resulted in a 20–30 year sentence, whereas an order to serve them consecutively would have resulted in a 40–60 year sentence. While different jurisdictions have different regulations regarding the imposition of concurrent or consecutive sentences, a general rule is that completely separate events must occur in order for a defendant to receive consecutive sentences. In this case, the rape happened during the kidnapping and multiple crimes, but only one (albeit prolonged) illegal event.

The U.S. Supreme Court Appeal

The U.S. Supreme Court heard Ernest Miranda's case on February 28–March 1, 1966. It was decided on June 13, 1966, along with three other cases that involved similar content. The issue involved the admissibility of statements obtained from someone during police interrogation, and the necessity to provide a procedure ensuring that the individual has been informed of his or her rights. The defense felt that Miranda's confession was in clear violation of his Fifth Amendment right against self-incrimination, because he was not informed of this right prior to questioning.

Miranda's attorneys would this time find a sympathetic ear in the foremost experts on U.S. constitutional law. The Court reversed Miranda's conviction in a 6 to 3 decision, holding that his Fifth Amendment rights had indeed been violated when his rights were not disclosed to him, including the right to have an attorney present to help him understand these rights. Among the dissenters, Justice White felt that the fact that Miranda did not receive the right to waive an attorney "has no significant support in the history of the privilege or in the language of the Fifth Amendment" (p. 1).

Miranda's confession could not be admitted into evidence. Writing the majority opinion, Chief Justice Warren held that there is a constitutional prerequisite for statements such as Miranda's confession: The subject must first be aware of the incriminating factors involved in making such statements. In other words, the possible negative consequences or risks must be disclosed to ensure that the subject is properly informed to provide consent.

The Legacy of *Miranda v. Arizona*

The principles outlined in the *Miranda* case were put into practice in the form of the "*Miranda* warning," a specific example of which is presented in Box 3.1. To this day, detainees may not be questioned before these rights have been disclosed. Many jurisdictions adhere very rigidly to the *Miranda* ruling, requiring police officers actually to read the warning verbatim from a card, and/or to read it in the detainees native language. While disclosure for police is different from that required in mental health and medical treatment, the *Miranda* case still clearly describes the importance of the disclosure facet.

The 1966 *Miranda* case was challenged in the U.S. Supreme Court

---

BOX 3.1. Where Are They Now?

Ernest Miranda was granted a new trial in 1966, in which his improperly informed confession was not allowed. He was nevertheless convicted again and spent the next decade in an Arizona correction facility. Upon release, he had several "run-ins" with the law.

On the night of January 31, 1976, Ernest Miranda was playing poker in a local flophouse section of Phoenix. He was celebrating the New Year when a drunken fight broke out involving two illegal Mexican immigrants. Miranda approached the men and noticed that one of them had a knife. As he tried to remove the knife from the drunken man's hand, Miranda was stabbed in the stomach, and again in the chest. He was pronounced dead upon his arrival to the hospital.

By the time the authorities arrived, Miranda's attacker had fled, but the authorities captured his accomplice. Thus, the story of Ernest Miranda begins with a final stroke of irony. Before they asked him to accompany them to Police Headquarters, two Phoenix police officers read the *Miranda* warning from a card, in both English and Spanish:

You have the right to remain silent.
Anything you say can and will be used against you in a court of law.
You have the right to the presence of an attorney to assist you prior to questioning and to be with you during questioning, if you so desire.
If you cannot afford an attorney, you have the right to have one appointed for you prior to questioning.
Do you understand the rights that have just been read to you?
Will you voluntarily answer my questions?

---

during the 2000 session. In *Dickerson v. U.S.* (2000), an attempt was made to make the only requirement for the admissibility of confessions be that a confession is made voluntarily, effectively removing the disclosure requirement. Proponents of this position claimed that *Miranda* warnings were not necessarily required by the U.S. Constitution; they were merely used to help protect rights that *were* necessarily guaranteed. The Court disagreed with this contention in a 7 to 2 decision, and the *Miranda* warning was preserved intact.

DEVELOPMENTS IN MEDICAL INFORMED CONSENT

The case of *Kaimowitz v. State of Michigan* (1972), addressed the issue of coercion as an annulment to informed consent in both medical and legal settings. Convicted sex offender Louis Smith was serving his sentence in a Michigan state prison, when he was released by the parole board. As a condition of his release,[2] Smith had to agree to psychosurgery.[3] In the interest of optimizing Smith's due process rights, the information given to him about the parole conditions (including the psychosurgery) and his agreement to those conditions was initially scrutinized through a screening committee of physicians, and a second committee composed of a law professor, a clergyman, and a layperson. All agreed that the requirements for informed consent had been satisfied. Prior to the surgery, Louis Smith was released and, not surprisingly, rescinded his agreement to the surgery. The Michigan Court agreed to hear his case. The defense argued that making the psychosurgery a condition of his release had made the situation itself "inherently coercive." The court in Michigan agreed, ruling that the institutionalization made this process inherently coercive so as to impinge upon his First Amendment right to privacy. Mr. Smith did not have to undergo the surgery. That condition of his parole having been dropped, he was allowed to remain out of prison.

A case that refined the definition of *informed* was *Canterbury v. Spence* (1972). In this case, doctors performed surgery on a 19-year-old patient with a ruptured disc. The procedure resulted in paralysis and other side effects. The medical custom in place at the time was for physicians themselves to judge how much disclosure was important to inform the patient adequately. This practice was referred to as the "reasonable professional" standard, whereby a court would assess whether or not a "reasonable professional" (i.e., physician) would have seen fit to disclose more information. Rather than supporting this view, the *Canterbury* court shifted the judgment to the patient. Using the criterion of "what the typical patient would want to know" (subsequently referred to as the "prudent patient" or the "materiality of risk" criterion), this case defined the elements of modern informed consent as the need for full disclosure of the possible effects of a therapeutic procedure. The Court elaborated, "Thus the test for determining whether a particular peril must be

---

[2] When a prisoner is let out on parole, a governing body (typically a parole board) sets forth conditions of release. Examples of such conditions may be to seek treatment, avoid contact with previous victims, and to check in regularly with a parole officer.

[3] *Psychosurgery* is a global term that may include any number of procedures whereupon the brain is physically altered to treat a mental disorder. It has always been considered somewhat of an extreme measure, reserved for only the most treatment-resistant patients. With increases in therapy and drug treatments for medical disorders, its practice is extremely rare today.

divulged is its materiality to the patient's decision: all risks potentially affecting the decision must be unmasked" (pp. 786–787). In so ruling, the *Canterbury* court set forth the first standard legal guideline that defined the "informed" part of a patient's informed consent. The impact of *Canterbury* was widespread, resulting in very detailed disclosures of potential risks and benefits to medical procedures, including those that come in written form with even over-the-counter medications.

How detailed should the informed consent be? Should every detail of treatment be included in the informed consent? How much is too much? Are there details that are not necessary to disclose prior to treatment? The current trend relies on the "details *ad nauseam*" model, in which hospitals give patients so much detail that they skip through all of the medical jargon and sign the form, without ever reading through the documents provided. When this happens, patients are ultimately signing an informed consent form, but are they getting the information they need when this happens? If not, then, are they truly "informed?"

INFORMED CONSENT: FROM MEDICAL TO MENTAL HEALTH SETTINGS

Mental health professionals are also heavily affected by the need to obtain informed consent. Treatment facilities must not only be capable of handling clients' rights with the utmost care but also providing a legal hearing when an involuntary admission of a client is involved. Today, most states have a civil commitment procedure that allows persons to be involuntarily committed into a mental health facility if they are a danger to themselves or to others. The details of this type of procedure are discussed at length in Chapter 8 of this volume. Suffice it to say for now that there are numerous procedural rules, all set forth to maximize the protection of patients' rights. However, involuntary commitment procedures only protect clients who will not *voluntarily* enter treatment, and voluntary entry implies informed consent. Yet, by definition, the mental capacities of people needing inpatient mental health treatment may be diminished (Madduz & Winstead, 2005). Certainly it is possible for the mental capacities of some individuals to be diminished enough to preclude them from being held responsible for their behavior, including consenting to treatment. The case *Zinermon v. Burch* (1990) clarified the need for informed consent when dealing with admissions into mental health facilities and set forth specific guidelines for mental health professionals to follow in order to ensure that voluntary consents to treatment represent the competent wishes of the patient.

The Case of *Zinermon v. Burch* (1990): The Importance of Capacity

On December 7, 1981, a concerned citizen found a man named Darrel Burch wandering aimlessly on the side of a Florida highway, hurt and confused. Burch was taken to Apalachee Community Mental Health Services (ACMHS), Inc. in Tallahassee, Florida. Apalachee is a private mental health facility nominated by the state to receive and treat persons suffering with mental illness. Upon his arrival, Mr. Burch was "hallucinating, confused, disoriented, clearly psychotic, wearing no shoes, and believed he was in heaven" (*Burch v. ACMIIS*, 1988, p. 2). Staff evaluation forms further indicated Mr. Burch's face and chest were bruised and bloodied, suggesting that he had fallen or had possibly been attacked. The admissions staff at Apalachee asked Mr. Burch to sign voluntary admission forms, in which he gave his consent for the facility to admit and treat him. He signed the forms and remained at Apalachee for 3 days.

During this period, Mr. Burch continued to display psychotic symptoms and confusion, continuing to believe he was in heaven. Apalachee staff notes on his second day of hospitalization indicated, "If he does not begin to clear will consider FSH [Florida State Hospital] on 12/10. I think he will sign voluntarily" (p. 2). While Burch was still at Apalachee, he was diagnosed with Paranoid Schizophrenia, and placed on psychotropic medication. On December 10, the Apalachee staff decided Mr. Burch was "in need of longer-term stabilization" (*Zinermon v. Burch*, 1990, p. 11), and referred him to FSH, in Chattahoochee, Florida. Later that day, Apalachee staff had Mr. Burch sign forms requesting voluntary admission to FSH, as well as a form authorizing treatment at FSH. Still psychotic and believing he was in heaven, Mr. Burch signed the forms and was transferred to FSH by a county sheriff.

Upon his arrival, FSH had Burch sign voluntary admission forms in addition to the forms signed at Apalachee. One form, called "Request for Voluntary Admission," indicated that the client was requesting treatment for his current mental condition and that he agreed to accept treatment as prescribed by the treatment team in accordance with provisions of expressed and informed consent. Burch signed these forms, along with two witnesses.

Dr. Marlus C. Zinermon, one of the doctors on the FSH staff, wrote a "progress note" on December 10, which explained that Burch was "refusing to cooperate," would not respond to questions, "appears distressed and confused," but "related that medication has been helpful" (p. 12). The next day, a nurse's records indicated that Burch could not explain his reason for hospitalization and still believed "this is heaven." Burch's behavior remained somewhat constant, and on December 23, he signed another form, which authorized the FSH staff to utilize all treatments, with the exception of electroconvulsive treatment. Dr. Zinermon himself signed this authorization form as a witness. At this point, Mr. Burch was medicated to the point of disorientation and maintained in that manner for almost a week. Dr. Zinermon then evaluated Burch again on December 29, and his report stated that Burch had been "disoriented, semi-mute, confused and bizarre in appearance and thought . . . not cooperative to the initial interview" and "extremely psychotic, appeared to be paranoid and hallucinating" (p. 13). Burch remained at FSH until May 7, 1982, 152 days after he was admitted to Apalachee. While hospitalized, Burch never had a formal hearing in regard to his hospitalization and treatment. He signed several forms authorizing his treatment. However, hospital staff notes indicated he was clearly psychotic, as well as hallucinating, which would seem to be a valid reason to authorize involuntary admission procedures. In fact, the state had already provided guidelines for such an admissions procedure with individuals experiencing those or similar symptoms.

The Case and Initial Appeal

After his release Mr. Burch brought these circumstances to the attention of the Florida Human Rights Advocacy Committee. Burch's complaint to the Committee stated he had been admitted to FSH without receiving proper admission procedures, and that he did not remember signing any of the multiple admission forms. Additionally, Burch alleged that he had been physically abused while at FSH. On August 4, 1983, the Advocacy Committee discussed this matter at its regular Florida State Hospital meeting. At that point, a letter was sent by the hospital in response to Burch's claim to the Advocacy Committee, stating that the "hospital administration was made aware that they were very likely asking medicated clients to make decisions at a time when they were not mentally competent" (*Burch v. ACMHS*, 1988, p. 3).

Burch sued ACMHS and the FSH employees who were involved with his admission or treatment under a part of the Civil Rights Act of 1871, which provides for compensatory relief for a plaintiff whose rights, privileges, or liberties are violated by state employees or representatives. The plaintiff must show that the conduct complained of was committed by a person acting under state law, and deprived him of rights, privileges, or immunities secured by the Constitution or laws of the United States.

Burch's complaint alleged that the state's staff members had taken part in admitting him as a voluntary mental patient at a time when he was incompetent to make such a decision. Thus, the staff had deprived him of his due process liberty, an infraction of the Fourteenth Amendment to the U.S. Constitution. At that point, the defense moved for dismissal of the complaint. The District Court agreed with the defense, and dismissed the complaint on the grounds that the employees' actions were unauthorized, and the state had no way of preventing such a deprivation of rights. Their ruling stated that the complaint was only against the hospital staff, and that the staff did not follow authorized state procedures for involuntary admission. In Burch's case, the Court felt that whatever compensation he received prior to his release was sufficient. Thus, for the time being, the main question as to whether or not Burch's rights had been violated remained shrouded in legal technicalities. However, Burch was successful on appeal, with the Eleventh Circuit Federal Appeals Court deciding that Burch had claimed deprivations of liberty for which the defendants could be held financially liable. The stage was set for an appeal to the highest court in the land.

The U.S. Supreme Court Appeal

Dr. Zinermon, the primary defendant in this lawsuit, presented his case to the Court on October 11, 1989. It was decided 4 months later, on February 27, 1990. Burch continued to assert that the hospital professionals should have been more aware of his condition during the time he was signing admission forms. Mr. Burch felt he should not have had to sign voluntary admission forms, but he should have been admitted by going through the involuntary admission process.

The Supreme Court ultimately handed down a (5 to 4) decision supporting Mr. Burch's claim. Most importantly, the Justices affirming this decision felt that Mr. Burch's diminished capacity gave him the constitutionally guaranteed right to receive procedural safeguards provided by Florida's involuntary commitment procedures, and that the hospital staff had failed to initiate such procedures. Furthermore, the Court held that liability of state employees was not disqualified by Section 1983, in which random, unauthorized actions by the hospital staff are protected by the fact that the state cannot predict such unauthorized actions. This reasoning suggested the state had procedural guidelines already in place, because this would have occurred at a specific point in this admission process when Burch received admission and consent for treatment forms. Burch's deprivation could also have been avoided if the state had set guidelines to limit individual employees' power to deprive patients of their constitutional liberties.

This case offers a reminder that an adequate release is a matter of fact, and not a matter of law. A signature on a release form is not sufficient evidence of informed consent. A person has to know what the release form is for, whatever its purpose. In other words, all relevant information not only need be disclosed but the person must also have sufficient mental capacity to appreciate the information and understand the consent. Otherwise the consent is not valid.

INFORMED CONSENT: THE STATE OF THE PRACTICE TODAY

Traditionally, convictions have been reversed whenever an appeals court has held that the judge erroneously admitted a confession in the absence of appropriate disclosure or capacity. The U.S. Supreme Court broke new ground in this area in *Arizona v. Fulminante* (1991). Oreste Fulminante was convicted and sentenced to death in part on the basis of an alleged coerced confession. The court agreed that the confession was coerced. However, in the face of significant other evidence against Fulminante, the Court held that the error in admitting the confession constituted a *harmless error,* a legal term meaning that the result of the proceedings would not have differed had the confession been properly omitted. There is no constitutional due process right to a *perfect* trial, merely to a *fair* one. This ruling, however, serves as another case in which psychological research might have been useful in challenging the Court's assumption. A long-developed body of research demonstrating the enormous impact that confessions can have on juries suggests that an erroneously admitted confession may be far from "harmless" by legal or lay definitions (Kassin, 1997). As case law, *Fulminante* also brings up the question of whether or not an improperly obtained informed consent, such as that signed by Mr. Burch, would be as legally problematic if the outcome would likely have been the same had a responsible guardian signed the consent. Perhaps a future case may bring this issue into a court of law, but for now, it remains unanswered.

This chapter provides cases for the purpose of gaining a better understanding of informed consent. Today, patients commonly receive information about the prescriptions they are taking, risks and benefits of treatments, and possible alternatives. Due in part to cases like that of Mr. Burch, the trend in American society is to include every detail of what may or may not happen. This degree of detail may actually do more damage than good, because many patients simply flip through all of the different forms, signing them without even reading them. It is unlikely that the average person could understand all of the relevant information even if he or she did read it all. Is this sufficient disclosure and capacity to consider any consent to be informed consent? Is informed consent not compromised when there is too much information, presented in complex terms the average adult cannot understand? Until these issues are challenged in courts of law, a person's signature is interpreted as indicating that the person has read and understood whatever forms he or she has signed.[4]

CASE REFERENCES

Arizona v. Fulminante, 499 U.S. 279; 1991 U.S. LEXIS 1854 (1991).

Burch v. ACMHS, 840 F.2d 797; 1988 U.S. App. LEXIS 3530 (1988).

Canterbury v. Spence, 464 F.2d 772 (D.C. Cir.), *cert. denied*, 409 U.S. 1064 (1972).

Dickerson v. U.S., 530 U.S. 428; 120 S. Ct. 2326; 147 L. Ed. 2d 405; 2000 U.S. LEXIS 4305 (2000).

Kaimowitz v. State of Michigan, Civil Action No. 73-19434-AW (Cir. Ct. Wayne County, Mich. July 10, 1973) (1972), reprinted in A. Brooks (1974). *Law, Psychiatry and the Mental Health System*. New York: Little, Brown, p. 902.

Miranda v. Arizona, 384 U.S. 436 (1966).

Salgo v. Leland Stanford Jr. Board of Trustees, 317 P.2d. 170 (1957).

Schloendorf v. Society of New York Hospital, 211 N.Y. 125, 105 N.E. (N.Y. 1914).

Zinermon v. Burch, 494 U.S. 113 (1990).

---

[4] In short, make sure to read all the fine print (including footnotes)!

CHAPTER 4

Confidentiality and Privileged Communication

When is it . . . that the psychotherapist came to play such an indispensable role in the maintenance of the citizenry's mental health? For most of history, men and women have worked out their difficulties by talking to, . . . parents, siblings, best friends and bartenders—none of whom was awarded a privilege against testifying in court. Ask the average citizen: Would your mental health be more significantly impaired by preventing you from seeing a psychotherapist, or by preventing you from getting advice from your mom? I have little doubt what the answer would be. Yet there is no mother–child privilege.
   —U.S. Supreme Court Justice Antonin Scalia,
       dissenting with the Court's 1996 decision to endorse
       the right of psychotherapy clients to privacy in courts
       of law (*Jaffee v. Redmond*, 1996)

Confidentiality is a basic ethical tenet of many professions. It essentially means that a professional has an ethical obligation to keep client information private unless legally compelled to disclose it. What a client considers private must stay private. Confidentiality forms the foundation upon which successful mental health services stand. *Privileged communication* is a legal term indicating that even a court cannot compel disclosure. It is a legal right established by the Constitution, subsequent legislation, and case law. While privileged communication typically falls within various professions' definitions of *confidential,* not all confidential communications are legally privileged in a court of law.

In understanding the term *privilege,* it is useful to consider whose "right" it is. This person is sometimes referred to as *the owner of the privilege.* From the point of mental health ethics, the owner of the privilege is generally the client. Thus, if a professional who is ethically required to maintain client confidentiality is hired by a judge (the client) to assess an individual (i.e., a defendant), then the defendant does not own the privilege (or have the right) to confidentiality. Thus, any communication with the defendant is not a privileged communication. Ethics then commonly dictate that this situation be spelled out to the person being assessed (i.e., "Anything you tell me may be forwarded to the judge"). In addition, there are some standard limits of confidentiality, such as when a client represents a harm to him- or herself or someone else, or in the case of suspected child abuse (both respectively elaborated upon in Chapters 5 and 21 in this volume). In this manner, the concepts of confidentiality and privileged communication become intertwined virtually any time a mental health professional comes into contact with the legal system.

THE TENSION BETWEEN MENTAL HEALTH CONFIDENTIALITY AND THE LEGAL SYSTEM

Confidentiality can be at odds with the goals of legal professionals who operate in a system founded on getting all relevant and available facts out on the table. Client confidentiality is a frequent source of tension between mental health and legal professionals. Yet the confidentiality between a defense attorney and a client is a most sacredly held foundation of American law, without which the legal system would quickly crumble. Confidentiality may seem to hinder the legal system when important facts need to be kept private, or when persons who own the privilege assert their rights to keep the information private. The potential loss of information to the courts may be significant. Therefore, important public policy reasons are required to extend confidentiality (the ethical concept), via privileged communication (the legal concept), to a new group (i.e., hypnotherapists, dentists, etc.). It has to be shown that breaches of confidentiality would greatly harm not only the group's work but also society. Not surprisingly, the attorney–client privilege, first adopted in England in 1577, is the strongest form of privilege.

Given the potential societal impact of affording such stringent privacy, how can the appropriateness of testimonial privilege be determined? The most widely recognized test derives from the thinking of the eminent legal scholar John H. Wigmore, who proposed what is essentially a cost–benefit analysis from society's perspective:

1. The communication must originate after an expectation of confidentiality is established (i.e., after a therapy client is told that his or her discussions will be kept confidential).
2. Confidentiality must be essential to the relationship between the parties (i.e., it would undermine the therapeutic process for the client to worry about in-session conversations being disclosed to others).
3. Any injury that would occur to the relationship by breaching confidentiality must be greater than any benefit gained by society by the breach. (I.e., a therapy client's disclosure that he or she was planning on killing someone likely warrants a breach of confidentiality by the therapist to authorities, in the interest of protecting society and the potential victim from the crime. However, a disclosure by a client that she or he had previously killed someone may not be sufficient cause for breach as the crime has already been committed and the victim cannot be helped.)

Yet even privilege itself is not an absolute shield. If the professional has a statutory right to privilege, the interpretation of when it applies is left to the courts and/or legislatures. As we will see, the right to claim the privilege ultimately belongs to the client, not to the therapist. If the client waives the right to privilege, the therapist *must* testify and, if asked, provide his or her records to the court. Additional failures of privilege arise due to the presence of third parties, insurance disclosures, dangerousness, child abuse, and certain child custody cases. Courts have interpreted the *Wigmore* criteria to mean that if information is given to a third party, there is no expectation of confidence and hence no privilege. This brings about an interesting quandary in group therapy. Could information disclosed in a therapy group be kept confidential given that other group members represent "third parties?" The answer is that, unless mandated otherwise by state law, the decision would likely lie with the individual court.

There are also problems of confidentiality related to insurance programs in general and employee assistance programs (EAPs) in particular. EAPs are programs that provide mental health benefits to company employees. Although employees are often assured of total confidentiality when referred to an EAP, there are several ways that employers can legally obtain information: (1) if the supervisor, even casually, suggested that the client contact the EAP, the supervisor is entitled to know what visits were made (though not the contents of the visits); (2) if the employee sues for wrongful termination, discrimination, breach of contract, or virtually anything else; (3) if the client is suicidal or threatens violence, or reports a child being abused. Also, if the client files a workplace injury claim, EAP records are often turned over to claims adjusters (not directly to the employer).

Several landmark cases in the last few decades have shaped today's confidentiality standards in the law. The first case below illustrates the nature of the psychotherapist–patient privilege and the patient–litigant exception to this privilege.

THE CASE OF *IN RE LIFSCHUTZ* (1970): THERAPIST–PATIENT PRIVILEGE AND PRIVILEGE WAIVER

The California case of *In re Lifschutz* (1970) was the first to assert clearly and formally that a constitutional right to privacy includes a psychotherapist–patient privilege. Contrary to the thinking of many mental health professionals of that era, the court emphasized that the patient, not the therapist, "owned" the privilege.

On June 3, 1968, Joseph F. Housek, the plaintiff, alleged to the court that an assault by defendant John Arabian caused him "physical injuries, pain, suffering and severe mental and emotional distress" (*In re Lifschutz*, 1970, p.1). In court, Mr. Housek disclosed having received psychiatric treatment from Dr. Lifschutz for a period of 6 months. When Dr. Lifschutz was called by the defense to testify and produce the plaintiff's records, he vehemently refused. He maintained that he would not violate his oath of confidentiality, which is critical in a psychotherapist–patient relationship.

During a second hearing on December 5, 1969, Dr. Lifschutz was again ordered to answer questions and to provide any relevant records. Dr. Lifschutz, supported by a considerable amount of correspondence from his colleagues, contended that an absolute privilege of confidentiality is essential to the effectiveness of the profession, and that any concern by the patients about the possible disclosure of confidential information, under any circumstance, would deter anyone from fully and effectively participating in the psychotherapy process. Dr. Lifschutz pleaded that the benefits of retaining the integrity of the psychotherapist–patient bond of confidentiality for all of society outweighed the potential detriments caused by withholding certain evidence.

Dr. Lifschutz again declined to disclose the relevant information and records, and was consequently jailed for contempt of court. Dr.

Lifschutz contended that he, as a psychotherapist, had the right to absolute confidentiality with his patients, in effect asserting that he was the
"owner of the privilege."

In making its ruling, the Court clearly disagreed. By the privilege
resting with the client, the needs of society could be protected both as
therapy clients (who *could* opt to keep information regarding their mental health out of public courtrooms) and as people protected by a legal
system that is informed by all relevant information. The California Court
acknowledged that confidentiality is crucial to the process of psychotherapy. Nevertheless, the Court explained that society's needs to ensure
access to information in legal proceedings outweigh the importance of
the confidentiality privilege.

How is society protected by a therapist disclosing information
about a client? The answer depends on what information the therapist
has. Remember that the defendant, who allegedly caused emotional
harm to the client, is also a member of society. Suppose that Dr.
Lifschutz knew that the client was actually as emotionally disturbed
before the alleged incident as after. Holding that information confidential would be harmful to the defendant. The court ruled that, as the
patient himself had waived his right to confidentiality by bringing his
"emotional" issues into court, the deterrence of patients and the suggested impairment of the therapy profession should not occur. Despite
the exception, the patient had retained full control over the confidentiality of his records and communications until he *voluntarily* raised the
issues in court. The Court added that the profession of psychotherapy
had flourished up to that point, in spite of the nonabsolute nature of
the confidentiality privilege.

The Court's conclusion that "the statutory psychotherapist–patient
privilege does not apply" (*In re Lifschutz*, 1970, p. 2). This is known as
the patient–litigant exception to the therapist–patient privilege, and was
overtly spelled out in a California law that stated:

> Where any person brings an action to recover damages for personal inju-
> ries, such action shall be deemed to constitute a consent by the person
> bringing said action that any physician who has prescribed for or treated
> said person and whose testimony is material in said action *shall testify.*

RELEVANT DECISIONS IN THE WAKE OF *LIFSCHUTZ*

Courts generally hold that even when confidential information is relevant to the issue of litigation, there are a variety of safeguards to protect

the privacy and integrity of the patient. Each court makes its decision by weighing the probative value of the evidence against the danger of undue prejudice.

Six years after the decision on the *Lifschutz* case, in *Caesar v. Mountanos* (1976), Dr. Caesar found himself in a very similar position to that of Dr. Lifschutz. Dr. Caesar refused to answer questions about one of his patients and was held in contempt of a California state court. Dr. Caesar then took the case to federal court, arguing privilege based on a federal right to privacy. The patient had filed suit against third parties, alleging that two separate automobile accidents had caused her pain and suffering beyond her physical ailments. The 9th Circuit U.S. Court of Appeals asserted that the constitutional right to privacy indeed protects the confidentiality of psychotherapist–patient communications. However, it rejected the argument that the privilege was absolute. Instead, the Court held that the privilege may be limited when necessary to advance a compelling state interest.

Two subsequent cases addressed different forms of the confidentiality privilege and the situational exceptions to such privilege. In *Pennsylvania v. Ritchie* (1987), the U.S. Supreme Court's ruling can be perceived as eroding the privilege. Ritchie was accused of sexually assaulting his daughter, and the judge was allowed to subpoena a state agency's confidential mental health file, over the defense's objections, to decide which material would be revealed.

In *State v. Szemple* (1994), Craig Szemple allegedly shot and killed a 15-year-old boy. After the State had rested its case, it later asked to reopen it on the basis of two alleged admissions of guilt: (1) a letter Szemple wrote to his wife, which her father inadvertently discovered; and (2) an admission that he killed "not one but three" to a minister of the Trinity Baptist Church (p. 4). The minister in turn reported the admission to Mr. Szemple's sister and brother-in-law. By a 4 to 3 decision, the New Jersey Supreme Court found that the marital privilege does not prevent disclosure, and also that in the priest–penitent privilege, the priest owns the privilege, a contrast to psychotherapy, where the privilege is owned by the client.

There has long been a concern about privilege in group therapy, because there are obviously third parties present when a patient makes a disclosure. Smith and Meyer (1987) provided data that loss of privilege for group therapy might impede a person's willingness to enter group therapy. Yet they also acknowledged that courts were not likely to extend privilege to group therapy. This proved so in the 1994 case of Hal Cobb, wherein the confidentiality of a therapy group was allowed to be broken in light of the probative value of the evidence (Meyer, 1995). Cobb electrocuted his pregnant wife in 1984 near Lexington, Kentucky, by dropping a hair dryer into her bathtub. The death was originally ruled an accident. In October 1991, in a therapy group for sex addicts in California, Cobb said, "It wasn't an accident. I killed her." He said he did it because she would not be able to accept his admission that he was homosexual, and because of his distress over just having learned of her unwanted pregnancy. Over objection, a fellow member of the therapy group was allowed to testify to these statements. Cobb was ultimately given a life sentence for first-degree murder, in part because he exhibited forethought, having twice previously dropped the hair dryer into his wife's tub "unsuccessfully."

The federal courts do not recognize a general physician–patient privilege. Federal recognition of a psychotherapeutic privilege has been avidly sought for years by those in mental health and was, in fact, proposed to Congress nearly 25 years ago by the top policymaking group of Federal judges in a recommendation that the Supreme Court itself endorsed. That proposal became enmeshed in a broader dispute on rules of evidence and was not adopted.

Instead, Congress adopted an open-ended privilege rule in 1972 that authorized the federal courts to recognize new privileges by applying the principles of established law interpreted in light of reason and experience. Some cases have alluded to the possibility of the psychotherapist–patient privilege actually being based in the U.S. Constitution.[1] For example, the 1976 *Caesar* case found that there was a constitutionally based privilege, and in the 1983 case of *In re Zuniga*, the 6th Circuit Federal Court found a psychotherapist–patient privilege under federal common law. However, these cases held limited precedent and applied only in the respective jurisdictions. Furthermore, each ruling had stated that the privilege could be waived were a trial judge to decide that the benefit of doing so outweighed the costs. These issues were finally addressed by the U.S. Supreme Court in the case of *Jaffee v. Redmond* (1996).

---

[1] Rights and liberties can emanate from a number of places, or a combination of places. Many rights are included in the U.S. Constitution, either directly or indirectly. Furthermore, any given right may be supported by any number of places or combination of places within the Constitution. Other rights may come from state or federal laws or state constitutions. Therefore, if a right is struck down in court, it is only struck down as emanating from the place contended by the attorneys in that case. Thus, the assertion here that the therapist–patient privilege may come from the U.S. Constitution is different from previously discussed assertions that were based on rights provided by the relevant states.

THE CASE OF *JAFFEE V. REDMOND* (1996): BROADENING THERAPIST–CLIENT PRIVILEGE

On June 21, 1991, Mary Lu Redmond, a police officer, investigated a report of a stabbing, on a *fight-in-progress* call. She shot and killed Ricky Allen, who Redmond said was holding a knife and chasing someone. Several siblings of the decedent witnessed the event and gave an alternative perspective that the decedent was walking rather than running, and that Officer Redmond had planted a knife on the decedent. Jaffee, the executor of Allen's estate, sued, and sought notes and records from Karen Beyer, a licensed clinical social worker who had counseled Redmond several times a week for 6 months after the shooting, a total of about 50 times. The trial judge rejected the social worker's assertion of privilege, and instead instructed the jury at the officer's civil trial that there was no justification for withholding the records, and that the jury was "entitled to presume the contents of the notes would be unfavorable" to the defense (*Jaffee v. Redmond*, 1996, p. 1).

The jury returned a verdict against Officer Redmond and her employer. An Appeals Court overturned the verdict on the basis of client–therapist privilege. Though they emphasized that the privilege was not absolute, they argued for a balance of interests test under which they supported the assertion of privilege in this case. Relatives appealed, arguing that the Appeals Court created too broad of a privilege. The 7th Circuit Court affirmed the Appeals Court logic, including the *balance of interests* test joining the 2nd and 6th Circuits in recognizing such a privilege, under Rule 501 of the Federal Rules of Evidence.

The Supreme Court ruled on June 14, 1996, that federal courts must allow psychotherapists and other mental health professionals to refuse to disclose patient records in judicial proceedings. By a vote of 7 to 2, the Court created a new evidentiary privilege, in both civil and criminal cases, similar to the lawyer–client and marital privileges the federal courts have recognized for years.

The decision, written by Justice John Paul Stevens, brings the federal courts into line with the 50 states, all of which now recognize some type of psychotherapist–patient privilege. The Court's new rule, which now becomes part of Rule 501 of the Federal Rules of Evidence, is more inclusive than some of the state privileges in extending the rule to cover clinical social workers.

"This case amply demonstrates the importance of allowing individuals to receive confidential counseling," Justice Stevens said. "If the privilege were rejected, confidential conversations between psychotherapists and their patients would surely be chilled" (p. 10).

Although the new privilege applies generally and is not limited to police officers, the Court found the law enforcement context of the case to be particularly persuasive. "The entire community may suffer if police officers are not able to receive effective counseling and treatment after traumatic incidents," Justice Stevens said, "either because trained officers leave the profession prematurely or because those in need of treatment remain on the job" (p. 10).

The decision went even further than the Appellate Court decision that it affirmed. The 7th Circuit had created not an absolute privilege, but a qualified one, to be balanced in appropriate cases by the *evidentiary need for the disclosure*. The Court made the privilege absolute, saying anything less would be worthless. "Making the promise of confidentiality contingent upon a trial judge's later evaluation of the relative importance of the patient's interest in privacy and evidentiary need for disclosure would eviscerate the effectiveness of the privilege," Justice Stevens said (p. 15).

Justice Antonin Scalia dissented from the creation of what he called "a privilege that is new, vast, and ill-defined" (p. 17). As alluded to in the quote at the beginning of this chapter, he suggested that people would be better advised to seek advice from their mothers than from psychiatrists,[2] "yet there is no mother–child privilege" (p. 18). He concluded that this new privilege would interfere with the truth-finding function of the courts and cause the courts "to become themselves the instruments of wrong" (p. 16).[3]

Finally, the Court recognized that it will have to define the details of the new privilege in cases it decides in the future. In a footnote, it sug-

---

[2] While Justice Scalia obviously believes that the advice he got from his mother was wonderful (or perhaps the advice he got from his therapist was horrible), no doubt many readers will take issue with his assertion. While his opinion did not matter in the end, it perhaps serves as an illustration of the personal projections that can enter into the decisions of even the highest court in the land.

[3] Interestingly, Justice Scalia took special issue with extending the privilege to clinical social workers. Perhaps more interestingly, Chief Justice Rehnquist joined the dissent on this issue. However, writing for the majority, Justice Stevens specified that the privilege should apply to clinical social workers, as well as to psychiatrists and psychologists, because the social workers' clients often "include the poor and those of modest means" (*Jaffee v. Redmond*, 1996, p. 22), arguing (we think correctly) that many of these clients may be more vulnerable. Most states, including New York, New Jersey, and Connecticut, specifically include social workers within their legislated psychotherapeutic privileges.

gested that there will be situations in which the privilege will have to give way to other social interests. By way of example, it suggested that "if a serious threat of harm to the patient or others can be averted only by means of a disclosure by the therapist" the privilege may not exist (p. 11).

CONFIDENTIALITY AND PRIVILEGE: HIPAA, POST-*JAFFEE*, AND BEYOND

In an attempt to encourage the streamlining of information in the health care system and protect the confidentiality of patient information in the age of electronic transfer, Congress enacted the Health Insurance Portability and Accountability Act (HIPAA; pronounced "hippa") in 1996. Certainly mental health professionals who have had to sit through hours of training on HIPAA, and patients who have to sign a receipt of their "confidentiality rights," may argue that the Act has had the immediate impact of increasing confidentiality in health care settings. Indeed, the days may be gone when receptionists yell back to the doctor, "Your 4 o'clock is here about the rash." However, we would agree with assessments that the implications of HIPAA for psychologists and most other mental health professionals should be minimal (Daw, 2002). Generally speaking, psychological ethics and many state laws require much stronger confidentiality than does HIPAA. Thus, a psychologist who violates HIPAA has probably already violated the ethical code. What HIPAA may do is call more public attention to patients' rights of confidentiality, ultimately making practitioners more likely to practice ethically. What HIPAA certainly does not address is the issue of legal privilege.

It is probably safe to predict that many exceptions to the therapist–client privilege will be recognized over the next several years. In addition to the dangerousness exception, it is almost certain that the Court will formally adopt other exceptions: in mandatory child abuse and other abuse/neglect situations; when the information is disclosed to a *third party*; for patient–litigant cases; and for court-ordered examinations (e.g., civil commitment). Because the Supreme Court has not given much guidance to lower Federal Courts on the nature of exceptions, there will likely be a long series of battles in District Courts and Courts of Appeals over any potential exceptions.

Other questions remain to be addressed directly: Does the therapist–patient privilege apply to group therapy? Does any disclosure of information to insurance companies breach the confidentiality in a way that destroys the privilege from that point on? Are professionals other than psychologists, psychiatrists, and social workers covered by the privilege? All this should ensure full employment for mental health lawyers, and it will mean that mental health practitioners should pay particular attention to the rules developed by federal and local courts. An alternative would be to seek Congressional action to define more precisely the contours of the federal psychotherapist–patient privilege. Congress has avoided making a decision about such privileges before, in part because once it deals with one testimonial privilege, it is likely to become embroiled in whether other privileges (notably a news reporter–source privilege) should also exist.

It is hard not to agree with Judge Rehnquist's comments in *Jaffee*, that a privilege subject to exceptions is not much of a privilege. This seems especially true when a therapist has to tell a client that whether or not what is said will be kept confidential will depend upon how a court *later* views it.

CASE REFERENCES

Caesar v. Mountanos, 542 F.2d 1064; U.S. App. LEXIS 7171 (1976).
In re Lifschutz, 2 Cal. 3d 415 P.2d 557; Cal. LEXIS 280 (1970).
In re Zuniga, 714 F.2d 632; U.S. App. LEXIS 25231 (1983).
Jaffee v. Redmond, 518 U.S. 1; 1996 U.S. LEXIS 3879 (1996).
Pennsylvania v. Ritchie, 480 U.S. 39; 1987 U.S. LEXIS 558 (1987).
State v. Szemple, 135 N.J. 406; 1994 N.J. LEXIS 411 (1994).

CHAPTER 5

Duty to Warn
and Protect

In Chapter 4 we introduced the concepts of confidentiality and privilege, and some of the legal precedent behind these most basic respective tenets of mental health and legal practice. As we discussed, the few exceptions to a therapy client's legal right to privileged communication include protecting the client or someone else from any imminent dangerous actions of the client. In these instances, the law and professional ethics mandate that the therapist take actions that, by definition, violate the confidentiality of the client (i.e., notifying the police or admitting the client to a hospital). Key determinants for the appropriateness of a confidentiality breach (i.e., imminence, level of potential harm) are embodied in the concept of dangerousness.[1] While dangerousness is discussed at length in Chapter 8, it is to a brief consideration of this concept that we next turn.[2]

---

[1] *Dangerousness* is a psychological term, although it is sometimes adopted directly in legislation. The legal counterpart to "dangerousness" is "dangerous propensities," which can apply not only to people but also to products and animals.

[2] Dangerousness and various forms of risk are themes that run throughout much of mental health practice. It makes sense that these issues would frequently either get people from the legal system into therapy (i.e., court-mandated treatment) or get a therapist and client involved in some legal action (i.e., *Tarasoff* warnings, or civil commitment proceedings): thus, the necessity that these concepts be continually developed throughout this text. The state of affairs in this chapter, where the reader has but an incomplete introduction to dangerousness, is actually representative of the relative unfamiliarity of general mental health practitioners who suddenly find themselves across from a dangerous client (compared to forensic specialists).

THE ROLE OF DANGEROUSNESS
IN DUTY TO WARN AND PROTECT

Understanding what dangerousness *is* relies largely on understanding what it *is not* (Miller, Amenta, & Conroy, 2005). The concept of dangerousness is often ambiguous, particularly across various reference sources. Different terms that may be used to define *dangerousness* include that to others, to self, or to property. However, dangerousness to property alone is not adequate grounds for a breach of confidentiality. Does it include emotional harm, cognitive harm, or economic harm, as well as physical harm? How severe or frequent must harm be to justify intervention? Although some experts suggest limiting dangerousness to acts intended to do physical harm to self or others, the courts have not always concurred, and positions on this matter vary from state to state.

Even given an agreement on the definition of *dangerousness*, the question remains as to how close in time the dangerous act is expected. Specifying the dangerousness as "imminent" can clarify this one parameter. But how does one define this parameter? Does "imminent" mean 2 hours, 24 hours, 2 days, or a week?

Even if acceptable definitions of *dangerousness* and *imminence* were agreed upon, only part of the problem would be solved. For the concept to become clinically useful, a reasonably accurate prediction of dangerousness is still required. The literature on the prediction of dangerousness and related concepts is likely the most rapidly expanding research track in forensic psychology today. While the accuracy in such predictions has increased well beyond what was believed possible even 10 years ago, almost none of this research has focused on an individual's imminent dangerousness within the next day or so. Thus, clinicians are left without much empirical guidance in making such an assessment. There is a strong tendency to overpredict dangerousness. This is not surprising given that professionals who fail to detect the dangerousness of clients who ultimately harm someone will be subject to significant professional and legal ramifications.

CASE LAW ON DUTY TO WARN AND PROTECT

There is a volume of case law establishing professionals' duty to warn and protect, as well as dictating the actual practices with which the duty is carried out. Our first case, *Tarasoff*, is undoubtedly the most well known and most influential case dealing with a professional's duty to warn and protect. Case law in this area began with two state court rulings that addressed requirements of clinicians to accurately assess a client's suicide potential. The ruling in *Meier v. Ross General Hospital* (1968) firmly established a basic duty of therapists to exercise adequate care and skill in "diagnosing" suicidality based on a duty to protect the client from his or her own actions. The Court in *Dinnerstein v. State* (1973) stated things a bit differently when it clearly established the principle that the clinician can be held liable if the treatment plan overlooks/neglects a patient's suicidal tendencies. The stage was now set for courts to address the issue of dangerousness to others.

The Case of *Tarasoff v. the Regents of the University of California* (1976): Dangerousness to Others and the Duty to Warn and Protect

Mr. Prosenjit Poddar attended a New Year's Eve party with his friends and acquaintances, among them Ms. Tatiana Tarasoff. Following the countdown to the new year, Tatiana and Poddar engaged in a ritual kiss, along with many of the others around them. Poddar, however, mistook this friendly engagement as a sign of love for him. Despite trying, Ms. Tarasoff could not convince him otherwise. She avoided him and, as it turned out, with very good reason. On August 20, 1969, in therapy with a psychologist at the University of California–Berkeley mental health clinic by the name of Dr. Lawrence Moore, Poddar expressed his frustration with Ms. Tarasoff's continued avoidance of his romantic approaches. He confided in Dr. Moore that he intended to kill Ms. Tarasoff. Believing that there may be some validity to his client's claim, Dr. Moore appropriately conferred with two of his colleagues. All agreed that Dr. Moore was correct in his concerns, and that police assistance should be sought to place Poddar in custody for observation and evaluation. Dr. Moore engaged the help of clinic staff, who called the campus police and told them about the situation. The staff requested that the police pick Poddar up for further evaluation, and warned them that Poddar might appear reasonably normal and under control. Dr. Moore also followed up with a letter to the Chief of Police, detailing the events that had taken place and his concerns about Ms. Tarasoff's safety.

Despite the warning, the police went to Poddar's house, talked to him, and decided that there was no problem. They did not detain Poddar. Following the officers' decision, the Director of the Department of Psychiatry then ordered that no action be taken to place Poddar under evaluation and that all of Dr. Moore's notes, including his letter to the police chief, be returned or destroyed.

Two months later, on October 27, 1969, Poddar killed Tatiana Tarasoff. The Tarasoff family sued the university health service, the university, Dr. Moore, and the campus police for failure to take appropriate action to protect Tatiana from Poddar.

The plaintiffs brought forth their case under three notable arguments: (1) The defendants had failed to detain a dangerous patient; (2) the defendants were negligent in not making sure that the intended victim, Tatiana,[3] was made aware of the potential danger she faced; (3) the defendants had breached their duty to safeguard the patient and the public. Essentially, Tatiana's parents were contending that the doctors not only failed to warn the victim of Poddar's intentions, but they also failed to successfully commit Poddar. Ironically, the campus police, who had failed to act on the detailed concerns and warnings of the psychiatrists, was the first group to be dropped from the suit as not legally liable according to California state statute.

Tarasoff at Trial

At trial, the plaintiff's objective was to demonstrate that a therapist, upon determining that a patient presents clear and imminent danger to another person, is obligated by law to warn and protect the predicted victim. This obligation could have been fulfilled by warning either the victim or others who might apprise the victim of the danger. Although the plaintiffs admitted that Dr. Moore did in fact initiate the process for Poddar's commitment, the plaintiffs maintained that the care was obviously insufficient to protect Tatiana, since Poddar's detention did not succeed *and* no appropriate warning was given.

The defendants' position was that they had no duty of care to Tatiana directly and were thus immune from any liability. Under state law, the therapists could claim immunity for not seeing through that Mr. Poddar had been committed (the plaintiff's first cause of action above), but there was no such legal immunity for failing to warn Tatiana. The defendants contended that the absolute confidentiality was crucial in therapist–patient relationships, and stated that having to warn third parties directly breaks the bond of confidentiality that is formed with the patient. It was arguably this confidentiality that allowed Poddar to make

---

[3] Throughout the case material, repeated reference was made to the fact that the psychiatrists should have notified either Tatiana or her parents, the logic being that the parents could have then warned their daughter. Interestingly, breaching confidentiality to the parents *could have* been interpreted as an unnecessary additional breach. Why notify more than one person when only one person was in danger? However, including the parents in the claims against the defendants likely served the legal purpose of solidifying their role in the process, and hence their right to sue.

his homicidal thoughts known to begin with, in turn allowing the therapists to try to take *some* action. The Court held that an exception to the confidentiality privilege occurs when the patient provides information suggesting physical danger to him- or herself or others. State law included a "dangerous patient" exception to confidentiality that balances patients' rights to privacy with the public interest in safety. However, despite most states having similar statutes, no prior state court had interpreted such a law as stating that a therapist must actually warn the target person in order to fulfill the duty to warn.

The defendants argued that an obligation to warn could not even be effective. In making this argument, the defense presented research that therapists could not accurately predict if or when a patient would become violent.[4] However, the defendants did in fact predict (as it turns out, accurately) that Poddar presented imminent danger. It was their subsequent failure to assert his detainment and to warn the appropriate people that was problematic.

California state law stated that no one person owes a duty to control the actions of another, unless a "special relationship" exists between the parties involved. In the *Tarasoff* case, the therapeutic relationship between Dr. Moore and Poddar fulfilled this "special relationship" requirement. Therefore, the court held that this exception extended Dr. Moore's duty to warn into a duty to *protect* Tatiana. Upon determining that the patient poses serious physical danger to himself or others, the therapist has the obligation to exercise reasonable care to protect the foreseeable victim. Essentially, the therapist owes a legal duty not only to his patient but also to his patient's potential victims. Upon weighing the potential damage that could be inflicted to therapy patients by requiring a breach of confidentiality against the possibility of saving a life, the court concluded that the latter is of primary interest.

The Legacy of *Tarasoff*

Although a therapist's duty to warn *and* protect was imposed by the majority, many experts have since argued that patients' constitutional rights of privacy, as well as their right to receive treatment, would be

---

[4] Again, although the current state of the literature suggests that clinicians can make reasonably accurate predictions of violence, the methods for doing so were not available in the mid-1970s. However, Mr. Poddar actually stating his intention to kill a specific victim, and providing his reason for doing so, would place him at high risk by most clinician's accounts today.

violated as a result. While a court of law has yet to express this sympathy, it is reasonable to believe that this inherent breach in confidentiality may deter violence-prone patients from seeking therapy. Arguably, this makes them more dangerous (or misses an opportunity to make them less dangerous), consequently endangering society. Establishing a duty to warn may also result in overreporting and inappropriately overcommitting mentally ill patients.

California clinicians to this day say that they will "Tarasoff" a client who is deemed a danger to themselves or someone else. Nevertheless, a long series of subsequent cases from that state and others further refined the duty to protect. The following summary highlights critical points and discusses important precedents contained in these cases.

Bellah v. Greenson (1978) offered some support for the concept that there is no *Tarasoff* "duty to warn" significant others of the possible suicidality of a client (but the court did specify that this refers to outpatient settings). Regarding dangerousness to others, courts have been divided on the issue of the requirement of specific threats and specific victims. State courts held that therapists could be sued for failing to protect even when there were no threats communicated (*McIntosh v. Milano*, 1979), and that the duty to warn was in effect if medical staff either "knew" or "should have known" about a client's dangerousness (*Leedy v. Hartnett*, 1981). In the same period, another California court further narrowed the duty to protect others by saying that a duty arises only when there *are* "specific threats to identifiable victims," (*Thompson v. County of Alameda*, 1980). In a famous case in 1983, John Hinkley's therapist was deemed immune from any duty to warn *because of* a lack of specific threat (*Brady v. Hopper*, 1983).

In *Jablonski v. United States* (1983), a case similar in reasoning to *McIntosh*, several therapists at a Veterans Administration hospital were sued for negligence in warning. Their patient had been convicted of rape many years earlier and had recently threatened the mother of his girlfriend, but their assessment indicated that he did not meet civil commitment criteria.[5] The primary therapist and his supervisor each warned the girlfriend that she might not be safe in the apartment she shared with

---

[5] This is actually a quite common state of affairs. Things essentially get confounded when the danger to self or others needs to be "imminent" in order to carry out an involuntary civil commitment. A patient may have a long-term history of violent behavior with significant periods of time in between incidents. There may be no reason to expect that another incident is on the immediate horizon; thus, this arguably dangerous person clearly does not meet civil commitment criteria.

the patient and that she should move out, which she eventually did, with additional encouragement from her minister and others. However, she subsequently visited the apartment, whereupon the patient killed her. The victim's estate sued for negligence on several grounds. The court ruled against the therapists, ruling in relevant part that they were negligent, because (1) they did not forecast the homicide based on the "psychological profile" of the patient, (2) did not request some prior records, and (3) the warning was vague and inadequate.

That same year, in *Hedlund v. Superior Court of Orange County* (1983), it was ruled that failure to warn constituted not only professional negligence but also personal injury. Therefore, the longer statute of limitations for personal injury would be applicable in consideration of whether or not a plaintiff may file suit. While they do vary across jurisdictions, the critical issues in these and other cases remain whether or not there is a "specific threat" to a "specific victim" and "foreseeable danger."

RECENT CASES ON DUTY TO WARN AND PROTECT

Most of the cases we consider in this book are important in large part because of their precedent value, especially when they are heard at the level of the U.S. Supreme Court. Other cases are important because they were the first to deal with an important issue. Some cases are important only because they provide a clear focus on a central issue. The previous cases culminate in what seems to be a clear picture of how and when to breach confidentiality in fulfillment of a duty to warn and protect. However, the importance of some cases is that they demonstrate areas of law in which a seemingly clear issue is really not clear when put into practice. Such are the two cases that follow.

The Case of *Almonte v. New York Medical College* (1994): Duty to Warn and Protect a Nonspecified Victim

Douglas Ingram, MD, was the training psychoanalyst/therapist for Dr. Joseph DeMasi. Dr. Ingram, an experienced and respected psychoanalyst, was at one time president of the American Academy of Psychoanalysis. He probably knew as much about confidentiality issues as anyone in the United States. Indeed, he chaired the Manhattan Task Force on Confidentiality for the American Psychiatric Association. Dr. DeMasi (the client) had recently returned from a vacation trip to South America. He described to Dr. Ingram (the therapist) how he had enjoyed his trip, especially his sexual encounter there with a young boy. Dr. Ingram, knowing immediately the ethical dilemma he was in, later confessed that he knew his life would change forever after that day.

In that and subsequent sessions, Dr. DeMasi clearly indicated that although he philosophically embraced the ideals of the Man–Boy Love Society, he would not have a sexual encounter with an underage person, because he knew that was illegal. He assured Dr. Ingram that he could control his urges in that regard, suggesting that there was no future danger to any other child. Yet cases of even suspected child abuse are cause for breach of confidentiality and notification to the authorities. So what should Dr. Ingram have done at that point? No case offers a clearer dilemma.

Dr. Ingram argued in later testimony that there was little he could do, because there was certainly no "imminent" danger, no "mental illness" as we traditionally conceive it, and Dr. DeMasi had clearly and consistently insisted he had not and would not act out where such behavior was illegal. However, Dr. Ingram did change his treatment relationship with Dr. DeMasi to standard psychotherapy, on the premise that Dr. DeMasi's philosophical position endorsing "man–boy love" precluded him from becoming a psychoanalyst. Dr. Ingram continued the therapy with the goal of changing Dr. DeMasi's views and to monitor his behavior and adjustment.

Four months later, DeMasi obtained work as a psychiatrist at the Danbury Hospital in Connecticut. There he had a sexual encounter with Danny Almonte, a juvenile. Mr. Almonte was subsequently in and out of juvenile correctional facilities, then was eventually imprisoned as an adult for assault. Mr. Almonte and his family eventually sued Dr. Ingram (Dr. DeMasi's therapist). They asserted that by not intervening differently toward Dr. DeMasi, Dr. Ingram had ultimately, albeit indirectly, contributed to Mr. Almonte's problematic life.

Many eminent experts supported Dr. Ingram's choice as to how he handled this case. The case is presented in many professional ethics trainings on duty to warn and protect. The great majority of professionals and students in these trainings seem to believe that although Dr. Ingram was in the wrong place at the wrong time, he did the right thing. The jury disagreed and in October 1998 found for Mr. Almonte. The attorneys immediately conferred and reached an agreement on damages totaling $1.3 million. It is impossible to tell what the jury may have awarded. A consensus of jury members indicated that they felt that Dr. Ingram should have gone to the hospital and/or medical training directors and worked to have Dr. DeMasi removed from medical practice. Dr. DeMasi did serve 5 years in prison and was paroled. While being considered for a return to prison following a parole violation, he disappeared.

While this is a civil case holding very limited precedent value, it nonetheless sends a clear message. Regardless of what professional ethics or state and federal law mandate, juries may in fact impose more stringent restrictions on professionals should a client turn violent. However, it is not the answer for mental health practitioners merely to be quick to jump toward breaching confidentiality in the hopes of later avoiding the wrath of a jury. The case that concludes this chapter serves to illustrate this point.

The Case of *Garner v. Stone* (1973): Confidentiality and the Duty *Not* to Warn and Protect

Gordon Garner, a Georgia police officer, had over the years developed difficulties in his work and personal functioning, his problems apparently fueled by alcohol abuse. He accepted a recommendation from superiors for psychotherapy. In August 1995, he began therapy with Dr. James Gonzalez. However, Dr. Gonzalez promptly referred Garner to Dr. Tony Stone, a psychologist with specialized experience in treating police burnout. When asked to sign a release of information form, Mr. Garner crossed out all parts except those allowing Dr. Stone to talk to Dr. Gonzalez. Disclosures in therapy led Dr. Stone to be concerned about Mr. Garner's dangerousness, particularly to some of his law enforcement colleagues. Dr. Stone wisely consulted an attorney who worked with the Georgia Psychological Association (GPA). The attorney clearly advised him to break confidentiality and contact the potential victims, advice that seemed clearly consistent with the *Ingram* decision discussed earlier. Nothing remarkable ensued except that Mr. Garner, an animal lover (at least by later avowal), was reassigned to an animal shelter. Part of his job there was to euthanize some of the animals, a task that reportedly caused him much psychological damage. Mr. Garner then sued Dr. Stone for breach of confidentiality.

Despite Dr. Stone's evident expertise and his apparent extra precaution in consulting with the GPA attorney, in December 1999, the jury found for Mr. Garner, awarding him $280,000. Garner's attorneys had successfully argued that the disclosures by Dr. Stone regarding their client's dangerousness had contributed to Mr. Garner's demotion into the psychologically damaging job at the animal shelter.

Perhaps there is a moral for mental health practitioners in these latter cases: Sometimes even professionals who go to extreme lengths to protect the rights of society and their clients do not win, which is why they should be well insured.

CASE REFERENCES

Almonte v. New York Medical College, 851 F. Supp. 34 (1994).

Bellah v. Greenson, 81 Cal. App. 3d 614; 1978 Cal. App. LEXIS 1607 (1978).

Brady v. Hopper, 570 F. Supp. 1333; 1983 U.S. Dist. LEXIS 13755 (1983).

Dinnerstein v. State, 486 F.2d 34; 1973 U.S. App. LEXIS 7497 (1973).

Garner v. Stone, 85 N.M. 716; 516 P.2d 687; 1973 N.M. LEXIS 1318 (1973).

Hedlund v. Superior Court of Orange County, 34 Cal. 3d 695; 669 P.2d 41; 194 Cal. Rptr. 805; 1983 Cal. LEXIS 237 (1983).

Jablonski v. United States, 712 F.2d 391; 1983 U.S. App. LEXIS 26766 (1983).

Leedy v. Hartnett, 510 F. Supp. 1125; 1981 U.S. Dist. LEXIS 11444 (1981).

McIntosh v. Milano, 168 N.J. Super. 466; 1979 N.J. Super. LEXIS 798 (1979).

Meier v. Ross General Hospital, 69 Cal. 2d 420; Cal. LEXIS 251 (1968).

Tarasoff v. the Regents of the University of California, 17 Cal. 3d 425; 551 P. 2d 334 (1976).

Thompson v. County of Alameda, 27 Cal. 3d 741; 1980 Cal. LEXIS 196 (1980).

PART III

Clinical Forensic Evaluation

Parts I and II presented the legal precedent for some of the basic procedures used in the legal system, and that dictate everyday mental health
practices. In Part III, we turn to a more specific area of mental health
practice, that of forensic evaluation. In Chapters 6–8, we review the
legal cases demonstrating the necessity of each type of evaluation, and
the legal cases that dictate how these assessments are conducted. In
Chapter 9 we discuss the legal precedent dictating the use and admissibility of two particularly controversial procedures in courts of law.

CHAPTER 6

Competency

Competency can be grossly defined as "sufficient ability." The concept of competency underlies many of the legal and ethical issues that confront mental health practitioners in their everyday duties. Virtually any mental health evaluation involves the issue of competency in its most general sense. Thus, the following discussion has implications on a broad range of fronts. For instance, a client must be competent to consent to treatment or assessment.

In forensic terms, competency is much more specific. *Competency* typically refers to a client's mental state during a specific period in a legal process. For instance, an assessment to determine a client's competency to stand trial would involve assessing the client's abilities prior to and/or during trial. In contrast, *criminal responsibility* (also known as insanity) concerns the client's mental state at the time a crime was committed, which may be years prior to the trial (responsibility is discussed in Chapter 7). American law now recognizes a number of specific competencies (e.g., to stand trial, to testify, to be executed, to make a will). However, this degree of sophistication was not always in place. Legal competency began with the fairly broad competency, that to stand trial.

COMPETENCY TO STAND TRIAL

The English criminal justice system first introduced a requirement that the defendant plead to the charge prior to the trial. It is believed that the concept of "competency" first arose as a reaction by the English courts to defendants who stood mute rather than making the required plea. The court in such a case then made a decision as to whether the defendant was "mute by malice" or "mute by a visitation by God." If "mute by malice," the court sought to force a plea by employing a process in which increasingly heavy weights were placed upon the individual's chest until he or she provided the required testimony (not surprisingly, it was also often the desired testimony). Malingering of competency is still an issue (Jackson, Rogers, & Sewell, 2005).

People who the court decided were "mute by a visitation of God" likely included many mentally ill individuals. If the court decided that a defendant fell into this category, he or she was spared the ordeal. The requirement that the defendant be competent gradually grew in sophistication, spurred on by the general concern that it was simply unfair to subject certain types of people to trial.

The modern view of competency to stand trial stems from the Fourteenth Amendment of the U.S. Constitution, which promises due process for all defendants. The due process concept is intended to safeguard the accuracy of criminal cases and to guarantee fair trials. It also helps to preserve the integrity and dignity of the legal process, while acknowledging society's idea of retribution (i.e., we want defendants to know why they are being prosecuted.) Since indigent defendants do not have the means to procure their own mental health experts for competency evaluations, the court is obligated to make such experts available. This became law with the case of *Ake v. Oklahoma* (1985). The U.S. Supreme Court ordered that indigent defendants must be provided psychiatric expertise at the point of sentencing in a capital case in which mental condition or dangerousness is at issue. *Funk v. Commonwealth* (1989) extended this to psychologists.

Although early American courts used the competency doctrine periodically, not until *Youtsey v. U.S.* (1899) did a federal court of appeals give the doctrine of competency constitutional status, by explicitly tying it to the Sixth Amendment. In this case, the Court found that "it is fundamental that an insane person can neither plead to an arraignment, be subjected to a trial, or, after trial, receive judgment, or after judgment, undergo punishment; . . . to the same effect are all the common-law authorities. . . . It is not 'due process of law' to subject an insane person to trial upon an indictment involving liberty or life" (pp. 940–941).

The competency doctrine was initially set in place to protect deaf, mute, and "lunatic" defendants, but questions eventually arose as to what type of defendant fits into the latter category. This issue was better defined with the *Higgins v. McGrath* (1951) case, which set forth a reasoned argument that competency to stand trial is not dependent on the presence or absence of a psychosis (or even delusions per se). In this case, Higgins was accused of using the mail for obscene purposes. He was evaluated by several psychiatrists, who all testified that he was a paranoid schizophrenic with persecutory delusions. The psychiatrists concluded that Higgins was incompetent, and he was committed under the incompetency statute. Higgins filed a writ of habeas corpus for a redetermination of competency. The Court replied that Higgins's delusions were not sufficient to bar his trial. The standards to satisfy due process in competency to stand trial cases were established by the Supreme Court in *Dusky v. U.S.* (1960).

The Case of *Dusky v. U.S.* (1959): Defining Competency to Stand Trial[1]

Milton R. Dusky's family life had been filled with discord, and his parents divorced when he was 16 years old. He claimed that they abandoned him after the divorce. By age 17, Dusky was married and working a full-time job. When Dusky turned 18, he joined the Navy but was released with a medical discharge due to anxiety and panic. After that, Dusky struggled with his anxiety but was able to maintain employment with some regularity until his wife left him in 1949. The two were reunited later the same year, and Dusky returned to work, this time at the Porter Electric Company, where he stayed for 7 years.

During this time, Dusky's many problems at home worsened his anxiety. Following a series of psychiatric evaluations and hospitalizations, he began to miss work frequently. He eventually became extremely agitated and contemplated suicide, but instead sought treatment at the Psychiatric Receiving Center in Kansas City, Missouri. Records there indicate he was treated from January 2 to January 4, 1956, from March 14 to April 13, 1956, and again on December 31, 1956. The diagnoses were "happy, dependent personality; potential suicide reaction depression; threats severe; family and social problem; pre-disposition severe; passive depressive personality, dependent type with alcohol addiction" (p. 6).

Dusky quit his job at the electric company in 1957 on his doctor's recommendation. He committed himself to a voluntary hospitalization at the Veterans Administration Hospital at Topeka, Kansas in July of the

---

[1] Unless otherwise noted, information for this case was gathered from *Dusky v. U.S.* (1959).

same year. There he was evaluated by a psychiatrist, who found him to be suffering from anxiety and alcohol problems, diagnoses that were confirmed a year later. Reports during his hospitalizations indicated that Dusky was preoccupied with thoughts of suicide, hostility, murder, and "sexual indulgence" (p. 2). Dusky also reported fantasies of beating his ex-wife (who had married his brother) and spells in which he felt like he "was somebody else or something" and did not know where he was (p. 6). Through that spring and summer, he was so confused and unable to work that his teenage son moved in with him to help. The residence was chaotic, with Dusky's son frequently bringing in friends, including two boys who would later be involved in the alleged offense that would land Dusky in court.

On August 18, 1957, Dusky's son allowed the landlady's dog to leave the house, and it was killed. Consequently, Dusky and his son were evicted. With no home, little money, and no work prospects, Dusky's anxiety peaked. In response, he took tranquilizers given to him by his doctor. Just for good measure, he also drank two pints of vodka per day.

By this time, Dusky was 33 years old. He had had little legal involvement, having only been investigated for a robbery and released without charge. At about noon on August 19, 1958, his situation took a drastic change for the worse. Dusky and two of his son's friends, 16-year-old Richard Nixon and 14-year-old Leonard Dischart, approached Allison McQuerry, a 15-year-old high school girl, on her way to a local drugstore in Ruskin Heights. She was walking there to have lunch with a friend. The three men, riding in Dusky's automobile, offered her a ride to the store. Since Nixon was an acquaintance, she accepted the offer. After dropping McQuerry off, the three men went to a store to buy vodka. There, Dusky and the two boys discussed picking up McQuerry again to have sex with her.

When the men returned to the area of the drugstore, they sought out McQuerry and promised to drive her to visit a girlfriend of hers, and to take her home afterwards. However, after she got in the car, they drove back across the Kansas state line to a desolate back road. Nixon and Dischart then forced McQuerry to undress, and they raped her. Dusky also attempted to rape the girl but was unable to do so. The assailants allowed McQuerry to dress and drove her to a store, where they released her temporarily to get some water. When the three saw McQuerry speaking to a man inside the store, they sped away, assuming that she was reporting what had just occurred.

Dusky and Dischart were arrested the following night. When authorities told Dusky he was being arrested for kidnapping, he reacted, saying "That is a pretty serious charge, isn't it?" Dusky's reaction demonstrated his appreciation of the charges (p. 4). The officer also informed Dusky that the charge referred to kidnapping the girl from Rusking Heights. Dusky demonstrated at least some familiarity with the allegation, replying, "That wasn't a kidnapping. She got in the car voluntarily" (p. 4). Dusky denied the charges on the day of his arrest, saying that his only intention was to drop the two boys off to see a girl. However, when questioned the following day as to whether the alleged crime really happened, Dusky responded, "Well it evidently did because I am here and charged" (p. 6). Although he did not remember events written up in the statement (e.g., driving the car back to the store), Dusky stated, "I must have [driven the car back] because everybody seen me, but I don't remember that I did" (p. 7).

Dusky was indicted on the kidnapping charges. Because the alleged crime had taken place across state lines, Dusky was tried in Federal Court, where he received a court-appointed attorney, Mr. James W. Benjamin. At his arraignment on September 12, 1958, Dusky pled not guilty, and his counsel requested evaluations concerning his competency to stand trial and his mental capacity and responsibility (insanity) for his crime. He was then sent to the Federal Medical Center (FMC) for Prisoners in Springfield, Missouri to be evaluated for both competency and responsibility. Dusky was held at FMC Springfield for 4 months of examinations and treatment.

At a competency hearing on January 21, 1959, an examination report from a FMC psychiatrist was used to help determine Dusky's level of competence. In the report dated October 30, 1958, the psychiatrist stated that Dusky was "oriented as to time, place, and person" and that he "denies complete memory of the events of the day of the alleged offense" (p. 2). The report also mentioned psychological testing performed in September 1958, from which Dusky was diagnosed with Schizophrenia.

The Chief of Neuropsychiatric Service at the FMC, Dr. Joseph C. Sturgell, also submitted a report dated October 30, 1958. The report indicated that FMC staff believed that Dusky was not competent to stand trial at the current time. Staff did, however, think it was likely that Dusky would be competent if he remained in the facility for an additional 60 days and weaned from tranquilizers. The report also stated that, due to Dusky's long history of depression, anxiety, alcoholism, and family problems, indicative of chronic mental illness, the staff were unable to establish whether Dusky had had the mental faculties required to differentiate between right and wrong on the day of the alleged kidnapping.

Another report by Dr. Sturgell, dated January 20, 1959, confirmed and expanded on the findings of the previous evaluations. In the report, he stated that Dusky's mental state had remained stable for approximately 6 weeks after the October 1958 report; however, his condition had deteriorated since then. He had since become "agitated, anxious, and hostile to people around him" and conveyed "discouragement with his situation and began to feel that he was being framed in the present offense" (p. 3). The report also indicated that Dusky was suffering from delusions, hallucinations, and ideas of reference. Thus, the staff believed that Dusky's condition had significantly worsened since his initial evaluation.

At the competency hearing, Dr. Sturgell, the only witness who testified, explained prior claims that Dusky was "oriented to person, place, time" to mean that Dusky "knows the day of the week and the day of the year, and he knows that you are his attorney and Judge Smith is the judge. This is orientation to person. He knows it all" (p. 3). Dr. Sturgell also went on to testify that Dusky understood his charges, was aware that the trial would occur with a judge and a jury, understood that he would be punished if found guilty, and knew that his attorney, whom he recognized, was present in order to protect his rights. However, Dr. Sturgell told the Court that, in his opinion, Dusky would not be able to assist adequately in his defense, because he was unable to understand the meaning of the events that occurred since his mental illness confused his thinking. He also believed that Dusky would be able to discuss particulars related to his crime; however, his statements would be filtered through a mentally ill mind. Consequently, Dr. Sturgell testified that Dusky's statements concerning his role in the offense could be inaccurate, as well as confused, due to the large amount of alcohol he had consumed prior to the crime.

Despite the doctor's testimony, the court found Dusky to be competent to stand trial, because he was oriented to person, place, and time, and, in the words of Dr. Sturgell, he "knows it all." The Court disagreed with Dr. Sturgell's finding that Dusky would not be able to assist his attorney properly. Despite Dusky's attorney's repeated objections, the trial began on March 2, 1959. The jury did not accept the insanity defense, and Dusky was sentenced to 45 years in prison.

Dusky's U.S. Supreme Court Appeal

Dusky and his attorney filed a petition with the U.S. Supreme Court, asserting that the trial court was in error for finding him competent to stand trial. The Supreme Court reversed the judgment, requesting another competency evaluation and a new trial, if Dusky was again found to be competent. Following new assessments, a new competency hearing was held on October 3, 1960. Testimony was again given by Dr. Sturgell and another FMC psychiatrist, Dr. John Kendall Dickinson. The experts testified that Dusky was again well oriented, but this time he was able to remember the events of the crime, and had "sufficient present ability to consult with his lawyer with a reasonable degree of rational understanding" and that he had a "rational as well as factual understanding of the proceedings in court against him" (*Dusky v. U.S.*, 1961, p. 2). The experts felt that Dusky was competent to stand trial, and Dusky's attorney agreed.

During the second trial, which took place in early October 1960, Dusky did not take the stand, nor did Dr. Sturgell testify. The second trial also included more expert testimony detailing Dusky's history of psychological problems. Again, Dusky received a guilty verdict but was sentenced to only 20 years in prison, with eligibility for parole in 5 years (compared to his 45-year sentence in the first trial).

The Legacy of *Dusky*

In *Dusky*, the Supreme Court established standards under which due process would be satisfied in matters of competency to stand trial. The accused must have (1) sufficient present ability to consult with an attorney with a reasonable degree of rational understanding, and (2) a rational, as well as factual, understanding of the proceedings taken against him. Thus, to be competent to stand trial, it is not sufficient for a defendant to be oriented to person, place, and time, as Dusky had been at his initial trial. Though the *Dusky* test could hardly be described as specific, it does help to define two broad areas—(1) cognitive and (2) interpersonal—of competency to stand trial. The cognitive area centers on the ability to know and understand the charges and legal processes taken against the defendant. The phrase "rational, as well as factual" has been widely interpreted to mean that the accused must understand not only the specifics of the allegation but also the potential consequences of the trial (i.e., a sentence, possible imprisonment), the relative merits of basic legal strategies, and so forth. Given that many laypeople do not understand legal procedures or the advice of their attorneys, "reasonable" understanding may be considerably less than perfect. The interpersonal area is concerned with the ability of the client to consult with an attorney. Note that what is required is "capacity" rather than *willingness* to assist one's attorney. If it is determined that the client "can, but will not," he or she is likely to be found competent, even if some mental disorder is involved in the "will not."

As mentioned earlier, the *Higgins v. McGrath* (1951) decision first clarified the concept that a defendant may have a diagnosable, severe mental disorder and still may possess sufficient capacity to "understand and assist." In actual practice, a great deal of sophistication about the criminal process is not required for defendants to be determined competent, and later decisions have held that the Constitution does not even require a "meaningful relationship" between a defendant and his attorney. In a later case, *Wilson v. U.S.* (1968), the Court held that amnesia in and of itself is not grounds for incompetency.

REFINING COMPETENCY PROCEDURES

The standards for due process in questions of competency to stand trial were established in *Dusky*, which also clarified for whom it is appropriate to question competency. However, the question then arose as to who is responsible for requesting a competency evaluation for a defendant. In *Pate v. Robinson* (1966), the U.S. Supreme Court ruled that the trial judge must order an inquiry into competency if a "bona fide doubt" exists as to the defendant's competency. The responsibility to request a competency evaluation was expanded to include all parties, including the prosecutor in *Drope v. Missouri* (1975).[2] However, confusion remains in applying the *Pate* standard, depending on how "bona fide doubt" is interpreted.

What happens when a defendant is evaluated and found incompetent to stand trial? Before 1972, defendants were sent to forensic hospitals for treatment until they were found competent, no matter how long the treatment lasted. In that year, in the case of *Jackson v. Indiana*, the U.S. Supreme Court ruled that individuals found incompetent for trial cannot be held indefinitely if there is no real chance of recovering competency. Mr. Jackson was a mentally retarded individual who was also deaf and mute. An Indiana court found that he was incompetent to stand trial for two counts of robbery totaling $9, and ordered him sent to a state hospital, where he spent the next 4 years. Since Mr. Jackson was

---

[2] One may wonder why a prosecutor would question a defendant's competency. In general, it is in the best interest of the prosecutor to ensure that competency is established, to avoid the issue being suggested on appeal.

not amenable to treatment to become competent, it was likely that he would have remained incarcerated for the rest of his life. Not only was Jackson never convicted of a crime, but he was also never given an opportunity to challenge the allegations against him. The Supreme Court found that such confinement violated his Fourteenth Amendment rights to due process, since he had not been convicted of any crime yet was forcibly incarcerated by the state. The Court decided that confinement following an incompetency determination must address the issue for which the commitment was requested; that is, it must be aimed at restoring competency, not just warehousing a mentally disordered defendant. If competency cannot be expected within a reasonable period of time, then the defendant must be released or civilly committed. The Supreme Court failed to define a "reasonable" period of time, and since the *Jackson* (1972) decision, various criminal jurisdictions have adopted a range of procedures. States typically allow from 1 to 5 years of treatment to restore competency.

Incompetency to stand trial is prone to a variety of abuses. One of the most troubling issues centers on the defendant's right against self-incrimination and the nature of examinations for competency. Courts have held that the defendant cannot object to a motion by the prosecution or the judge to initiate competency hearings. Because the information discussed with the examiner is usually not privileged, and because it may be useful to the prosecution in the event of an insanity plea or in the penalty phase of the trial, the defendant may unavoidably aid in his own prosecution. This possibility was vividly illustrated in the 1981 U.S. Supreme Court decision of *Estelle v. Smith*.

The case of *Estelle v. Smith* (1981) began when Ernest Benjamin Smith and a friend, Howie Ray Robinson, robbed a Dallas convenience store. Robinson shot a clerk during the course of the offense, and both men were indicted for capital murder. While they were awaiting trial, a judge asked Dr. James P. Grigson, a psychiatrist, to assess Smith's competency to stand for trial. Dr. Grigson spoke to Smith for about 90 minutes and concluded that he was competent. He filed no report with the court, but he forwarded a letter stating his conclusions. Smith's attorneys were not informed that a psychiatrist had examined their client.

Smith was found guilty on the evidence, and Dr. Grigson was called to testify at the sentencing hearing. He was admitted over the objections of Smith's attorney. He offered the opinion that Smith was a sociopath and that modern medicine could not treat his ailments. He also stated that he believed Smith would commit other crimes if he was freed. The jury promptly sentenced Smith to death.

Smith's attorneys filed an appeal that was subsequently heard in a Federal Appeals Court. The Court found that failure of the prosecutor to notify the defense that Smith would be evaluated by an expert who could be called to testify against him violated Smith's rights against self-incrimination and the right to effective counsel, as provided by the Fifth and Sixth Amendments, respectively. It thus emphasized several points: (1) the unreliability of psychiatric testimony; (2) the need to inform a client that statements can be used against him or her to predict future dangerousness; (3) the right to consult an attorney before submitting to such an examination and to have an attorney present during the examination in capital cases.

Although the Court held that Smith could not be compelled to undergo examination and have the results used against him, it did not specify how the results of incompetency evaluations could be used. Dr. Grigson's conduct would raise serious ethical concerns for most practitioners. But what of the responsible practitioners who try to aid the court in competency determinations? Can they be compelled to reveal any or all of the information they obtain, even though they did not intend to participate beyond the competency hearing?

The next obstacle for the courts was to determine what standard of proof would be used to declare competency and who has the burden of proof. Not until *Medina v. California* (1992) was this issue addressed. The findings upheld in this case were that unless the state automatically puts the burden of proof on the prosecution as to whether a criminal defendant is competent to stand trial, it falls upon the party making that assertion, usually the defendant. Also, in this case, preponderance of the evidence was affirmed as the standard of proof.

In other cases for seemingly different and higher standards for other aspects of the process, for example, in *Faretta v. California* (1975), the Court held that a waiver of counsel must be "literate, competent, and understanding, . . . voluntarily exercising his informed free will" (p. 836).

COMPETENCY TO STAND TRIAL INSTRUMENTS

Several specialized instruments have been developed to aid in assessing components of competency, but they do not necessarily simplify the process of deriving a final opinion. There are several types of competency to stand trial measures, including three checklists: the Competency Screening Test, the Georgia Court Competency Test (GCCT), and the Computer Assisted Competence Assessment Tool. There are two more comprehensive measures based on semistructured interviews: the Competency

Assessment Instrument (CAI) and the Interdisciplinary Fitness Interview (IFI), the Fitness Interview Test (revised edition), and the MacArthur Competence Assessment Tool—Criminal Adjudication (MacCAT-CA; Zapf & Roesch, 2005). The Miller Forensic Assessment of Symptoms Test (MFAST) has been found to be effective in detecting when individuals are feigning incompetency to stand trial (Jackson et al., 2005). Another instrument, the Competency Assessment for Standing Trial for Defendants with Mental Retardation (CAST-MR), was designed to assess competency in cognitively impaired defendants.

Issues covered on these instruments vary from understanding the charges against the individual and possible consequences of the trial to estimating the defendant's understanding of the roles of each person in the court. For example, a defendant who is being assessed for competency to stand trial may be asked, "What does the judge do?" or "Where does the judge sit?" Thus, it is assumed that a defendant who is able to understand the responsibility of each person in the courtroom has a clear enough understanding of the situation in which he will be placed for trial.

If a defendant is administered these competency instruments time after time in order to determine competency and if he or she is educated about the court system, could the defendant possibly be trained to be competent? If so, does the trained individual truly meet the standards for competency, or is it a situation of coaching the individual to pass a competency test? Mental health professionals and the court are beginning to address this issue, but no clear answers have been given. Another interesting trend that found new energy in the increased specification of competency criteria in psychometric assessments is that of specifying separate competencies (Zapf & Roesch, 2005).

OTHER COMPETENCIES

As competency at its most basic level entails the ability to cooperate with certain proceedings, it follows that different types of proceedings may require different abilities. Following is a nonexhaustive discussion of some such specific competencies.

Competency Prior to Trial

Another Supreme Court opinion from the same year as *Ford v. Wainwright* appeared to be inconsistent with the general thinking in that case. The Court, in the case of *Colorado v. Connelly* (1986), found that mental illness in a defendant, in and of itself, does not provide a basis to conclude that the confession was coerced or that there was an improper waiver of rights. As a result, the Court held that individuals can be convicted of crimes on the basis of confessions prompted by severe mental illness (in this case, command hallucinations representing the voice of God). This opinion seems to suggest that there are no competency requirements prior to initiation of formal legal proceedings in criminal cases, and an inquiry into a mentally disabled criminal defendant's "free will" is irrelevant in the voluntariness inquiry.

Competency to Be Executed

According to our society's view of retribution, defendants should be able to understand why they are being prosecuted and why they are being punished if found guilty. From this foundation flows the requirement that a defendant should be competent to be executed (Eisenberg, 2004). Much debate has resulted from this belief, because it could be seen as inhumane to bring someone to competency in order to be executed. For example, in 1995, hours before Robert Breechen was to be executed by lethal injection, an Oklahoma prison pumped his stomach and revived him from a drug overdose so he could be aware of his execution and know why he is being executed. This general concept finds its clearest precedent and articulation in *Ford v. Wainwright* (1986). In this case, the U.S. Supreme Court reaffirmed the position of many state courts that the Eighth Amendment prohibition of cruel and unusual punishment is violated when severely disturbed individuals are subjected to capital punishment. This is part of a more general principle that offenders must be competent at all stages of their involvement in the criminal justice system. In *State v. Perry* (1992), the Louisiana Supreme Court ruled 5 to 2 that an insane inmate (in this case as a result of schizophrenia), Michael Owen Perry, could not be forced to take medication (in this case, Haldol) to make him competent to be executed. Earlier he had twice been found incompetent to stand trial but was then found competent in a third hearing. In credentialing examinations, mental health professionals may be asked whether it is ethical to treat such an individual, thus making him "qualified" for the execution. The obvious answer is "no." But it may be argued that treatment gets him back into the process, including appeals, and so forth.

Competency to Serve as a Juror

In *People v. Pierce* (1995), the California Court of Appeals overturned Ronald Pierce's conviction for forced oral copulation, forcible sodomy, and false imprisonment on the grounds that one of the jurors who con-

victed him was not mentally competent to act as a juror. A psychologist
had testified that this juror had an IQ of 66, was a long-term resident of a
group home, and had a shortened attention span and an inability to comprehend testimony at a normal rate.

Competency to Be a Witness

Early common law classified possible witnesses as incompetent on the
grounds of things such as infancy, insanity, infamy, interest and infidelity.
For example, the testimony of all males under age 14 and females under
age 12 was rejected, as was that of blind, deaf, and mute individuals,
slaves, and infamous persons. To be a competent witness under current
law, one must have the ability to perform the duties and responsibilities
involved in accurately relaying information to the court. Thus, a person
may be competent to be a witness regardless of age, psychopathology, or
motivation, as long as these factors do not interfere with the ability to be
a witness. Competency to testify is typically a low standard, in order that
the courts do not lose useful information. It is essentially composed of (1)
the ability to perform adequately (i.e., adequately within the legal system) and (2) the ability to give testimony whose probative value is
greater than its prejudicial value.

Competency to Make a Will

The competency to make a will in known as *testamentary competence*.
The law of testamentary capacity is fairly straightforward, at least in its
statement. The testator (person for whom the will is made) must be able
to do the following:

1. Understand the nature and extent of his or her property.
2. Realize the persons who are the natural objects of his or her
   bounty (e.g., relatives and friends).
3. Understand the distribution of the property contained in the
   will.
4. Understand the nature of a will and be able to form an intent to
   make a disposition of property that will be carried out after
   death.
5. Generally know how these elements relate to each other and
   form an orderly scheme for the distribution of property.

It is important to note that neither eccentricities, mistaken beliefs,
old age, nor unreasonable provisions in the will establish incompetence.

The cognitive abilities just described generally require only limited understanding of basic information. As with all the "competencies," any tests used have to be relevant to function. Videotaping and/or psychological evaluation at the time the will is made, then filed with the will, provide a safeguard against any future challenges.

There are numerous legal grounds upon which the validity of a will or codicil (amendment to an existing will) may be challenged, via a challenge to testamentary competence from the claim that (1) the testator (person for whom the will is made) lacked *testamentary capacity* at the time the disputed will was signed, and (2) specific contents of the will resulted from *undue influence* exerted upon the testator by one or more persons. Often both allegations are made simultaneously. If lack of testamentary capacity is proven, the entire will is invalid; if undue influence is proven, those portions of the will that either result from or cannot be separated from the results of influence are invalid.

Competency to Waive Counsel

The standard for the defendant's competency to waive his or her right to counsel was initially set in the case of *Faretta v. California* (1975). In this case, the U.S. Supreme Court emphasized that the Sixth Amendment guarantees a criminal defendant a right to self-representation, even though it becomes clear the defendant may act to his or her own detriment. A defendant is not incompetent simply because he or she does not understand some or even many of the technical, legal issues (e.g., hearsay evidence).

The Case of *Godinez v. Moran* (1993): The Constitutional Basis for Separate Competencies

At about 4:30 A.M. on August 2, 1984, Richard Allan Moran entered the Red Pearl Saloon in Carson City, Nevada, with Tammy Cortez. Both Moran and Cortez sat at the bar with one other patron, Russell Rhoades. The only other person in the establishment at the time was bartender Sandra DeVere. Without provocation, Moran pulled his .45-caliber semiautomatic pistol from his belt and shot DeVere four times. Then, reaching around Cortez, Moran emptied his last four rounds into patron Russell Rhoades. Moran then instructed Cortez to collect all money from behind the bar, while he attempted to open the cash register. Opening the cash register proved to be too difficult, so Moran placed the entire thing in his vehicle. He again entered the bar to start fires in several places before he and Cortez fled the scene together. It is unclear whether DeVere and Rhoades both died while Moran and Cortez were at the Red Pearl Saloon or whether they were left to suffer in the burning building.

On August 11, 1984, nine days after the murders, Moran showed up alone at the residence of his ex-wife, Linda Vandervoort. They had been divorced for approximately 6–8 months. Again without warning or provocation, Moran opened fire with the same pistol used in the Red Pearl murders. Five of the shots hit Vandervoort and two shots penetrated the wall and entered the next-door apartment. Luckily, the resident of that apartment was not home at the time, but one bullet destroyed the glass top of a coffee table. With his last round Moran attempted suicide by aiming the gun at his abdomen and firing. The wound was not fatal, so Moran then attempted to kill himself by cutting his wrists. However, he was unable to find a knife or other sharp object to carry out his plan. The police arrived to find Moran in Vandervoort's bedroom. He reported to the authorities that the incident had been caused by intruders. However, 2 days later, while he was recovering from his self-inflicted wounds, Moran summoned the police to the hospital and confessed to all three killings, stating that he felt remorse for his actions.

The Trial Process

Moran pled not guilty to three counts of first-degree murder, one count of first-degree arson, and one count of robbery. The court raised the issue of his competency to stand trial given that he had attempted suicide during the crime, approximately 1 month prior to the start of the trial process. Thus, Moran was evaluated by two psychiatrists, Drs. Jurasky and O'Gorman. Both evaluations, taking place in September 1984, focused on Moran's competency to stand trial in accordance with the *Dusky* standards.

Dr. Jurasky offered the opinion that Moran was able to understand and assist counsel in his defense. He expressed concern that Moran's high levels of depression and remorse might interfere with his motivation to assist in his defense, but he ultimately concluded that these factors were not "necessarily a major consideration" (*Godinez v. Moran*, 1993, p. 14). Consistent with Dr. Jurasky's findings, Dr. O'Gorman also reported that Moran was "very depressed," but that he was capable of understanding the charges against him and assisting his attorney in his own defense. With the reports of two independent psychiatrists confirming Moran's competency to stand trial, the State announced that the death penalty would be sought as appropriate punishment.

Changing the Plea

Moran then appeared before the court on November 28, 1984, just 3 months after the crimes and his attempted suicide, stating that he wished to discharge the public defender, waive the right to counsel, and plead guilty to all three charges of first-degree murder. His explanation for the drastic change was that he wanted to prevent mitigating evidence from being presented during the sentencing phase. Although asked by the judge about factors (e.g., drug use) that might affect his mental state, Moran did not provide details about his current medications, and the issue was not further probed by the court. The only statement that Moran made about his medications was an ambiguous reply that he was taking "just what they give me in, you know, medications" (*Godinez v. Moran*, 1993, p. 15).

Moran was in fact taking three medications: Dilantin, Inderal, and Vistaril. All of these medications were listed in his medical records at the time he asked to change his plea and waive his right to counsel. Dilantin is an antiepileptic medication that can cause confusion. Inderal, a beta-blocker antiarrhythmic drug, can cause light headedness, depression, hallucinations, short-term memory loss, and disorientation. The last medication on record for Moran is Vistaril, which is a depressant that can cause drowsiness, tremors, and convulsions.

Moran's requests to waive his right to counsel and plead guilty were granted after the judge asked a few routine questions: Did Moran understand his legal rights and the charges against him? Was he aware of the rights that he was asking to waive? And was he being influenced to plead guilty through threats or promises? Court records indicate that Moran's responses to these questions were mostly monosyllabic. Moran also became confused by questions concerning his intent to kill his ex-wife. When asked if he deliberately planned and carried out the execution of his wife, he replied: "No. I didn't do it. I mean, I wasn't looking to kill her, but she ended up dead." The judge repeated the question, and Moran responded, "I don't know. I mean, I don't know what you mean deliberately. I mean, I pulled the trigger on purpose, but I didn't plan on doing it; you know what I mean?" He explained to Moran that "deliberate means that you arrived at or determined as a result of careful thought and weighing the consideration for and against the proposed action." Then he restated his question in closed-ended fashion by asking, "Did you do that?" Moran then responded, "Yes" (p. 15).

Even with Moran's confused presentation and the possible medication side effects, the Court decided that he was competent to stand trial and that he waived his right to counsel voluntarily and intelligently, allowing Moran to plead guilty and to represent himself at his sentencing hearing. Moran did not call any witnesses and did not present any mitigating evidence in his defense. The aggravating circumstances found for Moran included the fact that, in committing the murders, he knowingly created a great risk of death to others and committed the crime in a random fashion without a clear motive. On January 21, 1985, a three-judge panel found that the aggravating circumstances outweighed the mitigating circumstances in the case of each shooting, thus returning three death sentences.

The Appeals

Moran filed a petition with the Nevada State Court on July 30, 1987, for postconviction relief. He claimed that in November of 1984, he was not competent by the standard of the law to waive his right to counsel or to change his plea to guilty. Blaming his medications in part for his mental state during the trial, Moran told the court, "I guess I didn't care about anything. . . . I wasn't very concerned about anything that was going on . . . as far as the proceedings and everything were going" (*Godinez v. Moran*, 1993, p. 15). In an evidentiary hearing in April 1988, the State Court decided that Moran could not prove that his guilty plea was involuntary or that he was incompetent to waive his right to counsel. The court cited that "the record clearly shows that he [Moran] was examined by two psychiatrists both of whom declared him competent" (p. 6). The Supreme Court of Nevada also rejected Moran's appeal (*Moran v. Warden, Nevada State Prison*, 1989) and affirmed Moran's death sentence for the Red Pearl Saloon murders; however, he was given a life sentence for the murder of his ex-wife. At that point, the U.S. Supreme Court declined to hear the case, leaving the Nevada Supreme Court ruling intact (*Moran v. Whitley*, 1989).

Moran filed a habeas corpus[3] petition in the U.S. District Court for the

---

[3] In habeas corpus cases, prisoners assert that they are being unlawfully detained. This is a completely different process from a criminal appeal, in that it is a civil process initiated by the prisoner.

District of Nevada, but it too was denied. However, the 9th Circuit U.S. Court of Appeals found that the State Court should have considered questioning Moran's competency to discharge counsel and plead guilty when he changed his plea on November 28, 1984. Specifically, the Court of Appeals held that the trial Court's failure to request *another* competency evaluation when Moran asked to change his plea and discharge counsel was a violation of his right to due process. The Court of Appeals also stated that the standard of competency to stand trial is a lower standard than that to waive the right to counsel and plead guilty. Moran may have been competent to stand trial but not competent to waive counsel or plead guilty, since these decisions require greater or more involved abilities than those necessary to be competent to stand trial. The court argued that the correct legal standard for competency to waive counsel or to plead guilty is determining whether the defendant has the ability to understand his situation and to make a "reasoned choice" from his options.

The U.S. Supreme Court eventually agreed to hear the case on June 24, 1993, and reversed the most recent Appeals Court decision, stating, "Although the decision to plead guilty is a profound one, such a decision is not more complicated than the sum total of decisions that all criminal defendants . . . may be called upon to make during the course of trial" (*Godinez v. Moran*, 1993, pp. 1–2). The Court essentially ruled that the standard of competency is equal for all criminal defendants whether they plead guilty or not guilty. There is no reason why deciding to waive counsel would require a higher degree of competency than pleading guilty or waiving any other constitutional right.

Implications of *Godinez*

In this case, the Court found a very low and nonspecific standard for competency to plead guilty or waive the assistance of counsel, in that the competency for either is the same as it is for competency to stand trial. It is the *decision* to waive counsel, not the *ability* to act in one's own defense, that is the issue, and the Court stated that "a criminal defendant's ability to represent himself has no bearing upon his competence to choose self-representation" (*Godinez v. Moran*, p. 332).

It is also noteworthy that the Court here clearly rejected the consensus of the mental health field that competency is situation-based and is tied to specific functions to be performed:

> Requiring that a criminal defendant be competent has a modest aim: It seeks to ensure that he has the capacity to understand the proceedings and

---

BOX 6.1. Where Are They Now?

Richard Allan Moran was executed by lethal injection on March 30, 1996, for the murders of Sandra DeVere and Russell Rhoades. His was the first non-consensual execution (meaning that the defendant was continuing to appeal his case at the time of execution) in the state of Nevada since the 1961 execution of Thayne Archibald. It is unclear whether Tammy Cortez served time for her involvement in the Red Pearl murders and robbery. She is not currently listed as a resident in any Nevada prison.

---

assist counsel. While psychiatrists and scholars may find it useful to classify the various kinds and degrees of competence, and while states are free to adopt competency standards that are more elaborate than the *Dusky* formulation, the Due Process Clause does not impose these additional requirements (p. 334).[4]

This may call for some reevaluation of competency assessment instruments.

In a more recent case, the Court addressed the issue of competency to waive counsel in appeals cases. The Supreme Court ruled that one's right to represent oneself does not extend to direct appeals in *Martinez v. California Court of Appeal* (2000). Therefore, competency should not be at issue for any cases being seen on direct appeal.

STANDARD OF PROOF IN COMPETENCY CASES

In competency hearings and all other legal proceedings, ultimate issues are always decided upon by the finder of fact (either the judge or a jury). Thus, while experts provide courts with opinions as to the competency of a defendant, the fact finder makes the final decision. Different standards of proof apply depending on the issue at hand.

At the turn of the 20th century, U.S. courts were explicitly applying a "preponderance of the evidence" standard in competency hearings. Essentially, defendants needed to prove by the slimmest margin (51%) that they were incompetent. In Ohio, in *State v. O'Grady* (1896), juries

---

[4] Note that while the court discussed separate competencies as being the stuff of "psychiatrists and scholars," the legal precedent for separate competencies dated back at least to 1975.

were instructed that "the burden is upon the prisoner to show by a pre-ponderance of proof that he is insane" (p. 655). Specifically on compe-tency, the Tennessee Supreme Court, in *Jordan v. State* (1911), said that determination is "controlled by the preponderance of the proof" (p. 329), and Pennsylvania adopted similar terminology in 1913.

Until just recently, some states were using the more stringent "clear and convincing" (roughly 75%) standard of proof to determine compe-tency. In *Cooper v. Oklahoma* (1996), the Supreme Court supported pre-ponderance of the evidence as the standard in competency to stand trial, asserting that this is consistent with common law tradition, and that the presumption of competency along with the clear and convincing stan-dard that was used by Oklahoma, could have a person proceed to trial who more than likely was incompetent. In rejecting pleas for the tougher "clear and convincing" standard of proof, Justice Stevens said, "The consequences of an erroneous determination of competence are dire. Because [an incompetent defendant] lacks the ability to communi-cate effectively with counsel, he may be unable to exercise other rights deemed essential to a fair trial" (p. 14). Justice Stevens was concerned that a defendant could be put on trial even though it was more likely than not that he or she was incompetent. For instance, a defendant may be able to assist his or her attorney to the point that they can only prove incom-petency by 65–70%, failing to meet a "clear and convincing" standard.

THE FUTURE OF COMPETENCY

The defendant's level of competency can be questioned at any point dur-ing the trial about any decisions he or she must make. Hence, the issue of competency can affect all aspects of a trial. The courts have delineated guidelines for how and when to approach issues of competency for both legal and mental health professionals. The issue of how to bring someone to competency will need to be addressed in depth in the near future. For more information about current instruments and techniques for assess-ing the various competencies, readers are encouraged to examine Grisso (2002).

CASE REFERENCES

Ake v. Oklahoma, 470 U.S. 68 (1985).
Colorado v. Connelly, 107 S. Ct. 115 (1986).

Cooper v. Oklahoma, 517 U.S. 348; 1996 U.S. LEXIS 2649 (1996).

Drope v. Missouri, 420 U.S. 162 (1975).

Dusky v. U.S., 271 F.2d 385; 1959 U.S. App. LEXIS 3123 (1959).

Dusky v. U.S., 362 U.S. 402 (1960).

Dusky v. U.S., 295 F.2d 743; 1961 U.S. App. LEXIS 3290 (1961).

Estelle v. Smith, 451 U.S. 454 (1981).

Faretta v. California, 422 U.S. 806 (1975).

Ford v. Wainwright, 477 U.S. 399 (1986).

Funk v. Commonwealth, 379 S.E.2d 371 (Va. App. 1989).

Godinez v. Moran, 509 U.S. 389; 1993 U.S. LEXIS 4396 (1993).

Higgins v. McGrath, 98 F. Supp. 670 (D. Mo. 1951).

Jackson v. Indiana, 406 U.S. 715 (1972).

Jordan v. State, 124 Tenn. 81, 135 S.W. 327 (1911).

Martinez v. California Court of Appeal, 531 U.S. 1054; 121 S. Ct. 661 (2000).

Medina v. California, 505 U.S. 437 (1992).

Moran v. Warden, Nevada State Prison, 105 Nev. 1041; 810 P.2d 335; 1989 Nev. LEXIS 193 (1989).

Moran v. Whitley, 110 S. Ct. 207; 107 L. Ed. 2d 160; 1989 U.S. LEXIS 4580 (1989).

Pate v. Robinson, 383 U.S. 375 (1966).

People v. Pierce, 40 Cal. Rptr. 2d 254 (1995).

State v. O'Grady, 5 Ohio Dec. 654 (1896).

State v. Perry, 610 So. 2d 746, 1992 La. LEXIS 3170 (1992).

Wilson v. U.S., 391 F.2d 460 (D.C. Cir. 1968).

Youtsey v. U.S., 97 F.937 (6th Cir. 1899).

CHAPTER 7

Insanity and Criminal Responsibility

Reply to a plaintiff who claims his cabbages were eaten by
your goat: You had no cabbages. If you did they were not
eaten. If they were eaten, it was not by a goat. If they were
eaten by a goat, it was not my goat. And, if it was my goat,
he was insane.

—Irving Younger
(as quoted in McElhaney, 1987)

Perhaps no other legal concept raises as many moral ambiguities as the
concept of criminal responsibility. As alluded to in the opening quote, a
defense asserting a lack of responsibility, commonly known as an *insanity defense*, may sometimes be used as an approach of last resort. However, the very legitimate construct of criminal responsibility is much
more complex.

Criminal responsibility can be viewed as a singular concept, but in
judicial application it is very often interwoven with the defendant's competency to stand trial. Indeed, the issues of criminal responsibility and
competency to stand trial are often confused by mental health experts
involved in the judicial process. *Criminal responsibility* refers to the state
of the defendant's mind at the time of the alleged crime, and includes
the related concepts of insanity and diminished capacity (see Box 7.1).
Competency to stand trial (as discussed in Chapter 6) refers to a defendant's psychological state at the time of his or her trial. Such a temporal
distinction is of crucial importance in the assessment of these issues.

For a punishable criminal act to occur, two related but independent
factors—action and intention—must be present. First, an act or behavior

---

BOX 7.1. Criminal Responsibility: Related Concepts

There are two concepts related to criminal responsibility. *Diminished capacity* focuses on the inability to form a specific intent, that is, to have "mens rea." An argument of diminished capacity may be used to reduce a criminal sentence, but the individual has still been found guilty. Another related concept is *guilty but mentally ill* (GBMI). This at first seemed to be a promising concept, but it soon became clear that there were problems with it. It can on occasion be a way for a jury simply to avoid a difficult decision, in that GBMI makes it easier for a jury to convict in the "gray" area between sanity and insanity. Furthermore being found GBMI frequently does not entail reception of special mental health services as it implies, and it may actually be a negative bias when the person comes up for parole.

---

previously defined as illegal must occur, that is, the "actus reus" or the act itself. Second, the individual committing the act must have the general intent to do so, that is, the "mens rea," which also implies some degree of free will. As we will see, some states have abolished the insanity defense; in such situations, proving the absence of mens rea becomes a de facto insanity defense. Except for a few criminal statutes, for example, some product liability laws, both an illegal act and guilty mind must be present before a punishable crime has occurred.

The key issues in the evolving law on insanity are the following: What are the legal criteria for insanity? Who bears the burden of proof in an insanity defense (prosecutor or defense)? What is the appropriate legal standard (preponderance, beyond reasonable doubt, etc.)?

Rightly or wrongly, the insanity defense is often portrayed as a choice between liberty and security, for both the accused and society. Despite the behavioral sciences' strongest efforts to draw a firm line of distinction between "madness" and "badness," this boundary continues to shift under the interwoven social, political, economic, and other pressures of our society.

A delusional misfit aims to assassinate a popular political figure, but the intended target survives and continues as a nation's leader. In a dramatic and highly publicized trial, the would-be assassin is found insane and acquitted of the charges against him. A storm of protest follows as the outraged public, the press, and other political leaders push for restriction of the "insanity defense." This synopsis describes John Hinckley's 1981 attempt on the life of President Ronald Reagan and its aftermath, but it also describes events in the 1843 case of *In re M'Naughten*. Most of the cases discussed in this chapter incorporate similar scenarios.

Insane was from the Latin *sanus*, for healthy. *In* meaning not. Not healthy.
Or mad from Old English *gemaedde*. Meaning foolish, vain, boastful. . . .
Or *crazy* from Middle English *crasen*, which meant shatter. Break into
many pieces.

—James W. Hall, *Buzz Cut* (1996, p. 182)

THE CASE OF *IN RE M'NAUGHTEN* (1843): THE FIRST FORMAL TEST OF CRIMINAL RESPONSIBILITY

In re M'Naughten (1843) was a British legal case that set forth the first
formal legal test of insanity that would be used in the United States. Like
much of our legal tradition, the ruling in *M'Naughten* was derived from
English law. As early as the 1500s, English common law had recognized
that "lunatics and idiots" whose mentality approached that of a "wild
beast" could not be held responsible for otherwise illegal conduct. Still,
these issues were largely ignored until the trial of Daniel M'Naughten, a
paranoid schizophrenic wood turner[1] from Glasgow. M'Naughten held
the delusional belief that Britain's Tory party (and at other times the
Jesuits or the Pope) was responsible for his difficult lot in life, and he saw
Sir Robert Peel, Prime Minister and the head of the party, as his chief
persecutor. M'Naughten shot and fatally wounded Edward Drummond,
one of the Prime Minister's secretaries, as Drummond left his brother's
banking house in one of Queen Victoria's carriages. M'Naughten was
apprehended by a policeman as he tried to fire a second shot into
Drummond's back. An interview with M'Naughten revealed both his
delusional thoughts and his generally confused thinking.

It is now unclear whether he was actually trying to kill Peel or
whether the attack was an outburst of his disorder without such a clear
focus. In any case, the judge at M'Naughten's trial instructed the jury
that he should be acquitted if they believed that he was insane at the
time of the crime. Nine medical experts testified for the defense that
M'Naughten was clearly insane. The jury was apparently influenced by
the progressive thinking of Isaac Ray, from his 1853 text *A Treatise on the
Medical Jurisprudence of Insanity* (3rd ed.), which spoke of a defect of
reasoning due to "mental unsoundness" that "embraced his criminal act,"
and M'Naughten was acquitted. From M'Naughten's perspective, this outcome was somewhat superfluous, because he was committed to and

---

[1] Wood turning is the art of creating wooden objects on a lathe. The objects are typically
round or cylindrical and may include anything from baseball bats to ornate wooden pots.

spent the rest of his life, 22 years, in Broadmoor, a legendary mental institution.

On the day after M'Naughten's acquittal, the *London Times* published the following little proclamation on its editorial page:

> Ye people of England exult and be glad
> For ye're now at the mercy of the merciless mad

The reaction from Queen Victoria and the House of Lords, who feared politically motivated violence, was almost as swift, though the Queen did comment: "We do not believe that anyone could be insane who wanted to murder a Conservative Prime Minister." Her sarcasm was understandable, because there had been several earlier attempts to assassinate her. One of those attempts resulted in an early form of the "irresistible impulse" test, as articulated in *Regina v. Oxford* (1840) as "some controlling disease was . . . the acting power within him which he could not resist" (p. 950). This concept is important for its focus on volition. It had some modest influence for about 20 years and then faded, only to resurface many years later. Following M'Naughten's acquittal, the judges of England's highest court were convened and directed to determine a strict rule defining when an insanity acquittal would be justified. They settled on the following test:

> That the jurors ought to be told in all cases that every man is to be presumed to be sane, and to possess a sufficient degree of reason to be responsible for his crimes, until the contrary be proved to their satisfaction; and that to establish a defense on the ground of insanity, it must be clearly proved that, at the time of the committing of the act, the party accused was laboring under such a defect of reason, from disease of the mind, as to not know the nature and quality of the act he was doing; or if he did know it that he did not know he was doing what was wrong (*In re M'Naughten*, 1843)

Although the actual instructions to the jury in the *M'Naughten* trial were somewhat less restrictive, the test given above is generally associated with his name. This rule was adopted by U.S. courts and was the basic legal test of insanity in this country until the 1950s. It was confirmed as the standard in the District of Columbia in 1881, when Charles Guiteau was tried for the assassination of President Garfield. It continues to be used today in many state jurisdictions and forms a basis for the most recently enacted rule for federal courts, described in more detail later in this chapter.

The *M'Naughten* test, along with its heirs, has been widely criticized for a variety of reasons. For example, it has a narrow focus on "knowing" that apparently confines the evidence for insanity decisions to cognitive functions. Controversies also center on whether what is known should be wrongfulness (as in *M'Naughten*) or illegality, and whether this refers to abstract knowing or to the specific behavior at hand.

THE EVOLUTION OF INSANITY DEFENSE

The *M'Naughten* criminal responsibility standard was integrated into the law of the United States until the irresistible impulse or volition test was added. The question became whether the individual had been robbed of his free will to control his behavior due to mental disease or defect, despite knowing such behavior was wrong.

The case of *Durham v. U.S.* (1954) was an attempt to open up the lines of communication between experts and the courts, Judge David Bazelon of the District of Columbia Circuit Court of Appeals formulated what would become known as the *Durham* rule:

> Unless [the jury believes] beyond a reasonable doubt either that [the accused] was not suffering from a disease or defective mental condition, or that the act was not the product of such abnormality, you must find the accused not guilty by reason of insanity. . . . He would still be responsible if there was no causal connection between such mental abnormality and the act. (p. 7)

This "product" test requires the jury to determine whether a criminal act was causally connected to a mental disease or defect. It was originally viewed as a significant advance, because it would allow experts to testify in their own terms. However, courts still found it difficult to interpret the experts' data, and attorneys often introduced an extremely broad (and often irrelevant) range of information in an attempt to explain criminal acts as the product of mental illness. In practice, it produced such freewheeling testimony that juries were frequently confused and overwhelmed, and Judge Bazelon himself and the D.C. Circuit (wherein it was originally adopted) dropped the *Durham* rule in 1972 in *U.S. v. Brawner* in favor of the ALI rule discussed next. The *Durham* rule is not currently used in the United States, and it offers more historic than precedent value.

In 1962, the American Law Institute (ALI) concluded an extensive study of criminal responsibility by proposing a Model Penal Code, complete with a rule that combined concepts from the existing tests of insanity but was somewhat more flexible than *M'Naughten*. The ALI rule reads as follows:

> A person is not responsible for criminal conduct if at the time of such conduct, as a result of mental disease or defect, he lacks substantial capacity either to appreciate the criminality [wrongfulness] of his conduct or to conform his conduct to the requirements of the law. (American Law Institute, 1962)

The ALI standard provides a number of improvements over earlier tests. It embraces issues related both to cognition and to volition, essentially bridging the traditional gap between *M'Naughten* and irresistible impulse. Also, the traditional and narrow *know* is replaced by the term *appreciate*. In recognition of the difficulty that may arise in deciding which acts could not be resisted versus those that were simply not resisted, the ALI standard typically carries a caveat: The terms *mental disease* or *defect* do not include an abnormality manifested only by repeated criminal or otherwise antisocial conduct.

This exception appears to make the defense inaccessible to those with Psychopathy, or Antisocial Personality Disorder (discussed in Chapter 15, this volume). Though chronic antisocial conduct may lead to a formal DSM-IV diagnosis, the ALI standard would view this as a description of bad character rather than as a discrete impairment compromising the conduct of an otherwise law-abiding individual.

Two cases in 1965 speak to decisions about the appropriate application of the insanity defense. In *Whalem v. U.S.* (1965) the Supreme Court established the duty of a court to impose an insanity defense in a situation when it would be likely to succeed. Of course, the success rate of the not guilty by reason of insanity (NGRI) defense suggests this will be extremely rare. And in *Frendak v. U.S.* (1965), the Supreme Court established that a defendant's decision to waive an insanity defense is to be accepted as long as the defendant is competent to make that decision (i.e., the defendant's right to exercise a personal decision here overrides the state's *parens patriae* interests in protecting its citizens).

In *U.S. v. Brawner* (1972), the D.C. Circuit court essentially embraced the ALI rule. It was subsequently adopted by several states and the majority of federal jurisdictions (at least until the *Hinckley* case that follows). Other courts gradually began adopting the ALI rule or a similar combined cognitive and volitional test. Federal jurisdictions, in particular, embraced this standard over more traditional language, that is, until the trial for the attempted assassination of the President of the United States.

THE CASE OF JOHN HINCKLEY: PUBLIC OUTCRY SPURRING INSANITY DEFENSE REFORM

John Hinckley was born in Oklahoma in 1955 and moved to Dallas at the age of 4. Prior to his school years, his early childhood was essentially unremarkable. He quarterbacked his elementary school football team and played basketball in high school. At the age of 9, Hinckley became a fan of the Beatles. His interest in music and possible identification with John Lennon continued into his adulthood. When he was 12, Hinckley and his family moved to a prominent Dallas neighborhood, where they were treated as low on the social status ladder.

After graduating from high school in 1973, Hinckley moved to Evergreen, Colorado. He wanted badly to attend Texas Tech University, but he quit school a year later and moved from Lubbock back to Dallas. He wanted to be on his own and work in perhaps music or politics. A move to Hollywood in 1976 to sell his music did not pan out, but he did see the movie *Taxi Driver* some 15 times that summer. He was smitten with the young star of the film, Jodie Foster. In the spring of 1977, Hinckley returned to Lubbock.

Hinckley's overall adaptation and emotional adjustment were apparently beginning to decline at this point. In the next year, he began to experience a number of minor health problems for which he received medical treatment. In October 1978, he became interested in the American Nazi movement via the National Socialist Party. In August 1979, he purchased his first firearm, and in September of that year began to publish the *American Front Newsletter*, proselytizing his views. He appointed himself national director of the American Front and fabricated membership lists from 37 states. By then, he had moved 17 times since high school.

Hinckley experienced his first severe anxiety attack in 1980, and had gained 60 pounds since high school. He bought another gun. In May 1980, *People* magazine announced that Jodie Foster, star of *Taxi Driver* (and later *The Silence of the Lambs*), would be attending Yale University. Hinckley began to believe that he could win Ms. Foster's attention and love. After a disappointing telephone conversation with Ms. Foster on September 20, 1980, Hinckley wrote in his diary: "My mind was at the breaking point. A relationship I had dreamed about went absolutely nowhere. My disillusionment with everything was complete." He then purchased more weapons and began taking numerous flights around the country, including Colorado, Tennessee, Ohio, and Nebraska. Hinckley thought desperately about ways he could impress Jodie Foster to gain more favorable attention. His travels eventually took him to Washington, DC.

Attempted Assassination of the President

Just before 2:30 P.M. on March 30, 1981, a gunman approached President Reagan on a Washington, DC, street, aimed, and fired six shots from a .22-caliber revolver. The first shot struck presidential press secretary James Brady, who suffered extensive neurological damage and remains in a wheelchair to this day. The second shot struck Washington, DC, police officer Thomas Delahanty. The third bullet harmlessly hit a building across the street from the Washington Hilton. The fourth bullet struck secret service agent Timothy McCarthy. The fifth bullet struck the glass in the presidential limousine but did no human damage. The sixth and final bullet ricocheted off the limousine and struck Ronald Reagan in the chest. Reagan's and McCarthy's wounds were serious, but all those shot survived. A Secret Service agent later testified to his feeling of desperation as he attempted to stop the gunfire and attack that lasted only a few seconds.

The attempted assassination of President Ronald Reagan riveted public attention on the insanity defense. Hinckley's extensive history of maladjustment only served to aggravate public outrage rather than to mitigate his responsibility, possibly because the insanity defense was his only real option. After all, his actions were replayed countless times by the television networks, allowing people around the world to witness the offense in slow motion.

Prior to trial, in May and November of 1981, Hinckley's defense attorneys offered to have their client plead guilty to all counts if the prosecution would agree to recommend to the court that penalties on all counts run concurrently rather than consecutively. Under this arrangement, their client would be eligible for parole in 15 years. The prosecution declined the offer, viewing it as improper and unseemly to plea bargain a case involving the attempted assassination of the President.

Understandably, the shooting raised many questions about Hinckley's psychological motivation, history, and mental stability. Testimony in Hinckley's trial laid out his ultimate goal of capturing the admiration of movie star Jodie Foster. Lawyers for the prosecution and defense differed little on the factual events, but, not surprisingly, they differed considerably over the defendant's true psychological condition (Greenberg et al., 2005). The raising of the insanity defense resulted in a trial that lasted slightly over 7 weeks. Total costs for mental health experts approached half a million dollars, with two-thirds of that total spent by the prosecution.

The conflicting testimony from a wide variety of experts fueled the media frenzy surrounding the event itself. Evidence presented to the jury ranged from notes taken by Hinckley's ex-therapist, to documentation of an extensive inpatient evaluation at a federal forensic hospital, to computerized axial tomographic (CAT) scans of his brain. Confronted with this mass of evidence, the jury deliberated for 3 days. Applying the ALI standard, they found Hinckley NGRI on all 13 counts. He was automatically committed to Saint Elizabeth's Hospital in Washington, DC, for treatment. John Hinckley, would-be assassin of the President of the United States, would never serve a day in prison for his actions.

THE INSANITY DEFENSE REFORM ACT OF 1984

Outrage at the trial outcome, originally focused on Hinckley himself, was soon directed at "soft on crime" liberals and the "corrupt experts." Spotting the political opportunity, legislators jumped on the bandwagon. In the following weeks, 26 different bills were introduced to modify the federal insanity statute. Against this background, the Congress eventually passed a statute that established a "reformed" test for insanity in all federal jurisdictions (a quasi-ALI rule, without the conformity clause):

> It is an affirmative defense to a prosecution under any federal statute that, at the time of the commission of the acts constituting the offense, the defendant, as a result of a severe mental disease or defect, was unable to appreciate the nature and quality or the wrongfulness of his acts. Mental disease or defect does not otherwise constitute a defense. (United States Code, 1984, as cited in Meyer, 1995)

This test has been used in federal courts since 1984, and was affirmed in the follow-up Insanity Defense Reform Act (1988). It has been influential in redefining many state statutes. Under this federal rule, the volitional aspect of the ALI standard, known as the "conformity clause," is dropped. The burden of proof (traditionally on the prosecution) is now on the defendant to demonstrate insanity by clear and convincing evidence (instead of the more stringent "beyond a reasonable doubt"), indicating that the jury is to have a strong presumption of sanity. The similarity of this rule to the *M'Naughten* standard is clear, because there is little or no consideration given to volitional factors, although the more expansive *appreciate* terminology has been retained from the ALI standard. As an affirmative defense, the insanity issue must be raised in the initial pleading of the case at hearings well before the trial proper. See Table 7.1 for a comparative description of insanity standards.

Carrying this trend even further, in 1994, the U.S. Supreme Court allowed to stand a Montana Supreme Court decision in *Cowan v. State* (1994) that allowed Montana's abolition of the insanity defense, holding that this does not violate the Eighth and Fourteenth Amendments. Montana does have a mens rea requirement, but uses terms such as *knowingly, purposefully,* and *with malice.* A Montana defendant could therefore act purposefully and knowingly, and thus be responsible yet still not appreciate the illegality of conduct nor be able to conform his or her behavior to the requirements of law. A number of other states have followed suit and eliminated the insanity defense. As described in Box 7.2, such strong reactions may actually not address realistic problems.

TABLE 7.1. Comparison of Insanity Defenses

Test	Legal standard	Final burden of proof	Who bears burden of proof
M'Naughten	"Didn't know what he or she was doing or didn't know it was wrong"	Varies from proof by a balance of probabilities on the defense to proof beyond a reasonable doubt on the prosecutor	
Irresistible impulse	"Could not control conduct"	Same as above.	
Durham	"Criminal act was caused by mental illness"	Beyond reasonable doubt	Prosecutor
ALI— Brawner	"Lacks substantial capacity to appreciate the wrongfulness of the conduct or to control it"	Beyond reasonable doubt	Prosecutor
Present federal law	"Lacks capacity to appreciate the wrongfulness of his or her conduct"	Clear and convincing evidence	Defense

Note. Adapted in part from Morris (1986).

BOX 7.2. Soft-on-Crime Liberals and Corrupt Experts?:
The Case of Perception versus Reality

Due in large part to cases like that of John Hinckley, public perception is that slick attorneys can get guilty criminals off by persuading juries that a defendant is insane. But, does this perception reflect reality?

Henry Steadman and his colleagues (1993) studied 49 counties in a cross section of eight states between 1976 and 1987. Out of approximately 9,000 felony cases, only 1% included an insanity defense. Of this 1%, about 25% were acquitted, and only 7% of those acquittals were by a jury (about two cases out of the 9,000). Furthermore, the median length of confinement on a murder charge was 1,828 days (about 5 years) when the defendant was found guilty, and 1,737 days (4.7 years) when found NGRI. Could some of the legal rhetoric and political maneuvering around the insanity defense be "much ado about nothing"?

RELATED LAW

In *Wainwright v. Greenfield* (1986), the U.S. Supreme Court ruled that any silence on the part of the defendant after being apprised of *Miranda* rights was found to be inadmissible as substantive evidence to rebut an insanity defense. Later, in *Shannon v. U.S.* (1994), the U.S. Supreme Court held that federal trial courts are not required to inform jurors that a defendant found NGRI will be subject to civil commitment. The Court emphasized that it is not the function of a jury to consider the disposition or sentencing of a defendant, and that the jury should focus only on the issues given it by the trial court. The Court did note, however, that in special circumstances (e.g., when a witness states that a defendant would "go free"), it may be necessary for the trial court to give an instruction to counter such a misstatement. The Court essentially turned a blind eye to the fact that jurors may presuppose such an inaccurate belief.

SUMMARY

At present, a successful insanity defense is based solely on the defendant's inability as a result of mental disease or defect to appreciate the criminality of his or her alleged conduct. The burden of proof (i.e., whose responsibility it is to demonstrate the defendant's psychological state) has shifted from the prosecution and is now on the defense. The level of proof required for the prosecution was also reduced from

BOX 7.3. Where Are They Now?

In 1984, Hinckley's father, John Sr., sold his oil and gas prospecting company, the Vanderbilt Energy Corporation, reportedly for $26 million. He and his wife spent about $1 million during the 1980s on a national advertising campaign to increase public awareness about both mental disorders and the insanity defense.

Today, John Hinckley is still undergoing treatment at St. Elizabeth's Hospital. He may be released at the recommendation of the hospital and with approval of the presiding judge. Such a recommendation will occur only if the hospital feels that Hinckley no longer poses a threat to society or himself. But, should one release an individual who has been proven dangerous in the past, who may well be dangerous at some point in the future, but who is probably not immediately dangerous? Add to that the fact that his symptoms are likely decreased by medication and other interventions that he may receive more sporadically when released, and the complexity inherent in making such a recommendation for release is evident.

Hinckley's behavior in recent years has generally been without substantial blemish, while in earlier years he provided plenty of material to argue for retaining him in the hospital. In 1986, he exchanged letters with convicted serial murderer Ted Bundy; according to a psychiatrist, Hinckley wrote Bundy to "express his sorrow" for the "awkward position he must be in." In 1988, his obsession with Jodie Foster was still clearly evident as he wrote a mail order company to order a nude drawing of her; the year before, a search of his hospital room had uncovered 57 photos of the actress.

Unnoticed by the media, Hinckley began taking brief unsupervised visits to see his parents in Williamsburg, Virginia, in 2003. He did, however, make the news in late 2004 when, through his lawyers, Hinckley petitioned the court for extended visits away from the hospital. To date, his requests have been denied.

"beyond a reasonable doubt" to "clear and convincing evidence" when applied to the defense. Thus, the level of certainty required of the jury when viewing the evidence was reduced from an estimated 90–95% to more like 75%. Although these changes in federal law were significant, they only serve as models to state courts, who hear by far the greater number of insanity defenses each year.

The difficulty for professionals evaluating insanity is that they typically make their assessment long after the act was committed. The most relevant data set is objective information as to how the person was functioning around the time of the crime. The second most relevant data set is the person's mental health history prior to the crime.

Only then might the data as to the person's mental status at the time of the evaluation be relevant. However, mental health professionals often focus on this last data set, because it is so readily available (Meyer, 2006). Unfortunately, this data set is often likely to be contaminated by several factors: (1) The person may have spent time in jail or some other institution, which in itself could traumatize one's mental state; (2) the person may have received psychotropic medications; (3) the person might have some emotional reaction to increasing or continuing awareness of whatever damage he or she perpetrated; (4) the person has no doubt been aware that he or she is making a plea of insanity and would be inclined, either consciously or unconsciously, to provide data, whether true, enhanced, or false, to support that plea; (5) the person may have received subtle or direct coaching from his or her attorney to further the goal discussed in item 3; and (6) if the person spent time in jail, he or she likely received such advice–coaching from other inmates.

CASE REFERENCES

Cowan v. State, 112 S. Ct. 1371 (1994).

Durham v. U.S., 214 F.2d 862 (D.C. Cir. 1954).

Frendak v. U.S., 408 A.2d 364; 1979 D.C. App. LEXIS 463 (1965).

In re M'Naughten, 8 Eng. Rep. 718 (1843).

Shannon v. U.S., 114 S. Ct. (1994).

U.S. v. Brawner, 471 F.2d 969 (D.C. Cir. 1972).

Wainwright v. Greenfield, 474 U.S. 284 (1986).

Whalem v. U.S., 120 U.S. App. D.C. 331; 346 F.2d 812; 1965 U.S. App. LEXIS 5807 (1965).

CHAPTER 8

Civil Commitment
and Dangerousness

Civil commitment is the process by which someone is admitted to inpatient psychiatric care. The process may be initiated voluntarily by the individual. There are also established procedures for the involuntary commitment of people who are deemed dangerous to themselves or others. Various mental health professionals may be called upon to commit someone, or otherwise to participate in the process, so it is important to recognize that the particular procedures can vary widely by jurisdiction. Nevertheless, there is a common history to the development of most civil commitment procedures.

The concept of commitment came out of the historical concept of *parens patriae*, meaning "state or government as parent or caregiver." Aristotle was the first to define the government's role in mental illness. He noted that the government has two basic powers: (1) police power, and (2) *parens patriae* power. He described police power as the power of the government to protect its citizens from danger or harm. *Parens patriae* power gave the government a more parental role of caring for people who were otherwise unable to care for themselves. According to the *parens patriae* doctrine, it was the government's responsibility to provide needy citizens with their basic needs, protection, and education. Police power and *parens patriae* power were later combined to form the groundwork for involuntary civil commitment.

Care and protection of citizens' rights remain key aspects of law on civil commitment even today. However, by definition, civil commitment entails a loss of the individual's rights. Traditionally, a psychiatric inpatient could not decide how long to stay or when to leave. Therefore, questions naturally arise. Under what circumstances can a person be involuntarily committed? What rights does the person have during and following commitment? Does a person have a right to treatment? Does he or she have a right to refuse a specific treatment? How long can he or she be kept and who decides? These are some of the issues dealt with in the cases discussed in this chapter.

THE LEGAL DEVELOPMENT OF CIVIL COMMITMENT

In ancient Greece and Rome, the burden of care for the mentally ill was the responsibility of the family or close friends of the person. In the 16th century, civil commitment was first created as a government procedure. It was originally used not to treat persons with mental illness but as a way to rid the streets of so-called "undesirables."

The case of *In re Oakes* (1845) first articulated the basis for civil commitment in America. Mr. Oakes was an elderly Cambridge, Massachusetts, man. Over his objections, his family delivered him to the McLean Asylum in Belmont, Massachusetts. His behavior was somewhat unusual, but it is difficult to know now whether it was pathological or just socially unacceptable. Oakes was held at the asylum against his will, with no prior trial or judicial action. Ultimately, he petitioned for release. His request was eventually heard by the Massachusetts Supreme Court, which ordered that Oakes remain confined. At least four important (though not necessarily desirable) precedents were established in *Oakes*: (1) The state has a right to confine someone against his or her own free will; (2) caretakers should have the major role in decision making for the mentally disordered, including length of treatment; (3) civil proceedings do not require the same strict due process considerations as criminal matters; and (4) involuntary treatment is justified not only by the detainee's dangerousness but also for his or her own welfare. Although the opinion noted that both dangerousness and humanitarian concern for the afflicted were important issues, the *parens patriae* concept has been widely regarded as the basis for the Court's decision.

Several implications of the *Oakes* decision served to decrease the rights of those considered for commitment. The first of these was the notion that mentally disordered individuals lacked free will. This provided a rationale for not giving due consideration to their wishes. Additionally, the Court's opinion established a precedent for "paternalism," the idea that family and professional caretakers would make decisions for impaired individuals. These decisions were to be based solely on that patient's best interests. Unfortunately, the presumption that others would act in a person's best interest did not always have merit, and the realities of involuntary commitment rarely matched the expectations. Individuals were often confined, seemingly for arbitrary reasons, and were not always afforded their constitutional right to due process. The situation only began to change in the 1950s and 1960s, with the development of effective antipsychotic medications.

In the latter part of the 20th century, the trend moved away from civil commitment and back toward the family care approach first seen in ancient times. The civil rights movement also contributed to the devaluation of the *parens patriae* concept in the courts. Then, in 1967, in the case of *In re Gault* (also elaborated upon in Chapter 19), due process was operationalized for juveniles, and the effects were generalized to some degree to persons with mental illness in the area of civil commitment.

Currently there are three types of commitment for persons with mental illness: (1) inpatient commitment, which is commitment to an institution; (2) outpatient commitment, in which the person lives in the community but is monitored closely; and (3) criminal commitment, in which a person is found guilty of a crime but is found to be mentally ill and in need of specialized treatment.[1] Every state in the United States has passed legislation regarding civil commitment of persons who are a danger to themselves or to others. Each state has a different set of criteria determining the factors that warrant such commitment. For example, in Arizona, a person who is "persistently and acutely mentally disabled" can be involuntarily committed. Hawaii permits the involuntary commitment of a person who is "obviously mentally ill." The criteria set forth by these statutes are vague at best, and while states do have statutes governing dangerous persons, there are none dealing with the commitment of persons who do not pose a danger to themselves or to others.

---

[1] A finding of "guilty but mentally ill" (GBMI) is not to be confused with a finding of "not guilty by reason of insanity" (NGRI). GBMI suggests that the person did not meet insanity criteria and was thus responsible and "guilty" for the crime. However, this person *currently* shows signs of mental illness and should receive some form of treatment while incarcerated. NGRI suggests that the person was actually insane *at the time of the crime,* and does not necessarily mean anything about his or her mental state during trial or at sentencing. People found NGRI cannot be incarcerated. Technically, they are involuntarily committed. In some states, GBMI findings may merely require a brief additional mental health evaluation upon entry to prison. This evaluation may or may not lead to any additional steps to treat the individual.

COMMITMENT AND THE RIGHT TO TREATMENT

In the 1960s, a few cases challenged commitment as being merely a "dressed-up" form of confinement. In *Rouse v. Cameron* (1967), the Court considered whether those committed could be confined only for the purpose of custodial care, and concluded that there was a constitutional right to treatment (although this was not a Supreme Court case, and the Supreme Court has never found for such a right). The Court ruled that confinement alone did not serve the purpose of civil commitment, because there must be a "bona fide effort at treatment." It was not, however, necessary that the treatment be successful. A Federal Appeals Court that same year provided the first articulation of the concept of "least restrictive alternative" in *Lake v. Cameron* (1966). This doctrine dictates that any kind of forced treatment must be the least restrictive option available.

A case that followed a few years after *Lake* represented the most significant effort to define the right to treatment, spelling out very specific and concrete requirements, and influencing standards of inpatient care in many sectors. In *Wyatt v. Stickney* (1971), a lawsuit was brought about by patients complaining about the poor conditions at Bryce Hospital in Alabama. The Court's ruling defined the "minimal standard of care" in terms of appropriate patient-to-staff ratios, hours of active treatment per week, existence of continuing therapeutic programs, and the utilization of individualized treatment planning. Thus, patients forced against their will to reside in an inpatient treatment facility had a right to adequate treatment. But could specific treatments be forced upon civilly committed individuals? This question bore the most relevance with regard to drug treatments, some of which had significant adverse effects on those being treated.

THE RIGHT TO REFUSE TREATMENT: *RENNIE V. KLEIN* (1978)

In 1971, Mr. Rennie, a 40-year-old divorced man and a former pilot and flight instructor, first showed symptoms of mental illness. His symptoms became more serious in 1973, when his twin brother was killed. Shortly thereafter, Rennie was admitted for the first time to Ancora, one of five hospitals for the mentally ill operated by the state of New Jersey. He was depressed and suicidal, and was diagnosed as a paranoid schizophrenic. At various times during his stays, Rennie refused to accept prescribed drugs despite insistence of the hospital staff that they had a right to medicate him against his will. During his 12th admission to Ancora, which began in August 1976, after an involuntary commitment proceeding, Rennie instituted this suit.

The State District Court's decision became the first significant one to recognize that those who are civilly committed have a constitutional right to refuse medications. This Court also held that this right can be overridden, so long as the patient was given due process. To overrule the patient's refusal, four factors should be considered by an independent party: (1) the patient's capacity to decide on his or her particular treatment; (2) the patient's physical threat to other patients and staff; (3) whether any less restrictive treatment exists; and (4) the risk of permanent side effects from the proposed treatment. Although the U.S. Supreme Court later considered *Rennie*, it remanded it back to the state courts without any constitutional ruling. The District Court that had established the right to refuse treatment subsequently determined that, based on the four factors, Mr. Rennie's refusal was properly overridden by the hospital. The Court's reasoning in *Rennie* has remained very influential in other jurisdictions.

CIVIL COMMITMENT AND DUE PROCESS

By 1974, procedures to guarantee the due process rights of civilly committed individuals were in place in most jurisdictions. However, there was no consensus as to what specific criteria were needed to assure due process. In 1975, the U.S. Supreme Court addressed the due process requirements for civil commitment in *O'Connor v. Donaldson*. Such protections were clearly needed, because civil commitment represented a significant loss of personal liberty for what could be an indeterminate amount of time.

The Case of *O'Connor v. Donaldson* (1975): The Criteria for Involuntary Commitment

William Kenneth Donaldson was born in 1908 in Erie, Pennsylvania. He attended Syracuse University for a year and a half. After leaving school before obtaining a degree, he married (Olivia). In 1943, at 34 years of age, Donaldson was hospitalized for the first time. Married, with three children, and working in a General Electric defense plant, Donaldson had a "nervous breakdown" for which he was hospitalized for 4 months at Marcy State Hospital in Marcy, New York. During his stay, he was treated with electroshock therapy and released. Upon his release, Donaldson developed paranoia. Specifically, he believed he had become the victim of slander and harassment. He also believed that people were tampering with his mail, and that someone was putting medication in his food. Attempting to escape these threats, he changed his name twice, first in 1953, to Kenneth McCullough, and again in 1955, to Kenneth Donaldson. Early in 1956, he was admitted to Philadelphia General Hospital, treated for paranoid schizophrenia, and released. Later that year, then 48 years old, divorced, and unemployed, Donaldson went to visit his parents in Florida. During his visit, he made disturbing claims to his parents that someone was trying to poison him. His father feared that his son was suffering from "delusions" and contacted the authorities. After a brief hearing, a Pinellas County judge committed Donaldson to the Florida State Hospital on January 3, 1957. The committing judge stated that Donaldson was "being sent to the hospital for a few weeks to take some of this new medication," and that he was sure that Donaldson would be "alright" soon (*Donaldson v. O'Connor*, 1974, p. 2). Despite the judge's impression of what his ruling entailed, Donaldson would remain in the state hospital for nearly 15 years until his release in July of 1971.

At the time Donaldson was admitted, Dr. J. B. O'Connor was the Assistant Clinical Director of the ward; Dr. John Gumanis was a staff physician. During Donaldson's confinement, Dr. O'Connor was promoted to Superintendent and Dr. Gumanis was placed in charge of Donaldson's ward (*Donaldson v. O'Connor*, 1974). Donaldson was offered medication and electroshock treatments, but he refused them on the grounds that he was a Christian Scientist, that these treatments were against his religion, and that he did not think he was mentally ill and did not need treatment. Dr. Gumanis later testified that Donaldson had received "recreational" and "religious" therapies, but these consisted of nothing more than simply allowing him to attend church and engage in recreational activities. Dr. O'Connor elaborated that Donaldson was given "milieu therapy," which consisted of nothing more than keeping Donaldson in a large room with other patients. Neither Dr. O'Connor nor Dr. Gumanis referred to anything specific about this "therapy" that was in any way therapeutic. Over the 15 years, Donaldson essentially received nothing more than custodial care and did not receive treatment for the supposed illness for which he had been put there (*Donaldson v. O'Connor*, 1974).

During his first 10 years there, Donaldson consistently requested grounds privileges and occupational therapy but was on each occasion denied. Dr. Walter Fox, Director of the Arizona Mental Health Department, who later testified on Donaldson's behalf, examined hospital records and testified during the trial that "it would have been standard psychiatric practice to extend grounds privileges to a patient of Donaldson's background, condition, and history" (*Donaldson v. O'Connor*, 1974, p. 5). Asked why Donaldson was never allowed occupational therapy, neither Dr. O'Connor nor Dr. Gumanis could remember a reason for denying his requests. During his stay, Donaldson rarely even spoke with a psychiatrist. He testified that during the 18 months that Dr. O'Connor was directly in charge of his care, he only spoke with Dr. O'Connor about six times, and the total length of all the visits combined was approximately 1 hour. During the following 8 and one half years, when Dr. Gumanis was in charge of his care, Donaldson testified that he spoke to Dr. Gumanis for not more than a total of 2 hours (*Donaldson v. O'Connor*, 1974).

For the duration of his confinement, Donaldson never had a moment of privacy. For most of the time he spent at Florida State Hospital, he was confined to a locked room that contained 60 beds. While some of the beds were so close that their sides were touching, none were any farther apart than the width of a straight-back chair. While other rooms did contain chairs, there were none to be found in Donaldson's room. He kept his belongings in a cedar box beneath his bed. Donaldson estimated that about one-third of his ward consisted of criminals. He testified that these criminals were actually treated better than he was, because they received the attention of doctors who were required to give a monthly court report on behalf of each criminal. While there was an outside exercise yard for the patients, Donaldson testified that it was rarely used, and at one point during his confinement, no one went outside for 2 years (*Donaldson v. O'Connor*, 1974).

Both sides agreed at the trial that at no point during his confinement did Donaldson pose a danger to himself or to others. Dr. O'Connor himself admitted during his testimony that Donaldson had committed no dangerous acts toward others and had never been found to be suicidal or susceptible to injuring himself. In fact, no evidence was ever presented at trial to show that Donaldson had ever been dangerous or suicidal in his entire life (*Donaldson v. O'Connor*, 1974).

Dr. O'Connor claimed that Donaldson was never released, because he did not believe that Donaldson would be able to make a "successful adjustment outside the institution," though at the time of the trial, Dr. O'Connor could not remember why it was that he had earlier recorded that assumption about Mr. Donaldson. For some 14 years before his commitment, Donaldson had held a job, and upon his release, he successfully acquired a job in hotel administration (*O'Connor v. Donaldson*, 1975).

Not only had Donaldson demonstrated the ability to live outside of the institution on his own, but also on five different occasions during his confinement, responsible persons notified Dr. O'Connor that they were willing to provide Donaldson with care in a suitable and less restrictive environment. Among those offering to help was Helping Hands, a half-way house that would later be recognized by the Court as having successfully rehabilitated well over a thousand patients over the years. Yet O'Connor refused all offers.

Kenneth Donaldson was finally released on July 31, 1971, at the age of 62. Upon his release, he filed a lawsuit against Drs. O'Connor and Gumanis, who had kept him confined for nearly 15 years. Donaldson alleged that Dr. O'Connor, Dr. Gumanis, and other staff members had "intentionally and maliciously deprived him of his right to liberty" (*O'Connor v. Donaldson*, 1975, p. 1) as guaranteed by the U.S. Constitution under the Fourteenth Amendment. Dr. O'Connor claimed that he had been acting on "good faith" and simply kept Donaldson in the hospital for his own good (*O'Connor v. Donaldson*, 1975).

After a 4-day trial in November 1972, a jury returned a verdict awarding Donaldson a total of $28,500 in compensatory damages and $10,000 in punitive damages (*Donaldson v. O'Connor*, 1974). Drs. O'Connor and Gumanis appealed to the U.S. Supreme Court, and in 1975 the Court agreed to hear the case. The Court first had to decide the grounds for continued confinement and then decide whether Donaldson required the length of confinement that he received. The Court stated that involuntary confinement was "to prevent injury to the public, to ensure his own survival or alleviate or cure his illness" (*O'Connor v. Donaldson*, 1975, p. 10). According to these grounds, a person would have to be a danger to him- or herself or to others or be receiving treatment for a mental condition. When considering these criteria for continued confinement, the Court found that since Donaldson had at no time been a danger to himself or others, his length of confinement was not warranted. The Court decided that the so-called "treatments" Donaldson received during his confinement had in no way been therapeutic. In actuality, his long confinement had resulted in nothing more than simple custodial care. The Court stated that "a finding of mental illness alone cannot justify a State's locking a person up against his will and keeping him indefinitely in simple custodial care" (*O'Connor v. Donaldson*, 1975, p. 4). The Court stated, "A State cannot constitutionally confine in a mental institution, a nondangerous individual who is capable of surviving safely in freedom by himself or with the help of willing and responsible family members or friends and since the jury found . . . that [O'Connor] did so confine [Donaldson], it properly concluded that [O'Connor] had violated [Donaldson's] right to liberty" (*O'Connor v. Donaldson*, 1975, p. 4).

Civil Commitment Due Process in the Wake of *O'Connor*

With relatively concrete criteria for civil commitment now available for guidance, an issue remained for courts to decide: What level of proof was needed to satisfy these criteria? Recall from the introduction to this book that the *level of proof* refers to the degree to which a point must be proven in a court of law. For instance, "beyond a reasonable doubt" is a common level of proof in criminal cases, whereas a "preponderance of the evidence" is typically sufficient in civil trials.

In 1979, the case of *Addington v. Texas* provided significant discussion on this matter. In accordance with Texas law governing involuntary commitment at that time, Addington's mother petitioned that her son be indefinitely committed to a state mental hospital, after he was arrested on a misdemeanor charge of "assault by threat" against her. While in custody, Addington was found to be "mentally ill and [requiring] hospitalization in a mental hospital" by the county psychiatric examiner. Addington already had a long history or prior confinements, including temporary commitment on seven different occasions between 1969 and 1975 (*Addington v. Texas*, 1979, p. 5). The jury found that, based on "clear, unequivocal, and convincing evidence," Addington was mentally ill and required hospitalization for his own welfare and protection, as well as for the protection of others. Subsequently, Addington was indefinitely committed to the Austin State Hospital (*Addington v. Texas*, 1979, p. 3). Addington appealed, claiming that the trial court should have employed the stricter "beyond a reasonable doubt" standard of proof. While the Texas Court of Appeals agreed with Addington, the Texas Supreme Court reinstated the initial judgment made by the trial court. In *Addington*, the U.S. Supreme Court decision ultimately placed the burden of proof on the petitioner (the person seeking to have someone committed) and the state, which must demonstrate by "clear and convincing evidence" that the detainee meets the statutory criteria for commitment. This level of proof is a compromise, reflecting the loss of a liberty interest in civil commitment, but also acknowledging that the purpose of the "confinement" would be to receive treatment that was in the patient's best interest.

It is noteworthy that states can adopt a more, though not a less, stringent level of proof if they wish. For example, Texas adds the word "un-equivocal" to the "clear and convincing" standard, making it that much more stringent. Kentucky requires proof of commitment criteria beyond a reasonable doubt for persons with mental illness, yet affords persons diagnosed with Mental Retardation (MR) only a clear and convincing standard. In *Heller v. Doe* (1993), the U.S. Supreme Court upheld Kentucky's practice. The Court found it constitutional and not in violation of the Fourteenth Amendment *equal protection* clause. The rationales for the more easily met standard for MR was that the diagnosis of MR was viewed as usually more specific and accurate, and treatment for MR was usually less invasive (thus offering a lesser loss of liberty; see also Bersoff, Glass, & Blain, 1994).

Thus were laid out the procedures needed to guarantee the protection of individuals' due process rights upon seeking their involuntary commitment to a mental institution.

CIVIL COMMITMENT AND THE
AMERICANS WITH DISABILITIES ACT

In *Olmstead v. L.C.* (1999), the Supreme Court held that treatment on an inpatient basis may violate patients' rights under the Americans with Disabilities Act (ADA), following declaration by the states' mental health professionals of the appropriateness of community-based treatment. It was decided that states have the responsibility to provide the most integrated setting appropriate; thus, holding a patient in an inpatient setting would represent unfair and illegal discrimination based upon a disability. While the Court took steps to prevent this holding from creating unwarranted deinstitutionalization, a trend toward more lenient discharges may indeed result. Of important note is that this ruling is based upon the ADA rather than upon a constitutional right. Therefore, changes in the ADA could remove the precedent implications of this ruling.

An interesting aside to the *Olmstead* decision came in the form of three other Supreme Court cases from the same year, in which the Court limited ADA's relevance to certain individuals. In *Sutton v. United Airlines* (1999), the Court ruled that successful corrective measures (in this case, corrective lenses for myopia, but potentially applicable to psychotropic medication) precluded protection under the ADA. Furthermore, the court ruled that disallowing someone to perform a specific job on the basis of a disability does not violate the ADA on a per se basis. The logic in this ruling is that the person is free to seek other employment; thus, the life area of "work" is not severely limited by the disability. In *Albertsons v. Kirkingburg* (1999), the Court stated more broadly that mitigating circumstances must be taken into account when deciding the applicability of the ADA to a specific case. Also in the *Albertsons* decision, the Court included the ruling that although clients can seek waivers of federal regulations for requirements (in this case Department of Transportation requirements), these waivers are considered "experimental"; thus, individual companies cannot be required to acknowledge such practices. The impact of these findings for mental health professionals remains to be played out in the courts. However, the potential impact is quite significant because clients with mental disabilities who receive successful treatment may in fact lose their protection under the ADA. We next turn to the issue of what happens when the commitment is the result of criminal proceedings.

INDEFINITE CIVIL COMMITMENT AND THE DANGEROUS CRIMINALLY INSANE: TREATMENT OR CONFINEMENT?

Civil commitment of individuals who have been convicted of a crime has paralleled the commitment of noncriminals. An early case in the area was *Baxtrom v. Herold* (1966). In the 1960s, New York State maintained a significant population of "criminally insane" patients in the Mattacawan and Dannemora hospitals. These were completely separate from the public mental hospitals and served primarily to warehouse convicted offenders believed too dangerous and mentally disordered to be released. Johnnie Baxtrom had been convicted of a crime, found mentally ill, and then detained in one of these security hospitals throughout the maximum length of his sentence and beyond. He sued. Eventually, the U.S. Supreme Court found this system of detainment unconstitutional. It ruled that there is a denial of equal protection to a person civilly committed at the expiration of a prison sentence if there is no jury review, when a jury review is available to all others who are civilly committed. The court ordered that Mr. Baxtrom be released or processed through state civil commitment procedures, as any other citizen would be, and he and nearly a thousand other criminally insane individuals were either transferred to public hospitals or released. Subsequent research on the Baxtrom patients revealed that the frightening predictions of their potential for violence in the less restrictive hospital and community settings were exaggerated. Only about 20% (although some commentators have argued that this is an underestimate based on design flaws) engaged in assaultive acts during the next 4 years. Some would argue that such results prove that civil commitment is problematic, since 80% were not violent (as far as we know). Others would argue the same results support the value of civil commitment, since 20% is far higher than the rate of such violence (which is likely around 1–2%) expected in the general population.

In *Barefoot v. Estelle* (1983), the U.S. Supreme Court addressed the controversial issue of mental health professionals' opinions on dangerousness, and the value that should be awarded to them in making decisions to commit. In *Barefoot*, the Court heard testimony that even trained mental health professionals had poor accuracy in making predictions of future dangerousness. Yet the Court held that there are no constitutional barriers for mental health experts to testify in capital cases about long-term dangerousness. The Court stated, "The suggestion that no psychiatrist's testimony may be presented with respect to defendant's future dangerousness is somewhat like asking us to disinvent the wheel" (*Barefoot v. Estelle*, 1983, p. 15).

Paradoxically, the psychiatric testimony presented in *Barefoot* also demonstrates how a jury can be misled (Greenberg et al., 2005). Barefoot was convicted of murdering a police officer. He had five prior arrests for nonviolent offenses. Although neither of the two psychiatrists who testified for the prosecution had examined Barefoot, both diagnosed him as a *sociopath* (the term then in use for what we would now likely call a *psychopath* (See also Chapter 15 on Psychopathy). Most importantly, both also told the jury that such a person would commit violent acts in the future. One of the psychiatrists, Dr. James Grigson, claimed that his predictive accuracy was "100% and absolute" and the other, Dr. John Holbrook, claimed accuracy within a reasonable psychiatric certainty. The jury found it probable that Barefoot would commit acts of violence in the future, and that there was no known cure for his condition (the latter statement is one with which even a number of modern researchers might generally agree). Consequently, he was sentenced to death and executed (*Barefoot v. Estelle*, 1983, p. 20).

Five years later, Dr. Grigson was involved in another case in which his role was again noteworthy. In *Satterwhite v. Texas* (1988), the Supreme Court disallowed the testimony of Dr. Grigson, noting that there was no clinical interview or even any significant face-to-face contact with the patient, Mr. Satterwhite. The Court concluded that his opinions were not admissible, because they were not based on anything that could be reasonably interpreted as acceptable psychiatric practice.

In 1983, the ruling in *Jones v. U.S.* endorsed a different means of obtaining the relevant information for a civil commitment. The U.S. Supreme Court held that it is constitutionally acceptable to hold a ruling of Not Guilty by Reason of Insanity (NGRI) as a per se commitment. Thus, the Court permitted using the finding of NGRI to establish mental illness[2] and the violence of the crime to establish dangerousness. Of course, unlike most prison sentences, there is in theory no limit as to how long a civilly committed person may be held.

A current hot topic in forensic mental health and in law enforcement (and society in general) is the indefinite civil commitment of dangerous sex offenders after they have been released from prison. This provocative area carries with it several unique considerations, such as the fact that the offender was actually deemed *guilty* (as opposed to NGRI) in a court of law (for more discussion, see Chapter 18 on sexual predation and community notification in this volume). But what if the state is seeking indefinite commitment for the person for who was found *not* guilty by reason of insanity in a court of law? The Supreme Court faced this issue in the early 1990s in the case of *Foucha v. Louisiana*.

The Case of *Foucha v. Louisiana* (1992): Dangerousness and Mental Illness as Criteria for Indefinite Commitment

The decision in *O'Connor v. Donaldson* (1975) helped lay the groundwork for the Court in the case *Foucha v. Louisiana* (1992). Terry Foucha was charged with aggravated burglary and illegal discharge of a firearm. He was initially found incompetent to stand trial. Four months later, Foucha was found competent to stand trial, and the trial ensued. At trial, doctors testified that, at the time of the offense, Foucha was unable to distinguish right from wrong and was thus insane. On October 12, 1984, the Court ruled that Foucha was NGRI. The trial Court stated that, at the time of the offense, Foucha did not know right from wrong and could not appreciate the consequences of his actions. Furthermore, the Court held that Foucha was dangerous to himself and to others, and he was not only insane at the time the offense was committed but also at the time of the trial. Foucha was subsequently committed to the East Feliciana

---

[2] A blatant contradiction exists in this ruling, because an NGRI ruling refers to mental illness at the time of the crime, which may be years removed from the time of the trial. Thus, the mental illness present at the time of the crime may have long subsided, yet the person may be committed for mental illness.

Forensic Facility until such time as doctors or the Court recommended otherwise.

In March 1988, a three-member panel from the facility collaborated to determine Foucha's current mental state and whether he could be released without being a danger to himself or others. Later that month, the panel reported that Foucha showed no signs of mental illness other than having Antisocial Personality Disorder. In fact, he had showed no other signs of mental illness since his admission and should therefore be discharged. Upon receiving the panel's recommendation, the trial judge convened a "sanity commission" consisting of two doctors who would assess Foucha and testify to his mental state. The commission agreed with the panel from Feliciana, but they stated that they could not guarantee that Foucha would not be a danger to himself or others if released. The court consequently held that Foucha was in fact a danger to himself and others, and returned him to the Feliciana mental facility. This decision was upheld by the State Supreme Court of Louisiana and subsequently appealed to the U.S. Supreme Court in 1992.

In *Foucha*, as in *O'Connor v. Donaldson* (1975), the U.S. Supreme Court was faced with making a decision regarding the grounds for which a person can be forced to remain at a mental institution. Is the argument that a person could possibly pose a threat to him- or herself or to others reason enough to keep the person admitted to an institution when he or she shows no signs of mental illness? The Court did not think so. In May 1992, the Court reversed the decision of the lower courts, stating that the state of Louisiana "violates the Due Process Clause because it allows an insanity acquittee to be committed to a mental institution until he is able to demonstrate that he is not dangerous to himself and others, even though he does not suffer from any mental illness" (*Foucha v. Louisiana*, 1992, p. 2). In other words, continuing to keep Foucha committed despite the lack of any presence of mental illness would require the courts to develop additional grounds on which to keep him confined. For example, if Foucha was to be kept against his will after the finding that he no longer suffers from a mental illness, he was entitled to civil commitment proceedings (*Foucha v. Louisiana*, 1992).

As we see in Chapter 18 on sexual predation and community notification, the U.S. Supreme Court has since allowed personality disorder to be considered a mental illness with sex offenders (*Kansas v. Hendricks*, 1997). If similar reasoning were applied to the *Foucha* case today, Mr. Foucha could have been detained. He had been diagnosed with Antisocial Personality Disorder and was admittedly dangerous. So far, the courts have not resolved these obviously contradictory rulings.

SUMMARY

As illustrated in this chapter, the courts have indeed considered civil commitment from a variety of angles. The precedents set forth by both the *O'Connor* and *Foucha* decisions guarantee important rights to persons for whom involuntary commitment to mental institutions is being sought. The *O'Connor* decision stated that an individual diagnosed with a mental illness cannot be confined simply for custodial care. Unless found to be a danger to him- or herself or to others, an individual must be receiving treatment for an illness to remain involuntarily committed. Other cases have guaranteed a right to treatment and a right to refuse treatment once committed, and have stressed the importance of mental illness as a requirement for commitment.

Despite open questions about the applications of law, civil commitment today honors a number of due process rights. Although they vary somewhat across jurisdictions, these rights generally include: (1) right to an attorney; (2) notification of charges and when hearings occur; (3) hearings on the issue, with a statement of charges; (4) the standard of proof being stated; and (5) commitment procedures that follow rules of evidence.

CASE REFERENCES

Addington v. Texas, 441 U.S. 418; 1979 U.S. LEXIS 93 (1979).
Albertsons v. Kirkingburg, 527 U.S. 555; 1999 U.S. LEXIS 4369 (1999).
Barefoot v. Estelle, 463 U.S. 880; 1983 U.S. LEXIS 110 (1983).
Baxtrom v. Herold, 383 U.S. 107 (1966).
Donaldson v. O'Connor, 493 F.2d 507; 1974 U.S. App LEXIS 8960 (1974).
Foucha v. Louisiana, 504 U.S. 71; 1992 U.S. LEXIS 2703 (1992).
Heller v. Doe, 113 S. Ct. 2637 (1993).
In re Gault, 387 U.S. 1 (1967).
In re Oakes, 8 *Monthly Law Reporter* (Mass. 1845).
Jones v. U.S., 463 U.S. 354 (1983).
Kansas v. Hendricks, 521 U.S. 346; 1997 U.S. LEXIS 3999 (1997).
Lake v. Cameron, 124 U.S. App. D.C. 264; 364 F.2d 657; 1966 U.S. App. LEXIS 6103 (1966).

O'Connor v. Donaldson, 422 U.S. 563 (1975).

Olmstead v. L.C., 527 U.S. 581; 119 S. Ct. 2176; 144 L. Ed. 2d 540; 1999 U.S. LEXIS 4368 (1999).

Rennie v. Klein, 462 F. Supp. 1131; 1978 U.S. Dist. LEXIS 14441 (1978).

Rouse v. Cameron, 373 F.2d 451 (D.C. Cir. 1966), later proceeding, 387 F.2d 241 (1967).

Satterwhite v. Texas, 486 U.S. 249 (1988); but see *Perry v. Locke,* 488 U.S. 272 (1989).

Sutton v. United Airlines, 1996 U.S. Dist. LEXIS 15106; 6 Am. Disabilities Cas. (BNA) 116 (1999).

Wyatt v. Stickney, 334 F. Supp. 1341 (M.D. Ala. 1971).

CHAPTER 9

Hypnosis and the Polygraph

Hypnosis and the polygraph are two techniques that have provided significant controversy in the legal arena. Although it is difficult to pin down an exact definition for hypnosis, the practice has received at least modest acceptance in the courts. Yet the more easily definable polygraph historically has been rejected by the courts. We first consider the evolution of forensic hypnosis.

HYPNOSIS

Since the dawn of ancient recorded history, various methods of influence that are clearly hypnotic in nature are easily detected.[1] In 1955, the British Medical Association became the first professional organization to designate hypnosis as an accepted treatment modality and as a proper subject for medical research. The Canadian Medical Association and the American Medical Association formally recognized the therapeutic value of hypnosis in 1958, and the American *Psychological* Association in 1960 recognized hypnosis as a branch of psychology; in 1961, the American *Psychiatric* Association endorsed hypnosis as a valid therapeutic procedure. As we will soon see, case law dealing with hypnosis goes back to

---

[1] References to forms of hypnosis in the terms of "temple sleep" or being enchanted by the "evil eye" can be traced back as early as 3000 B.C. An Egyptian stone tablet from the reign of Ramses XII is said to be the earliest record of a hypnotic session.

the 19th century. Partly spurred on by legal challenges to the practice, methods designed to measure hypnosis stem from the same era.

Measurement of Hypnosis

It is generally accepted in the hypnosis field that people are on a continuum as to their ability to experience a hypnotic state. A number of psychometric scales have been developed for the assessment of this hypnotic susceptibility. The first hypnosis scales were developed in the 1880s. Updated forms continue to be in use today. Among these are the Stanford Hypnotic Susceptibility Scale, Forms A, B, and C (Weitzenhoffer & Hilgard, 1959, 1962, 1963), the Harvard Hypnotic Susceptibility Scale (Shor & Orne, 1962); the Barber Suggestibility Scale (Barber & Glass, 1962); and the Hypnotic Induction Profile (HIP; Spiegel & Bridger, 1970). The major scales currently in use, the Stanford and Harvard scales, are controversial regarding what they actually measure. In 1962, Form C of the Stanford Scales was developed, and is now generally referred to as the "gold standard" of hypnotic scales. The general premise of these scales is for the subject to perform various tasks, or ignore various stimuli, that would be very difficult to perform or ignore were the subject not aided by the hypnotic state. While these scales have been extensively researched for both reliability and validity, they remain face valid and are subject to dissimulation, or faking (Miller & Stava, 1997).

Hypnosis in the Courtroom

Legal cases involving the use of hypnosis can be traced back as far as the mid-1800s (Knight & Meyer, 2006). Expert testimony concerning hypnotically refreshed memory in a U.S. court has been dated back to 1846, and the first formal report of legal cases focusing on hypnosis appeared in the *American Journal of Insanity* in 1848.

In a historically important case, *People v. Ebanks* (1897), the defense attempted to show through hypnotically enhanced testimony that Ebanks's alleged amnesia was simply a result of his not being at the crime scene. Upon appeal, the California Supreme Court denied the admissibility of such evidence and would not allow the expert to testify, setting a precedent of "per se inadmissibility" (see Table 9.1 for a comparison of approaches to evidence admission). The Court specifically noted in *Ebanks* that "the law does not recognize hypnotism," and by extension would not accept any testimony based on the practice. In other words,

TABLE 9.1. Approaches to Evidence Admission

Approach	Is the evidence admitted?	Considerations
Per se admission	Yes	None
Per se exclusion	No	None
"Requirements"	Maybe	Legally predetermined set of requirements that *must* be met.
"Guidelines"	Maybe	Legally predetermined set of guidelines that *may* be considered by the judge.
"Totality of the circumstances"	Maybe	Who has a vested interest in the ruling (i.e., the defendant, the state)? What are the risks–benefits to each of these parties of admitting–not admitting the testimony in the specific case? Taking all of this into consideration, should the testimony be admitted?

once hypnosis occurs, the testimony is tainted and is automatically not admissible.

Austin v. Barker (1906) became an important precedent case for several decades. Edith Austin had a baby in August 1901, but reported that she had no idea how this had come about. She was hypnotized by her father's attorney in a sort of pre-DNA-era paternity test. Under hypnosis, she allegedly had a recovered memory of having sex with a man named David Barker at the appropriate time, and recalled that Mr. Barker had also hypnotized her. Ms. Austin sued Mr. Barker to get him to accept his paternal responsibilities. After three trials, the Court eventually absolved Mr. Barker of any responsibility on the basis of what amounted to a legal technicality. The Court ruled that what Edith recounted under hypnosis was impermissible hearsay, and was thus not a "true" memory.

In 1923, the U.S. Supreme Court gave the U.S. legal system a criterion by which to assess the admissibility of scientific techniques into courts of law. In *Frye v. U.S.* (1923; discussed in detail in Chapter 2 on admission of expert testimony and the eyewitness, this volume), the Court ruled that a procedure must have "gained general acceptance in the particular field in which it belongs" to be allowed into evidence. Although the *Frye* case is discussed in the Polygraph section below, because it involved the use of a lie detection test, its application as legal precedent regarding hypnosis would not be recognized for several decades.

Before the application of the *Frye* standard, courts continued to delineate rulings specific to hypnosis. In the critical case of *Harding v. State* (1968/1969), Baltimore resident Mildred Coley reported to police that she had been robbed and stabbed by three black males. However, police noticed that she had actually been shot rather than stabbed, and requested that she be hypnotized to aid her recollection. Under hypnosis by the chief psychologist from the local state hospital, Ms. Coley produced enough information to implicate a Mr. Harding in the assault. Based on the investigation that had hinged entirely on the hypnotically refreshed memory, Harding was found guilty. The Maryland Court of Appeals acknowledged the earlier *Austin v. Barker* case that disallowed hypnosis. However, the Court ultimately ruled that hypnosis was acceptable in this instance because it involved (1) a thorough evaluation by (2) a well-trained professional, who (3) had not used leading questions. The ruling in this case was subsequently interpreted as a setting forth minimal "guidelines" to be considered in determining whether to admit hypnotically refreshed testimony (see Table 9.1 for a comparison of the "guidelines" approach to other approaches). The *Harding* court also stated that testimony produced from hypnosis "concerns the weight of the evidence which the trier of facts, in this case, the jury, must decide" (p. 306). In other words, not only were the guidelines important for a judge to consider in overruling *Austin*, but they should also be considered by the *jury* (or judge) in weighing hypnotically refreshed testimony.

Harding remained the primary precedent case in the nation for admissibility of hypnosis until another Maryland court reversed the ruling in *Collins v. State* (1981). Not surprisingly, Harding opened the courts up to numerous cases that included hypnotically refreshed testimony. From the mid-1800s up to *Harding*, only about 50 appellate cases concerning hypnosis had been filed in the United States; after *Harding*, and up until 1993, about 750 such cases (about 96% of which were criminal) were filed. Developing in parallel to this explosion in legal interest, an interest in empirical evaluation of hypnosis was pioneered by Dr. Martin Orne (Knight & Meyer, 2006).

Forensic Hypnosis and the Influence of Dr. Martin Orne

In the 1970s, Martin Orne MD, PhD, in conjunction with numerous criminal attorneys, studied the process of hypnosis, focusing on the influence of investigative hypnosis on related testimony. The work of Dr. Orne has been cited in more than 30 legal cases in the Supreme Court and in infamous cases such as those of Kenneth Bianchi (discussed in detail below) and Patty Hearst. Orne's influence in these cases had an enormous impact on the admissibility of hypnotically refreshed testimony.[2]

The Case of the Hillside Strangler: The Veracity of Hypnosis in a Forensic Setting

Kenneth Alessio Bianchi, born on May 22, 1951, was the son of a prostitute who immediately gave him up for adoption. He was diagnosed as having epileptic (petit mal) seizures at age 5, for which no treatment was sought. He also suffered periodic urinary incontinence from a deformed kidney. By age 11, Bianchi manifested compulsive lying, indifference toward school, and frequent eruptions of anger. These problems in school persisted, despite Kenneth having a significantly above-average IQ of 116. Although psychological treatment was recommended and sought, his adoptive mother discontinued it when the psychologist suggested that she needed treatment as well.

At age 18, Bianchi entered into a marriage that lasted less than 6 months.[3] He eventually became bored with his life in Rochester, New York. In 1976, he moved to Los Angeles, California, to live with his cousin Angelo Buono. Bianchi's engagement in illegal behavior began almost immediately. Within the first couple months of moving, Bianchi, Buono, and Buono's son Anthony exploited a prostitute by jointly using her services and then refusing to pay her. When the prostitute asked for her money, Buono showed her a police badge and told her to leave. Bianchi later applied to and was rejected by two police departments. Things were not going entirely well for him, and stressors were building. After a rejection by a woman he had been dating, Bianchi began stalking her. He broke into her apartment, urinated into her diaphragm, and placed a condom filled with semen over her doorknob.

---

[2] Orne's research culminated in his publication in a 1979 special issue of the *International Journal of Clinical and Experimental Hypnosis*. A second article in that issue offers experimental support for Orne's assertions by Hilgard and Loftus (1979). As a side note, Dr. Loftus went on to establish herself as a current preeminent expert in the area of eyewitness memory and testimony.

[3] Readers familiar with the material in Chapter 15 in this volume may recognize that Bianchi's behavior fits a pattern consistent with Psychopathy, even prior to his formally being charged with any crime.

By May 1977, Bianchi had obtained a job at a tile company. He impregnated one of his coworkers, Kelli, and had her move in with him. At around the same time, he opened an office, fraudulently portraying himself as a "psychologist." When asked to explain his frequent absences from work, Bianchi told his boss and Kelli that he had cancer and was getting chemotherapy. This excuse eventually failed, and Bianchi and Buono decided to become pimps, "hiring" two young girls to work for them. They named this new business venture "Foxy Ladies." They frequently had sex with the girls and occasionally beat them. Yet Kelli remained loyal. However, due to the abuse, the girls eventually ran away. Buono and Bianchi were furious and made plans to kill a prostitute for retribution. Picking up the first victim, Bianchi raped and strangled her as Buono drove. During Thanksgiving week of 1977, they killed five more women in 9 days, leaving their bodies in the hills surrounding Los Angeles. The press, not knowing that there were multiple perpetrators, named the case "Hillside Strangler."

The murders continued, becoming increasingly violent and sadistic. At some point, Bianchi began killing prostitutes on his own, without the aid of Buono. After strangling a total of 10 women, he stopped out of fear of being caught. Occasional leads caused the police to question Bianchi several times. Threats from Buono to turn himself and Bianchi in caused Bianchi to move to the small town of Bellingham, Washington. There he soon strangled two more women. But in January 1979, he got caught. The similarity of these murders with the previous 10 alerted officials that Bianchi might be Los Angeles's "Hillside Strangler."

The evidence against Bianchi was substantial, and his attorneys recommended the insanity defense. Bianchi refused and insisted he was innocent. The case would soon become a battle of expert mental health witnesses. Two experts (Drs. Allison and Moffett) were appointed by the court; three experts (Drs. Watkins, Lunde, and Markman) were hired by the defense, and two (Drs. Orne and Faerstein) by the prosecution. Several of these individuals had national reputations. Most importantly for our discussion here, both John Watkins and Martin Orne had well-deserved international reputations in the hypnosis community.

Dr. Watkins saw Bianchi on March 21 and 22, 1979. He reported that while hypnotized, Bianchi presented another personality, Steve, who admitted to the murders. Dr. Allison concurred with the veracity of these statements. Dr. Orne then assessed Bianchi and claimed that Bianchi's performance indicated faking on specific tests for malingering in hypnosis (see Table 9.2). Also, Dr. Orne noted that Bianchi had not presented a third personality until just after Dr. Orne purposely

TABLE 9.2. Techniques Employed by Dr. Orne to Assess Kenneth Bianchi

Technique	Hypnotized patient	Malingering patient	Kenneth Bianchi
Double hallucination—Patient is asked to hallucinate a vision of a person who is actually in the room out of the patient's view. Hypnotist then points to the actual person and asks, "Who is that?" giving the patient the impression that two of the same person are present.	• Will generally not acknowledge the illogical nature of the situation. • Will correctly identify both the hallucination and the actual person.	• May draw extra attention to the illogical nature of the situation. • May fail to identify the real person or may stop identifying the hallucination as the same person to make the situation logical.	Repeatedly pointed out the illogical nature of the situation when asked to hallucinate his attorney. He repeatedly asked, "How can Dear Brett [his attorney] be in two places at once?"
Single hallucination—Patient is asked to hallucinate a vision of an object and is repeatedly asked to describe it in significant detail.	Will commonly describe seeing the outline of background objects through the hallucination (i.e., will see the outline of a chair if asked to hallucinate someone sitting in a real chair).	Will not describe seeing the outline of the background object through the hallucination. (This result is actually interpreted as equivocal.)	Did not describe seeing the outline of background objects.
Suggested anesthesia—Hypnotist draws an imaginary circle on the back of patient's hand and tells patient that he or she will have no feeling inside the circle. Hypnotist then alternates touching patient's hand inside and outside of the circle. Patient is asked to close his or her eyes and respond "yes" if he or she feels a touch and "no" if he or she does not feel a touch.	• Will respond "yes" to touches inside the circle. • May respond "yes" to touches inside the circle. • Will most likely respond "no" to touches inside the circle, despite the illogical nature of such a response.	• Will respond "yes" to touches outside the circle. • Will not respond at all to touches inside the circle, thus maintaining the logic that the area is numb.	• Responded "yes" to touches outside the circle • Did not respond to touches inside the circle.

149

remarked that it was very unusual for a true multiple personality to only have two personalities. Through these observations, Dr. Orne concluded that Bianchi had not only fabricated the claims of multiple personality but had also simulated the hypnotic trance to begin with (Miller & Stava, 1997). Dr. Orne eventually concluded Bianchi had Antisocial Personality Disorder. Throughout the trial, and despite Dr. Orne's evidence, Dr. Allison maintained his position that Bianchi truly had multiple personalities.[4] Dr. Watkins visited Bianchi on occasion after he was imprisoned, and recently reported to one of us (Meyer) in a phone conversation that he still believes that Bianchi truly has multiple personalities.[5]

Following quickly on the heels of Dr. Orne's report indicating that Bianchi was faking his hypnosis, Bianchi immediately offered to plead guilty to five of the California murders and two Washington State murders. The prosecution accepted. Bianchi was sentenced to life plus 5 years in California and to two consecutive life sentences in Washington State. In return, he promised to provide testimony sufficient to convict Buono, but later reneged by giving testimony that favored Buono. Luckily, prosecutors convicted Buono without Bianchi's aid.

In 1978, Dr. Orne filed an amicus brief in a California case in which he anticipated the formal adoption of a set of rules for the acceptance of hypnotically enhanced testimony. In the 1981 case of *State v. Hurd*, the New Jersey Supreme Court adopted six procedural rules or safeguards for hypnotically enhanced testimony. Known as the *Hurd* rules,[6] they are the precedent for most procedural safeguards employed today. The rules are as follows: (1) The session should be conducted by a licensed psychologist or psychiatrist; (2) the hypnotist should be independent of, and not responsible to, the prosecutor or the defense; (3) any prior information provided to the hypnotist should be in writing; (4) before inducing hypnosis, the facts the subject has should be obtained and recorded; (5) the session should be recorded; videotaping is desirable, not mandatory; and (6) only the hypnotist and subject should be present at prehypnosis meetings, the session itself, and any debriefing.

---

[4] Interestingly, Dr. Allison later seemed to change his mind after working for some time as a prison psychologist.

[5] Dr. Watkins presents a cogent defense of his position in a 1984 article, "The Bianchi Case: Sociopath or Multiple Personality?" in volume 32 (pp. 67–101) of the *International Journal of Clinical and Experimental Hypnosis*.

[6] The *Hurd* rules have also been called the *Orne* rules, noting the contributions made by Dr. Orne.

Hypnosis as Expert Testimony

In 1923, the U.S. Supreme Court had provided the *Frye* standard (that a procedure needed to have gained general acceptance in its field) for the admission of expert testimony. Interestingly, this standard was not applied to hypnosis (despite the field's inherent use of scientific experts) for over half a century.

Finally, in *State v. Mack* (1980), the 2nd Circuit Court of Appeals invoked the *Frye* rule in establishing the admissibility of hypnotically refreshed testimony. The *Mack* case effectively stemmed the tide of cases flowing from *Harding*, because the latter ruling required consideration of case-specific circumstances. Yet the case-specific circumstances of the *Mack* case included a poorly trained hypnotist and an utter lack of expert testimony. In *Mack*, the Appeals Court ruled that hypnotically refreshed testimony was in fact *not* generally accepted in the field, and was thus per se inadmissible. In the landmark case, *People v. Shirley* (1982), the California Supreme Court mandated a sweeping "per se inadmissible" rule for hypnotically refreshed testimony. In this case, Shirley, a young Marine, was accused of rape but said the alleged victim's participation was voluntary. The victim's testimony was changed by hypnosis performed by the prosecuting attorney the very night before her testimony. The court made no reference to *Frye* and indicated that any case-by-case analysis of hypnotic procedures would be too costly.

Notably, the testimony in neither of these cases holding per se inadmissible precedent would have been allowed under the *Hurd* rules. But a problem that remained with the *Hurd* rule approach was that it had not yet received U.S. Supreme Court attention and was thus of limited precedent value. That situation actually did not improve until 1987, when the Court heard the case of *Rock v. Arkansas*.

The Case of *Rock v. Arkansas* (1987): U.S. Supreme Court Acknowledgment of *Hurd* Criteria

In *Rock v. Arkansas*, Vacua Lorene "Vickie" Rock was charged with shooting her husband. She had partial amnesia for the details of the shooting. The two had been fighting and physically struggling, when one of them pulled out a gun. As they continued to struggle, the weapon discharged, and Frank was fatally wounded. Mrs. Rock reported that she had only a vague memory for what happened. Her attorney sent her to be hypnotized by a qualified professional to enhance her memory. While in the trance, her recall was that her finger was never on the trigger. In response, her attorney then sent the weapon to a laboratory for analysis. The laboratory report indicated that the trigger mechanism was defective and could have discharged without someone pulling the trigger.

Since Arkansas had already adopted a "per se" exclusionary rule for evidence obtained while under hypnosis, the trial Court refused to permit the testimony or the resulting laboratory analysis. The U.S. Supreme Court, in a 5 to 4 decision, with Justice Blackmun writing the decision, held that it was a violation of one's constitutional rights (based on the Fifth, Sixth, and Fourteenth Amendments) to preclude arbitrarily or absolutely the hypnotically refreshed testimony of the defendant in a criminal trial. The Court wrote:

> Hypnosis by trained physicians or psychologists has been recognized as a valid therapeutic technique since 1958, although there is no generally accepted theory to explain the phenomenon, or even a consensus on a single definition of hypnosis. . . . The popular belief that hypnosis guarantees the accuracy of recall is as yet without established foundation and, in fact, hypnosis often has no effect at all on memory . . . The most common response to hypnosis, however, appears to be an increase in both correct and incorrect recollections. (p. 59)
>   . . . We are not now prepared to endorse without qualifications the use of hypnosis as an investigative tool; scientific understanding of the phenomenon and of the means to control the effects of hypnosis is still in its infancy. (p. 61)

In light of recommendations made by Dr. Orne, the Court expanded upon the *Hurd* rules and established the following procedural requirements: A psychiatrist or psychologist must be experienced in the use of hypnosis and should also be able to qualify as an expert in order to assist the court; the professional conducting the hypnotic session should not be employed by the prosecution; any information given to the hypnotist by law enforcement personnel must be recorded; before inducing hypnosis, the hypnotist should obtain from the subject a detailed outline of the facts as the subject then remembers them; all contacts between the hypnotist and the subject must be recorded; only the hypnotist and the subject should be present during any phase of the hypnotic session.

The Court asserted that the recognized difficulties with such testimony can be handled through cross-examination or by adopting appropriate rules of evidence. The Court specifically noted that this does not apply to civil trials, and left open the question as to the issue of a nondefendant witness in a criminal trial.

While there remain no U.S. Supreme Court rulings on hypnosis in civil litigation, the topic was addressed in 1995 at the State Supreme Court level. On May 28, 1996, the California Supreme Court let stand the Appeals Court decision from *Borawick v. Shay* (1995), which affirmed the use of a "totality of circumstances" rule of admissibility, as opposed to any per se inadmissibility rule. The California Court suggested a case-by-case analysis on a "nonexclusive" list of factors very similar to the *Hurd* rules. In part influenced by the new *Daubert* rule (1993), the Appeals Court had found that the exclusion of posthypnotic testimony may give way to lost opportunity for individuals to convict their abusers. However, the Court also noted that admitting testimony that concerns hypnosis creates danger in the fact that a lay jury will have to speculate on the potential problems of this type of testimony.

THE POLYGRAPH

There are lies, damned lies, and statistics.
—Mark Twain

Champagne . . . is better than a lie detector. It encourages a man to be expansive, even reckless, while lie detectors are only a challenge to tell lies successfully.
—Graham Greene

Various techniques have been employed in an attempt to assess deception (Boyd et al., 2006). The polygraph, or "lie detector" test,[7] is a well-known example of such a technique. While the admissibility of polygraph testimony is suspect in court, the polygraph is often used as an investigative measure. The use of a failed polygraph is oftentimes enough to entice an accused individual to plead guilty. The classic example of this occurred in the city of Radner, Pennsylvania. An investigating officer placed a metal colander on a suspect's head, attached wires between the colander and a nearby copy machine, and placed a paper in the copier that read "He is lying!" Periodically, the officer surreptitiously hit the copy button, and showed the suspect the resulting "He is lying!" copy. The suspect did confess, but fortunately this confession was thrown out.

---

[7] *Polygraph* is actually not synonymous with *lie detector*. A polygraph is merely a machine that simultaneously tracks and records multiple physiological measurements. Lie detection is a specific application of a polygraph machine.

The polygraph measures a number of physiological reactions that are theoretically associated with arousal that occurs when one is lying. Two primary emotions are involved when one is lying: the fear of being caught in this act and the feeling of guilt associated with the act (Ekman, 1985). Fear elicits preparation for a fight-or-flight response in most animals, including humans. Physiological arousal results when the body is prepared to enter into a flight-or-fight response. Specifically, the autonomic nervous system becomes activated, and the result is increased heart rate, sweating, and increased respiration, among other things. The polygraph test relies on the assumption that deliberately lying to an authority will elicit these emotions and resulting psychological arousal. The four monitored reactions are associated with the autonomic nervous system: abdominal and thoracic breathing patterns, cardiovascular activity, and galvanic skin response (Grubin, 2002). At least in theory, specific patterns emerge when someone is lying to the polygraph administrator. However, the types of responses thought to indicate lying can occur for reasons other than deception (i.e., use of stimulants, including caffeine, and stress). Thus, particular care and specific training are needed when administering and recording results from a polygraph test. As we will see, even special care in these areas may not be enough to make the technique accurate.

Historical Evolution of Polygraphy Techniques

William Moulton Marston, the subject of the decision in *Frye v. U.S.* (1923), was the first person to use the phrase *lie detector*, although his early technique involved only a periodic assessment of systolic blood pressure that was undoubtedly ineffective.[8] John Larson was one of the first to use a combination of techniques, blood pressure and respiration; thus, he can be reasonably construed as the pioneer of the modern polygraph. He used these measures in solving his first case, a shoplifting case, but, realistically, the primary potency of the technique (as in many modern cases) was in generating a confession. Larson is credited with developing the relevant–irrelevant technique in which responses to case-relevant questions are compared to responses from irrelevant questions. To his credit, Larson always remained a bit skeptical of the validity of the polygraph. Leonard Keeler furthered the polygraph by developing

---

[8] When Marston later left psychology and developed the Wonder Woman cartoon, he retained his lie detections interest when he gave her the "Lasso of Truth."

a portable version of the instrument and by using the polygraph to help solve the second most publicized child homicide, that of Annie Lemberger in 1933.

John Reid is likely the most recognized figure in the history of the polygraph, no doubt because of his development of the commercial use of the polygraph and for founding the original school for polygraphers. In the mid-1940s he strongly attacked the relevant–irrelevant approach as being too imprecise, and in response came up with the "control question" technique. Using control questions (e.g., "Did you ever steal something of value in your life?"), the examiner attempts to set a baseline of response to emotional topics. These responses are then contrasted to specific and relevant questions (e.g., "Did you take the money from the desk drawer in Mr. Smith's office?"). Clive Backster also founded his own polygraphy school. He emphasized making decisions based only on the data from the polygraph. In contrast, Reid emphasized combining the polygraph data with behavioral cues. Backster is also infamous for having hooked up a galvanic skin response machine to a plant, and concluding that the plant might be reading his mind.

Another major polygraphy figure, David Lykken, is primarily responsible for the Guilty Knowledge Test, which uses, indeed, requires, some knowledge of the crime that would not be available to someone who was not a direct witness to the crime (e.g., the cash that was taken was in (1) an envelope on the desk, (2) a desk drawer, (3) an open safe under the desk, (4) a vase, (5) a fake book). By providing a number of these questions, one can determine the probabilities that the person being examined showed an emotional response only to the crime-related material. If enough details about the case are available, the guilty knowledge technique is clearly superior to other techniques. However, most polygraphers have little training in it.

Factors Confounding Polygraph Assessment

Many factors may impact upon the applicability of the polygraph to determine deception. For instance, personality traits (i.e., Psychopathy) can greatly affect a person's lying performance; some individuals lie with great ease; others are greatly disturbed by it. By nature, some people are more prone to anxiety and would therefore most likely perform poorly on a polygraph, whereas others are calm in a multitude of situations and/or feel little guilt or remorse when doing wrong. In essence, a person's entire psychology can greatly impact his or her experience of being deceitful, and by extension, his or her physiological reaction to lying.

The results of the polygraph can also be compromised through techniques (purposeful or accidental) such as taking relaxant medications, practicing relaxation/meditation to develop internal relaxation cues, putting a small cut on a toe and then pressing it at appropriate times to disrupt baseline measurements, and so on (Marquand, 1997). And a person can always use the most effective countermeasure to obtain exams from private polygraphers until he or she passes one, or take several practice polygraphs. With the proliferation of the Internet, websites abound that address methods of beating the polygraph.

Confounding these issues further, it is extremely difficult to conduct research on the use of the polygraph in lie detection. The primary problem is that it is nearly impossible to conduct an experiment that truly replicates what is often at stake for the real-world examinee who is lying to authorities. Can people lie better when there is less at stake (i.e., a $5 study participation fee)? Or can people lie better when the stakes are higher (i.e., when trying to dodge a murder conviction)? What are the differences in physiological arousal between lying about having committed a murder and fearing that one will be wrongly accused? We return to concerns about the research on polygraphy in a later section. First, we turn to what the courts have to say about polygraph testimony.

The Polygraph in the Courtroom

Court decisions regarding the validity of the polygraph vary widely. Variations occur for reasons ranging from doubt as to the scientific merit of the polygraph to the fear that it will affect the jury's role in making judgments of credibility. As with hypnosis, use of the polygraph in court is largely dependent on the acceptability of expert testimony on its use. Recall from earlier discussion that the 1923 decision in *Frye v. U.S.* set the stage for expert admissibility.

Frye was actually a case involving Marston's systolic blood pressure deception test, described earlier. Again, the Court ruled that to be allowed into evidence, a technique has to be "sufficiently established to have gained general acceptance in the particular field in which it belongs." The *Frye* "general acceptance" test became the dominant rule governing the admissibility of expert testimony for 70 years and is still used in California, Florida, Illinois, and New York. Most courts hare refused to admit testimony about the polygraph under *Frye*. A continuing dilemma for courts under the *Frye* standard is determining what "field" decides if a technique is scientifically acceptable. For the polygraph, is it physiology, psychology, medicine, or specifically polygraphy?

The latter option seems most logical, but the field itself has very weak credentialing standards, and the U.S. Supreme Court has severely limited the right of government to regulate such certifications (*Peel v. Attorney Registration and Disciplinary Commission*, 1990).

The more recent *Daubert* rule (1993),[9] currently in use regarding admissibility in federal court and in most states, allows the judge more discretion in the decision of what is "scientifically acceptable." However, in 1995 alone, some federal courts rejected polygraph testimony under *Daubert* (*U.S. v. Posado*, 1995; *U.S. v. Galbreth*, 1995), while others simply rejected it (*U.S. v. Sherlin*, 1995). The latter ruling went so far as to describe polygraphy as infringing upon the right of the jury to determine the truthfulness of a witness's claims (Faigman, 2003). Not until the 1998 case of *U.S. v. Scheffer* did the U.S. Supreme Court address the issue.

The Case of *U.S. v. Scheffer* (1998): Polygraph Admissibility in the Wake of *Frye* and *Daubert*

In *U.S. v. Scheffer* (1998), the U.S. Supreme Court directly considered the polygraph. A general court martial of several charges convicted Airman Edward Scheffer. Since he had been working with the Air Force's Office of Special Investigations (OSI) to investigate drug allegations, he was routinely asked to take a drug test. On this occasion, he asked for a 1-day delay, stating he only urinated once a day. When he requested further delays, he was ordered to take a polygraph and was asked (1) whether he ever used drugs while in the Air Force, (2) whether he had ever lied in providing any information to OSI, and (3) whether he had told anyone but his parents that he worked for OSI? He answered "No" to all of these questions, and the examiner concluded there was no deception. However, a later laboratory test showed that he used methamphetamines, and he was court-martialed.

The various appeals developed when his polygraph evidence was not considered, because then President George Bush (the father) had promulgated an executive order that decreed the results of polygraph tests to be inadmissible for any purpose in military courts. The Supreme Court eventually ruled in 1998 that Sheffer had no constitutional right to tell a court-martial that he had passed a polygraph exam. In this 8 to 1 decision written by Clarence Thomas, with Justice Stevens as the lone

---

[9] Both the *Frye* and *Daubert* approaches are discussed in detail in Chapter 2, this volume.

dissenter, the Court emphasized that a defendant's constitutional right to present evidence, as discussed earlier in this chapter in Vickie Rock's case, does have reasonable restrictions. However, it did not rule out various jurisdictions admitting polygraph evidence, and in sifting through the opinions, a 5 to 4 majority appeared to be against a per se inadmissibility rule but did not conclude that polygraph evidence was unreliable, or that it invades the province of the jury.

Thus, the current state of affairs is that jurisdictions are left to their own devices for considering the admissibility of polygraph testimony. But what are the courts to consider when determining this admissibility? Proponents of the polygraph (i.e., law enforcement agencies) rely on a body of literature that they interpret as indicating an 80–99% accuracy rate. Opponents interpret the same literature as being, at best, inconclusive and, at worst, "junk science." Exactly what does the existing research say? This was the question posed by National Research Counsel in 2000.

The 2003 National Research Counsel Review of the Scientific Evidence on the Polygraph

The National Research Counsel was formed by the National Academy of Sciences in 1916 to assist the Academy in its mission to inform federal lawmakers about advancements in science and research that impact upon public policy. At the turn of the millennium, the Counsel convened a committee to conduct a review of the scientific literature on the reliability and validity of the polygraph. This committee was formed by some of the most eminent researchers in lie detection and related fields. In January 2001, the committee began its work that culminated 19 months later in the publication of a formal report. Notably, the work of the committee spanned the events of September 11, 2001. These events significantly heightened the country's awareness of the importance of lie detection in national security.

In its publication (Moore, Petrie, & Braga, 2003), the Committee stated that, "Almost a century of research in scientific psychology and physiology provides little basis for the expectation that a polygraph test could have extremely high accuracy" (p. 2). The Committee referenced many of the concerns discussed earlier regarding factors other than deception that may cause polygraph results to indicate lying. From this, the Committee expressed concern that this problem "suggests that further investments in improving polygraph technique and interpretation will bring only modest improvements in accuracy" (p. 2). Perhaps what is of most concern in the Committee's research summary is the following statement:

> . . . there is evidence suggesting that truthful members of socially stigma-tized groups and truthful examinees who are believed to be guilty or believed to have a high likelihood of being guilty may show emotional and physiological responses in polygraph test situations that mimic the re-sponses that are expected of deceptive individuals. (p. 2)

Despite the Committee's stated concerns that additional research in polygraphy would, at best, yield modest gains, it strongly encouraged governmental support of research looking at polygraphy and alternative means of detecting deception. We interpret the Committee's report as being strong evidence for the exclusion of polygraph testimony under both *Frye* and *Daubert* criteria. However, only the future will tell whether the report spurs any bias against the practice in U.S. courts of law.

CASE REFERENCES

Austin v. Barker, 110 A.D. 510; 96 N.Y.S. 814; 1906 N.Y. App. Div. LEXIS 15 (1906).

Borawick v. Shay, 68 F.3d 597 (1995).

Collins v. State, 52 Md. App. 186; 447 A.2d 1272; 1982 Md. App. LEXIS 317 (1981).

Daubert v. Merrell Dow Pharmaceuticals, 113 S. Ct. 2786 (1993).

Frye v. U.S., 295 F. 1013 (D.C. Cir. 1923).

Harding v. State, 5 Md. App. 230; 246 A.2d 302; 1968 Md. App. LEXIS 367 (1968/1969).

Peel v. Attorney Registration and Disciplinary Commission, 496, U.S. 91; 110 S. Ct. 2281; 110 L. Ed. 2d 83; 1990 U.S. LEXIS 2909 (1990).

People v. Ebanks, 117 Cal. 652, 665 (1897).

People v. Shirley, 641 P.2d 775 (Calif. 1982).

Rock v. Arkansas, 483 U.S. 44 (1987).

State v. Hurd, 432 A.2d 86 (N.J. 1981).

State v. Mack, 292 N.W.2d 764 (Minn. 1980).

U.S. v. Galbreth, DC NM, Cr. No. 94-197 MV (1995).

U.S. v. Posado, 57 F.3d 428; 1995 U.S. App. LEXIS 15157 (1995).

U.S. v. Scheffer, 523 U.S. 303; 118 S. Ct. 1261; 140 L. Ed. 2d 413; 1998 U.S. LEXIS 2303 (1998).

U.S. v. Sherlin, CA 6, No. 94-6111 (1995).

PART IV

Civil Rights and Civil Law

Having laid the foundation for basic courtroom procedures, and for both everyday and forensic mental health practice, we now turn to the topic of mental health issues in civil (as opposed to criminal) law. Civil precedent cases dictate mental health practice by establishing or specifying rights afforded to clients and by demonstrating the historical background of group discrimination. Cases under civil jurisdiction also provide roles for mental health professionals, such as in performing assessments in contested civil disputes. Furthermore, virtually any legal proceeding is awash in issues of civil rights.

Chapter 10 deals with the movement toward guaranteed civil rights for same-sex couples. The issues presented here are not only interesting from a psychological perspective but also can have an impact upon mental health practice directly (i.e., the appropriateness for child custody placement with a homosexual parent or couple). As this chapter demonstrates, this particular civil rights movement is still very much in its infancy. As the 2004 Presidential election demonstrated, the topic is of enormous interest and impact to today's society. Chapter 11 explores areas of civil law that may involve mental health professionals in their role of substantiating damages through assessment. Chapter 12 concludes this section with a look at specific civil rights afforded to prisoners, a population whose most basic right to freedom has been taken away. This chapter presents some of the legal precedents that helped pave the way for similar rights for both individuals with specific mental illnesses (the focus of Part V) and for juveniles (the focus of Part VII).

CHAPTER 10

Sexual Orientation
and Civil Rights

Though the conduct be the desire of the bisexually or
homosexually inclined, there is no necessity that they
engage in it.　　　—U.S. 5th Circuit Court Judge
　　　　　　　　　Reavely, writing for the
　　　　　　　　　majority in *Baker v. Wade* (1985)

Congress shall make no law respecting an establishment of
religion, or prohibiting the free exercise thereof. . . .
　　　　　—First Amendment to the U.S. Constitution

No state shall . . . deny to any person within its jurisdiction
the equal protection of the laws.
　　　　　—Fourteenth Amendment to the U.S. Constitution

Mental health issues are intertwined throughout most of the issues relating to civil rights of gay men and lesbians.[1] Such is made clear in the filing of amicus briefs by the American Psychological Association for many
of the major cases in the area. The general premise of these briefs has
been the assertion that homosexuality is not considered a mental disor-

---

[1] Most of the case law in the area relates to same-sex couples; hence, we typically stick
with "gay men and lesbians." A case later in the chapter involved a bisexual woman, and
the case law on same-sex partnerships would apply to a bisexual individual when engaged
in a same-sex relationship. For instance, a bisexual man could marry a woman in any jurisdiction in the United States with full rights. But if he wished to marry another man, the
relevant law discussed in this chapter would apply. The legal situation gets even trickier
when it comes to transgendered individuals, with little or no case law directly addressing
the issue. Thus, in not commonly including bisexual and transgendered individuals, we
wish not to be exclusive, but to include only the same-sex relationships addressed directly
in the law.

der. Mental health issues become even more relevant in areas such as the psychological impact on children who are exposed to same-sex relationships by parents, caretakers, or other role models, as we see later.

HOMOSEXUALITY AND SODOMY LAW

As evidenced by the opening quote of this chapter, misunderstanding about homosexual activity continues even among the best educated of our society. Throughout history, bisexual, gay, and lesbian individuals have been condemned by religious, legal, and medical leaders alike (Slovenko, 2002). Prior to the mid-1980s, homosexual acts were strictly forbidden as illegal in many jurisdictions, falling under the crime of sodomy.[2] Then the issues began to come to the attention of the judiciary, a body arguably less prone to public and religious opinion.

While the traditional definition of *sodomy* encompassed only a very circumscribed number of sexual acts, the contemporary legal definition (which, of course, varies from one jurisdiction to another) is typically expanded to include any sexual activity that could be considered *unnatural* or *perverted*. These terms lend themselves to much interpretation and are essentially moral questions, allowing the introduction of religious bias and opinion. A theme to keep in mind throughout this chapter is the degree to which opponents to gay civil rights base their opposition on religious grounds. Officially acknowledging a religious link would immediately bring a law into conflict with the First Amendment of the U.S. Constitution, as quoted at the beginning of the chapter. However, when listening to a publicly expressed rationale for limiting gay civil rights, it is difficult to conclude that religious views do not play a significant role. This grounding in morality would become the basis of one of the early challenges to sodomy laws, as we see later.

The legal gay civil rights movement began at a very basic level, with gay men asserting their right to engage in consenting intercourse.[3] Oth-

---

[2] It is important here to make the distinction that *sodomy* traditionally meant any sexual act that is not penile–vaginal intercourse (including oral and anal sex). Thus, sodomy laws made those acts illegal for whoever practiced them, not just for gay men and lesbians. Practical enforcement of these laws was, of course, a different issue, with prosecution of consenting opposite-sex partners virtually unheard of.

[3] While sodomy cases typically involve consensual sex between two men, any precedent would presumably apply to lesbian relationships as well. Sexual activity between lesbians has evoked less legal (and arguably public) reaction on sodomy grounds than that between gay men.

erwise, the assertion of any other right as a gay citizen would mean admitting to the crime of sodomy.

SEXUAL INTERCOURSE AND THE RIGHT TO PRIVACY

One would expect that if protection of gay individuals' right to engage in consensual intercourse were ever to be upheld by legal doctrine, such a finding would occur through the U.S. Constitution. The most obvious avenue for a constitutional challenge to consensual sodomy laws would be to maintain that any such act was protected by the Fourth Amendment right to privacy.[4]

In 1982, Atlanta Georgia resident Michael Hardwick asserted his right to privacy after he was arrested for sodomy for engaging in consensual intercourse in his bedroom with another man. The charges against him were eventually dropped, but Hardwick filed suit against Georgia's Attorney General (Bowers). Hardwick claimed that the sodomy law simply endorsed the popular belief that all sodomy was immoral, regardless of consent. By only one vote, the U.S. Supreme Court rejected his claim in the case of *Bowers v. Hardwick* (1986). The Court ruled that laws cannot be invalidated merely because they represent "essentially moral" choices, and that *nothing* in the U.S. Constitution "would extend a fundamental right to homosexuals to engage in acts of consensual sodomy" (p. 6). This ruling dealt a devastating blow to gay civil rights advocates. While the statute had only been challenged on the basis that it violated an individual's Fourth Amendment right to privacy, the Justices generalized their denial of the rights to *all* areas of the Constitution, despite the slim majority.

For the time being, solace was not to be found in the U.S. Constitution. However, the failure of the U.S. Supreme Court to find a specific constitutional protection is not necessarily the final word. Citizens may also be guaranteed *additional* rights under individual state constitutions. Six years after the *Hardwick* decision, citizens wishing to engage in consensual, same-sex relationships would find protection in the Constitution of the Commonwealth of Kentucky.

---

[4] The "right to privacy" is not included verbatim in the U.S. Constitution. Justice Brandeis first hinted at it in his dissenting opinion in *Olmstead v. U.S.* (1928), when he interpreted the Fourth Amendment as including "the right to be let alone." He elaborated that this right was "the most comprehensive of rights and the right most valued by civilized men," (as cited in *Kentucky v. Wasson*, 1992, p. 8). The first specific mention of the right by the U.S. Supreme Court majority came in 1965, in the case of *Griswold v. Connecticut*.

The Case of *Kentucky v. Wasson* (1992): State Extension of Privacy and Equal Protection Rights in the Absence of Federal Protection

Lexington, Kentucky, is a small, picturesque city in the middle of Kentucky's horse country and home to the University of Kentucky. Strolling along in a downtown parking lot, Jeffrey Wasson struck up a conversation with a friendly male stranger. At some point, the conversation turned toward sexual banter. Wasson eventually made the suggestion that the two men return to his home. When asked to elaborate, Wasson suggested homosexual intercourse. He at no time suggested either an exchange of money or intercourse anywhere other than in his home. The stranger, an undercover Lexington police officer, informed Wasson that he was under arrest for solicitation to commit sodomy.

At trial, Wasson's attorneys contended that the underlying charge of sodomy violated their client's rights to privacy and equal protection under the U.S. Constitution *and* the Kentucky Constitution. They argued the state violation despite specific wording in the Kentucky sodomy statute stating that "consent of the other person shall not be a defense" (KRS 510.100). Nor was it defensible for a sodomy defendant to contend that the act was part of a private (rather than commercial) relationship. In fact, Wasson and his attorneys alleged that this very language intentionally discriminated against homosexual individuals, based merely on their sexual orientation.

The prosecution offered no witnesses, arguing only that Kentucky citizens had the right to deem homosexual intercourse immoral, and elected officials could deem immoral acts illegal and punishable by law. Furthermore, there was an English common law tradition of punishing sodomy as a crime that predated the Kentucky Constitution. And even the U.S. Supreme Court had held in *Bowers v. Hardwick* (1986) that there was nothing in the U.S. Constitution that "would extend a fundamental right to homosexuals to engage in acts of consensual sodomy" (p. 6). Why should the Kentucky Constitution provide more protection than the U.S. Constitution?

Coming to Wasson's defense were a number of expert witnesses, including a cultural anthropologist, a Presbyterian minister, a social historian, a medical professor, a psychologist, a therapist, and a "sociologist and sex-researcher." In their collective testimony, they discussed the prevalence of homosexual activity throughout history, the scientific opinion that homosexuality was not a mental disorder, and the prevalence of "sodomy" acts among heterosexuals. Organizations representing a wide variety of public interests filed briefs on Wasson's behalf, including the American Psychological Association (APA), the Kentucky Psychological

Association, the Kentucky Chapter of the National Association of Social Workers, and nine different religious organizations. Among the APA's statements were the following:

> (1) homosexuality is common, unlikely to change, is not a disorder, and does not affect one's ability to contribute to society;
>
> (2) the proscribed sexual conduct is a normal and important aspect of the private sexual expression of gay men and lesbians, most of whom, like most heterosexuals, form long-lasting relationships in which sexuality is important;
>
> (3) the statute is harmful to the health and well-being of [state] citizens because it is not a public health measure, but rather, is counterproductive to public health goals, is psychologically damaging to gay men and lesbians and is likely to reinforce hostility, discrimination, and violence against gay people and interfere with law enforcement efforts to deter violent crimes against gay men and lesbians; and
>
> (4) gay people share many of the characteristics of other groups accorded heightened protection under equal protection doctrine, e.g., there is a history and prevalence of prejudice and discrimination against gay people. (online source: www.apa.org)

The initial trial Court was impressed by the litany of responses on behalf of Jeffrey Wasson and held that the Kentucky sodomy statute indeed violated his right to privacy as guaranteed by the Kentucky Constitution. However the Court disagreed that any equal protection rights had been infringed upon and refused to rule on the basis of the U.S. Constitution. The case was thrown out.

The prosecution appealed the decision to the Kentucky Court of Appeals. The Appeals Court actually *extended* the initial ruling to include an equal protection violation. Again, the Court declined to rule on the basis of the U.S. Constitution. On appeal, the Kentucky Supreme Court ultimately upheld the decision. While it did not officially rule on the matter, the State Supreme Court even predicted that the Kentucky statute might indeed fall prey to U.S. Constitutional challenge. While the statute in question in the earlier *Bowers* case applied equally to same- and opposite-sex partners, the Kentucky law applied specifically to same-sex acts. As is discussed below, this prediction by the Kentucky Supreme Court would prove correct.

State and Federal Reaction in the Wake of *Wasson*

The rulings in individual state cases, including *Wasson*, carry only limited precedent value. The U.S. Supreme Court ruling in *Bowers* remained the only federal opinion on the matter. However, similar rulings in other states, including that of a lesbian couple from Tennessee (*Campbell v. Sundquist*, 1996), continued to strengthen precedent for the protection of same-sex couples under state constitutions. The question lingered as originally posed by Jeffery Wasson's prosecutor: Why should a state constitution provide more protection than the U.S. Constitution?

In the 2003 term, the U.S. Supreme Court agreed to hear the case of *Lawrence v. Texas*, which, like *Wasson*, involved a state law specifically prohibiting homosexual acts. As predicted by the Kentucky Supreme Court, the U.S. Supreme Court ruled 6 to 3 that the Texas law was indeed unconstitutional. In *Lawrence*, the U.S. Supreme Court could have opted to restrict its ruling to laws specifically targeting homosexual partners. Such a ruling would have left the precedent-setting *Bowers* case intact. However, the Court more broadly ruled that the liberty rights afforded by the Fourteenth Amendment included the right of homosexual partners to engage in sexual intercourse. The Court further legitimized the role of gay and lesbian couples in society, stating that they

> . . . are entitled to respect for their private lives. The State cannot demean their existence or control their destiny by making their private sexual conduct a crime. Their right to liberty under the Due Process Clause gives them the full right to engage in their conduct without intervention of the government. (p. 15)

The *Bowers* ruling was specifically overturned, with the Court opining that its "continuance as precedent demeans the lives of homosexual persons" (p. 13). In dissent, Justice Scalia (joined by Chief Justice Rehnquist and Justice Thomas) declared that the Court "has taken sides in the culture war" and "signed on to the so-called homosexual agenda" (p. 27).

SEXUAL ORIENTATION AND THE RIGHT TO MARRY

At about the same time that Jeffrey Wasson was appealing his case through Kentucky courts, other individuals began trying to assert their right to marry a partner of the same sex. In 1990, Craig Dean and Patrick Gill attempted to obtain a marriage license in the nation's capital. Their request was denied; they filed suit in the D.C. Superior Court in November of that year, alleging that the failure of the District to recognize their marriage was a violation of the jurisdiction's Human Rights

Act. While the couple's assertions were ultimately denied by the District's Superior Court and Court of Appeals (*Dean v. District of Columbia*, 1995), the case raised the recognition of the issue throughout the country (Katsh & Rose, 2002).

In the same year, a Hawaii court ruled that denial of same-sex marriages violated that state constitution (*Baehr v. Lewin*, 1993). Realizing that every state would then need to recognize any same-sex marriage that took place in Hawaii, state politicians reacted with legislation specifically prohibiting same-sex marriages. The federal Defense of Marriage Act of 1996, overwhelmingly endorsed by the House and Senate and signed into law by President Clinton, laid the issue of reciprocity to rest for the time being. The Act formally denied federal recognition of any same-sex marriage and protected the right of any state to do the same (Katsh & Rose, 2002).

Individual states are free to endorse same-sex marriages, yet no state has done so at the time of this writing. In 2000, the Vermont legislature adopted the concept of "civil unions," an institution available to same-sex couples that guarantees them many of the rights and benefits afforded to married couples. While Vermont is frequently credited with inventing the civil union concept, Denmark actually enacted similar legislation 11 years earlier (see Box 10.1 for a timeline of gay marriage issues in the international community).

In November 2003, the Massachusetts Supreme Court ruled that the existing ban on gay marriages violated the state constitution. Legislation amending Massachusetts law to exclude same-sex marriage failed to pass in February 2004. The debate reached a fever pitch later that year, when newly elected San Francisco Mayor Gavin Newsom opened marriage ceremonies in the city to same-sex couples. Nearly 4,000 marriages were performed before the California Supreme Court halted the practice on March 11, 2004. On August 12, that same Court ruled that the Mayor's move had been in violation of California law. The pending lawsuit broadly asserting the constitutional rights of same-sex couples to marry promises to bring legal precedent on the issue. The controversial *Lawrence* ruling, discussed earlier, will likely be widely cited in the cases that are to follow.

PARENTING AND VISITATION RIGHTS

A related but separate right to marriage is the right to participate in the upbringing of children. Rights related to childrearing continue to be a

---

BOX 10.1. Gay Marriage in the International Community

1989

- Denmark offers civil unions and legally equates them with marriage.

2001

- Holland allows gay and lesbian citizens to marry with full rights of adoption.

2002

- France, Germany, Switzerland, Norway, Sweden, and Iceland allow civil unions.

2003

- Belgium legalizes same-sex marriages.
- Ontario and British Columbia provinces in Canada allow same-sex marriage.
- European Parliament urges resistant southern European member nations to endorse same-sex marriage.

2004

- Canadian Supreme Court considers national legislation redefining marriage to include same-sex couples.
- French court annuls the marriage of a gay couple.
- Australian government amends marriage law to include only heterosexual couples.

---

struggle for gay, lesbian, and bisexual couples and individuals. The legal opposition to such rights has rested on a number of arguments, including the following:

1. Homosexual activity itself is immoral.
2. Homosexual lifestyles include additional immoral or deviant components (i.e., increased promiscuity).
3. Exposure to such activity is detrimental to child development.
4. Children raised in the presence of bisexual, gay, or lesbian parents will be exposed to their parents' sexual activity to a sufficient degree to be detrimental.[5]

Implicit in these concerns is that the children would probably grow up to be accepting of a homosexual lifestyle and not see it as deviant.

---

[5] Of course, one problem with this particular assumption is immediately evident, in that even children exposed to heterosexual parents' sexual activity could suffer detrimental effects.

The state of the law up to the mid-1990s was that some jurisdictions felt that the concerns listed here were sufficient to warrant denial of custody to parents who engaged in homosexual activity. Clouding the picture was the fact that in many of these cases, the homosexual parent had (or was portrayed as having had) an "extramarital" homosexual affair. Thus, precedental case law in the area is based on cases in which the parents' behavior was problematic, *independent* of their sexual orientation. Many of these dilemmas and concerns were played out in the state of Missouri in the child custody battle between Janice and Joe DeLong.

THE CASE OF *DELONG V. DELONG* (1998):
MAINTAINING THE "BEST INTERESTS OF THE CHILD"

Twenty-four-year-old Janice had just begun her career as a school-teacher when she married Fredrick Joseph DeLong III, in June 1985. He was 12 years her senior and a prominent attorney in their Missouri community. Joe brought with him into the marriage a son (Joe IV) from a previous marriage, of whom he (Joe III) was the primary custodian.

From the outset, Joe's marriage to Janice was anything but unconditional. As a term of the marriage, Janice had to submit to a psychological evaluation from "his psychologist" (p. 2).[6] During the evaluation, Janice disclosed to Joe's psychologist that she "was sexually attracted to both men and women and that she had engaged in sexual activity with women in the past" (p. 2). She did, however, state that she was committed to a monogamous relationship. These results were disclosed to Joe, who the court document reports was "satisfied with [Janice's] psychological profile" (p. 2).

Adding to the formality of the affair, Joe asked Janice to sign a prenuptial agreement drafted by his attorney. Janice had two of her own attorneys survey the agreement. When one of her attorneys recom-

---

[6] The situation here illustrates an instance in which "his therapist" was probably acting in violation of the Psychological Ethics Code. The insinuation is that the psychologist was serving as Joe DeLong's therapist. For a therapist to agree to perform a psychological assessment upon a current client's pending love interest would constitute a dual relationship. Such an arrangement would pretty clearly violate the bounds of professional ethics. Even if "his psychologist" meant "the psychologist who Joe hired to assess his wife," the problem would be the potential coercion of Janet to participate. "His therapist's" later referral of Janice to an attorney who was in favor of the prenuptial agreement probably constituted an additional violation. In many states, ethics violations are also criminal actions, punishable by suspension of professional license, fines, and/or jail time.

mended that she reject the agreement, another attorney (to whom Janice had been referred by Joe's psychologist) replaced him at Janice's request.

The marriage progressed relatively positively for the next few years, during which the couple gave birth to three children. By 1991, Janice had concluded that the marriage was not working out. She later admitted to having two homosexual affairs during the marriage. Convinced that there was absolutely no hope for reconciliation, Janice filed for divorce in 1994. After the couple's separation, Janice admitted to having had a third homosexual relationship, and Joe admitted to having had a heterosexual relationship during the separation period. In the divorce petition, Janice requested that she be deemed the primary custodian of their three children, while Joe would continue to have joint custody. Joe responded with a request that he be deemed the sole custodian, with Janice having limited visitation rights. He alleged that such an arrangement was in the best interests of the children based upon her homosexual extramarital affairs.

At trial, both parents presented evidence about their parenting skills, including opposing expert witness mental health professionals who had conducted formal custody evaluations. Janice contended that her homosexual relationships were kept discreet from the children in that they only knew the other women as "friends" of their mother.

The trial Court found particular trouble with Janice's "engagement 'in a promiscuous series of four homosexual affairs,' her repeated denial and concealment of 'her adulterous lesbian activity,' her intention to continue 'exposing her lesbian lovers to her children,' and her 'immaturity in seeking after repeated new love relationships' " (p. 4). The trial Court ultimately ruled that Joe receive sole custody of the children. Furthermore, the Court restricted Janice's visitation rights, ordering her to "keep any and all aspects of the homosexual lifestyle away from the minor children during the children's periods of visitation with her" (p. 4). The Court ordered that nobody be in the children's presence who was known by Janice to be a lesbian or to have engaged in lesbian activity. Nor were the children ever to be in the presence of any unrelated female with whom their mother was living. Most interesting, given that the court was trying to "protect" the children from "any and all aspects of [her] homosexual lifestyle," was an order that the mother conduct a "telling session" with the two older children in which she was to inform them that "she is homosexual" (p. 4).

Janice appealed the decision to the Western District Missouri Court of Appeals. The grounds of the appeal were succinctly summarized by Justice Robert Ulrich:

She argues that the court's rulings regarding custody and visitation were not based on the best interests of the children but solely on the fact that "she is homosexual." Mother alleges that instead of a focus on the best interests of the children, "the courtroom became a battleground in which sexual orientation was the principal issue" and that Father and the guardian ad litem became obsessed with dissecting her sexual life, "uncovering every detail of any kiss, touch or other intimate contact she may have engaged in with a member of the same sex." (p. 4)

Justice Ulrich concluded that Missouri legal precedent, while divided, indicated a per se assumption on behalf of Missouri courts that the "best interests of the child" was to live with their heterosexual parent. But, the Court further concluded, "A per se approach necessarily ignores the heterosexual parent's fitness to be custodian, and the application of this approach could conceivably result in an award of custody to the heterosexual parent without any evidence regarding his or her inappropriate *heterosexual* conduct or parenting skills" (p. 12, emphasis added).

The Court clearly ruled that the standard by which custody decisions must be made was the "best interests of the child." If evidence can be presented that the parent's homosexual activity is detrimental to the children, then it should be considered a factor, as would any other testimony. While the trial court in the *DeLong* case had allowed significant testimony as to the presence of homosexual acts, there was no evidence on the record regarding how such acts may detrimentally affect the DeLong children. With regard to the limited visitation ordered at trial, Justice Ulrich concluded that the goal of the trial Court in doing so was, in its words, to "keep the negative influence of homosexuality away from the children" (p. 12). Since there was no evidence of any negative influence, the trial Court had mistakenly applied the law to the case. As such, the custody decision and visitation restrictions were unanimously remanded back to the trial Court, which was ordered to consider "*all* factors relevant to the children's welfare" (p. 12, emphasis added).

Rather than try his hand back at the trial court level, Joe DeLong appealed to the Supreme Court of Missouri. The American Psychological Association (APA) filed a brief on Janice's behalf that concluded the following:

1. The appellate court's ruling that a mother's sexual orientation cannot be presumed to be detrimental to her children is supported by a considerable body of scientific research on children of lesbian parents, finding that children raised by gay parents are as healthy psychologically and socially as those raised by heterosexuals, and that there is no significant

difference between the two groups on sexual identity and gender role issues; and

2. Research on parenting issues indicates that lesbians and gay men are as fit parents as heterosexuals, homosexuality is not a mental disorder, and the two groups have comparable parenting skills. (online source: www.apa.org)

Ultimately, the appropriate criterion was determined to be the "best interests of the child," negating the per se rule. However, in applying the "best interests" standard, the trial Court upheld its initial custody decision but relaxed the visitation restrictions.

THE CURRENT STATE OF GAY PARENTS' RIGHTS

The *DeLong* decision offers a precedent precluding a per se denial of parental custody or visitation to a homosexual parent. However, in most jurisdictions, evidence of the detrimental impact of a parent's relationships may be introduced as a factor to be considered in the custody determination. The detrimental impact of homosexuality can be argued directly (i.e., through the child witnessing "immoral and deviant" acts) or indirectly (i.e., the parent's homosexual status will negatively affect his or her income potential and subsequently impact the child). At a minimum, the gay parent is afforded an individualized assessment of the particular facts of his or her case. For now, the specific way in which any potential detrimental impact is considered is left to the jurisdiction, either through legislation or judicial discretion.

HOMOSEXUALITY AND CHILD CARE/MENTOR ROLES

An interesting point that probably escaped many readers of the *DeLong* case was that Janice DeLong was employed as a teacher. Thus, her impact upon children extends far beyond her biological children. What do the courts have to say about children's exposure to a bisexual, gay, or lesbian teacher? Not surprisingly, there is a body of case law on the matter, but again one that excludes U.S. Supreme Court precedent. Further clouding the picture is the fact that many cases include instances in which the instructor engaged in some type of outward endorsement of homosexuality or gay rights. For instance, a teacher may counsel a gay student that "it's OK to be gay," arguably infringing upon the rights of the parents to parent their child.

The impact that teachers have on society's youth is not limited to instructional material presented in class. Teachers also "teach" by serving as role models and mentors (Eisenmenger, 2002; Fulmer, 2002). And mentoring and modeling imply that the students are taking on the traits of the mentor or model. What then do the courts say when the mentors of our children are homosexual? Some argue that homosexuals serving as mentors to children are modeling immoral and deviant behavior and thus should be relieved of their positions.

Of course, the degree to which courts are willing to accept "homosexual attitudes" as being harmful continues to vary widely by jurisdiction. To address this question, courts have to deal with several component questions: Is homosexuality immoral and deviant? If so, are students of homosexual teachers exposed to their teachers' sexuality to a degree necessary to cause harm? Given that these questions may never be answered to everyone's satisfaction, the ultimate question becomes: Can a school system fire a teacher based on his or her sexual orientation that involves a strictly private part of his or her life?

The only limitation upon any employment discrimination that comes from the level of the U.S. Supreme Court happened in 1989. In the case of *Price Waterhouse v. Hopkins* (1989), Ms. Hopkins was told that her success in the company (an accounting firm) was dependent upon her "walking, talking, and dressing more femininely" (p. 1). The Court ruled 6 to 3 that such a judgment based upon physical gender roles constituted discrimination based on gender. The 9th Circuit Court of Appeals extended the *Hopkins* ruling to effeminate males in 2001, in the case of a Washington, D.C. restaurant worker (*Nichols v. Azteca Restaurant Enterprises Inc.*, 2001). Thus, the law would seem to protect masculine women and feminine men against whom any discrimination occurs based on gender-discordant appearance alone.

However, both *Hopkins* and *Nichols* failed to address the issue of homosexuality per se. In fact, these cases actually make it seem as if homosexual citizens will be afforded increased protection if they are more openly flamboyant. While the cases may provide some precedent regarding employment discrimination in general, they do not speak to the application of this law as it applies to those employed in child mentor roles. In such instances, being more "openly" gay may leave one open to more criticism as being "harmful" to the children.

It seemed as if the U.S. Supreme Court would deal more directly with the child mentor issue when it heard the case of *Boy Scouts of America v. Dale* in 2000. Dale was an assistant scoutmaster in New Jersey and an avowed activist for gay civil rights. When he was relieved of his scouting duties due to his homosexuality, he filed suit against the Boy

Scouts of American (BSA). The Court ultimately ruled in favor of the BSA, in what initially seemed like a defeat for gay civil rights. But the Justices handed down a very specific ruling, failing to comment on the ultimate issue. The Court ruled that the BSA was an "expressive" private organization, teaching and fostering certain beliefs in its participants, including disapproval of homosexual behavior. Thus, to force the BSA to accept a homosexual leader would violate its First Amendment protection of free speech. In short, the BSA spoke out against homosexuality and had the constitutional right to do so. For the time being, the issue of bisexual, gay, and lesbian individuals as child role models remains without unitary clarification.

FUTURE DIRECTIONS IN GAY CIVIL RIGHTS

A major roadblock to the progression of gay rights is the reluctance by courts and legislative bodies to recognize these citizens as a "cognizable group," thus affording them protection under antidiscrimination law. In 1992, an interesting attempt was made by the State of Colorado to rectify this debate once and for all. The Second Amendment to the Colorado State Constitution was proposed and passed by majority vote. It effectively precluded any Colorado jurisdiction from protecting citizens from discrimination based upon sexual orientation. It was eventually struck down by Colorado Courts (*Evans v. Romer*, 1993, 1994) and the U.S. Supreme Court (*Romer v. Evans*, 1996) as being contrary to the Fourteenth Amendment of the U.S. Constitution. This approach was interesting in that it essentially recognized homosexual citizens as a group *and* declared that they could be discriminated against. The U.S. Supreme Court ruling against the Amendment was a significant victory for gay civil rights in federal court. In commenting to this end, the Court stated, "The resulting disqualification of a class of persons from the right to seek specific protection from the law is unprecedented in our jurisprudence" (p. 4). Thus, the precedent value of this ruling is limited to legislation that so brazenly violates civil rights.

The *Lawrence* ruling discussed earlier illustrates a willingness on behalf of the U.S. Supreme Court to hear cases on the issue of gay rights, and perhaps a willingness to rethink old patterns. The avenue by which a precedent-holding case seems most likely to come at the time of this writing is around the issue of same-sex marriage. But until further U.S. Supreme Court attention, there will be a lack of uniformity across jurisdictions in all relevant matters. Thus, perhaps the best "bottom line" for each of the rights discussed in this chapter is, "It depends on the jurisdiction."

CASE REFERENCES

Baehr v. Lewin, 852 P.2d 44 (1993).

Baker v. Wade, 774 F. 2d 1285 (1985).

Bowers v. Hardwick, 478 U.S. 1039; 107 S. Ct. 29; 92 L. Ed. 2d 779; 1986 U.S. LEXIS 2828 (1986).

Boy Scouts of America v. Dale, 530 U.S. 640; 2000 U.S. LEXIS 4487 (2000).

Campbell v. Sundquist, 926 S.W.2d 255 (1996).

Dean v. District of Columbia, 653 A. 2d 307 (1995).

DeLong v. DeLong, 1998 Mo. App. LEXIS 69 (1998).

Evans v. Romer, 854 P.2d 1270; 1993 Colo. LEXIS 628 (1993).

Evans v. Romer, 882 P.2d 1335; 1994 Colo. LEXIS 779 (1994).

Griswold v. Connecticut, 381 U.S. 479 (1965).

Kentucky v. Wasson, 842 S.W.2d 487; 1992 Ky. LEXIS 140 (1992).

Nichols v. Azteca Restaurant Enterprises Inc, 256 F.3d 864; 2001 U.S. App. LEXIS 15899 (2001).

Price Waterhouse v. Hopkins, 490 U.S. 228; 1989 U.S. LEXIS 2230 (1989).

Romer v. Evans, 517 U.S. 620; 1996 U.S. LEXIS 3245 (1996).

CHAPTER 11

Personal Injury

Court Proceedings and Assessment
of Psychological Damages

Psychologists, particularly those who conduct forensic assessment, can choose to take on personal injury cases in which the assessment and "quantification" of psychological damages are key components. See, for instance, Greenberg (2003) for a particularly thorough discussion of the assessment of psychological damages in personal injury cases. But the case law concerning personal injury is pertinent to a much wider mental health audience. Professional negligence claims are a form of personal injury suit that potentially impact upon all mental health practitioners. Mental health clients at one time or another may have been either survivors and/or perpetrators of some personal injury (i.e., discrimination, violent crime, familial abuse), and these areas may frequently be the primary focus of treatment or case management. Whether or not clients are ever involved in an actual case, the rights violated are elucidated in this area of law. In this chapter, we address the evolution of personal injury law, with particular emphasis on the changes that have affected psychologists and other mental health professionals.

THE LAW OF PERSONAL INJURY AND TORTS

Personal injury law has evolved within what is known as "tort" law, which is a subdivision of civil law, and has undergone significant changes in recent years (Greenberg, 2003). *Tort* is probably derived from the Norman word for "wrong." The word is also rooted in the Latin *tortus*, meaning "crooked, dubious, twisted." Tort law is an extremely complex area of law, with terminology and concepts that are well outside the realm of understanding for most nonlawyers. As such, our review for this chapter merely scratches the surface enough to provide a background for understanding the precedent-setting cases presented herein.

In the U.K. and U.S. legal systems, a tort is not a crime; it is a civil wrong. It generally refers to intentional or negligent wrongs to another person for which the offender may be responsible or "liable." A wide range of civil wrongs can be conceptualized as torts, including false imprisonment, invasion of privacy, malpractice, some forms of product liability, defamation that results in personal injury of some sort, and intentional or negligent infliction of emotional trauma.

The number of personal injury cases has mushroomed in recent decades, as exemplified by the fact that all patrons to a McDonald's drive-through must now read a sign informing them that their coffee will be, of all things, "very hot." Perhaps the political–social influence of attorneys on their colleagues in the judiciary (virtually all of whom are also attorneys) and in the legislative and executive branches of governments (many of whom are also attorneys) has kept lawmakers from placing any limits on suits that make it to court, except in cases of pure deception and malingering.

LIABILITY CRITERIA FOR PERSONAL INJURY

Individuals may be legally responsible or liable for injuring someone if their actions are either (1) *intentional*, that is, meant to cause the injury; or (2) *negligent*, that is, not undertaken with appropriate caution. A person found liable in a personal injury case is usually ordered to pay "damages" to the injured party. In cases of negligence, these are called "compensatory" damages, designed to compensate the person for the injury. In cases of intentional injury, "punitive" damages may be allowed, in addition to compensatory damages. Punitive damages are designed to punish the responsible person. To prove the *negligent* infliction of emotional injuries, allowing only compensatory damages, claims must first meet the four basic elements of a tort: (1) *Duty*: The defendant had a legal duty to conform to a standard of conduct; (2) *Breach*: The defendant breached that duty; (3) *Causation*: The breach *proximately caused*[1] the harm; and (4) *Damages*: The law must allow for compensation for the particular harmful action.

To prove the *intentional* infliction of emotional injuries, thus also allowing punitive damages, the problematic act must meet four *additional* required elements: (1) an intention to inflict, or "substantial certainty"[2] that the injury would result; (2) the defendant's conduct was "extreme and outrageous"; (3) the act directly or proximately caused the injury; and (4) the emotional injury was severe (or, in reality, is at least evident). In practice, less severity is accepted to the degree the causal behavior is outrageous.

EARLY LAW RECOGNIZING PSYCHOLOGICAL INJURY

Nineteenth-century courts hesitated to recognize emotional damages at all. The reasons included a lack of legal precedent; the possibility of fictitious lawsuits, since psychological damages are largely subjective; the difficulties of connecting emotional distress to a physical event, when it could have some other cause; and the danger of a huge flood of litigation if precedents were overturned and emotional damage were recognized. Early cases highlighted some of the difficulties inherent in claims of psychological injury, primarily relating to criteria 3 and 4 cited earlier for the establishment of a basic tort. Namely, how was psychological harm to be defined, and what may constitute a proximate cause of this harm? Furthermore, was it even possible to determine reasonable damages for psychological harm?

Historically, if a court were to acknowledge emotional injury at all, there was a requirement that it be associated with a physical injury. In 19th century England, the courts ruled that mental pain or anxiety alone could not be compensated. The prevailing legal view up through

---

[1] *Proximate cause* is a legal term meaning that the wrongful act caused the harm in a sufficiently direct manner. For instance, if someone gets hit in the head by a rock thrown by another person, the act of rock throwing is the *direct* cause of the injury. On the other hand, if someone gets cut by broken glass that resulted from someone throwing a rock through a window, the act of rock throwing may be deemed a *proximate* cause of the injury. The rock itself did not directly hit anyone.

[2] The distinction here refers to the fact that the defendant need not intend to harm a specific victim. Nor does the defendant necessarily need to set out with the purpose of harming someone. Drinking and driving is an example that may be deemed to have a *substantial certainty* of harming someone, even though the drunk driver may not intend to harm anyone.

the 19th century was that emotional suffering or psychogenic pain from a personal injury incident was not appropriate for remedy, because the law could not place a value on mental pain or anxiety. To allow redress for emotional trauma, the trauma had to be directly related to evident physical disorder that was in turn a direct result of the "impact" in the personal injury incident. This doctrine was known as the "impact rule."

English courts were by this point beginning to abandon the impact rule. Interestingly, however, in *Bell v. Great Northern Railway Co.* (1890) and subsequent cases, U.S. courts continued to embrace it. Problems with the impact rule are demonstrated in the absurd ruling in the 1897 case of *Jones v. Brooklyn Heights Railroad*. The defendant alleged that a miscarriage and subsequent emotional damage occurred when her automobile and a slow moving train bumped together. There was no physical damage to the defendant, nor had the train actually "impacted" her body. Nevertheless, the view of the Court was that the incident had indeed caused emotional damage, and the victim should receive compensation. Thus was concocted the position that a small light bulb had fallen from the roof of the defendant's automobile when hit by the train and hit the plaintiff on the head. This "impact" was cited as the physical cause of her emotional trauma. A 1928 Georgia case, *Christy Bros. Circus v. Turnage*, illustrates how the impact rule, and its associated problems, were carried into the 20th century. In this case, horse manure fell into Ms. Turnage's lap while she was at the circus. The court allowed recovery for damages, because there was an impact of the manure on her lap, even though there was no *physical* damage.

An evolution took place in personal injury law when courts began to recognize that negligent or intentionally harmful actions created a "zone of danger" around the perpetrator. Under this concept, a litigant was permitted to recover damages for psychological harm from the fear experienced by being in the "zone of danger" generated by the defendant's negligence or malice. A person could thus recover damages as a witness to a trauma, so long as he or she was sufficiently close to the trauma that he or she could have also been injured. The decision in the 1928 case of *Palsgraf v. Long Island Railroad*, though not a clear precedent case to the "zone of danger" rule, articulated a related "orbit of danger" idea. Cases that endorsed these ideas later helped to establish the concept of "proximate cause."

Thus, prior to 1968, in order to sue for emotional damage arising from an event, one had to have either suffered an impact (e.g., being shot), or to have been in close enough proximity to the event to have suffered an impact (e.g., being shot *at*). This next case is the critical one in the evolution of the "zone of danger" rule.

The Case of *Dillon v. Legg* (1968): Redefining the "Zone of Danger" for Emotional Damages

On September 27, 1964, David Legg was driving south on Bluegrass Road near its intersection with Clover Lane in Sacramento, California. Crossing at the intersection was 2-year-old Erin Dillon. Legg's vehicle struck and killed Erin. Erin's older sister Cheryl witnessed the accident, as did their mother, Margery Dillon, who had been standing some few yards farther away from the intersection.

Following traditional "zone of danger" precedents, a lower court in California permitted the surviving daughter to recover for damages, asserting she was in the "zone of danger," because she was within the range where she could have been injured and may have feared for her own safety. But they dismissed the mother's claim, stating that she was not in the "zone of danger" and thus could not recover for emotional trauma.

On appeal, the California Supreme Court reinstated the mother's claim. The clearly documented set of facts in the case then allowed an opportunity to comment on the arbitrariness of the "zone of danger" rule. The Court stated:

> We can hardly justify relief to the sister for trauma which she suffered upon apprehension of the child's death and yet deny it to the mother merely because of happenstance that the sister was some few yards closer to the accident. (p. 8)

The California Supreme Court further asserted that the concept of "zone of danger" actually encompasses the area of exposure to emotional as well as physical injury, elaborating:

> The courts, today, hold that no distinction can be drawn between physical and emotional injury flowing from the physical injury; indeed, in light of modern medical knowledge, any such distinction would be indefensible. As a result, in awarding recovery for emotional shock upon witnessing another's injury or death, we cannot draw a line between the plaintiff who is in the zone of danger of physical impact and the plaintiff who is in the zone of danger of emotional impact. The recovery of one . . . is as much compelled as that of the other. (p. 24)

In *Dillon v. Legg*, the Court generated three criteria that further helped to clarify the zone of liability: (1) The plaintiff must have a close relationship with the victim; (2) the plaintiff must be in close proximity to the scene of the accident; and (3) the emotional shock has to be the "sensory and contemporaneous result" of the incident. Together, these criteria are termed the *related bystander* test.

Refining *Dillon v. Legg*

Many and varied interpretations have sprung from *Dillon v. Legg*. A major question that continues is: What is a "close relationship"? Certainly mother–child or brother–sister would qualify. But what about stepfather–stepdaughter, good friends, tennis partners, or a stepgrandmother? Many states would not find some of these relationships to be compelling ones (in fact, some states do not even accept the "zone of danger" concept).

Other states have expanded upon definitions of "zone of danger." In *Chen v. Superior Court* (1997), a bystander was allowed to recover for emotional distress resulting from negligence based on hearing the injury-causing event. The Second District Court of Appeals in Los Angeles ruled that the parents of Lucy Chen, who were in other rooms of the house when an unsecured kitchen island crushed Lucy, could recover emotional distress damages. It had been previously determined that bystanders may recover emotional damages if they are (1) closely related to the injured person, (2) present at the scene of the injury-producing event and are aware that the victim is being injured, and (3) suffering emotional distress beyond what would be expected in a disinterested witness (*Thing v. Chusa*, 1989). In the *Chen* case, it was determined that the awareness was not limited to visual observation.

EMOTIONAL INJURY WITHOUT PHYSICAL HARM

Other cases have addressed the question: What compensation may individuals seek should no *physical* harm come to anybody, even the primary person who was harmed? For example, in a 1980 case that involved an incorrect medical diagnosis, the claimant was compensated for his psychological distress resulting from marital problems. *Molien v. Kaiser Foundation Hospital* (1980) involved a husband that successfully sued a physician who had negligently misdiagnosed his wife's condition as syphilis. There was no physical harm or impact to anyone involved, and the husband did not directly observe the doctor making or reporting the diagnosis. Nevertheless, the California Supreme Court recognized the husband's right to gain compensation because of psychological distress. The misdiagnosis was ultimately deemed the proximate cause of marital upset and eventual divorce.

However, the trend away from a strictly physical "zone of danger" rule has not been uninterrupted. In the 1994 federal case, *Consolidated Rail Corp. v. Gottshall*, the claimant's close friend collapsed and died while they worked under intense time pressure on a railroad work crew. The claimant had helped with cardiopulmonary resuscitation (CPR), and several hours later had to return to work within sight of the corpse that had not been removed from the scene. The claimant felt ill over the next several days in hot and humid weather, became preoccupied with his own health, and several days after that was hospitalized for Post-traumatic Stress Disorder and major depression. A lower court had awarded damages based on the claimant being in the zone of emotional danger that should have been foreseen by the defendant. Thus, the lower court had broadened the "zone of danger" concept to include non-physical danger. However, the U.S. Supreme Court later affirmed the strictly physical "zone of danger" rule as best reconciling Congress's intent for federal cases. See Box 11.1 for another situation where the line between physical and emotional damage pertains.

ASSESSING PAIN AND SUFFERING

In *Thompson v. National Railroad Passenger Corp.* (1980), the U.S. Supreme Court recognized five types of compensatory damages: (1) expenses incurred; (2) pain and suffering and fright; (3) permanent injury (disability); (4) impaired earning capacity; and (5) impaired enjoyment of life. Loss of enjoyment of life was therein defined in terms of "the limitations on the person's life created by the injury," thus setting forth the distinctiveness of the loss of enjoyment of life for collecting damages.[3]

---

[3] As an example of how psychological assessment can aid in personal injury cases, a specific scale, the Lost Pleasure of Life Scale, has been shown to be effective in assessing damage that has resulted from a personal injury (Andrews, Meyer, & Berla, 1996). This measure can be used to systematically rate and quantify the impact the injury may have had on the injured individual's life enjoyment. A conceptual framework is used to guide in the acquisition of information and the development of a judgment concerning the severity of the injury.

BOX 11.1. Torts and Sexual Harassment

Sexual harassment is another form of tort with some specific legal character-istics. For instance, there is by definition no need for any nonconsensual physi-cal act to have taken place. The U.S. Supreme Court has established that a per-son who may at first have willingly engaged in an ultimately harmful behavior (i.e., sexual intercourse) may still bring a suit for sexual harassment (*Meritor Savings Bank v. Vinson*, 1986). Thus, the harm caused in sexual harassment cases may be primarily psychological or emotional in nature, and it is in assess-ing these damages that forensic psychologists may play a role. However, to prove sexual harassment, a plaintiff need not prove psychological damages, since detracting from the person's job or unfairly preventing him or her from advancing may be wrongs in and of themselves (*Harris v. Forklift Systems*, 1993).

The area of pain and suffering has also generated the need for testi-mony by mental health professionals. Despite the previously mentioned ruling in *Thompson*, the U.S. Supreme Court was not finished dealing with the issue of awards for pain and suffering. The case that follows presents some of the legal concepts associated with such awards as they pertain to personal injury cases.

THE CASE OF *MOLZOF V. U.S.* (1992): COLLECTING DAMAGES FOR "LOST PLEASURE OF LIFE"

Mr. Robert Molzof had undergone lung surgery at the Veterans Adminis-tration (VA) hospital in Madison, Wisconsin. Following surgery, he was placed on a ventilator to provide him with oxygen, but ventilator's alarm system was disconnected. The ventilator tube itself later became discon-nected, leaving Mr. Molzof deprived of oxygen for approximately 8 min-utes before it was discovered. Shirley Molzof, Robert's wife, sought to recover damages from the U.S. government after her husband suffered irreversible brain damage from this apparent negligence of the federal VA employees.

The United States admitted liability, and the case proceeded to trial in order to determine the amount of compensatory damages. The Dis-trict Court ordered the hospital to provide continuing medical services for Mr. Molzof at the existing level of care free of charge, and awarded damages of $75,750 for supplemental care that was not provided by the hospital, such as physical and respiratory therapy, and doctor visits. The court did, however, decline to award damages for Mr. Molzof's loss of pleasure of life.

Unfortunately, Mr. Molzof died after the District Court's final judgment was entered. His wife, however, appealed the denial of loss of pleasure of life as a personal representative of his estate. The government argued that the pain and suffering damages were punitive in nature, and punitive damages against the government are prevented by federal law. The U.S. Court of Appeals affirmed the judgment of the District Court, ruling that any award for loss of enjoyment of life could not compensate the patient's loss, due in no small part to the fact that he had been in a coma and would not have been able to enjoy the settlement. Any such award would therefore be strictly punitive in nature and was thus barred. Ultimately the U.S. Supreme Court reversed this judgment and ruled that separate damages for loss of enjoyment of life were legitimate and recoverable. In effect, this award approved the earlier precedent case, *Thompson v. National Railroad Passenger Corp.* (1980), thus setting forth the distinctiveness of the loss of enjoyment of life for collecting damages.

LIMITS ON PUNITIVE DAMAGES

Another critical and timely issue is whether there should be limits to judgments on punitive damage awards. Judges and juries have as a rule been given tremendous leeway in the determination of these judgments. Although punitive damages are awarded in a relatively small proportion of cases, there is a clear concern that "runaway juries" may award huge punitive damage awards. While the cases in this subarea do not typically involve mental health issues, the law elucidated in these precedents applies to a wide range of personal injury cases, including those in which mental health professionals regularly participate.

In *TXO Products Corp. v. Alliance Resources* (1993), the U.S. Supreme Court, although badly split on the reasons for its decision, gave great latitude to states in permitting the award of very large punitive damages as long as there are basic guidelines to juries concerning the award of such damages. In this case, the jury granted $10 million for punitive damages even though only $19,000 in actual damages was awarded. The Court considered several factors in the ruling, stating:

> We do not consider the dramatic disparity between the actual damages and the punitive award [problematic] in a case of this character . . . The puni-

tive damages award in this case is certainly large, but in light of the amount of money potentially at stake, the bad faith of the petitioner, the fact that the scheme employed in this case was a part of a larger pattern of fraud, trickery and deceit, and petitioner's wealth, we are not persuaded that the award was so "grossly excessive" as to be beyond the power of the State to allow. (p. 2723)

While there is perhaps legal justification for rulings in support of extremely high punitive damages, public perception seems to be that such cases constitute miscarriages of justice and motivation for attorneys to seek out frivolous cases with which to clog up the country's court-rooms. Limits may not even reduce excessive awards, as has been expected. In fact, caps tend to increase both the variability and amount of awards in low severity of injury cases, but tend to reduce them some-what in high severity of injury cases, thus increasing the already nega-tive perception that jurors tend to overaward in low-severity cases and underaward in high-injury cases (Meyer, 1995).

An aid to avoiding inappropriate awards is built into the legal sys-tem in the form of judicial review; that is, trial judges are typically given the authority by the state to review an award of punitive dam-ages by juries and to reduce them as appropriate. In fact, in the 1994 case of *Honda Motor Co. v. Oberg*, the U.S. Supreme Court held that an Oregon law that provided no procedure for a judge to routinely review an award of punitive damages violated the due process rights of the defendant. Recently, the U.S. Supreme Court endorsed the broaden-ing of yet another form of check and balance. In the 2001 case of *Cooper Industries v. Leatherman Tool Group*, the Court was called upon to decide what level of deference the Federal Appeals Courts should use in reviewing the amount of punitive damages awarded by a lower trial court. The Court gave Federal Courts of Appeal considerable latitude in reducing punitive damages that may be deemed excessive. The practical effect of the *Cooper* decision may ultimately be to reduce the size of punitive damages, but it also will likely encourage those against whom punitive damages are awarded to appeal to the federal level.

Given the tendency for these types of cases to be appealed, it would seem to make sense for the legal system to adopt rules for calculating punitive damages. We end the chapter with an Alabama case that has had a significant impact on the way that damage awards are initially determined. The relevance of this case for forensic mental health profes-sionals is that the case introduces language (i.e., guidelines) that are widely cited as precedent in personal injury cases today.

THE CASE OF *BMW V. GORE* (1996):
GUIDELINES FOR CALCULATING PUNITIVE DAMAGES

In 1983, BMW of North America adopted a nationwide policy allowing cars that were damaged in the course of manufacture or transportation to be sold as new, without even the dealer's knowledge, as long as the cost of the repair did not exceed 3% of the suggested retail price (i.e., as much as $1,200 for a $40,000 vehicle). In 1990, Dr. Ira Gore purchased one of these cars for $40,750.88 from an authorized dealer in Birmingham, Alabama. The vehicle he purchased had been damaged and then partially repainted at the distributor's vehicle preparation center, at a cost of $601.37, prior to its shipment to the dealer.

Dr. Gore drove the car for approximately 9 months before taking it to an independent automobile detailing shop, Slick Finish. He had not noticed any flaws in the car's appearance but took the vehicle in to make it look "snazzier than it normally would appear." The detailing shop informed Dr. Gore that the car had received a touch-up paint job. He sued the distributor and alleged that the failure to disclose that the car had been repainted constituted fraud.

An Alabama jury, viewing the practice as consumer fraud, awarded Gore $4 million. They reached this amount by multiplying $4,000 (their estimate of his loss of "value," because he now owned a repainted car; the actual paint repair cost was only $600) by 1,000 (records indicated that about 1,000 repainted BMWs had been sold in all 50 states in the 10 years prior to their decision). The Alabama Supreme Court ruled that the jury could not rely on "acts that occurred in other jurisdictions," but then inexplicably only cut the award in half (though only 14 BMWs had been touched up in Alabama during those 10 years). The Supreme Court of Alabama expressed the view that

> 1) a jury could not use the number of similar acts that a defendant had committed in other jurisdictions as a multiplier when determining the dollar amount of a punitive damages award, and 2) a reasonable punitive damages award in the case at hand was $2 million. (p. 1)

On certiorari, the U.S. Supreme Court, in a 5 to 4 decision written by Judge Stevens, held that such punitive damages were so "grossly excessive" as to violate the constitutional requirements of due process of law. "Elementary notions of fairness . . . [require he] receive fair notice not only of the conduct that will subject him to punishment but also of the severity of the penalty a state may impose" (p. 5).

Justice Stevens said the jury's decision failed three "guideposts," refusing to delineate them as actual rules.[4] These "guideposts" were (1) the "degree of reprehensibility of the defendant's conduct" (i.e., whether people's health or safety was at risk or whether there was bad faith, noting there was no affirmative misconduct, or no false statements, or even reason for BMW to think it violated Alabama laws); (2) the ratio between compensatory and punitive awards (here it was 500:1. Justice Stevens said the Court could continue to reject "the notion that the constitutional line is marked by simple mathematical formula," but when it is a "breathtaking 500 to 1," one "must surely raise a suspicious judicial eyebrow"); and (3) the difference between any punitive award and any relevant criminal or civil sanctions. In Alabama, the fine for violating the state's Deceptive Trade Practices is $2,000, and Justice Stevens noted that in New York, the fine for a first-time violation of Consumer Protection laws is $50.

In the 2003 term, the U.S. Supreme Court stood behind its position in *BMW* that excessive punitive damages violated defendants' rights to due process when it limited the original jury award in *State Farm Mutual Auto Insurance Co. v. Campbell*. It is noteworthy that the *BMW* decision focused on economic loss as opposed to personal injury. However, the "guideposts" delineated in the ruling generalize to punitive damages in emotional damage cases and may provide the basis for cases involving assessments conducted by mental health practitioners. Thus, *BMW* is an example of a legal decision dictating an area of mental health practice that originally had no direct mental health aspect. It is a bit unclear exactly how the guideposts will translate to such cases, because no clear precedent yet exists.

CASE REFERENCES

Bell v. Great Northern Railway Co., 12 S.W. 321 75 Tex. 50 (1890).
BMW v. Gore, 517 U.S. 559 (1996).
Chen v. Superior Court, 54 Cal. App. 4th 168 (1997).
Christy Bros. Circus v. Turnage, 144 S.E. 680 38 Ga. App. 581 (1928).

---

[4] Such a seemingly timid method of response (i.e., forwarding "guideposts" rather than setting rules) is seen quite commonly in judicial rulings, and it seems especially frustrating in rulings handed down by the U.S. Supreme Court. Why can the Supreme Court not accept that it is the court of last resort and state clear rules, and answer questions that even the dullest of us could see as logically following from the decision? Rather, the practice seems to be to wait for another case in which the same questions will again be raised.

Consolidated Rail Corp. v. Gottshall, 512 U.S. 532 (1994).

Cooper Industries v. Leatherman Tool Group, 69 U.S.L.W. 4299 (2001).

Dillon v. Legg, 68 Cal. 2d 728 (1968).

Harris v. Forklift Systems, 114 S. Ct. 367 (1993).

Honda Motor Co. v. Oberg, 512 U.S. 415 (1994).

Jones v. Brooklyn Heights Railroad, 23 A.D. 141 48 N.Y.S. 914 (1897).

Meritor Savings Bank v. Vinson, 477 U.S. 57 (1986).

Molien v. Kaiser Foundation Hospital, 27 Cal. 3d 916 (1980).

Molzof v. U.S., 911 F.2d 18 (7th Cir. 1991), ret'd, 112 S. Ct. 711 (1992).

Palsgraf v. Long Island Railroad, 248 N.Y. 339; 1928 LEXIS 1269 (1928).

State Farm Mutual Auto Insurance Co. v. Campbell, 123 S. Ct. 1513 (2003).

Thing v. Chusa, 48 Cal. 3d 644 (1989).

Thompson v. National Railroad Passenger Corp., 44 U.S. 1035 (1980).

TXO Products Corp. v. Alliance Resources, 509 U.S. 443 (1993).

CHAPTER 12

Prisoners' Rights to Medical and Mental Health Treatment

In colonial times, punishment consisted of fines, public humiliation, and executions; the sole function of prisons was to house accused persons before and during trial. The shift from public sanctions to incarceration occurred in 1785, with the opening of the first American prison that exclusively held convicted criminals as a form of punishment. Sentences were tailored to be proportionate to the severity of the crime (Harvard Law Review Association, 2002).

By the mid-19th century, the possibility of rehabilitating and re-forming prisoners became increasingly popular. Prisons began to design moral training programs to prevent recidivism. Treatment specialists were hired to resolve the problems underlying prisoners' criminal behavior. Legislators eventually incorporated indeterminate sentencing to encourage rehabilitation. This system allowed for release when prison officials deemed a prisoner to be reformed, and not before (Harvard Law Review Association, 2002).

Today, upon conviction, a person loses his or her right to be free from confinement but retains the great majority of the human rights established by the U.S. Constitution. Until recently, the legal trend was for prisoners to acquire ever more protections under the law. For instance, *Bounds v. Smith* (1977) guaranteed the right of prisoners to access legal materials or assistance. This guarantee was later limited in *Lewis v. Casey* (1996), demonstrating a shift away from increasing prisoners' rights.

Fundamental to many prisoners' rights are the procedural protection granted by the Due Process Clause of the Fourteenth Amendment and the Eighth Amendment's protection against cruel and unusual punishment. These particular rights bear heavily on mental health–related issues such as involuntary commitment or treatment. However, recent decisions have placed limitations even on these basic human rights. Following are some of the most influential cases in the last few decades that have shaped today's legal standards in relation to prisoners' rights, including prisoners' right to due process.

PRISONERS' RIGHTS TO TREATMENT

Cases in the area of prisoners' rights are often extensions of previous rulings concerning nonincarcerated citizens, as in the case law on civil commitment. As we discussed in Chapter 8, the U.S. Supreme Court had made it clear in *Rouse v. Cameron* (1967) that the purpose of civil commitment (in this instance, for someone found not guilty by reason of insanity) had to be for treatment rather than confinement or punishment. Otherwise, the commitment constituted a violation of equal protection and due process, both of which were guaranteed under the Fourteenth Amendment. Yet, in the case of a convicted inmate, confinement is among the primary goals of the system, and presumably the inmate received due process throughout the trial process. Thus, any further due process rights were potentially rendered moot. How, then, do the rules regarding rights to treatment apply in prison?

As discussed in Chapter 3, two necessary components of informed consent for treatment are that the person who is to receive it know all relevant information plus have the mental capacity to make a decision. However, in dealing with prisoners' rights to informed consent, coercion becomes an issue. As we saw in Chapter 3, the case of *Kaimowitz v. State of Michigan*, (1972) addressed this issue specifically with regard to inmates. Psychosurgery was to be a requirement for Louis Smith's parole. The Michigan Court concluded that institutionalization made the informed consent process "inherently coercive," thus intruding on the First Amendment right to privacy. An unforeseen fallout of this ruling was the cessation of the traditional practice wherein pharmaceutical companies would build their own research center/hospital in the middle of the prison compound to facilitate inmates' "voluntary" participation in a variety of drug study protocols. Following *Kaimowitz*, it could no longer be assumed that any signed consents would be considered valid in a court of law, and the potential risks (and potential resulting lawsuits) from drug studies were too many.

Prior to 1976, it had not been established that inmates even had a right to receive treatment while in prison. Then, in *Estelle v. Gamble* (1976), the U.S. Supreme Court acknowledged inmates' rights to appropriate care and treatment under the Eighth Amendment. Incarceration in the absence of needed treatment would constitute cruel and unusual punishment. However, the court held that "deliberate indifference" to these rights had to be proven in order for the inmate to sue.

An interesting situation occurs when inmates need mental health treatment that is beyond the scope of that provided by the correctional facility. Clearly defined procedures for voluntary and involuntary commitment exist for the protection of the rights of nonincarcerated citizens, as discussed in Chapter 8. However, prior to 1980, correctional systems had no definite due process guidelines for the unwilling transfer of inmates from prison to a mental institution. For that matter, there had not been any formal legal declaration that due process rights even existed for inmates. The Supreme Court took up these issues that year in *Vitek v. Jones* (1980).

The Case of *Vitek v. Jones* (1980): Due Process and Civil Commitment of Prisoners

On May 31, 1974, Mr. Jones was convicted of robbery and sentenced to serve 3–9 years in a Nebraska state prison. Seven months later, he was placed in solitary confinement at the penitentiary hospital, where he set his mattress on fire. He was severely burned and was immediately treated in the burn unit of a private hospital. After this incident, and based on the findings that he was mentally ill and could not receive proper treatment in prison, Mr. Jones was involuntarily transferred from the state prison to the security unit of the Lincoln Regional Center, a state mental hospital.

According to Nebraska statute at the time, if a designated physician or psychologist found that a prisoner suffered from a mental disease or defect that could not be given proper treatment in prison, the Director of Correctional Services could transfer the prisoner to a mental hospital for examination, study, and treatment. The statute provided that the prisoner was to be returned to the Department of Corrections if, prior to the end of his sentence, treatment was no longer necessary. If the state determined that, upon the expiration of the prisoner's sentence, he or she was still in need of treatment, civil commitment proceedings would have ensued for the purpose of retaining him or her in the mental institution, but not until then. A Nebraska law authorized the Director of Correctional Services to place a state prisoner in any available, suitable, and appropriate residence facility or institution, and to transfer him or her from one place to another.

Mr. Jones filed a suit challenging the constitutionality of that law. The lawsuit specifically contended that the law violated Mr. Jones's right to due process. Mr. Jones further contended that involuntary commitment to a mental institution did not fall within the usual conditions of confinement for which he had already received due process. Furthermore, the medical nature of the issue in question did not justify doing away with due process requirements.

The District Court determined the statute to be unconstitutional as applied to Mr. Jones, stating that his transfer to a medical hospital without adequate notice and the opportunity for a hearing was in direct violation of the liberty interest that is protected by the Due Process Clause of the Fourteenth Amendment. Such transfers must be "accompanied by adequate notice, an adversary hearing before an independent decision-maker, a written statement by the fact-finder of the evidence relied on and the reasons for the decision, and the availability of appointed counsel for indigent prisoners." The District Court enjoined the State from transferring Mr. Jones to Lincoln Regional Center without following the requirements for due process.

The U.S. Supreme Court agreed. Justice White noted that "the stigmatizing consequences of a transfer to a mental hospital for involuntary psychiatric treatment, coupled with the subjection of the prisoner to mandatory behavior modification as a treatment for mental illness, constitute the kind of deprivations of liberty that requires procedural protections" (*Vitek v. Jones*, 1980, p. 2). Although the Court acknowledged that a valid conviction extinguishes the right to freedom from confinement, it held that this does not authorize the involuntary commitment to a mental institution without granting new and complete due process protections.

Since 1980, the word *Vitek* has become well known among treatment providers in the correctional field. To *Vitek* an offender means that a treatment provider invokes a procedure designed to protect the inmate's due process rights, while attempting to keep the inmate in an inpatient treatment program or send the inmate to a mental hospital against his or her wishes. See Box 12.1 regarding a prisoner's right to sue following neglect.

BOX 12.1. Neglect and the Prisoner's Right to Sue

The U.S. Supreme Court addressed the issue of neglect in the case of *Farmer v. Brennan* (1994). A person diagnosed by a prison psychiatrist as transsexual (preoperative) was allowed to be transferred to the general prison population of the U.S. Penitentiary at Terre Haute, a prison that allegedly had a violent environment and a high level of inmate assaults. The inmate was beaten and raped 2 weeks later. The Supreme Court held for the inmate and reaffirmed *Estelle v. Gamble* (1976) in finding that prison officials were "deliberately indifferent" rather than just negligent, and so supported these officials' potential liability for compensatory and punitive damages.

Increased recognition of prisoners' rights continued into the early 1990s. Then, in 1996, the U.S. Supreme Court ruled that to bring a suit against a prison, an inmate must show "actual injury" as opposed to simply claiming that a right was being violated (*Lewis v. Fletcher,* 1996). Perhaps the most far-reaching impact of this latter ruling was that it limited the ability of inmates to use class-action suits to bring about any widespread reform.

Involuntary Medication of Prisoners

In *Knecht v. Gilman* (1973), inmates claimed that those with behavior problems were given aversive therapy, consisting of an injection of apomorphine, which caused vomiting lasting from 15 minutes to an hour. A Federal Court held that this treatment could be considered cruel and unusual punishment if administered without truly informed and voluntary consent. In *Washington v. Harper* (1990), the due process requirements for the involuntary medication of prisoners were further elucidated.

The Case of *Washington v. Harper* (1990): Due Process and Involuntary Medication of Prisoners

Walter Harper, sentenced to prison in 1976 for robbery, served 4 years in the Washington State Penitentiary, where he spent most of the time in the mental health unit. During this time, Harper consented to treatment with antipsychotic medications commonly used to treat mental disorders such as schizophrenia. In 1980, Harper was given parole, with the contingency that he continue receiving psychiatric treatment, including the antipsychotic drugs.

In December 1981, Harper was committed to the Washington State

Hospital in Seattle to receive treatment for his illness. He had at that point already been noncompliant with his treatment. Hospital staff predicted that Harper would become violent and that his condition would deteriorate if he did not continue to take the antipsychotic drugs. After violating his parole by assaulting two nurses, Harper was returned to prison.

Back in prison, Harper was sent to the Special Offender Center (SOC), a correctional institute designed to diagnose and treat convicted felons suffering from serious mental disorders. There Harper was diagnosed with Manic–Depressive Disorder (later he would also be diagnosed with Schizoaffective Disorder, and eventually with Schizophrenia), and subsequently treated with antipsychotic medication. Harper consented to the medication for almost a year. In November 1982, he adamantly refused to continue taking the antipsychotic drugs.

Upon his refusal, the treating psychiatrist sought to involuntarily medicate Harper under the SOC policy, which stated that if a psychiatrist ordered such medication, an inmate could be involuntarily treated only if he (1) suffered from a "mental disorder" and (2) was "gravely disabled" or posed a "likelihood of serious harm" to himself or others. After a hearing, and upon a finding that the above conditions were met, a special committee consisting of a psychiatrist, a psychologist, and a Center official, none of whom could be currently involved in the inmate's diagnosis or treatment, could order involuntary medication, if the panel agreed with the psychiatrist.

A psychiatric security attendant made the first request for involuntary administration of antipsychotic drugs to Harper, after Harper allegedly pulled the officer's hand through a food slot. The request read, "This inmate is in need of involuntary medication. He is a threat to the safety and security of the institution" (Washington v. Harper, 1990, p. 34). Harper had a long history of serious, assaultive behavior toward inmates and staff. Doctors said his condition worsened when he did not take his medication. It was also noted that Harper's opposition to medication was partly rooted in his desire to self-medicate with street drugs, especially cocaine. Nevertheless, forced administration of antipsychotic medication may not be used as a form of punishment; instead, it must be prescribed in line with the patient's best medical interest.

Harper was quoted as saying in one of the SOC hearings that he "would rather die than take medication." He accused the prison staff, saying "Well all you want to do is medicate me and you've been medicating me. . . . Haldol paralyzed my right side of my body. . . . You are burning me out of my life. . . . You are burning me out of my freedom" (p. 25).

However, the panel agreed that Harper was in need of forced medication; he was involuntarily given the medication he had been refusing.

Harper filed a suit in State Court claiming that the failure to provide a judicial hearing before the involuntary administration of antipsychotic medication violated the Due Process Clause of the Fourteenth Amendment. He contended that prison staff were utilizing the medication to sedate him and to suppress his potentially violent outbursts, with disregard for the medical implications that such drugs would have in his mental and bodily function.[1] Harper demanded that the State must first find him incompetent and then obtain court approval for involuntary medication. The State argued that the SOC policy contained adequate procedural safeguards to protect the prisoner's interests, specifically, the independence of the decision maker from the institution's interests, as well as the deferred reliance on medical professionals to diagnose and treat inmates using appropriate and ethical medical expertise. The State maintained that its interest and duty was to combat the danger posed to other inmates, as well as staff members, by a violent, mentally ill prisoner. The Court ruled that an inmate with a serious mental illness may be involuntarily medicated if he is dangerous to himself or others, and if the prescription is in his medical interest. The Court found that the SOC policy's administrative hearing procedures met procedural due process, stating, "It is less than crystal clear why lawyers must be available to identify possible errors in medical judgment" (p. 23).

However, the Washington State Supreme Court reversed the decision, ruling that "the State could administer such medication to a competent, nonconsenting inmate *only if, in a judicial hearing* at which the inmate had the full panoply of adversarial procedural protections, the State proved by 'clear, cogent, and convincing' evidence that the medication was both necessary and effective for furthering a compelling state interest" (p. 9, emphasis in original). In summary, the Washington State Supreme Court determined that Harper's being deprived of a judicial hearing prior to his treatment violated the requirements for due process.

---

[1] Even though extensive research supports the therapeutic effectiveness of antipsychotic medication, serious side effects may occur. Even the Court acknowledged that these drugs can cause irreversible and even fatal side effects. For example, the Prolixin injections that Harper was receiving may induce catatonic-like states, alter electroencephalographic (EEG) recordings, and cause the brain to swell. The list of adverse reactions includes bizarre dreams, hypertension, nausea, vomiting, headache, constipation, blurred vision, impotence, jaundice, eczema, tremors, and muscle spasms. Some antipsychotic drugs may cause tardive dyskinesia, a motor syndrome that can be fatal in up to 30% of cases.

The U.S. Supreme Court ultimately agreed. According to the Court, Harper possessed a significant liberty interest in avoiding the forceful administration of antipsychotic drugs. Justice Stevens said about involuntary medication that "the violation of a person's bodily integrity is an invasion of his or her liberty . . . [and] . . . it is particularly intrusive if it creates a substantial risk of permanent injury and premature death." He also stated that "when the purpose or effect of forced drugging is to alter the will and the mind of the subject, it constitutes a deprivation of liberty in the most literal and fundamental sense." He described the right to be left alone as "the most comprehensive of rights and the right most valued by men" (p. 24). The Court elaborated that "the liberty of citizens to resist the administration of mind altering drugs arises from our Nation's most basic values, [and as such] . . . it deserves the highest order of protection" (p. 24). Notably, though, the Court technically only required an in-house review.

The Case of *Riggins v. Nevada* (1992): Forced Medication to Achieve Competency

A primary reason the rights of prisoners need to be specifically considered independent of the rights of nonincarcerated citizens is that the prisoners are denied many fundamental rights. In the cases discussed in this chapter so far, these rights were taken away only after the inmate received due process in the form of a trial (or perhaps the inmate waived the right to trial by pleading guilty). However, it is possible that issues of medication and treatment may be tied directly into the trial process, thus *directly* affecting due process itself. Such was the case in the 1992 case of *Riggins v. Nevada*.

In November 1987, David Riggins rode with a friend to the apartment of Paul Wade. While his friend waited in the car, Riggins went into the apartment. About one and a half hours later, Riggins returned to the car. Sometime later, when unable to reach him by telephone, Wade's girlfriend went to his apartment, where she found him dead. He had been stabbed to death (*Riggins v. State*, 1991). Forty-five hours later, David Riggins was arrested for the murder and robbery of Paul Wade (*Riggins v Nevada*, 1992).

Upon his arrest in 1987, Riggins complained to a psychiatrist that he was hearing voices and having trouble sleeping (*Riggins v. Nevada*, 1992). He told the psychiatrist that he had taken the drug Mellaril in the past and it had helped his symptoms to abate. After the psychiatrist completed a 10-minute examination, he prescribed for Riggins 100 milligrams of Mellaril a day, explaining that he chose that drug because it had helped Riggins's symptoms to subside in the past. When Riggins continued to hear voices, he requested that his psychiatrist increase the dosage. His psychiatrist agreed, eventually increasing his dosage to 800 milligrams a day (*Riggins v. State*, 1991).

In June 1988, the defense pled not guilty by reason of insanity (NGRI), and moved to suspend the administration of the drug until the end of the trial on the grounds that it not only infringed on Riggins's freedom but also that continued administration of the drug would prevent the jury from seeing Riggins's mental state firsthand. The following month, the District Court denied Riggins's motion in a one-page order that failed to give a reason for its decision. The following November, the case went to trial, and Riggins continued to take 800 milligrams of Mellaril each day throughout the duration of the trial (*Riggins v. Nevada*, 1992).

During the trial, in which Riggins testified on his own behalf, he testified that on the night of the murder, he had used cocaine before going to Wade's apartment and stated that Wade was trying to kill him and that voices in his head said that killing Wade would be justifiable homicide (*Riggins v. Nevada*, 1992, p. 6). In November 1988, after a trial that lasted 4 days, a jury found Riggins guilty of robbery and murder in the first degree. Subsequently, he was sentenced to death (*Riggins v. Nevada*, 1992).

Three years after the decision, in 1991, Riggins took his case to the Nevada Supreme Court, with the claim that he had been denied a fair trial due to the fact that he was forced to take Mellaril during the trial (*Riggins v. Nevada*, 1992). Because Riggins pled NGRI, the fact that he endured forced medication of the drug Mellaril was of the utmost importance. For jurors to make a fair decision based on all of the evidence, they in fact needed to see all of the evidence, and included in this evidence was Riggins's mental state. Riggins' attorneys argued that since his mental state was an important piece of evidence, it would be a violation of his Fourteenth Amendment rights to due process of law to prevent him from presenting his nonmedicated self at trial. According to the Fourteenth Amendment due process of law is required before a person can be denied "life, liberty or property." Given the fact that the District Court had denied the defense's motion to suspend Riggins's taking the medication, his liberties were violated. In other words, his freedom to choose to discontinue the use of Mellaril was taken away from him without due process.

Riggins also claimed that being forced to take this medication

---

BOX 12.2. Notes on the *Riggins* Dissent: What Is the Effect of Antipsychotic Medication on Courtroom Behavior?

Antipsychotic drugs such as Mellaril can make even severely psychotic people seem to be in complete control of their behavior (Durrant & Thakker, 2003). Taking such a medication could indeed have masked Riggins's true demeanor. A defendant's demeanor in the courtroom is one of the most important items to take into consideration when the jury is making a decision about a person's mental condition. In his dissent, Justice Springer of the Supreme Court of Nevada commented that psychotropic drugs have come so far in the past three decades that they can "so well mask underlying mental disorders that persons who are agreed by all to be mentally incompetent and thus unfit to stand trial can be drugged into a mental state in which psychotic symptoms disappear" (*Riggins v. State,* 1991, p. 6). Justice Springer also stated in his dissent that "an expert cannot draw a verbal picture of a defendant's condition that is anywhere near as reliable as would be an observation of the defendant in an undrugged, natural state" (p. 6). While an expert witness did testify as to the effect the medication would have on Riggins's behavior, it was no replacement for seeing this behavior firsthand. Allowing the jury to see Riggins while medicated would cloud their view of Riggins's illness. Seeing Riggins in a nonmedicated state would allow the jury to have a more accurate view of how he might have behaved at the time of the murder.

---

before and during trial violated his rights guaranteed to him by the Sixth Amendment of the federal Constitution. According to the Sixth Amendment, in a criminal prosecution, one is entitled to "appear and defend" on one's own behalf when faced with an accusation (*Riggins v. State,* 1991). In other words, a defendant has the right to appear at his own trial and confront his accusers. Riggins claimed that he was unable to do this, because he was unable to appear as "himself"; instead, he was forced to appear at his trial as a medicated version of himself. Riggins claimed that taking medication at the time of his trial affected not only his outward appearance but also his testimony. See Box 12.2 for an explanation of the effects of medication on psychotic symptoms.

In 1991, the Supreme Court of Nevada upheld the decision given by the District Court, stating that the expert testimony given during the trial describing the effects the drug Mellaril would have on the defendant was sufficient evidence. They further held that the District Court did not violate the defendant's rights by denying his motion to suspend taking the medication (*Riggins v. Nevada,* 1992). The following year, Riggins took the case to the Supreme Court.

Riggins's Supreme Court Appeal

The United States Supreme Court was faced with the same challenges as the previous courts. It had to decide whether or not Riggins's rights, according to the Sixth and Fourteenth Amendments, had been violated as a result of his forced medication. To make its decision, the Court looked to its arguments in *Washington v. Harper* (1990).

On May 18, 1992, the U.S. Supreme Court reversed and remanded the decision made by the Supreme Court of Nevada. The Court found that Riggins's rights guaranteed to him by the Sixth and Fourteenth Amendments had been violated as a result of the administration of forced medication to him by the State. The Court stated that the District Court's original decision to deny Riggins's motion to suspend medication was a violation, due to the fact that the State Courts had "failed to make findings sufficient to justify the forced administration of the drug to the defendant during his trial" (*Riggins v. Nevada,* 1992). The Court found that while Riggins's dosage of medication was increased prior to trial, it was not to control how dangerous he was. Instead, the increased dosage appeared to be more of a way to ensure that Riggins would be seen as appropriate during trial. The State also failed to prove that forcible medication was necessary to obtain a decision of Riggins's guilt or innocence, and that medication could not have been replaced with a less intrusive method of treatment (*Riggins v. Nevada,* 1992). Justice Kennedy commented, "When the State commands medication during the pretrial and trial phases of the case for the avowed purpose of changing the defendant's behavior, the concerns are much the same as if it were alleged that the prosecution had manipulated material evidence" (p. 10).

The Legacy of *Riggins v. Nevada*

In his concurring statement, Justice Kennedy expressed "that absent an extraordinary showing by the State, the Due Process Clause [Fourteenth Amendment] prohibits prosecuting officials from administering involuntary doses of antipsychotic medicines for purposes of rendering the accused competent for trial" (*Riggins v. Nevada,* 1992, p. 10). However, the *Riggins* Court also had to deal with the added dimension that Riggins was asserting insanity. Thus, the *Riggins* decision was not a pure look at the issue of medicating defendants to achieve competency. In 2003, the U.S. Supreme Court took up the case of *Sell v. U.S.*, which provided a clearer look at the medicated competency issue. Dentist Charles

---

BOX 12.3. Psychology versus Psychiatry:
Differing Views on Least Intrusive Treatment

In his commentary on the *Sell v. U.S.* (2003) decision, Smith (2003) notes:

> Another example of an area in which psychologists may be called upon to assist
> trial courts is where trial courts must consider less intrusive treatment alterna-
> tives than medication. The question of alternative modes of psychotherapy will
> become important. It is interesting that the [*Sells*] Court cited conflicting *amicus
> curiae* briefs from the two APAs. The American Psychiatric Association's brief
> indicated that "alternative treatments for psychosis commonly are not as effective
> as medication," while the brief for the American Psychological Association indi-
> cated that "non-drug therapies may be effective in restoring psychotic defendants
> to competence." This same disagreement may be played out in trial courts consid-
> ering the availability of non-medication alternatives to restoring competency to
> stand trial.

Sell was charged with fraud and found incompetent to stand trial due to
unmedicated psychotic symptoms. The Court ultimately ruled that an
inmate could be legally medicated against his or her will if a trial court
determined that

1. The individual facts of the case suggest that important governmental interests are served by getting the defendant competent
   and proceeding to trial.[2]
2. The forced medication is substantially likely to significantly further those state interests.
3. Any less intrusive interventions are unlikely to provide the same
   benefits.
4. The medication is also in the best medical interest of the defendant.

The *Sell* Court urged that other rationales for forced medication (i.e.,
dangerousness) be exhausted before competency. Smith (2003) notes
that these guidelines suggest ways in which mental health professionals
may be involved in such proceedings. In particular, he notes that these
guidelines may bring differing treatment approaches to the legal forefront (see Box 12.3).

---

[2] The Court specifically noted that the government's interest in keeping criminals away
from society may be lessened in instances of incompetency, because incompetent defendants are commonly held in mental hospitals or forensic jail units.

CURRENT AND FUTURE TRENDS:
SEX OFFENDER TREATMENT VERSUS
SELF-INCRIMINATION

The 1990s also saw a proliferation of legislation that restricted the rights of incarcerated sex offenders (Herman, 2005). Two types of such legislation, community notification and indefinite commitment, are discussed in depth in Chapter 18. These laws linked nonparticipation in treatment to continuation of incarceration. For example, Kentucky requires incarcerated sex offenders to successfully complete a specialized treatment before they can be considered for parole. Thus, under these laws, treatment participation can carry with it some very high stakes.

Now consider the fact that a fundamental requirement of most sex offender treatment programs is that the offender must admit to committing the offense. Many take this further and require offenders to own up to even previously unknown crimes. In a treatment setting, this is known as offenders taking ownership of their problem (after all, you cannot treat a problem your client does not "have"), but in legal settings, this is known as admitting guilt. And make no mistake about it, a prison treatment program (while afforded some rights of confidentiality) is very much a legal setting. Thus, the situation becomes one in which offenders face serious legal ramifications if they do not admit guilt. This seems on its face an unacceptable condition from a constitutional standpoint. Yet the U.S. Supreme Court has actually ruled otherwise. In *McKune v. Lile* (2002), the Court heard the case of an offender who had the choice of participating in a Kansas sex offender treatment program or being subject to reductions in visitation rights, earnings, work opportunities, television time, and risking transfer to a maximum security prison. The first step of the treatment program required a detailed description of *all* sexual behavior, the thoroughness of which was verified by polygraph. Added to this was an independent Kansas statute that required all prison treatment staff to report knowledge of any new sex offense against a child. This seems to be a recipe for self-incrimination, traditionally precluded by the Fifth Amendment of the U.S. Constitution. While divided 5 to 4, the Court upheld the Kansas procedure. A key issue in the ruling was the fact that Kansas had only very rarely used information gained through the treatment process in criminal proceedings against the offender. Thus, on the whole, the procedure did not impose "substantial penalties." Given this last consideration and the division of the Court, it is unclear how similar future cases may be decided. At present, there seems to be room for interpretation based on case-specific facts (Smith,

2002). What is clear from the ruling in *McKune* is that the new millennium seems only to be bringing a continuation of the trend of restricting prisoners' rights. While one may expect the legal pendulum eventually to swing back in the direction of protecting prisoners, such a change has yet to be seen in a significant legal ruling.

CASE REFERENCES

Bounds v. Smith, 430 U.S. 817; 97 S. Ct. 1491 (1977).
Estelle v. Gamble, 429 U.S. 97; 97 S. Ct. 285 (1976).
Farmer v. Brennan, 511 U.S. 825; 114 S. Ct. 1970 (1994).
Knecht v. Gilman, 488 F.2d 1136; 1973 U.S. App. LEXIS 6674 (1973).
Lewis v. Casey, 518 U.S. 343; 116 S. Ct. 2174 (1996).
Lewis v. Fletcher, 518 U.S. 343 (1996).
McKune v. Lile, 536 U.S. 24; 122 S. Ct. 2017; 153 L. Ed. 2d 47; 2002 U.S. LEXIS 4206; 70 U.S.L.W. 4502 (2002).
Riggins v. Nevada, 112 S. Ct. 1810 (1992).
Riggins v. State, 107 Nev. 178; 808 P.2d 535; 1991 Nev. LEXIS 27 (1991).
Rouse v. Cameron, 373 F.2d 451 (D.C. Cir. 1966), later proceeding, 387 F.2d 241 (1967).
Sell vs. U.S., 539 U.S. 166; 123 S. Ct. 2174; 156 L. Ed. 2d 197; 2003 U.S. LEXIS 4594 (2003).
Vitek v. Jones, 445 U.S. 480; 1980 U.S. LEXIS 31 (1980).
Washington v. Harper, 494 U.S. 210; 1990 U.S. LEXIS 1174 (1990).

Specific Mental Diagnoses in the Law

At times, the law deals specifically with particular mental diagnoses that may be found in the DSM-IV-TR (American Psychiatric Association, 2000). In Part V we review the legal precedent and mental health issues in three such instances.

Chapters 13 and 14 explore both the history and prevalence of substance abuse and Mental Retardation in the legal system, as well as some of the legal ramifications that the respective diagnoses carry with them. Chapter 15 presents what can be called the darker side of mental illness. While less frequently mentioned in legal proceedings than addictions and Mental Retardation, Psychopathy and Antisocial Personality Disorder have an enormous cost to the health and well-being of society, and in particular, the legal system (Meyer, 2006). Many of the concepts contained within this section, particularly in Chapter 15, are helpful in understanding the issues surrounding violent crime, to which we turn in Part VI.

CHAPTER 13

Alcohol and Drug Abuse and Dependence

There can be no single program for the elimination of an illness as complex as drug addiction which carries so much emotional freight in the community. . . . The addict should be viewed as a sick person, with a chronic disease which requires almost emergency action.
> —U.S. Supreme Court Justice Douglas, quoting addictions treatment expert Charles Winick in *Robinson v. California*, 1962, p. 10

Substance abuse disorders are among the most prevalent mental health problems in the United States. The Substance Abuse and Mental Health Services Administration (SAMHSA, 2002) estimated that 14.5 million Americans ages 12 and older were either dependent on or abusing alcohol or illicit drugs in the year 2000. Numerous studies have also indicated a correlation between substance abuse and criminality (Newcomb, Galaif, & Carmona, 2001; Miller & Brown, 1997), and alcohol is involved in a significant number of deaths, including driving accidents, homicides, and suicides (Durrant & Thakker, 2003; Caces & Stinson, 1991). Often other mental disorders exist comorbidly with substance abuse, complicating the process of diagnosis and treatment. Many individuals with comorbid disorders are arrested in an attempt to manage their problematic behavior, and the majority of those arrested frequently exhibit symptoms of substance abuse disorders (Abram & Teplin, 1991). Yet few jails are equipped to provide treatment for this population or even to perform acute intervention and stabilization (Steadman, Callahan, Robbins, & Morrissey, 1989).

207

ADDICTION: MORAL DEFICIENCY OR ILLNESS?

Historically, society has viewed substance addiction as a moral deficiency on the part of the individual (Miller & Brown, 1997). Abuse of
alcohol or drugs was seen as a willing but immoral choice for which the
individual was responsible. During the 20th century, another view
emerged of addiction as a medical disease meriting treatment. It held
that most addictive disorders were biologically or genetically based, and
resulted in impaired self-control for which the individual should not be
held responsible. This medical or "disease" model of addiction generally
assumed that

1. Addictive disorders, particularly alcoholism, reflect a physiological disorder, possibly genetically determined.
2. People who are addicted have virtually no control over their
   intake of the substance because of this dysfunction.
3. With some substances, especially alcohol, people with addictions permanently retain their status as addicted even when they
   are able to abstain (Meyer, 1995, 2006).

DEFINING ADDICTIONS IN THE LEGAL SYSTEM

How does the legal system conceptualize individuals with substance
addictions? Over the years, the courts have been influenced by the
prevailing social understanding of addiction, as well as by scientific
research. The medical model and the moral deficiency model of addiction mentioned earlier have affected the manner in which legal decisions have been made: The medical model maintains that addiction is
a disease, and that addicted persons have virtually no control over
their intake of substances, because addiction is a physiological disorder. The moral deficiency model, on the other hand, makes the claim
that addiction is a willful lack of self-control on the part of the individual, and as such, that individual is liable for any actions and/or behavior that occurs as a result of substance use. This distinction can make a
world of difference in the proceedings of legal cases. As will be seen in
the cases presented in this chapter, the Courts are influenced by both
of these paradigms. For instance, can someone be arrested for merely
being an alcoholic or for being a drug addict? Under the medical
model, this would mean arresting them for a disease over which they
had little to no control. Would this not constitute some violation of

personal liberties? Not surprisingly, the courts have been asked these same questions.

THE CASE OF *ROBINSON V. CALIFORNIA* (1962): IS BEING ADDICTED A CRIME?

February 4, 1962, on a Los Angeles street, Officers Brown and Lindquist of the LAPD questioned and physically examined one Mr. Robinson. Officer Brown observed physical evidence suggestive of narcotic use, including "scar tissue and discoloration" on the inside of Robinson's right arm, and "what appeared to be numerous needle marks and a scab which was approximately three inches below the crook of the elbow" (p. 4) on his left arm. Officer Lindquist, having over 10 years of experience as a member of the LAPD Narcotics Division, examined Robinson's arms the next morning in the Central Jail in Los Angeles. Allegedly, Robinson later admitted under questioning by the officers that he had occasionally used narcotics for 3 or 4 months, three or four times a week, usually at his place with friends.

A California statute made it a misdemeanor for an individual to "either use narcotics or to be addicted to the use of narcotics" (p. 5). As such, Robinson was charged in the L.A. Municipal Court with being addicted to narcotics. Officers Brown and Lindquist testified about the observations they had made and presented photographs taken of Robinson's arms shortly after his arrest. Lindquist went on to admit the scabs were several days old at the time of his examination, and that Robinson was neither under the influence nor exhibiting withdrawal symptoms when he saw him. The State's expert corroborated Robinson's claim and testified that no needle mark or scab was newer than 3 days old, with the most recent mark possibly being 10 days old.

The officers also presented Robinson's alleged confession of drug use to the Court. The State's evidence, based solely on this admission, was that he had used narcotics at least seven times in the 15 days prior to his arrest. At trial, Robinson denied having ever had these conversations with the two police officers, and also denied ever using narcotics or being addicted to narcotics. He stated that the marks on his arm were due to an allergic condition contracted during his military service. Robinson even had two witnesses who testified to his assertions.

The judge instructed the jurors to convict Robinson if they agreed either that he had the "status" of being an addict or had committed the "act" of using. He further explained that the jurors did not have to include in the verdict the particular act or status they agreed upon, stating, "All the [Prosecutor] must show is either that the defendant did use a narcotic . . . , or that . . . he was addicted to the use of narcotics" (p. 16). The jury found Robinson guilty, a verdict requiring at least 90 days' imprisonment. In accordance with the judge's instructions, the jury never specified whether it convicted on the act of drug use or the status of being addicted.

The Appeals Process

Robinson appealed the ruling, but the Appellate Court supported the conviction. However, the U.S. Supreme Court ultimately reversed the decision on June 25, 1962. While the differing opinions among Justices in the 3 to 2 decision illustrated fundamental differences of opinion regarding the nature of addiction, the majority endorsed the medical model of addiction as a disease. Justice Stewart, writing for the majority, viewed the criminalization of chronic addiction as cruel and unusual punishment, because this would leave the offender subject "to arrest at any time before he reforms" (p. 5). The Eighth Amendment to the U.S. Constitution prohibits cruel and unusual punishment, and thus prohibits punishment of the status of addiction. Justice Douglas agreed with the majority and clarified that it is justifiable to punish an addict for illegal *acts*, but he did not see how simply *being an addict* could be punished as a crime under the Constitution. Justice Douglas elaborated that confinement for the purpose of treatment was *not* cruel and unusual punishment, but that convicting the addict of a crime was cruel and unusual because "the purpose of convicting someone is not to cure, but to penalize" (p. 15). Furthermore, confinement for treatment purposes or to protect society from a dangerous addict was achievable under civil commitment procedures. Justice Douglas concluded that to allow addiction or any other sickness to be a punishable crime would be a "barbarous" action in "this age of enlightenment" (p. 15).

Justices Clark and White disagreed and dissented with the Court's opinion. In his opinion, Justice Clark indirectly endorsed the moral deficiency model of abuse. He argued that Robinson had actually demonstrated self-control over his drug use, because he was neither under the influence of any substances nor experiencing any withdrawal symptoms the day he was arrested. Justice White also did not view Robinson as a helpless victim of disease, since there was no evidence of a loss of self-control during the arrest. Justice White viewed the State statute as appropriate in circumstances such as Robinson's versus a civil commitment for addicts who have lost their self-control and represent a danger.

The Legacy of *Robinson*

The impact of this case today is clear: The definition of *addiction* as a disease was legally adopted, and as such, states were prohibited from making addiction a criminal offense. Otherwise, an addict would always be vulnerable to the possibility of arrest. Such interpretation is founded on an acceptance of the medical model of addiction as a disease. As with any other disease, one cannot be prosecuted for having an addiction. To do so would constitute cruel and unusual punishment. Four years later, in *Easter v. District of Columbia* (1966), the U.S. Supreme Court ruled that criminalizing addict status also violated the Fourteenth Amendment right to equal protection.

While these rulings initially seem to be a wholesale endorsement of the medical model, courts were faced with the competing need for government to curtail unruly behavior engaged in by addicts. If it could be argued that an otherwise illegal behavior engaged in by an addict was a result of the addiction, was the behavior excusable as part of the disease? Defense attorneys certainly argued that this was the case. While upholding previous rulings that conviction for the *status* of being addicted was unconstitutional, the U.S. Supreme Court held in *Powell v. Texas* (1989) that a person might be convicted of *behaviors* stemming from addiction. Powell, arrested in Austin, Texas, for public intoxication, was found guilty and fined $20. His addiction was never disputed in court. Thus, argued his attorney, Powell's appearance in public was a result of his intoxication, which was itself a result of his disease (alcohol addiction), none of which was of his own free will. Therefore, any punishment would be constitutionally cruel and unusual and banned by the Eighth Amendment. However, the majority opinion held that the Eighth Amendment protection did not apply, since Powell was not convicted for the *status* of being a chronic alcoholic, but rather for the *behavior* of being in public while drunk on a specific occasion. As such, the Court held that there was no attempt to punish a status or even a condition, but simply to regulate behavior. Curiously, the Court also specifically noted that to find Powell innocent would open the floodgates for other types of criminal defendants going free on the basis of other "compulsions," suggesting that the ruling may have also been influenced by concern for opening a legal Pandora's Box.

Throughout the 1960s and into the 1980s the assumptions in the medical model were thus adopted as legal precedent. Meanwhile, however, a growing body of observations and research has developed suggesting that the assumptions of the medical model are not entirely accurate. For example, some alcoholics are able to return to a pattern of social drinking even after many years of chronic alcohol abuse (Meyer & Weaver, 2006). There is also clear evidence that many alcoholics, even while in the status of chronic alcoholism, can refrain from the first drink (a bedrock assumption in Alcoholics Anonymous). The current evidence suggests that the loss of control in substance abuse may be intermittent and not be apparent at all times in all situations (Madduz & Winstead, 2005; Lyvers, 2000; Miller & Chapell, 1991). Current research indicates that addictions are multidetermined. Inconsistent with a purely physiological disease model of addiction, psychological treatments are among the most effective, with client motivation to change a prerequisite for success (Miller & Brown, 1997). Even the U.S. Supreme Court seemingly rendered a verdict endorsing the moral deficiency model in *Traynor v. Turnage* (1988), in which it upheld the Veterans Administration definition of primary alcoholism as "willful misconduct" (that is, *not* the result of a medical or other psychological disorder). This evolution in court rulings parallels a similar trend in addictions research and treatment in which addicts are seen as more accountable for their actions (see, e.g., DiClemente [2003]). In such a way, the legal and scientific conceptualizations of addictions are becoming more complex and sophisticated, stepping away from the relatively black-and-white moral deficiency and medical models (Durrant & Thakker, 2003). While many individual theories of addiction currently exist, an approach that is appealing in its breadth of consideration is the biopsychosocial approach that emphasizes the biological, psychological, and social aspects of addiction, and targets treatment toward each aspect as is relevant to the individual addict.

Thus, by the 1990s, the court had acknowledged that addiction itself was a disease and was thus out of the control of the afflicted addict. Addiction itself could not be punished. However, the subsequent rulings permitting the punishment of behavior related to, or even stemming from, the addiction meant that states merely had to mind the wording of statutes to gain a similar practical effect as punishing the disease itself. However, as with other topics, the court had not seen the last case challenging the culpability of addicts. It was on the role of addiction in the division between intentional and unintentional crime that the court would next focus its lens.

INTOXICATION AND INTENTIONAL CRIME

Intentional crime is that committed "knowingly and purposely." That is to say, the perpetrator sets out to commit an act that he or she knows to be a crime. Generally, a crime committed without specific intent (i.e., manslaughter) carries with it a much less severe penalty than a crime committed with specific intent (i.e., first-degree murder) even though the other facts of the crime are exactly the same (in these examples, the perpetrator's actions caused someone to die.) With substance intoxication at the time of the crime, intentionality becomes a confounded issue, because substance abuse obviously impairs one's judgment. The U.S. Supreme Court addressed this issue in the following case.

The Case of *Montana v. Egelhoff* (1996): Voluntary Intoxication and Criminal Intent

Early in July 1992, 31-year-old James Egelhoff and a friend went to pick psilocybin mushrooms in the Yaak area near Troy, Montana. Egelhoff had in his possession a .38-caliber handgun, which he kept in a holster on his right hip. Another pair, Roberta Pavola and John Christianson, also in the Yaak area to pick mushrooms, were camping nearby. The four people met and got to know each other before Egelhoff's friend eventually departed.

On Sunday, July 12, 1992, Egelhoff, Pavola, and Christianson sold their mushrooms. The three bought beer, went to a party, and eventually left in Christianson's station wagon. Egelhoff and Christianson restocked their goods at a local IGA grocery store at around 9:30 P.M. Shortly before midnight, the Lincoln County Sheriff's department got a report of a station wagon they would later determine as Christianson's driving "in an erratic manner" on Highway 2.

Responding to the call, Sheriff's officers soon found the station wagon wrecked in a ditch alongside the road. Christianson and Pavola were dead in the front seat; Egelhoff was in the backseat yelling obscenities. Christianson and Pavola had died not from the accident but from gunshot wounds to the head. Egelhoff's gun was on the floor near the driver's brake pedal. The revolver had four loaded rounds and two empty casings. Detective Clint Gassett was called at approximately 1:00 A.M. and met Egelhoff at Libby hospital. Egelhoff was intoxicated, verbally abusive, and physically combative. Detective Gassett and others tried to physically restrain him, but he continued acting uncontrollably for the next several hours. At one point, another detective attempted to take Egelhoff's picture, but Egelhoff managed to kick the camera out of the detective's hands. Egelhoff's blood alcohol content had been .36% (over four times that typically needed for DUI) 1 hour after his arrival at the hospital.

Egelhoff at Trial

Egelhoff was tried for two counts of deliberate homicide in the District Court of the 19th Judicial District in Lincoln County, Montana. Forensics testing presented evidence of gunshot residue on Egelhoff's hands, suggesting that he had fired the weapon. Egelhoff's attorney argued that his client's blood alcohol level of .36% one hour after being brought to the hospital excluded him from being physically capable of shooting Christianson and Pavola. Egelhoff further stated that he suffered a blackout due to the alcohol, and therefore could not remember the events that night. Dr. Knecht, who examined Egelhoff in the Libby Hospital emergency room the morning after his arrest, confirmed that Egelhoff had likely suffered from an alcoholic "blackout." However, Dr. Knect also testified that an intoxicated person experiencing a blackout was capable of walking, talking, and functioning, with others unable to tell that person experienced a blackout at all.

The jury was instructed that voluntary intoxication could not be taken into consideration in determining whether Egelhoff acted "knowingly and purposely," key elements of the offense of deliberate homicide with which he was charged. The jury ultimately found Egelhoff guilty on both counts for the deaths of Christianson and Pavola. Egelhoff was sentenced to 40 years on each count, with an additional 2 years on each count for use of a weapon.

The Appeals Process

Egelhoff appealed the verdict to the Supreme Court of Montana. He asserted that he was denied due process by the jury instruction that voluntary intoxication could not be taken into consideration in determining his mental state, a key consideration in the determination of guilt for *deliberate* homicide. Due process essentially guarantees the ability of a defendant to mount a defense against any allegations. Egelhoff's counsel argued that the instruction given to the jury was unconstitutional, because it lessened the State's burden of proving whether or not the defendant acted "knowingly" or "purposely." It also shifted the burden of proof of this element from the prosecution to the defendant. The counsel argued that it was unconstitutional to deprive the defendant of due process by essentially removing relevant facts from the jury's consideration.

The Supreme Court of Montana concluded that Egelhoff was indeed denied due process by the jury instruction. The prosecutor appealed this decision to the U.S. Supreme Court, which ultimately reversed the State Supreme Court decision, holding that the instruction to ignore his intoxication had *not* violated Egelhoff's right to due process.

In a 5 to 4 decision, Justice Scalia delivered the opinion of the Court, arguing that the instruction was not unconstitutional, because the due process law does not give an absolute right to present relevant evidence. Examples of such a matter would be if the evidence is "incompetent, privileged, or otherwise inadmissible under standard rules of evidence" (*Taylor v. Illinois*, 1988, cited in *Montana v. Egelhoff*, 1996, p. 6). Relevant evidence may also be excluded due to the defendant's noncompliance with procedures, or if the evidence will likely induce "unfair prejudice, confusion of the issues, misleading the jury, or cause undue delay" (p. 6). Justice Scalia also expressed the belief that "drunks" are not violent just because alcohol makes them that way, but also because of a learned belief that drunks behave violently. On whole, the Court saw this as further support of the view that an intoxicated criminal should not be excused of his crimes. They felt that permitting evidence of intoxication may have falsely persuaded the jury to accept the argument that the defendant was physically incapable of committing such a crime, and therefore felt the evidence was rightly precluded from the jury's decision making.

Justice Souter specifically dissented with the majority opinion, reasoning that although there are sometimes valid reasons for not permitting relevant evidence, the State failed to offer such a justification for excluding relevant evidence in this particular case. This, of course, was not an endorsement of Egelhoff's defense, merely an endorsement that he should have been allowed to present his intoxication as part of his defense.

The Legacy of *Egelhoff*

At the time of this writing, James Egelhoff was still serving time as an inmate in the Montana Department of Corrections. The impact that his case has today is that a State Court still has the power to exclude evidence of intoxication from the jury in determining whether or not a defendant acted knowingly or purposely in committing a crime. Again, the logic behind this practice is that the jury may be falsely persuaded by the defense that the defendant was physically incapable of committing the crime due to being under the influence of a substance, or he may also be excused of the crime altogether. In the Court's view, one cannot simply say he or she is addicted and therefore be afforded a minimized sentence. If that were the case, then it would be the defense of a majority of people who commit a crime. The fact remains that even if substance abuse is a medical illness, one still "willfully engages" in the act of using/abusing to some degree, and is therefore found to have willfully committed any "resulting" crime.

ADDICTIONS CASE LAW: LOGICALLY CONSISTENT OR CONSISTENTLY ILLOGICAL?

The cases just reviewed demonstrate that the law can seem curiously at odds with itself at times. Even the founding assumptions (i.e., medical model) underlying basic issues can be interpreted differently across jurisdictions. Perhaps, as with most areas of law, there seems to be a healthy dose of personal agenda injected into many rulings. Although, arguably, even the approach taken by mental health practitioners toward addictions is subject to the same criticism. A curious and interesting ruling to this end occurred in New York State's highest court, on June 14, 1996. The Court ruled that Alcoholics Anonymous (long considered by many as the primary treatment method for alcoholism) "engages in religious activity and religious proselytization." The New York Supreme Court, in a 5 to 2 ruling, declared that state prison officials were wrong to penalize an inmate who stopped attending the organization's self-help meetings because he said he was an atheist or an agnostic. The high Court said that state prison officials violated the constitutional rights of the inmate, David Griffin, a former heroin addict who complained that he found the Alcoholics Anonymous (AA) meetings objectionable on the grounds of his agnostic or atheistic views, which he had held since the 1950s. Prison officials were ordered not to tie the man's eligibility for a family reunion program to his refusal to take part in the Alcoholics Anonymous sessions at Shawangunk State Prison. "A fair reading of the fundamental A.A. doctrinal writings discloses that their dominant theme is unequivocally religious," (*Griffin v. Coughlin*, 1996, p. 6) the Court said. "Adherence to the A.A. fellowship entails engagement in religious activity and religious proselytization" (p. 6).

BOX 13.1. Other Addictions Case Law

With addictions and drug abuse being such a wide open subspecialty within mental health, numerous other cases comprise the case law in this area. Some of the more interesting and important rulings follow.

On Drug Testing

- In *Skinner v. Railway Labor Executives Association* (1989), the Supreme Court upheld a private railway's right to drug-test employees who may have violated particular safety rules. The railway had the right to do this without a warrant, and without evidence or even suspicion that the person was under the influence of drugs at the time of the accident/event.
- In *Treasury Employees v. Von Raab* (1989), the Court upheld drug testing as a condition of employment or promotion when the government could demonstrate some compelling public safety interest.
- In *University of Colorado v. Derdeyn* (1993), the Supreme Court found that it was unconstitutional to require a random urinalysis of student athletes, trainers, managers, and cheerleaders. The Court held that the school–state's interest in maintaining drug-free athletic teams did not override Derdeyn's privacy interests, and that this testing program was a violation of the Fourth Amendment as an "unreasonable search."

On Mandatory Sentencing for Drug Crimes

- In *Harmelin v. Michigan* (1991), a first-time offender possessing 650 grams of cocaine and given life without parole appealed on grounds that it is cruel and unusual punishment, but the Supreme Court ruled this is not prohibited by the Eighth Amendment. A 1997 RAND Corporation study suggested that mandatory sentencing is less cost-effective than treatment.

Disparities Among Drugs and Drug Prosecutions

- In *Chapman v. U.S.* (1991), the convicted defendant in a drug possession case appealed, saying that the relevant statute was based on weight of lysergic acid (LSD)-laced substance in its entirety (e.g., the whole sugar cube rather than just the substance itself) and thus led to disproportionate weight, but the Supreme Court said no to appeal.
- In *U.S. v. Armstrong* (1996), the Supreme Court in an 8 to 1 decision held that statistical disparity in the prosecution of minorities for possession of crack cocaine (approximately 90% of those convicted of federal crimes involving crack are African American) is not sufficient as a defense for prosecution; in order to pursue this line of defense, defendants would have to show that there were "similarly situated" white defendants that the government declined to prosecute on crack charges and instead were charged with powdered cocaine crimes (which carry lighter sentences).
- *U.S. v. Ursery* (1996) found that ordinary civil forfeiture is not a punishment. Included was a case in which a Michigan man forfeited the value of his house because he had processed marijuana there. Chief Justice Rehnquist, in his majority opinion, said that federal forfeiture statutes aimed at drug-related crimes, "while perhaps having certain punitive aspects, serve important non-punitive goals" (p. 16) such as encouraging property owners to make sure their property is not used for illegal purposes.

Legal ambiguities always arise from case to case, and the rulings themselves are often subjectively interpretable. See Box 13.1 for some more samples of cases to which this applies. Mental health research will likely continue to play a role in informing the conceptualization of addiction in the legal system. After all, mental health professionals have demonstrated that they are best able to rehabilitate individuals with chemical dependency. Mental health professionals may also assist in clarifying who is in fact physiologically addicted and who is merely engaging in willful misconduct. This distinction may in turn assist in deciding whether or not the individual charged acted knowingly and purposely.

Primarily though, mental health professionals will continue to contribute greatly to the rehabilitation of addicts. This rehabilitation can serve effectively to put the addict back into mainstream society as a productive member. The legal system may be the initial intervention, but ultimately a well-trained professional of the mental health field can make the greatest reform.

CASE REFERENCES

Chapman v. U.S., 500 U.S. 453 (1991).

Easter v. District of Columbia, 124 U.S. App. D.C. 33; 361 F.2d 50 (1966).

Griffin v. Coughlin, 88 N.Y.2d 674; 1996 N.Y. LEXIS 1522 (1996).

Harmelin v. Michigan, 501 U.S. 957 (1991).

Montana v. Egelhoff, 116 S. Ct., 64 L.W. 4500 (1996).

Powell v. Texas, 492 U.S. 680 (1989).

Robinson v. California, 1962 U.S. LEXIS 850 (1962).

Skinner v. Railway Labor Executives Association, 489 U.S. 602 (1989).

Taylor v. Illinois, 484 U.S. 400; 108 S. Ct. 646 (1988).

Traynor v. Turnage, 485 U.S. 535 (1988).

Treasury Employees v. Von Raab, 489 U.S. 656 (1989).

U.S. v. Armstrong, 116 S. Ct. 1480, 64 L.W. 4305 (1996).

U.S. v. Ursery, 518 U.S. 267; 116 S. Ct. 2135; 135 L. Ed. 2d 549; 1996 U.S. LEXIS 4256 (1996).

University of Colorado v. Derdeyn, 863 P.2d 929; 1993 Colo. LEXIS 887 (1993).

CHAPTER 14

Mental Retardation

The word "habilitation," . . . is commonly used to refer to
programs for the mentally-retarded because mental
retardation is . . . a learning disability and training
impairment rather than an illness.
> —H. Bartow Farr III, writing the *Amicus Curiae* Brief
> for the American Psychiatric Association in
> *Youngberg v. Romeo* (1982)

No state shall make or enforce any law which shall abridge
the privileges or immunities of citizens of the United
States; nor shall any state deprive any person of life, liberty,
or property, without due process of law; nor deny to any
person within its jurisdiction the equal protection of the
laws.
> —Article 1 of the Fourteenth Amendment to the
> U.S. Constitution

Understanding Mental Retardation relies in part on an understanding of
the intelligence quotient, or IQ score. The average IQ score observed in
the general population is 100, with a standard deviation of 15. Therefore,
any score 15 or more points above or below 100 signifies a significant
deviation from "average." As measured with the most sophisticated standardized psychological tests assessing IQ,[1] the range is from 45 to 160.

---

[1] For IQ assessments with adults (ages 16–89), the "gold standard" test is the Wechsler
Adult Intelligence Scale, Third Edition (WAIS-III; Wechsler, 1997); for children ages 6–
16, it is the Wechsler Intelligence Scale for Children, Fourth Edition (WISC-IV; Wechsler, 2003); and for children ages 2½–7, it is the Wechsler Preschool and Primary Scale of
Intelligence, Third Edition (WPPSI-III; Wechsler, 2002).

Mental Retardation is a psychiatric disorder diagnosed when individuals have significant impairment in intellectual functioning (IQ < about 70, or 2 standard deviations below the mean), and significant impairment in more than one area of daily functioning. Furthermore, there must be evidence that these impairments began prior to age 18 (American Psychiatric Association, 2000). The diagnosis can be further broken down into groups by level of severity, which are divided primarily on the basis of the IQ score into the groups below. Note the room afforded to clinical judgment based upon the level of impairment in daily functioning. For instance, an IQ score of 52 could put the person in either the "mild" or the "moderate" group, depending on the evaluator's assessment of the person's "impairment in daily functioning."

- Mild—IQ of 50–55 to around 70
- Moderate—IQ of 35–40 to 50–55
- Severe—IQ of 20–25 to 35–40
- Profound—IQ below 20–25

The state of the law today includes significant protections against discrimination for individuals with Mental Retardation. However, this has not always been the case. The development of basic civil rights for individuals with Mental Retardation is a progression that has come along only in the past few decades.

Individuals with Mild Mental Retardation can achieve a fairly high level of functioning in the community with appropriate training, but individuals suffering from more severe forms of Mental Retardation or those who do not receive adequate training can require significant assistance just to complete the most basic of daily living tasks. As such, appropriate care of mentally retarded individuals often involves treatment in an institutionalized setting.

Prior to the 1970s mentally retarded persons were confined in psychiatric hospitals and asylums, often labeled as "deviants," and housed together with mentally ill criminals. A common claim made by treatment staff was that the individuals were receiving "milieu therapy." By placing patients in the presence of others, the assumption was that individuals with Mental Retardation would develop social skills by participating in the social "milieu." In reality, this amounted to little more than warehousing, with little attention paid to therapeutic activities. Much of the legal impetus for the change in this system can be traced back to the story of a single institution.

The first part of this chapter outlines events occurring at Pennhurst

State School and Hospital of Pennsylvania. These events eventually led to a civil lawsuit filed by 12 "retarded citizens" and three organizations, to over 70 court publications, and to at least three precedent-setting U.S. Supreme Court decisions. The cases in this story, and various shortcomings and pitfalls of each, spurred on the deinstitutionalization movement in America and eventually helped to spark Congressional reform of the rights of individuals with all disabilities.

As such, this case illustrates not only the troubled mental health care system in Pennsylvania but also the plight of thousands of mentally ill individuals who suffered at the hands of budget cuts and public apathy toward their situation, and the many employees who fought to change a system that seemed indifferent. The story of Pennhurst State School and Hospital[2] is that of a civil rights movement, and it is characterized by strength, courage, and a strong commitment to change.

THE CASE OF PENNHURST STATE SCHOOL AND HOSPITAL: THE SLOW START ON THE PATH TO CIVIL RIGHTS AND REMEDIES

Located in Spring City, Pennhurst was one of Pennsylvania's largest institutions for the mentally disabled. Founded in 1908, the institution was overpopulated and understaffed from the start. During the 1960s, Pennhurst housed over 4,000 residents. By the mid-1970s this number had decreased to around 1,200, although the facility was still considered inadequate for that number of residents. One can hardly imagine what the situation must have been like when the population was over three times that number.

The following are some of the abuses documented as facts of law supported by evidence in the initial proceedings. Residents of Pennhurst averaged 15 minutes of beneficial treatment time per weekday, and none at all during weekends. In a treatment program designed to "increase the residents' attention span and to teach them to sit and tolerate the presence of others," residents were being placed in a room to watch television (*Halderman v. Pennhurst*, 1977, p. 11). Young clients with cerebral palsy were found sitting about on the floor, and they received little to no physical therapy. Of the 511 residents on a waitlist

---

[2] Except where expressly noted, historical information about the Pennhurst School was gleaned from *Halderman v. Pennhurst* (1977).

for occupational therapy in April 1977, some had been on the list for over 3½ years. Around the same time, over 300 residents were unable to communicate verbally, but only 20 were receiving communication treatment. Abuses of residents did not stop with treatment negligence. Physical and chemical restraints were used with residents in lieu of therapeutic interventions provided by adequate staff. This included the placement of one female resident in physical restraints for a total of 112 days (2,593 hours) in the months of June through October 1977 (the girl's aggressive behavior later decreased significantly upon implementation of appropriate treatment). While these are individual reports, similar abuses of most residents were commonplace. Less common, but no less horrific, were reports of residents suffering beatings by staff, and even reports of sexual assaults.

Halderman v. Pennhurst

In response to these and other atrocities, the parents of Pennhurst resident Terri Lee Halderman filed suit against the Hospital. In July 1974, other residents and former residents began to join in a class action suit, eventually totaling 12 individuals and a parents' group representing 200 additional clients. On January 17, 1975, the U.S. District Court for the Eastern District of Pennsylvania added as fellow plaintiff none other than the United States of America, intervening on behalf of the rights of her disadvantaged citizens. It was not quite *The World v. Pennhurst*, but it was close. Pennhurst's defense was that there was no specific level of treatment mandated by Pennsylvania law or by the U.S. Constitution.

After hearing 32 days of testimony, the District Court ruled overwhelmingly in favor of the plaintiffs. The Court found the following:

> That when a state institutionalizes individuals because they are retarded, the United States Constitution (Eighth and Fourteenth Amendments) and the laws of Pennsylvania require the state to provide such minimally adequate habilitation as will afford a reasonable opportunity for them to acquire and maintain such life skills as are necessary to enable them to cope as effectively as their capacities permit. (*Halderman v. Pennhurst*, 1977, p. 45)

With respect to the specific individuals named in the suit (including Hospital Superintendent C. Duane Youngberg and various other system administrators), the Court held that they were not liable. In fact, the Court found that no evidence supported specific abuses perpetrated by any of these individuals charged. Quite the contrary, most of these individuals had been actively involved in seeking reform in the system. However, Pennhurst Center (as it was known by then) as an organization was liable. As such, the Court ordered that staff make immediate alternative placement arrangements for all residents and provide all staff with alternative employment. Pennhurst Center was to close and never again treat individuals with Mental Retardation.

Pennhurst's Appeals of *Halderman*

The District Court had based its ruling solely on the Developmentally Disabled Assistance and Bill of Rights Act (DDA) of 1975.[3] It had not founded its decision on constitutional grounds. In 1981, the U.S. Supreme Court reversed this decision, holding that the Act was merely a recommendation that institutions that receive federal funds provide their residents with "appropriate treatment" in the "least restrictive" environment (*Pennhurst v. Halderman*, 1981). Because the components of the DDA were merely recommendations, the District Court had no jurisdiction to sanction the hospital, even though it had specified that the treatment of Pennhurst residents was unconstitutional. The case was remanded back to the District Court, which ultimately upheld the entire ruling, this time on the basis of Pennsylvania State Statute. Again, the U.S. Supreme Court remanded the ruling, this time stating that the District Court's injunction violated Pennsylvania's protections under the Constitution's Eleventh Amendment[4] (*Pennhurst v. Halderman*, 1984). While at least one court had held that the constitutional rights of hundreds of Pennhurst residents were being egregiously violated, the case seemed hopelessly deadlocked with regard to how to fix the problem. Given these jurisdictional technicalities, the Supreme Court had yet to rule on the Constitution's promise of treatment in the least restrictive setting. However, another Pennhurst resident was waiting in the wings to have his day in court. The wheels of justice were turning slowly, but they were turning.

---

[3] The DDA illustrates a commonly used tactic in which the legislature sidesteps requiring states to do something, most commonly because such a requirement would be unconstitutional. Here, states were given the choice of whether or not to comply with the DDA, but declining to endorse the Act meant forfeiting any funds provided by the federal government to care for and treat the developmentally disabled.

[4] The Eleventh Amendment of the Constitution of the United States states that "the Judicial power of the United States shall not be construed to extend to any suit in law or equity, commenced or prosecuted against one of the United States by Citizens of another State, or by Citizens or Subjects of any Foreign State."

THE CASE OF *YOUNGBERG V. ROMEO* (1982):
A CONSTITUTIONAL RIGHT TO TREATMENT AND SERVICES

Born with profound Mental Retardation, Nicholas Romeo spent the first 24 years of his life under the care of his parents in South Philadelphia. Upon the death of his father in the early 1970s, Nicholas's mother Paula found herself unable to care for her son. Through the Philadelphia Common Pleas Court, Nicholas was admitted to Pennhurst State School and Hospital on July 11, 1974. At Pennhurst, treatment staff allegedly used restraints against him inappropriately several times. Furthermore, similar to the claims of many other Pennhurst residents, Nicholas was reportedly receiving little to no appropriate treatment. Staff failed to protect Nicholas from over 70 injuries (some self-inflicted, others inflicted by fellow residents). As described in court records, the injuries "included a broken arm, a fractured finger, injuries to sexual organs, human bite marks, lacerations, black eyes, and scratches. Moreover, some of [Nicholas's] injuries became infected, either from inadequate medical attention or from contact with human excrement that the Pennhurst staff failed to clean up" (*Romeo v. Youngberg*, 1980, p. 2). In response to these claims, Nicholas's mother filed suit against Pennhurst's Superintendent, Duane Youngberg, as well as Director of Resident Life, Richard Mathews, and the Director of Unit 9, Margurete Conley.

While the Romeos lost the initial jury trial, this case fueled the battle to acquire civil rights for individuals suffering from Mental Retardation. The situation was eloquently summed up in the beginning of the U.S. Court of Appeals reversal of the trial decision, which stated, "The present controversy inhabits the twilight area of developing law concerning the constitutional rights of the involuntarily committed mentally retarded" (*Romeo v. Youngberg*, 1980, p. 2). However, the U.S. Supreme Court held that a state has an obligation to provide the institutionalized mentally retarded "minimal habilitation," along with at least "minimal services" that permit (1) the least restraint possible, and (2) basic safety. However, in so ruling, the Court recognized that these standards were somewhat open to interpretation. Thus, Justice Powell, writing for the plurality, elaborated:

> In determining whether the State has met its obligations in these respects, decisions made by the appropriate professional are entitled to a presumption of correctness. Such a presumption is necessary to enable institutions of this type—often, unfortunately, overcrowded and understaffed—to continue to function. A single professional may have to make decisions with respect to a number of residents with widely varying

needs and problems in the course of a normal day. The administrators, and particularly professional personnel, should not be required to make each decision in the shadow of an action for damages (*Youngberg v. Romeo*, 1982, p. 19)

The Supreme Court thus established that a state does have a legal obligation to provide some level of treatment for involuntarily institutionalized individuals with Mental Retardation. However, Romeo's suit was against Pennhurst Superintendent Duane Youngberg and other staff. Given the Supreme Court's provision regarding the deference to professional opinion, Romeo's suit against the Pennhurst staff was eventually dismissed by the U.S. 3rd Circuit Court of Appeals in 1984 (*Romeo v. Youngberg*, 1984). Thus ended over a decade of court battles involving Pennhurst State Hospital and School.

THE AMERICANS WITH DISABILITIES ACT OF 1990: THE INFLUENCE OF STATE COURTS ON FEDERAL LEGISLATION

All of the rights guaranteed in the *Pennhurst* decisions were specifically limited by each court to individuals who were involuntarily committed. Thus, at that point, individuals who signed voluntary admissions to treatment were not guaranteed adequate treatment, nor were they guaranteed treatment in the least restrictive environment.

The development of guaranteed civil rights for individuals with Mental Retardation was agonizingly slow, even by legal system standards. Indeed, the establishment of guaranteed civil rights for prisoners convicted of crimes preceded the provision of similar rights to the mentally retarded by almost a decade. Clearly, the struggle embodied in the *Pennhurst* cases and in similar cases throughout the land does not represent a bright spot in this country's protection of its citizenry. As such, the 101st Congress of the United States sought to "establish a clear and comprehensive prohibition of discrimination on the basis of disability," when they enacted the Americans with Disabilities Act (ADA) in 1990. In 1999, the Supreme Court held that treatment similar to that faced by Pennhurst residents violated the ADA in *Olmstead v. L.C. by Zimring* (1999). The U.S. Supreme Court has since been sharply criticized as limiting the ADA with every opportunity, for example, by denying state employees subjected to discrimination the right to seek money damages (*University of Alabama v. Garrett*, 2001); however, the ADA remains the most powerful protection for individuals with a wide variety of disabilities, including Mental Retardation.

MENTAL RETARDATION AND CAPITAL OFFENDERS

An area of mental health law that has recently stirred significant public and scientific debate is the state-sponsored execution of mentally retarded offenders. Since 1985, the cases of John Paul Penry and Daryl Atkins have examined the question of whether the death penalty is cruel and unusual punishment for those with Mental Retardation (Eisenberg, 2004).

Johnny Paul Penry had been convicted of capital murder in Texas and sentenced to die by lethal injection. The *Penry* case was complicated by issues of mitigating factors. The jury had not been adequately instructed in the first trial to include the issues of Penry's Mental Retardation and childhood abuse as mitigating factors. Because of this, Penry's case was argued (for the second time) to the U.S. Supreme Court in March 2001. In the retrial, the defense relied heavily on issues pertaining to Penry's Mental Retardation.

The Supreme Court's decision arrived on June 4, 2001. Justice O'Connor, writing the 6 to 3 decision, overturned Penry's sentence on the grounds that the Texas jury was told to consider Mental Retardation as a mitigating factor but was given no avenue to put any such consideration into effect (*Penry v. Johnson*, 2001). The decision laid important groundwork, but it failed to address explicitly the issue of executing mentally retarded offenders.

All states allowing capital punishment had anxiously awaited the decision, only to be left again without direction. By this time, the political climate was in full swing from previous years, with states expressly banning execution of mentally retarded criminals by legislation. Before the *Penry* decision was handed down, the Missouri Senate and Texas's own House of Representatives each passed bills categorically banning the execution of mentally retarded individuals. Similar legislation was also pending in Connecticut. The state of Florida soon passed its own bill banning imposition of the death penalty on mentally retarded defendants. North Carolina followed, and the Texas legislature soon passed a similar bill, but Governor Rick Perry vetoed the bill on June 18, 2001.[5]

---

[5] In the interest of being able to take a more "pure look" at the primary issue, the U.S. Supreme Court agreed to hear the case of *McCarver v. North Carolina* on the 2001 docket. McCarver is a convicted murderer whose IQ has been measured as low as 67. All hope would have been lost when the state of North Carolina passed a retroactive ban on executing mentally retarded offenders (effectively mooting the *McCarver* Supreme Court appeal) had it not been for the case of Daryl Renard Atkins.

THE CASE OF *ATKINS V. VIRGINIA* (2002):
EXECUTION OF OFFENDERS WITH MENTAL RETARDATION

Throughout his schooling, Daryl Renard Atkins had been moved through various specialized courses, managing to achieve a grade point average (GPA) of only 1.26 out of 4.0. Report cards to the family documented significant behavior problems and a general lack of motivation in academic activities. He never graduated from high school (*Atkins v. Commonwealth of Virginia*, 2000).

By the age of 18, Daryl had a series of prior felony convictions, including the violent offenses of robbery and maiming. Daryl and his friend, William Jones, spent time hanging out at his father's house, abusing various drugs and drinking beer. On a mid-August evening in 1977, their friend Mark arrived to hang out with the pair. Mark brought with him a gun.

That evening Daryl and William went to the local convenience store, where they abducted and robbed Eric Nesbitt, a 21-year-old Airman First Class working at Langley Air Force Base. After abducting Nesbitt, the three men forced him to drive to a local bank and make a withdrawal, and then drove to a remote location with the plan to tie Nesbitt up and escape.

After reaching the destination and allowing Nesbitt to leave the car, Daryl began shooting him. The attack was apparently unprovoked and surprised William, who fought with Daryl for control of the gun. Daryl shot Nesbitt eight times and wounded himself in the struggle with William. Eric Nesbitt was left to die at the scene, while Daryl and William drove (in Nesbitt's car) to the emergency room. The lifeless body of Eric Nesbitt was found later. William dropped Daryl off at the emergency room, asked for some money, and drove off to spend the night in a Newport News hotel.

Authorities eventually evaluated a security videotape from the bank and were able to identify both Daryl Atkins and William Jones. Atkins was arrested at his home, and Jones, attempting to elude the authorities, was eventually picked up at a motel.

At trial, Daryl Atkins laid the blame upon William Jones, insisting that Jones had been the leader of the crime spree—an account that differed dramatically from an earlier statement. In stark contrast, the prosecutor put up a convincing case against Atkins, allowing victims from Atkins's previous crimes, as well as Eric Nesbitt's mother, to testify. Citing Atkins's prior felony convictions, the prosecutor argued for imposition of the death penalty based on the dangerousness of Atkins, as well as the vile nature of the crime. Perhaps the most damning argument was that had Daryl Atkins been put away for earlier crimes, Eric Nesbitt would still be alive.

Knowing that its client was facing the death penalty, the defense attempted to submit into evidence as much mitigating information as possible. A forensic psychologist from the Richmond area, Dr. Evan Stuart Nelson, testified at trial that Atkins had an IQ of 59. Dr. Nelson also testified that it was unlikely that Mr. Atkins would be violent in prison, having proven his ability to maintain his behavior in such a setting before. However, perhaps damning to the defense's case, Dr. Nelson also testified that he could offer no reason as to why Mr. Atkins should not be able to appreciate the wrongfulness of his act despite his limited mental abilities.

In Virginia, capital murder juries are given the initial task of determining guilt, followed by a second hearing, after which they recommend a sentence to the judge, who later passes final sentence. Just prior to the jury retiring for initial deliberations in the *Atkins* case, the defense declined an instruction by the judge for the jury to consider Mental Retardation as a mitigating factor. The Virginia jury returned a verdict of guilty and later recommended the death penalty, finding that Mr. Atkins represented a continued risk for violence, and that the crime had been "outrageously or wantonly vile."

Before the Court at the final sentencing hearing, the defense counsel unexpectedly reversed its earlier decision and objected to the death sentence on the grounds that the jury had not considered Atkins's Mental Retardation as a mitigating circumstance. The judge ultimately ruled that the objection was untimely, and held that Daryl Reynard Atkins be executed by the Commonwealth of Virginia.

Defense counsel appealed to the Supreme Court of Virginia, renewing its objection, and further argued that to subject its mentally retarded client to the death penalty would constitute "cruel and unusual punishment" from which he was protected by the Eighth Amendment of the U.S. Constitution. The higher State Court eventually ruled that the trial judge had in fact erred in not providing the jury with an instruction to consider Atkins's Mental Retardation as a mitigating circumstance. However, the argument that Mental Retardation categorically excluded Atkins from the death penalty was deemed baseless. The Texas case of *Penry v. Lynaugh* was cited as precedent for both of these findings. Following the ruling, the case was remanded for a second hearing with a new jury, in which Daryl Atkins would receive a new recommended sentence. While imposition of the death penalty would still be given to the jury as an option, the jurors would be expressly instructed by the judge to consider evidence of Mr. Atkins's Mental Retardation as a mitigating circumstance.

Opponents of capital punishment thought the *Atkins* case would be one in which the courts could reexamine the "pure" issue of executing mentally retarded offenders. However, the proceedings of Atkins's second trial illustrate that this argument was far from pure. In this new sentencing hearing, the veracity of Dr. Nelson's diagnosis of Mental Retardation was hotly contested.

At the time of the hearings, the fourth edition of the *Diagnostic and Statistical Manual of Mental Disorders*, (DSM-IV; American Psychiatric Association, 1994) served as the basis for mental disorder diagnoses in courts of law. Diagnosis of Mental Retardation under DSM-IV required the finding of three characteristics. As mentioned earlier, these are valid measurement of an IQ below around 70,[6] impairment in more than one area of daily functioning, and onset of the problems before the age of 18. The prosecution would attack Dr. Nelson's diagnosis on each of the three diagnostic criteria. Dr. Nelson had himself admitted in court that Atkins's performance on the IQ test would likely have been better were it not for "depression" he was suffering due to the trial proceedings. The doctor had also explained that Mr. Atkins met diagnostic criteria for Antisocial Personality Disorder, some key traits of which are manipulation and disregard for rules and law.

In addition, the prosecutors brought in their own expert witness, Stanton Samenow, PhD. Dr. Samenow testified that he "sharply disagreed" with the diagnosis of Mental Retardation, making the claim that Atkins was of at least average intelligence. While Dr. Samenow had not given Mr. Atkins a formal IQ test, he cited Atkins's use of complex words and knowledge of current events as evidence supporting this finding. Furthermore, Dr. Samenow stated that some of the questions he used to come to his conclusion were from formal psychological tests. Dr. Samenow elaborated on Atkins's history of poor motivation in academic settings, offering this as the reason for his seemingly limited mental abilities. Dr. Samenow also attacked the Mental Retardation diagnosis on the basis that Mr. Atkins's deficits in adaptive functioning did not extend beyond academic settings (the second diagnostic criterion). Again, Dr. Samenow

---

[6] Of interest here are the citations by the defense that Atkins had scored "below the 20th percentile in almost every standardized test he took (*Atkins v. Virginia*, p. 8, emphasis added)." By definition, an IQ below 70 represents mental ability at or below the 2nd percentile, significantly worse than 20th.

described a history in which Mr. Atkins *chose* not to excel, rather than lacked the capacity to do so (*Atkins v. Commonwealth of Virginia*, 2000).

After hearing this testimony and being instructed to consider the evidence of Mental Retardation as a mitigating factor, the jury again recommended imposition of the death penalty. Judge Prentis Smiley agreed, and Atkins was again sentenced to death. This time, on appeal, the Supreme Court of Virginia upheld the ruling that Daryl Atkins be put to death. While this was not the final word, it is of interest that Dr. Samenow, the prosecution's expert witness, was sharply (and very astutely) criticized by a Virginia Supreme Court Justice for giving Atkins questions from outdated psychological tests. (Dr. Samenow reported giving Atkins questions from the original versions of the Wechsler Memory Scale and Wechsler Adult Intelligence Test, while these tests were already into their second and third editions, respectively.) The Court intimated that this practice violated the ethical guidelines for forensic psychologists, a code by which Dr. Samenow was bound. Interestingly, the Court also specifically criticized Dr. Samenow for using "a test developed in 1939" (*Atkins v. Commonwealth of Virginia*, p. 10), referring to the Thematic Apperception Test, even though the 1939 version is still the one appropriate for use today. Nonetheless, the dissenting judge summarized, "Indeed, I am perplexed that Dr. Samenow, who did not administer a complete IQ test to the defendant and admittedly asked the defendant questions based upon bits and pieces of outdated tests to supposedly evaluate the defendant, would opine that this defendant possesses at least average intelligence" (p. 10). With regard to the defense's objection that a mentally retarded offender be executed, the Virginia Supreme Court cited the lack of clarity in diagnosis in its statement, "We are not willing to commute Atkins' sentence of death to life imprisonment merely because of his IQ score" (p. 7).

The U.S. Supreme Court agreed to hear the appeal of the *Atkins* case, and limited it to the specific issue of whether execution of mentally retarded offenders violates the Constitution's Eighth Amendment protection against cruel and unusual punishment. Ruling on the case on June 20, 2002, the court explicitly held that execution of mentally retarded offenders constituted cruel and unusual punishment. Invoking a previously held standard for deciding what constituted "cruel and unusual," in summary, Justice Stevens explained the Court's reversal of the *Penry* decision:

> Much has changed since *Penry*'s conclusion that the two state statutes then existing that prohibited such executions, even when added to the 14 States

that had rejected capital punishment completely, did not provide sufficient evidence of a consensus. Subsequently, a significant number of States have concluded that death is not a suitable punishment for a mentally retarded criminal, and similar bills have passed at least one house in other States. It is not so much the number of these States that is significant, but the consistency of the direction of change. Given that anticrime legislation is far more popular than legislation protecting violent criminals, the large number of States prohibiting the execution of mentally retarded persons (and the complete absence of legislation reinstating such executions) provides powerful evidence that today society views mentally retarded offenders as categorically less culpable than the average criminal. The evidence carries even greater force when it is noted that the legislatures addressing the issue have voted overwhelmingly in favor of the prohibition. Moreover, even in States allowing the execution of mentally retarded offenders, the practice is uncommon. (*Atkins v. Virginia*, 2002, p. 2)

The Court cited the relative lack of legislative response to the execution of 16- and 17-year-old criminals as making these reactions to the execution of mentally retarded offenders even more telling. America was not calling for decreasing the culpability of all offenders whose mental abilities were less than the average adult. The message was clearly specific to offenders with Mental Retardation. However, the Court made clear to that the ruling might not apply to all offenders who had ever received a Mental Retardation diagnosis, so long as the diagnosis itself could be disputed as a fact of law. The Court specified that the manner in which Mental Retardation is defined for the purposes of capital punishment exemption be left to each state. Thus, while the immediate effect of the ruling for Daryl Atkins was to reverse his death penalty, the Commonwealth of Virginia might choose to try him again. If, during the course of another trial, he was found (not by mental health professionals, but by jurors) not to be mentally retarded, he might again be sentenced to death (see Box 14.1).

FUTURE DIRECTIONS IN MENTAL RETARDATION LAW

There are areas of case law dealing with Mental Retardation that have not been covered in this chapter, and these issues will provide the grounds for future case law revisions. One such area may be the right of mentally retarded citizens to parent children. Another area may be refinement in the degree to which school systems must provide services to integrate students with Mental Retardation into normal classrooms.

BOX 14.1. Where Are They Now?

William Jones pleaded guilty in September 1988 to the abduction and robbery of Eric Nesbitt. In exchange for his testimony against Daryl Atkins, authorities agreed to drop all charges except the murder charge and one handgun charge. The prosecutors also agreed not to seek the death penalty against Jones. Jones was sentenced to life in prison, without the possibility of parole, for his role in the murder. At the time of this writing, he was listed as a resident at the Augusta Correctional Center near Stuarts Draft, a small town in Virginia's scenic Shenandoah Valley. Following the U.S. Supreme Court ruling, Daryl Atkins was moved from his cell on Virginia's death row at the Sussex I State Prison, not far from where the murder took place. As of the time of this writing, the Commonwealth of Virginia has not stated either way its future intentions for pursuing another trial.

The areas of law discussed in this chapter are subject to review and refinement in the future, for while institutionalized individuals with Mental Retardation have a constitutional right to the least restrictive and appropriate treatment available, the fact remains that the "least restrictive alternative" may be nothing more than a theoretical fantasy. Virtually every jurisdiction has a long waitlist of individuals for whom community-based treatment has been recommended. However, without increased funding for organizations to provide such treatment, the lists will only lengthen. The sad fact is that the term *least restrictive environment* has been practically redefined as "least restricted environment *currently available*." What may courts have to say about this state of affairs in the future? The ban on executions of mentally retarded offenders may also serve to increase rather than decrease activity in U.S. courts. The Supreme Court ruled that it was illegal to execute an offender who was mentally retarded *as a matter of law*. Thus, the validity of diagnoses are likely to be challenged more frequently and more thoroughly. Even in the *Penry* and *Atkins* cases, evidence was presented at trial that the diagnosis was unfounded.

To be sure, we have not seen the last courtroom debate regarding Mental Retardation. The only question that lingers is, "Where will we go from here?"

CASE REFERENCES

Atkins v. Commonwealth of Virginia, 260 Va. 375, 534 S.E.2d 312 (2000).
Atkins v. Virginia, 122 S. Ct. 2242; 2002 U.S. LEXIS 4648 (2002).

Halderman v. Pennhurst, 446 F. Supp. 1295; 1977 U.S. Dist. LEXIS 12200 (1977).

McCarver v. North Carolina, 533 U.S. 975; 2001 U.S. LEXIS 5345 (2001).

Olmstead v. L.C. by Zimring, 527 U.S. 581; 1999 U.S. LEXIS 4368 (1999).

Pennhurst v. Halderman, 451 U.S. 1; 1981 U.S. LEXIS 12 (1981).

Pennhurst v. Halderman, 465 U.S. 89; 1984 U.S. LEXIS 4 (1984).

Penry v. Johnson, 2001 U.S. LEXIS 4309; 69 U.S.L.W. 4402 (2001).

Penry v. Lynaugh, 487 U.S. 164 (1988).

Romeo v. Youngberg, 644 F.2d 147; 1980 U.S. App. LEXIS 11999 (1980).

Romeo v. Youngberg, 734 F.2d 7; 1984 U.S. App. LEXIS 23070 (1984).

University of Alabama v. Garrett, 531 U.S. 356 (2001).

Youngberg v. Romeo, 457 U.S. 307; 1982 U.S. LEXIS 128 (1982).

CHAPTER 15

Psychopathy and Antisocial Personality Disorder

Oh, he is a monster, a pure psychopath. So rare to capture one alive.

> —Dr. Chilton's description of Hannibal Lecter
> to Special-Agent-in-Training Clarice Starling
> in *The Silence of the Lambs*

. . . for psychopaths . . . , the social experiences that normally build a conscience never take hold. Without the shackles of a nagging conscience, they feel free to satisfy their needs and wants and do whatever they think they can get away with. Any antisocial act, from petty theft to bloody murder, becomes possible.

> —Robert Hare, *Without Conscience: The Disturbing
> World of the Psychopaths among Us* (pp. 75–76)

I picked prostitutes because I thought I could kill as many of them as I wanted without getting caught.

> —Gary Ridgeway, aka the Green River Killer, during his
> November 2003 guilty plea for the murders of 48
> women in Washington State in the 1980s. (Ridgeway's
> plea bargain spared him from execution.)

The general concept of Psychopathy has been written about for at least a century (Meyer, 2006). No doubt the concept itself has been recognized for significantly longer. However, relatively recent refinements in the measurement of the construct have opened it up to increased scientific scrutiny and application (Hare, 1996a). Moreover, legislation in the forms of community notification and civil commitment for sex offenders (each discussed in length in Chapter 18, this volume) has heightened the need for accurate risk assessments, a task to which the construct of Psychopathy[1] has proven particularly well suited. Psychopathy as discussed in the mental health literature (and in this chapter) does not parallel legal uses of the same term (Hart & Hemphill, 2003), and legal uses themselves are inconsistent across rulings and jurisdictions. However, increased reliance on the establishment of "mental disorder" by courts in sexual predation legislation may be moving us toward a common definition, because Psychopathy will undoubtedly play an important role in many sexual predation cases. In fact, U.S. society may be moving toward permanent detention of criminal psychopaths, but more on that later. For now, we begin with a discussion of how the assessment of Psychopathy got to where it is currently.

DEFINING THE CONSTRUCT: PSYCHOPATHY, SOCIOPATHY, OR ANTISOCIAL PERSONALITY?

Psychopathy, sociopathy, and antisocial personality are three labels that refer to the same basic syndrome, with subtle but very important distinctions. These distinctions can best be understood by tracing the evolution of the diagnosis from early writings to the way it is being used today.[2]

In about 1800, Philippe Pinel coined the term *manie sans délire* to reflect the fact that these individuals manifest extremely deviant behavior (*manie*) but show no evidence (*sans*) of delusions, hallucinations, or other cognitive disorders (*délire*). Late in the 19th century, Johann Koch introduced the label *psychopathic inferiority*, which became the accepted term.

One of the earliest published definitions of the psychopathic per-

---

[1] People are fairly familiar with the term *psychopath*, and its use in common language closely mirrors technical definitions. A psychopath is said to have "Psychopathy," much as an anxious person has anxiety. Psychopathy is not to be confused with *psychopathology*, which is a general term that is essentially synonymous with *mental illness*. Also similar is *psychosis*, a fairly broad subset of psychopathology characterized by loss of touch with reality (i.e., delusions and/or hallucinations). For instance, schizophrenia is a form of psychosis, and people with such a psychosis are described as psychotic.

[2] We have merely addressed enough of the historical development of the Psychopathy construct to illustrate its meaning. A much more detailed description is available in Millon, Simonsen, and Birket-Smith (1998).

sonality was that of Cleckley in 1941, who defined the sociopath by a list of 16 characteristics typically observed in these individuals:

1. Superficial charm and good "intelligence"
2. Absence of delusions and other signs of irrational thinking
3. Absence of "nervousness" or psychoneurotic manifestations
4. Unreliability
5. Untruthfulness and insincerity
6. Lack of remorse or shame
7. Inadequately motivated antisocial behavior
8. Poor judgment and failure to learn by experience
9. Pathological egocentricity and incapacity for love
10. General poverty in major affective reactions
11. Specific loss of insight
12. Unresponsiveness in general interpersonal relations
13. Fantastic and uninviting behavior with drink, and sometimes without it
14. Suicide rarely carried out
15. Sex life impersonal, trivial, and poorly integrated
16. Failure to follow any life plan

The first significant evolution in labeling the disorder reflected an evolution in beliefs about the etiology, or cause, of the disorder. *Psycho*path suggested a flaw internal to the person. The view that society was ultimately to blame was better conveyed by the term *socio*path. The original *Diagnostic and Statistical Manual of Mental Disorders* (DSM) labeled the disorder "sociopathic personality" to emphasize the American Psychiatric Association's belief that the origin of the disorder was primarily environmental. In DSM-II (1968), the American Psychiatric Association relabeled the disorder as Antisocial Personality Disorder. Individuals with Antisocial Personality Disorder (APD) were characterized as unsocialized, impulsive, guiltless, selfish, and callous persons who rationalize their behavior and fail to learn from experience. With this subjective definition, clinicians had difficulty making the diagnosis reliably. This complication in turn hindered research. Authors of the DSM-III-R (1987) increased the diagnostic reliability of APD by defining it more in terms of observable criminal behaviors. This definition has remained virtually unchanged in the current DSM-IV (1994) and DSM-IV-TR (2000). The American Psychiatric Association (2000), now generally defines APD as "a pervasive pattern of disregard for, and violation of, the rights of others that begins in childhood or early adolescence and continues into adulthood" (p. 701). The diagnostic list includes a number of behavioral indicators of these violations. This diagnostic method significantly improved the diagnostic reliability of the disorder but at the expense of construct validity. That is to say, the diagnosis no longer captured the people previously referred to as psychopaths.

A return to the traditional conceptualization of Psychopathy emerged from research conducted at the University of British Columbia. Robert Hare described psychopaths as actually making up a subset of individuals who are diagnosable with APD. From this research came the assessment instrument that has evolved into the current "gold standard" in Psychopathy assessment, the Psychopathy Checklist (PCL). The PCL used a definition that included both the behavioral aspects of APD and the personality characteristics originally spelled out by Cleckley. The original PCL included 22 items based on both Cleckley's list *and* DSM-III-R criteria for APD. The original PCL items are as follows (Hare et al., 1990):

1. Glibness/superficial charm
2. Grandiose sense of self-worth
3. Need for stimulation
4. Pathological lying
5. Conning/manipulative
6. Lack of remorse or guilt
7. Shallow affect
8. Callous/lack of empathy
9. Parasitic lifestyle
10. Poor behavioral controls
11. Promiscuous sexual behavior
12. Early behavior problems
13. Lack or realistic goals
14. Impulsivity
15. Irresponsibility
16. Failure to accept responsibility
17. Many short-term relationships
18. Juvenile delinquency
19. Revocation of conditional release
20. Criminal versatility
21. Previous diagnosis as a psychopath or similar
22. Drug or alcohol not direct cause of antisocial behavior

Many of the PCL items follow directly from Cleckley's list, such as lack of remorse or guilt. Other PCL items are more observable approximations of Cleckley's criteria. For example, the PCL-R's "grandiose sense of self-worth" and "many short-term relationships" follow respectively from Cleckley's "pathological egocentricity" and "incapacity for love."

For the revised version of the PCL (PCL-R), the last two items were discontinued because of their low correlations with PCL total scores and poor interrater reliability. This procedure resulted in the 20-item PCL-R (Hare, 1991). Each of the 20 items are rated on a scale from 0 (does not apply to this individual) to 2 (applies to this individual) by a clinician following a diagnostic interview and exhaustive collateral review of available data. The improved validity of PCL-defined Psychopathy over APD has actually played out in numerous research studies. For instance, prison inmates with high PCL scores are more likely to recidivate than nonpsychopathic inmates diagnosed with APD (Hare, 1996b).

The PCL-R items break down into two factors (Hare, 1991). Factor 1 (items 1, 2, 4, 5, 6, 7, 8, and 16) delineates core personality traits, and Factor 2 (items 3, 9, 10, 12, 13, 14, 15, 18, and 19) reflects chronic antisocial behavior (Harpur, Hakstian, & Hare, 1988; Hare et al., 1990). Research (Cooke & Michie, 2001)[3] further dividing each factor into two related facets (for a total of four facets) resulted in the publication of the second edition of the PCL-R (PCL-R2) by Hare in 2003.

The PCL-R2 represents the cutting edge of Psychopathy research and conceptualization today. But familiarization with the PCL's list of criteria does not underscore the impact that Psychopathy can have on an individual. Nor do the items begin to convey the impact a psychopath can have on his or her victims. As suggested in the first quote at the beginning of this chapter, the popular concept of the psychopath can be quite frightening, even entertaining. As the other opening quotes suggest, reality can be at least as chilling, a point further illustrated in the following case.

THE CASE OF JOHN WAYNE GACY[4]:
AN ILLUSTRATION OF PSYCHOPATHY IN A SERIAL MURDERER

Growing up in the suburbs of Chicago, John Wayne Gacy was always a sickly youth. His mother, a nurse by trade, insisted that he suffered from

---

[3] Cooke and Michie (2001) recommended a three-factor model, but only after rejecting the group of items retained in the PCL-R2 (Hare, 2003) as a fourth factor. Thus, they originally identified the fourth factor; they just did not use it.

[4] Information for the following case was gleaned from Sullivan and Maiken (1983).

a heart condition. While medical examination would later dispel the heart condition as myth, Gacy was eventually diagnosed with psychomotor epilepsy that included seizures and occasional blackouts. His mother started treating the seizures with prescription barbiturates when Gacy was around age 5. Gacy's abusive father consistently ridiculed him as "worthless" and "queer." Incidents including cross-dressing and awkward sexual encounters bolstered the concerns of both Gacy and his father. Gacy later recounted entertaining homosexual thoughts at an early age.

Gacy began his first job at age 14, delivering goods for a local grocery, and also established himself in several volunteer organizations. Never able to impress his father, these activities did earn him positive regard with local citizens and public officials alike. Nevertheless, the constant onslaught of verbal abuse from his father prompted Gacy to quit high school during his senior year and run away from home.

Gacy temporarily took up residence in Las Vegas, Nevada. He lost his job in a mortuary when some of the cadavers ended up mysteriously unclothed on mornings after which Gacy had worked the night shift. Having failed, Gacy returned home to Chicago after his father reluctantly agreed. After moving back home, Gacy took a business course at a local community college and got a job as a shoe salesman where his charming demeanor helped him excel. It was also during this time that he had his first homosexual experience. It would not be his last.

In 1964, Gacy married his first wife, Marlynn. Her father, owner of a chain of Kentucky Fried Chicken restaurants in Iowa, offered Gacy a managerial position. The couple lived fairly happily for the next few years; their son was born in 1966, and their daughter, a year later. Gacy even seemed to be getting along well at work and was establishing a positive reputation through his charitable work with a local organization. His favorite activity was entertaining sick children as Pogo the clown.

However, covert behavior, of which Gacy's family was not aware, was going on behind the scenes. Gacy had begun a series of homosexual relationships with young boys, including some of his own employees. One evening, Gacy boldly offered money in exchange for sexual favors to the 15-year-old son of a fellow community volunteer. The boy was unable to fight off Gacy's coercion. Overcome with guilt afterward, the boy told his father, who immediately reported the story to the police. The police searched Gacy's home but found nothing out of the ordinary, except for some pornographic videotapes hidden in Gacy's bedroom. Pessimistic about the likelihood of a conviction based entirely on the boy's self-report, the prosecutor was unwilling to follow up on the rape charge. However, the videotapes found in Gacy's home contained images of oral sex, an illegal act of sodomy in the conservative state of Iowa.[5] For his possession of the tapes, Gacy would stand trial on the charge of sodomy.

During the interim before trial, Gacy maintained his innocence. His wife stood by him, believing that the tapes were meant for their enjoyment together. Such behavior was familiar to the couple; they had engaged in frequent acts of "wife swapping" with other couples in the community. Despite his wife's support and the charges pending against him, Gacy continued his adulterous affairs with underage boys.

These affairs soon escalated into violence. During one encounter, Gacy tried to force one of his 16-year-old male employees to perform oral sex on him. When the young man objected, Gacy flew into a fit of rage. Before it was over, the boy found himself chained up and being choked. He survived and went to the authorities. But, again, police did not have enough evidence. Gacy denied the incident and proudly proclaimed that he would take a polygraph test. He did so and failed, twice. However, Gacy's positive public image and mere willingness to subject himself to the polygraph were enough to gain his support with most people in the community. But the problems were just beginning, and Gacy's wife was slowly losing faith in her husband.

Soon afterward, two more young men, ages 18 and 15, each reported that Gacy paid them for what he termed "sexual experiments being carried out by the Governor of Iowa." Shortly after those allegations were made, the legal system reared its lethargic head and Gacy was convicted of the original sodomy charge. He was sentenced to the maximum of 10 years in the Iowa State Penitentiary. On the day that the sentence was read, Gacy's wife filed for divorce. He would never see her or their two children ever again.

Pillar of the Community Imprisoned for Sodomy

While serving his time in prison, Gacy was the model prisoner. Psychological assessments documented an IQ of 118 ("high average") and a style of providing an excuse for every criminal accusation. His psychopathic traits had finally come under the scrutiny of professionals who

---

[5] Oral sex as criminal sodomy is discussed at length in Chapter 10, this volume. Until recently, such laws were actually very common and were not restricted to conservative jurisdictions.

knew what to make of them. Gacy would twist the truth and make it sound as if he were the victim, suggesting that he had no remorse whatsoever for the crimes he had committed against the young men. He was given a fitting diagnosis: APD. However, given his track record of community service and his "model inmate" status, the parole board quickly decided to give Gacy a second chance. The psychologists had recommended otherwise. Having successfully manipulated the Iowa system, Gacy promptly moved back to his hometown of Chicago.

Back in Chicago, and true to form, Gacy soon reestablished his "pillar of the community" status. He formed his own general contracting company and stayed quite busy. His reputation was as a loudmouth braggart, but he was always first at the scene to give a helping hand, and he treated his employees and patrons well. He paid almost double the hourly wage of most other jobs. Through such treatment, Gacy soon developed a network of young men with whom to engage in sexual activity. What people either did not recognize or simply did not connect to Gacy was that these young men were disappearing.

It was through one of his usual "work" encounters that Gacy met a young man named Rob Piest. Rob worked in a pharmacy where Gacy had been hired to do some remodeling. Rob was unhappy with his job, and told a friend and coworker that he was going to talk to Gacy about getting a new job. Piest went out the back door of the pharmacy, presumably to meet Gacy, and was never seen alive again. However, Piest, unlike the other young men with whom Gacy consorted, was from a caring, affluent family that pushed police to investigate the disappearance. The primary suspect was the last person to have contact with Piest: John Wayne Gacy.

The Police Investigation: Ferreting Out the Psychopath

During the ensuing investigation, Gacy again showed his true psychopathic colors, and the police were there to document it. Accounts of Gacy's behavior during the investigation read like a rundown of items on the PCL-R2 (Hare, 2003; see Box 15.1 for a sample scoring). He constantly tried to charm the officers into accepting favors from him, and he flaunted their appearance to others, claiming that they were his bodyguards. In his grandiosity, Gacy nagged the local officers to admit that they were really FBI agents.

Connecting Gacy to more and more missing young men, authorities believed they might be investigating multiple murders. Through their investigatory efforts, the police determined that Gacy frequently engaged

BOX 15.1. Sample PCL-R Scoring[6] for John Gacy

Item 1:   Glibness/Superficial Charm   Score: 2
Many people considered Gacy charming, and this helped his business, his advancement in civic organizations, and his ability to coerce young men. However, some characterized him as an insincere, boisterous braggart, suggesting a superficial quality to his charm.

Item 2:   Grandiose Sense of Self-Worth   Score: 2
Gacy's reputation as a braggart is also suggestive of his grandiosity. He boasted to friends that police following him were "personal bodyguards" and convinced himself that they must be "FBI" instead of local officers. Officers also noted a "press conference" quality to interviews.

Item 3:   Need for Stimulation/Proneness to Boredom   Score: 2
Gacy's chronic use of numerous illicit drugs and his participation in many activities supported a "life in the fast lane" quality. Officers' accounts of Gacy's routine when he was being followed suggested an almost a hypomanic quality, including very little sleep.

Item 4:   Pathological Lying   Score: 2
Gacy continuously lied to the officers assigned to follow him. Whenever officers countered his unlikely claims with factual information, Gacy was quick to put a slightly different spin on the story and lead the officers away from the original botched fabrication.

Item 5:   Conning/Manipulative   Score: 2
Gacy used deceit as an instrumental tool to achieve goals. This quality is particularly evident in Gacy's modus operandi for most of the murders. He also appeared very "cooperative" with the authorities at times, in an attempt to develop beneficial relationships with them.

Item 6:   Lack of Remorse or Guilt   Score: 2
When asked by police how he felt about conning, torturing, and killing the 27 young men, Gacy blamed his victims: "They shouldn't have tried to con me. I never killed anyone who didn't try to take advantage of me." He never apologized or admitted wrongdoing.

Item 7:   Shallow Affect   Score: 2
Gacy was apparently able to exhibit strong, pleasant emotions, and he certainly expressed extreme rage and anger. However, his emotions were often inconsistent with the situation, as in the "press conference" quality to his interviews while being investigated and arrested for murder.

(continued)

---

[6] This is a sample assessment scored solely from available reference materials and is for illustration purposes only. We did not conduct an actual clinical assessment of John Gacy, nor is this information drawn from any such assessment.

BOX 15.1. (continued)

Item 8:   Callous/Lack of Empathy   Score: 2
Gacy's participation in community organizations may demonstrate empathy, or may have been a way to meet potential victims. More relevant and observable was his willingness to blame his victims for their own murders and failure to recognize his negative impact on others.

Item 9:   Parasitic Lifestyle   Score: 0
Gacy was able to sustain gainful employment as the head of his own contracting company and was successful at several other jobs and positions.

Item 10:   Poor Behavioral Controls   Score: 2
Gacy was described by those close to him as short-tempered and hot-headed. He also threatened police, saying that his personal hitman would "take care of" the officers if they were too obtrusive. He was quick to calm down from rage but could not resist his impulse to murder.

Item 11:   Promiscuous Sexual Behavior   Score: 2
Gacy had sexual relations with the 27 young men he killed and numerous others. He had charges brought against him for sexual assault and was involved in "wife swapping."

Item 12:   Early Behavior Problems   Score: 0
Gacy's father was extremely overbearing and abusive. Gacy's reaction to this was to be extremely passive rather than acting out with behavioral problems.

Item 13:   Lack of Realistic, Long-Term Goals   Score: 0
The only argument that could possibly be made for this item was the difficulty Gacy encountered burying all of the bodies below his house. However, this item refers more to employment and life goals. General lack of forethought is addressed in the next item.

Item 14:   Impulsivity   Score: 2
In his disposal of the bodies, Gacy clearly lacked planning or forethought. Additionally, he never appeared to worry much about the legal ramifications of his actions. The killings themselves, while probably premeditated to an extent, seemed to be somewhat impulsive.

Item 15:   Irresponsibility   Score: 2
Gacy's sloppy construction work elicited many complaints from customers. He also showed no responsibility to his children and virtually no adherence to societal norms.

Item 16:   Failure to Accept Responsibility for Own Actions   Score: 2
Gacy was always ready with some excuse for his behavior, and he blamed his victims for causing him to murder them by making him mad.

BOX 15.1. (*continued*)

Item 17:   Many Short-Term Marital Relationships   Score: 1
Gacy had two marriages and at least one sustained and committed homosexual relationship. In the objective scoring for this item, three relationships warrant a score of 1.

Item 18:   Juvenile Delinquency   Score: 0
Gacy had no history of behavioral problems prior to adulthood.

Item 19:   Revocation of Conditional Release   Score: 0
Gacy was released under supervision but never had parole revoked.

Item 20:   Criminal Versatility   Score: 2
Gacy had numerous types of offenses, including theft, drug use, assault/murder, weapons possession, rape, DUI, kidnapping, and various other crimes.

---

young men in a particular "erotic" game, in which Gacy would handcuff the young men and act as if he were choking them with a rope that he twisted with a hammer. The authorities were suspicious that this game was the particularly manipulative and gruesome method Gacy used for his killings.

In the end, Gacy's pathological confidence in his ability to manipulate the authorities led to his demise. After inviting officers into his house, one of them noticed a putrid smell coming from the heat ducts. Police obtained a search warrant for Gacy's residence. What they found in the crawlspace below the house would shock the conscience of the entire country. Meticulously searching the three-foot space between the ground and floor joists above, police found the badly decomposed remains of a corpse in what looked like a small, shallow grave. Gacy had continued to live with this victim decomposing just a few feet from his living room. But the body was far too decomposed to be that of Rob Piest.

For days, neighbors and members of the press continued to watch body bag after body bag being taken from Gacy's home to the coroner's waiting van. In all, John Wayne Gacy was responsible for the deaths of the 27 young men buried under or around his home, and six others buried at various other locations. Among the dead was the tortured body of Rob Piest. True to his callous nature, Gacy later summarized for authorities how he felt about the killings: "They shouldn't have tried to con me. I never killed anyone who didn't try to take advantage of me" (Sullivan & Maiken, 1983).

Not surprisingly, Gacy did not fare well at trial. The crux of his attorney's argument throughout trial was that Gacy was too mentally ill to be given the death penalty. Prosecutor Bill Kunkle argued to the jury in closing arguments, "If this is not an appropriate case for the death penalty, then there *is* no death penalty in Illinois" (Sullivan & Maiken, 1983, p. 374). The jury agreed.

PSYCHOPATHY VERSUS INSANITY

A basic tenet of the U.S. legal system is that a person whose commission of a crime is largely caused by a mental disorder should be held less accountable for their actions. But what if that mental disorder is Psychopathy? If psychopathic individuals are as impulsive as research suggests, does that not constitute some explanation for any crime committed? If so, how is the legal system to deal with psychopathic offenders (Sales & Shuman, 2005).

While the Supreme Court has not ruled on this matter, lower courts have commented, although not always consistently. The driving conceptualization behind most rulings is that APD and Psychopathy represent deviations in character rather than disorders of the mind. This interpretation was first put forth with in the 1960s, when courts were vacillating on the appropriateness of tests for insanity between the *M'Naughten* rule and the newly proposed American Law Institute (ALI) rule (see Chapter 7, this volume). In the case of *U.S. v. Currens* (1961), the 3rd Circuit U.S. Court of Appeals rejected the *M'Naughten* rule on the basis that it emanated from a time "in which belief in witchcraft and demonology" (p. 15) dominated conceptualizations of mental illness. As such, the *Currens* Court favored the ALI approach.

As a basis, the ALI rule required the presence of a mental illness. Most relevant to the discussion here, it also included a "caveat paragraph," which stated that for a finding of not guilty by reason of insanity, the mental illness could not comprise only criminal conduct or antisocial behavior. While the *Currens* Court fully endorsed this caveat, it failed to hold that psychopaths were sane per se, deferring instead to the judgment of the jury or fact finder in each individual case.

In 1968, U.S. courts were somewhat divided on the issue. In *U.S. v. Smith*, the 6th Circuit Court of Appeals flat-out rejected the caveat paragraph of the ALI rule. However, that same year, in *U.S. v. Chandler*, the 4th Circuit Court of Appeals cautioned against such a rejection, stating, "Should the law extend its rule of immunity from its sanctions to all those persons for whose deviant conduct there may be some psychiatric explanation, the processes of the law would break down and society would be forced to find other substitutes for its protection" (p. 12). The 9th Circuit Court of Appeals sided with the *Smith* Court 2 years later in 1970, in *Wade v. U.S.*, flatly rejecting the caveat paragraph as essentially meaningless, since even a diagnosis of APD or Psychopathy would not be based solely on prior antisocial acts.

While federal courts continue to exclude the caveat paragraph from use, many state insanity laws do incorporate it. In either type of jurisdiction, defendants are not per se precluded from pleading insanity on the basis of APD or Psychopathy. However, such an attempt would be practically futile in the absence of at least a significant secondary mental disorder, rendering any "diagnosis" of Psychopathy effectively moot.

What then *is* the legal significance of Psychopathy in the courtroom? While its use as a mitigation of criminal responsibility is suspect, the construct is enjoying increased importance in one particular legal setting: the prediction of future dangerousness.

PREDICTIONS OF DANGEROUSNESS: THE INCREASING LEGAL IMPORTANCE OF PSYCHOPATHY

Clinical prediction of future violent behavior is having an increasingly profound impact on legal proceedings (Miller et al., 2005). A trend toward giving more weight to perceived dangerousness seems to be gaining ground in the U.S. legal system. With recent court decisions, sex offenders may be civilly committed until the time at which they are assessed and judged no longer to be a risk to reoffend (see Chapter 18, this volume). Given the poor rehabilitation prognosis of sexual offenders, this procedure could amount to indefinite removal from society for many of these individuals. In a similar manner, the enactment of sex offender registration laws in most jurisdictions has served effectively to deprive sex offenders of civil liberties beyond the duration of their initial imprisonment. These, and other laws like them, while enjoying public support, serve to underscore several legal and ethical issues related to the prediction of dangerousness. Is it ethical for individuals' civil liberties to be revoked or modified on the basis of a crime they have not yet committed? Is this perhaps a forfeiture that one makes upon committing a violent crime? These laws are but a glimpse of the myriad issues with which society must strike a balance.

It is in making predictions of future risk that the construct of Psychopathy has much to offer. An overview of the research on the matter drives home the increasing legal importance of not only the construct itself but also its accurate and ethical measurement and presentation in court.

The PCL-R and Risk Assessment Research

From early on, the original PCL showed promise over currently available methods of assessment in the prediction of general and violent recidivism (Serin, Peters, & Barbaree, 1990; Hart, Kropp, & Hare, 1988). Studies regarding recidivism rates and PCL-R scores suggest a strong relationship between Psychopathy and several different recidivism outcome measures. Psychopathy has been shown to be predictive of general recidivism, and violent recidivism (Hemphill, Hare, & Wong, 1998), both sexual (Porter et al., 2000; Rice & Harris, 1997; Serin, Malcolm, Khanna, & Barbaree, 1994; Hall & Hirschman, 1991) and nonsexual (Hart & Dempster, 1997). And research is now demonstrating that Psychopathy's predictive ability may generalize to younger offenders (Forth & Burke, 1998; Forth, Hart, & Hare, 1990) and to European populations (Grann, Langstrom, Tengstrom, & Kullgren, 1999).

A rather significant line of research has specifically addressed the role of the Psychopathy construct in violent acts that are impulsive (i.e., reactive or spur-of-the-moment) versus those that are instrumental in nature (i.e., to silence a witness or to meet sexual needs). Crimes committed by psychopathic individuals have been shown to be more characteristic of instrumental violence (Williamson, Hare, & Wong, 1987), but individuals who engage in increased instrumental violence also show increased involvement in impulsively violent acts (Cornell et al., 1996). Psychopathy does appear to be able to predict whether or not an offender has ever engaged in an instrumentally violent act (Cornell et al., 1996), and there is some evidence that Factor 1 scores are particularly predictive (Dempster, Lyon, Sullivan, Hart, Smiley, & Mulloy, 1996, as cited in Hart & Dempster, 1997). Given this new data, Hart and Dempster then make the claim that a "prototypical psychopath—one who manifests the full range of psychopathic symptomology—tends to be impulsively instrumental" (p. 227). Thus, the prototypical psychopath will utilize violent measures to achieve a goal in the absence of excessive external motivation to do so. Violent means are merely another option that the psychopath has in his or her repertoire of instrumental behaviors.

Several reviews and studies have addressed the comparative violent recidivism rates of high, low, and mixed Psychopathy groups. One particular method for assigning group membership was to designate those with PCL-R scores lower than 17 as nonpsychopaths, those with scores of 30 or higher (this is the typical cutoff score for a PCL-R "diagnosis" of Psychopathy) as psychopaths, and anyone scoring between 17 and 29 inclusive as "mixed" (Serin & Amos, 1995). Violent recidivism rates were reported to be anywhere from two to five times higher for psychopathic versus nonpsychopathic groups, and in the Serin and Amos study, a cutoff score of 30 provided for 80% correct classification of violent recidivism. Much smaller differences were found between the predictive validity of mixed and nonpsychopathic groups than between that of mixed and psychopathic groups (Hemphill et al., 1998; Serin, 1996; Serin & Amos, 1995). This increased similarity between mixed and nonpsychopathic groups tends to lend credence to the validity of Psychopathy as an actual "illness," as has other research (Rice, 1997). Not only has research supported the hypothesis that psychopaths are more prone than nonpsychopaths to violent recidivism, but they are also likely to experience recidivism more quickly upon release than are nonpsychopathic and mixed groups (Serin & Amos, 1995).

Psychopathy, as measured by the PCL-R, has also shown predictive ability over and above that of various other predictors. Studies assessing this phenomenon have researched the PCL in conjunction with criminal history of both a nonviolent (Harris, Rice, & Cormier, 1991) and a violent (Harris, et al., 1991; Serin, 1996) nature, as well as a number of demographic variables (Hart et al., 1988). While research also indicates that various mentally disordered presentations are predictive of violence (Rice & Harris, 1995; Calcedo-Barba & Ordonez, 1994; Link & Stueve, 1994), studies concurrently assessing the roles of mental disorder and Psychopathy demonstrated the PCL-R's unique predictive utility beyond mental health factors (Rice & Harris, 1995; Rice, Harris, & Cormier, 1992), including APD (Grann et al., 1999; Serin, 1996; Harris et al., 1991).

Given the predictive capabilities of Psychopathy and the PCL-R, we have only seen the beginning of the importance of Psychopathy assessment in court. While Psychopathy is not currently recognized as an official diagnosis in the American Psychiatric Association's DSM-IV-TR, it may become one of the most important labels with respect to sex offender registration laws and sex offender civil commitments. Yet there are limits on imposing on individuals legal ramifications for their status (i.e., status of being an alcoholic; see Chapter 13, this volume). With the possible exception of drug addictions, no other diagnosis impacts upon the legal system in the manner and to the degree as Psychopathy. We may see, in the near future, higher courts directly addressing the role of Psychopathy in the U.S. legal system.

CASE REFERENCES

U.S. v. Chandler, 393 F.2d 920; 1968 U.S. App. LEXIS 7445 (1968).

U.S. v. Currens, 290 F.2d 751; 1961 U.S. App. LEXIS 4649 (1961).

U.S. v. Smith, 404 F.2d 720; 1968 U.S. App. LEXIS 4760 (1968).

Wade v. U.S., 426 F.2d 64; 1970 U.S. App. LEXIS 10089 (1970).

Violent Criminals
and Violent Crime

In Part VI, we delve into legal cases that are pertinent to violent criminal offenses. In Chapter 16, we address a misunderstood area in which knowledge gained from mental health research may be used to track down an offender based upon the methodology used in his or her crimes. In Chapter 17, we present a history of capital punishment, from its roots in the earliest of legal "code" to recent decisions of the U.S. Supreme Court. The section closes with Chapter 18 on sex offenders, a controversial area that is frequently the topic of nightly newscasts across the nation.

CHAPTER 16

Criminal Psychological Profiling

Perhaps no other aspect of forensic mental health has captured the imagination of the public, the media, and entertainment industries more than has psychological profiling. Profiling is very much a field in its infancy, with little agreement between reality and media portrayals, and not much better agreement among those who practice profiling on even the most basic issues. That being said, it seems important to begin with the first known case demonstrating the application of profiling in an investigation. This account also remains one of the more sensational and successful examples.

THE CASE OF THE MAD BOMBER

In New York City in 1940, a merger of smaller power companies had recently formed the Consolidated Edison Electric Company, or "Con Ed." That year, an odd package wrapped in newspaper and bound with string was found in a Con Ed building and turned over to police. Authorities determined that the package was an unexploded "dud" bomb. A similar device was found about a year later.

Over the next 16 years, more than 30 of the bombs (not all of them duds) would be placed around the city, but not before an odd (if not patriotic) moratorium. At the outset of World War II, police headquarters received a letter stating that the bombings would stop during the war. In the interim, the bomber continuously taunted investigators with letters that included paranoid rants about "The Consolidated Edison," as he referred to the company. As promised, the bombing resumed shortly after the war's end.

By the early 1950s, targets of the bomber included such landmarks as Grand Central Station, the New York Public Library, and various subway buildings. All bombs were wrapped in newspaper and tied with similar string, details that are currently known as the crime's "signature." The media dubbed the bombings the work of the "Mad Bomber." In 1956, the Mad Bomber completed his 17th "successful" bombing, when an explosion injured six people at the Paramount Theater in Brooklyn.

Letters continued to arrive at police headquarters. They included detailed information that could only be known to the bomber and suggested that the bomber was either a Con Ed employee or, more likely, a disgruntled ex-employee. However, the company's personnel files from the relevant time period were a jumble of various filing systems from the smaller companies that had merged into Con Ed. Despite evidence from each crime scene and the plethora of letters received by both police and local media, the investigators had absolutely no suspects. In the face of public pressure to make an arrest, the authorities took the unusual move of consulting with Dr. James Brussell, a psychiatrist, who at that time was serving as the city's Commissioner of Mental Hygiene. Dr. Brussell was known and trusted by the police, who thought he might be able to help given the pathological rants evident in the letters.

Dr. Brussell agreed to take a look at all of the evidence. After examining descriptions of each incident and each of the bomber's letters, Dr. Brussell offered investigators a description of the man he thought they were seeking. He suspected that the bomber was Roman Catholic, about 50 years old, and of eastern European decent. The bomber suffered from paranoia and likely a chronic physical ailment. He would be unmarried and living with a female relative. Moreover, predicted Dr. Brussell, the bomber wanted to be caught. Brussell's boldest prediction: When the bomber was eventually caught, he would be wearing a double-breasted suit, buttoned. Dr. Brussell suggested that contacting the bomber through the newspaper might draw a response from him.

Newspapers began to plead with the bomber to clarify his grievances with Con Ed. He responded with a letter stating that he had been injured in a plant accident; more importantly, he provided the specific date of the accident. Further investigation provided authorities with the file of an employee of one of the smaller original companies who was injured on the specified date. The employee's name was George Metesky and he was found residing in Connecticut. Subsequent letters corroborated Metesky's identity as the Mad Bomber.

In the aftermath of the case, police denied that Dr. Brussell's profile had had any impact on the investigation. However, at the very least, Metesky fit Dr. Brussell's profile to an uncanny degree (see Table 16.1). Metesky was a 53-year-old Roman Catholic of eastern European decent. He was later diagnosed with paranoia and tuberculosis (a chronic physical ailment), and he lived with two sisters. When police arrived at his home to arrest him, they found bomb-making paraphernalia on the premises. Metesky, dressed in street clothes, then provided authorities with an immediate confession. He was so polite and cooperative that police agreed to his request to go up to his room to change clothes before they took him in. When he emerged from the stairwell, he was wearing a double-breasted suit—buttoned.

SERIAL CRIME AND THE REFINEMENT OF PSYCHOLOGICAL PROFILING

The refinement of profiling coincided with increased focus of law enforcement and media on serial crime in the 1960s and 1970s. When an offender commits a series of crimes with breaks between offenses,[1] he or she is said to be a serial offender. The crime itself can be anything from murder to theft. While we most commonly hear of serial murder or rape, other crimes, such as serial bombings or arson, may also be the focus of profiling. Serial crime was acknowledged little before the 1970s. However, there is no way to know whether serial crime was less prevalent before then, or whether law enforcement agencies simply did not have the technology to track and thus recognize serial criminals in the same way they can today.

In serial crime, information from multiple crime scenes is available and needs to be incorporated into a unitary investigation. This information can demonstrate trends in the offender's behavior (i.e., escalating violence, increasing boldness) that can help predict future behavior and give insight into psychological functioning. The repeated offenses suggest some sort of compulsion at work, increasing the potential relevance

---

[1] When a series of crimes is committed without an appreciable break between them, the crime is considered a "spree" crime rather than a serial crime. Varying opinions exist regarding what constitutes an "appreciable" break, a question that itself would make for interesting research.

TABLE 16.1. George Metesky's Fit with Dr. Brussell's Profile

Brussell's Profile	George Metesky
Roman Catholic	Roman Catholic
About 50 years old	53 years old
Of eastern European decent	Of eastern European decent
Suffered from paranoia	Later diagnosed with paranoia
Likely a chronic physical ailment	Had tuberculosis
Unmarried	Never married
Living with a female relative	Lived with two sisters
Would be caught wearing a buttoned, double-breasted suit	Put on buttoned, double-breasted suit before leaving with police

of psychological expertise. The repetition also means that investigation of the initial crime failed to capture the perpetrator, at least for as long as it took him or her to reoffend. In such cases, authorities may seek the assistance of a criminal profiler to augment the investigatory techniques already being used on the case.

The Federal Bureau of Investigation (FBI) was the first agency to invest sizable effort into developing a methodology for psychological profiling. In the interest of making the technique more widely available, the FBI diversified into offering profiles to assist other law enforcement agencies, and eventually to teaching non-FBI agents to develop their own profiles.

WHAT IS CRIMINAL PSYCHOLOGICAL PROFILING?

There are two kinds of psychological profiles, each constructed in different ways. In the first, the profiler may study details of the case (possibly including crime scene photos and descriptions of the offense and victim) and offer a description of the type of offender who has likely committed the crime. In the second method, a general profile may be constructed of the typical person who supposedly commits a certain *type* of crime. For example, the FBI may gather information about all serial arson cases with which they have worked. From this data, they may be able to spot certain common characteristics (i.e., most or all were white males age 20–30, with a history of fascination with fire). In this manner, the FBI may compose a profile for typical serial arsonists. The brief history of case law on psychological profiling suggests that courts have yet to observe this distinction. Thus, even reviews on the subject fail to delineate the distinction, and courts cite as precedent cases involving one type, while their case at hand involves the other.

There are several ways in which an accurate psychological profile may benefit law enforcement efforts. Some of the primary goals of profiling include identifying both demographic (i.e., race, age, etc.) and psychological (i.e., controlling, easily humiliated, reclusive) characteristics of the offender; predicting items that the offender may have in his or her possession (i.e., "souvenirs" of victims' jewelry, photos of victims) that may be listed on search warrants; and providing suggestions for interview/interrogation tactics that may work best with the offender (i.e., play into his or her inflated ego; Holmes & Holmes, 1996). There are also ways in which an inaccurate profile may hinder an investigation. An inaccurate profile may divert the focus away from proper suspects (i.e., predicting an offender in his early 20s, causing the police to miss the actual offender, who is in his late 40s).

Both types of profiling employ the practice of applying tenets (or beliefs) about known offenders to new cases in which the offender is not known. An example of such a belief is that serial murderers tend to pick victims within their own ethnicity. This and many other tenets largely grew from research conducted by the FBI in the early stages of profiling development in the 1970s. This research consisted almost exclusively of interviews of known offenders. Thus, the researchers recognized, for instance, the pattern that most violent serial offenders shared a common ethnicity with their victims. From this observation came the tenet, "Serial offenders kill within their own race." From this tenet flows the practice of profiling an unknown offender as being of the same race as his or her victims. Other tenets were developed and applied in similar manners (Schechter, 2003).

At first blush, this reasoning seems straightforward, but potential problems exist with the application of this logic. Take, for example, the following: People tend to consort with other people who are similar to them, and it is not uncommon for neighborhoods to be populated with people who are similar to each other. Police are more likely to make an arrest when the offender has some link to the victim (and is thus more likely similar to the victim[2]) than when there is no way initially to link a perpetrator to the victim. When there is no link between victim and per-

---

[2] The type of "link" we refer to here may be quite simple. For instance, living in the same neighborhood would be a sufficient link for victim and perpetrator to have an increased likelihood of similarity. It is not necessary for the two to be more closely related, or even known to each other, for this argument to apply.

petrator, the perpetrator may be more likely to elude detection and stay free. Free criminals cannot be researched by interviewing known offenders (since they are *unknown* offenders). Thus, perpetrators who are similar to their victims may be overrepresented in a sample of prisoners who got caught (but were available for research). Perpetrators who are unlike their victims may not be nonexistent, they may just be nonresearched.

PROFILING PRACTITIONERS
AND THE STATE OF THE SCIENCE

Most profilers are professional law enforcement personnel, with a few others coming from academic backgrounds such as criminology and sociology. It may come as somewhat of a shock to would-be forensic psychologists that criminal profiling will represent a minute to nonexistent component of their professional careers. The vast majority of forensic mental health practitioners have nothing to do with criminal profiling, with many writing the practice off as unscientific and a stretch on the bounds of ethical mental health practice. Indeed, the practice of profiling is founded largely on case study research. As discussed earlier, there are problems when this type of research alone provides the foundation for an entire practice. Thus, profiling would certainly benefit from an increase in methodologically sound research based on principles of offender and personality psychology.

Complicating the research issue, professionals in the field have yet to agree on standards for teaching, credentialing, and practice. In his recent text on profiling, Brent Turvey (2002) summarized how the scientific inquiry that is needed for the field to grow is being hindered by disagreements among profiling practitioners:

> The nature of these ego-based disagreements in the criminal profiling community has been at times civil, at times belligerent, and at times openly vicious. They have caused hurt feelings along individual and agency lines, as well as between the academic, mental health, and law enforcement communities. The unending byproduct has been a pathological failure of practicing criminal profilers to resolve interprofessional, interpersonal, and/or inter-agency differences and communicate effectively with each other. The competent minds involved in the work are often unable to appreciate each other due to the egos of their supervisors, or their own personal pride. The incompetent are deeply concerned about the very real fear of being exposed as a fraud and protect themselves by hiding their methods by being obscure or intellectual. (p. xvii)

Despite the problems with psychological profiling, there are compelling cases in which profiles seem to have provided a significant contribution to a criminal investigation. Just as it would be ludicrous for any law enforcement investigation to proceed solely on the basis of a psychological profile, so too would it be ridiculous to abandon the practice in its entirety.

Much of the literature (including case law) on psychological profiling tends to focus on cases in which the profile was helpful to an investigation, or at least turned out to be accurate after the offender was caught. We are much less likely to hear of instances in which the profile was inaccurate (as in the Virginia sniper case in 2002) and possibly hindered the investigation. If an offender is never caught, there is no way to know whether the profile has led the investigation astray, or whether there is some other reason why an offender has not been apprehended.

Thus, we believe researching psychological profiling demands special attention to cases in which the profile was incorrect. When an accurate profile leads to the apprehension of an offender, the sensational accounts that follow can color our perceptions of the practice as a whole. We offer this critical approach not as a means of "debunking" the practice, but rather a means of stimulating further improvement in profiling methods.

CASE LAW ON PSYCHOLOGICAL PROFILING

Case law has addressed the appropriateness of profiling in two distinct phases of the legal process: use in initial investigation, and as evidence at trial. In a criminal investigation, police must establish "probable cause" to investigate an individual legally (i.e., with surveillance or property searches). Courts have generally ruled that criminal profiles are legally sufficient for establishing probable cause for investigating someone who fits the profile. These cases typically involve profiles conducted specifically for that investigation and include a Colorado Court of Appeals case (*People v. Genrich*, 1996). The second type of precedent case involves limitations placed upon the admissibility of profile evidence in court. Courts are more divided in this type of case, which typically involves instances in which general profiles are offered by the prosecution. Many have ruled that the profile essentially constitutes inadmissible character evidence, unnecessarily tying many assumed characteristics to the person. Examples of cases limiting admissibility of profile testimony include cases from Ohio (*State v. Haynes*, 1988) and Georgia (*Penson v. State*,

1996; Ingram, 1998). However, the Pennsylvania State Supreme Court has even suggested that profile evidence may establish enough connection between separate murders to introduce information about a prior crime at trial (*Commonwealth v. Hawkins*, 1993).

A case that addresses both the use of a profile during an investigation, and admissibility at trial is *Pennell v. State of Delaware* (1991). While the case holds somewhat limited precedent value, having not made it to the U.S. Supreme Court, the sentiments expressed by both Delaware courts are echoed in rulings from various other jurisdictions.

The Case of *Pennell v. State of Delaware* (1991): Profile "Fit" Establishes Probable Cause to Investigate

Shirley Ellis was plying her trade as a prostitute, walking the street on a cold November evening in her Delaware hometown. Up pulled a dark-blue panel van; the driver invited her to come closer. Shirley and the man eventually agreed upon a price, and the two headed in the van toward a secluded area. The deal did not go as planned for Shirley. She was bound and gagged with duct tape, and was brutally tortured by the stranger. He pinched her breasts with pliers and beat her about the head with a hammer. Shirley died of strangulation and multiple blunt-force traumas to the head. Her partially clothed body was found on November 29, 1987, at construction site. Her body was covered with bruises and cuts from the torture.

That following summer, another prostitute named Catherine DiMauro was walking the streets near the area where Shirley Ellis had disappeared over 6 months earlier. Like Shirley, Catherine was visited by the man in the blue van, and like Shirley, her ride in the stranger's van would be her last. On June 29, 1988, New Castle County Police detective James Hedrick received a call that Catherine's body had been found at the Fox Run construction site. Arriving at the scene, Hedrick saw her nude, tortured, lifeless body, with the ligature marks around her neck suggesting that she had been strangled. The near absence of blood at the scene and tire tracks leading up to the body suggested that the killer had done his work elsewhere and had come to the construction site only to dispose of the body. The medical examiner later removed numerous blue fibers from Catherine's body. The causes of death were listed as strangulation and multiple blunt-force head traumas.

Detective Hedrick learned of Shirley Ellis's strikingly similar murder case that the Delaware State Police were investigating. When the investigating officers compared notes on the two cases, it became evident that there was a serial predator loose who was targeting prostitutes. An inter-agency task force was formed to investigate the murders. An undercover operation was started that June, in which female police officers posed as prostitutes. The task force had little evidence to go on, and they requested a psychological profile from the FBI's Investigative Support Unit. Special Agent Steve Mardigian constructed the profile, predicting that the of-fender was a white male between ages 25 and 35, employed in the con-struction trades, who lived near where the bodies were found. Most omi-nously, the profile stated that the killer would likely continue killing until he was stopped.

Police issued warnings about the murders to local prostitutes. As of yet, authorities did not have enough information to warn the women about any specifics. Many of the prostitutes continued working in small groups for safety. When the next victim, Margaret Finner, turned up in late August, witnesses were able to connect Margaret to the blue van. Police now had a description of a vehicle. Also back from the crime labo-ratory were the blue fibers found on the body of Catherine DiMauro. The fibers were consistent with blue carpet fibers that might be found in a vehicle.

The police were closing in, but not before the killer claimed Michelle Gordon as his fourth victim. Recovered from a local canal, Michelle's badly decomposed body provided little evidence. The killer was getting better at covering his tracks.

On the evening of September 14, 1988, Steven Pennell left his modest trailer home and got into his blue panel van to cruise for pros-titutes. He negotiated a deal with a prostitute but dropped her off at a convenience store before performing his regular acts on her. She was perhaps Delaware's luckiest prostitute that evening. As Pennell drove away, neither he nor the woman noticed the unmarked sedan pulling out behind.

Later that evening, Renee Lano was walking nearby on Route 40. She was relatively new to the Delaware prostitution scene, having only been there since June. She knew all about the missing girls and contin-ued to walk the streets despite the danger. She had noticed a blue van cruising past her several times. Staying in a fairly well-lit area made many cruisers avoid her, so she eventually moved into a darker, more secluded area. Eventually, the driver of the blue van braved a conversa-tion, pulling to the curb in front of Renee. The driver beckoned her nearer. As she stepped up to the van, she noticed the blue carpet. Stand-ing in the door, she teased the stranger with her conversation, telling him she had a headache and haggling over prices. This man was different from the others Renee had encountered in her walks along Route 40. He was much more sullen and serious, and he made her very uneasy. The stranger asked Renee if she was a police officer, to which she replied, "No." She was lying.

Officer Renee Lano had been recruited as a prostitute decoy by the team investigating the serial murders. She had been briefed on the FBI profile. She knew that Margaret Finner had last been seen getting into a dark-blue panel van, and she knew that blue vehicle carpet fibers had been found on Catherine DiMauro's body. Officer Lano had been in the unmarked car following the van earlier that evening. From the license check they had run when the van dropped off the unknown prostitute at the convenience store, she knew the driver to be Steve Pennell. Maintaining her rapport with Pennell, Officer Lano gently pressed him for information. He related to her that he was in his early 30s and employed in construction. Pennell fit the FBI profile. Standing in the doorway of the van, Officer Lano decided that she had what she needed, almost. She pretended to be dissatisfied with Pennell's price offer. Stepping out of the doorway, Officer Lano reached down and plucked a few strands of blue carpet fiber from the van's door. This split-second decision would prove a crucial part of the investigation and almost its demise. Walking off as Pennell pulled away, Officer Lano radioed back to her surveillance team, "It's him."

Laboratory results indicated that the blue fibers obtained by Officer Lano were microscopically indistinguishable from those found on the body of Catherine DiMauro. Police now had someone upon whom to focus their investigation. Pennell was placed on 24-hour surveillance. He was observed repeatedly cruising the area of highway where he had encountered Officer Lano. On September 30, 1988, officers pulled Pennell over for a traffic violation. A resulting search of the blue van yielded a bloodstain. Subsequent search warrants for Pennell's property yielded a knife, eight pairs of pliers, a bag of unused flexicuffs, and rolls of specialized duct tape, similar to that found on some of the bodies.

Pennell was arrested and charged with the first-degree murders of Shirley Ellis and Catherine DiMauro. Local and national pretrial publicity made it difficult to seat a jury for the case. Finally, the trial began on September 26, 1989, and the prosecution sought the death penalty. During the 2-month trial, DNA and fiber evidence linked Pennell to Catherine DiMauro, and FBI profiler John Douglas testified that the unusual nature of the wounds on each victim suggested that they were all killed by the same person. Ultimately the jury convicted Pennell for both murders,[3] sentencing him to die by lethal injection.

The rulings were appealed to the Delaware Superior Court and ultimately to the Delaware State Supreme Court. In both cases, the defense argued that Office Lano had no probable cause to grab the carpet fibers from Pennell's van. The defense reasoned that since the fibers were seized illegally, all subsequent evidence was also illegal "fruit of the poisonous tree." Were the defense's argument successful, all evidence would be thrown out, and Pennell would go free on the legal technicality. Each Court eventually held that the seizures were constitutional, due in large part to the psychological profile. Pennell himself had provided Officer Lano with personal information that fit the profile, thus providing her with probable cause to seize the fibers as evidence. The seizure of the fibers was not "unreasonable."[4]

Another challenge was leveled against the initial rulings on the basis that FBI profiler John Douglas's testimony at trial improperly introduced information from the profile. The defense argued that profile evidence was inadmissible, because the technique did not meet the *Frye* requirements for the admissibility of expert testimony (see Chapter 2, this volume.) The Delaware State Supreme Court claimed that Douglas's testimony was based on his experience in his field; thus, it was not subject to the *Frye* test. The Court did, however, acknowledge that to have entered profile evidence would have constituted inadmissible evidence as Pennell would have been "in a sense, being accused by a witness who was not present at any of the crimes." The State Supreme Court ultimately decided that Douglas had adequately avoided discussing the offi-

---

[3] Pennell later plead "no contest" to the murder of Michelle Gordon. He was never charged in the death of Margaret Finner. This is an example of a common practice in which some criminal acts are not initially charged, but rather are saved in the event that something goes wrong with the initial prosecution. Even if a perpetrator is released from the current charges, he or she could immediately be placed under arrest for the remaining crime(s).

[4] Both Courts held that the reasonable nature of the search was supported by the profile *and* eyewitness reports of one of the victims being seen getting into a van similar to Pennell's. Interestingly, FBI Agent John Douglas recounts in his best-selling book that the profile initiated the suspicion of the perpetrator driving a van. He suggested that the undercover operation initially focused upon drivers of vans because of the profile rather than the eyewitness accounts (Douglas & Olshaker, 1995). Yet court records fail to reflect this version of the story. We may never know whether the courts would have upheld the undercover operation based, at least initially, solely on a profile.

cial profile. Douglas had stuck, the Court found, to discussing the crimes' unifying "signature," which provided a crucial link between victims.

The Impact of *Pennell* on the Practice of Profiling

The Delaware State Supreme Court ruled that profile evidence would have been inadmissible at trial, since it would have constituted an accusation by a "witness who was not present at any of the crimes." This logic is similar to sentiments expressed in other rulings regarding the admissibility of profile evidence. The general sentiment is that profile evidence introduced into court would constitute inadmissible character evidence, since it comes from a witness who does not know the defendant. At the same time, profiling has been defended by numerous courts, albeit not yet the U.S. Supreme Court, as being appropriate evidence for probable cause for surveillance and property search.

DEMYSTIFYING THE PSYCHOLOGICAL PROFILE

Both cases in this chapter include profiles that turned out to be very accurate. It is just this kind of case that provides the media with fuel for sensationalism and provides some professionals with a rationale for dogmatically eluding scientific scrutiny. Is there a rational explanation for how profilers can come up with such an accurate profile? A critical look at the available information provides some insight.

Developing the Profile: Specialized Training, Omniscience, or Just Plain Common Sense?

A process that sometimes gets lost in the storytelling is the development of the profile. The prediction that an offender will be wearing "a double-breasted suit, buttoned" quite sensational. The entertainment industry exacerbates this problem with fictional "profilers" who use dreams, visions, and other paranormal phenomena to catch their quarry. Rest assured, there is a simpler explanation.

Pennell's court records provide a relatively simple example for examination. Recall that the profile stated that authorities were most likely looking for a white male between ages 25 and 35, employed in the construction trades, who lived nearby, and that the killer would keep killing. The FBI knew from its research that most serial killers are white males, and most kill within their own ethnicity. The crimes were fairly "sophisticated" in that the killer had made arrangements to have the necessary tools and seclusion to torture the women, and was comfortable enough to spend some time with them. This sophistication tended to rule out an offender younger than age 25. Violent behavior decreases, even in some of the most violent offenders, after the age of 35. The use of a hammer, pliers, and duct tape, and the dumping of the bodies in construction sites suggested someone familiar with the construction trades. Killers often dump bodies in areas within which they are relatively comfortable, so the proximity of the two bodies suggested that the offender either lived or worked nearby. The women were not sexually assaulted, suggesting that the perpetrator killed them for the sake of killing, not to hide a rape or other infraction. In short, there was no real motive. Offenders who commit multiple, motiveless murders are not likely to stop.

How, then did Dr. Brussell come up with his predictions in the Mad Bomber case? To begin with, Dr. Brussell knew the age when paranoia peaks (35) and added the 16 years the bomber was active, yielding a perpetrator in his 50s. Furthermore, most bombers to that date had been males of eastern European decent. And most eastern Europeans were Roman Catholic. Metesky's letters, which used fanciful wording, suggested that the author wrote not from experience in social interactions but from reading books. Reasoning that the bomber had a significant mental illness, Dr. Brussell predicted that the bomber might live with a female relative, who would be more likely to take care of him. What about for the most famous of his predictions: the double-breasted suit, buttoned? The meticulous attention to detail in the creation and packaging of the bombs suggested a suit over street clothes, and that it would be buttoned. The rigidity of the bomb construction over the entire course of the bombings suggested unwillingness to change, hence the double-breasted suit that was about 3 years out of style at the time.

Thus, the profiles of the Mad Bomber and Steve Pennell were developed through a rational application of existing knowledge to the evidence at hand. To the extent that profilers' knowledge is guided by accurate research, they engage in a logical process with a scientific basis and reasonable odds of success. And therein lies some explanation for times when the profile is off. There is room in even the best mental health and legal research methodology for error. Thus, anytime one applies what is known from research to an individual case, the application may or may not be accurate. Profiler and profiling author Ronald Holmes perhaps summarized this observation best: "When we do crime scene analysis or psychological profiles, we tend to play the odds." Thus, significant but low-probability characteristics of an offender may go unnoticed until there is direct evidence to be incorporated into the profile. For instance, unabomber Ted Kaczynski's paranoid and schizoid pathologies (each occurring in less than 3% of the general population) were not evident until authorities received his "Manifesto," which bore out this pathology in excruciating detail. "Playing the odds" also suggests a degree of luck when profiles turn out to be exceedingly accurate.

"Playing the Odds": When the Odds Do Not Play Out

As we have continuously suggested, the documented cases in which psychological profiles have been incorrect and may have hindered the investigation are rare. The famed Dr. Brussell himself was relatively unsuccessful in subsequent profiles in cases, including the Boston Strangler. However, "playing the odds" does not mean that profilers are "guessing." Rather, a profiler is attempting to apply the rules of probability to the case at hand. If valid research shows that 90% of all serial murderers kill within their own race, then a number of linked victims who were all white would indeed suggest a white offender.

Yet this does not always work out. First, it is important to note that any given case may simply fall into the percentage to which the rule never did apply. In our oversimplified example, the offender could fall in the 10% who did kill outside of their race. Such may have been the case in the 2002 Washington, DC, area sniper case. In this case, the profile of a white male, ages 25–35, and acting alone was far from the two non-white offenders, one of whom was only 17. Were it not for some clever detective work by the investigators, law enforcement might still be looking for a sniper who fit the profile.

Given the stakes, it seems too simplistic to chalk this example up to an instance that just fell outside the odds. Rather, we think it underscores a potential problem that is closer to the foundation of psychological profiling: Maybe some of the original tenets are faulty, at least as applied to contemporary offenders. Perhaps more offenders these days are offending outside of their racial group. Perhaps they always were, and police are just getting better at catching perpetrators who have no relationship to their victims.

Even if the tenets appear consistent, one possibility is that they are somewhat self-fulfilling. For example, when the profile (based on the tenets) is correct, it increases the likelihood of an arrest and conviction. When the profile is incorrect, it either hinders the odds of arrest or may

BOX 16.1. Where Are They Now?

After his arrest, Metesky's (the Mad Bomber's) neighbors would later describe him as a very sullen man, rarely smiling. Yet postarrest pictures of Metesky show him beaming. In fact, it is difficult in some pictures to distinguish him from the surrounding authorities, who were also quite pleased with his arrest. It would appear that even Dr. Brussell's prediction that the bomber wanted to be caught may have been accurate. Perhaps one reason for this was that Metesky had been able (at least in his mind) to soil Con Ed's reputation through his manipulation of media attention on the case. After confessing to the charges against him, George Metesky was committed to the Matewan State Hospital for the Criminally Insane. While there, he adamantly resisted treatment for his paranoia; however, with medical attention, his tuberculosis was cleared up. Interestingly, he had incorrectly attributed the accident at Con Ed's subsidiary as the cause of his tuberculosis, and healing that disorder rectified his perceived slight to a significant degree. Metesky was released in 1973, whereupon he moved back to his family home in Connecticut. From there, he lived out the rest of his life in a relatively uneventful manner. George Metesky, New York City's infamous "Mad Bomber" and the first criminal to fall prey to the technique now known as psychological profiling, died in 1994, at the age of 90.

Steven Pennell's case was taken to court three times, in addition to his criminal appeals. His case holds Delaware precedence as establishing the right of a trial judge to keep juror information from the press. A Delaware newspaper alleged that in doing so, the trial judge violated press members' First Amendment rights to the information. Due to the extensive pretrial publicity, the judge ordered the information sealed, an order that was subsequently upheld in the Delaware Superior and Supreme Courts (*Gannett v. State v. Pennell*, 1990). From his conviction until early 1992, Pennell resided in the secure unit of the Delaware Correctional Center in Smyrna, Delaware. Sentenced to death after a June 1986, law mandating the means of death to be lethal injection, Pennell was not given the choice to die by hanging, as is given to Delaware death row inmates sentenced prior to that date (the most recent offender who chose to be put to death by hanging in the Delaware gallows was Billy Bailey on January 25, 1996). On March 14, 1992, 34-year-old Steven Brian Pennell was led from his cell to a temporary building (a permanent lethal injection chamber was not constructed until the summer 2000). Here, he was strapped down and administered an intravenous injection of lethal chemicals that ended his life.

do nothing at all. Thus, among incarcerated offenders upon whom profiles were used, we would expect to see a higher proportion of those for whom the profile (and thus the tenets) were correct. Therefore, even updated offender interviews may uphold the tenets, when what has really happened is that those not fitting the tenets remain at large. The ultimate conclusion: The tenets of psychological profiling may be founded in faulty or at least incomplete information.

PSYCHOLOGICAL PROFILING: WHAT DOES IT ALL MEAN?

Profiling is a very misunderstood practice. Even those who research, teach, and conduct profiles may misunderstand some significant areas of the process. Court rulings that fail to recognize different types of profiles illustrate this point. Yet psychological profiling continues to be used to an increasingly greater extent. While some may dismiss the practice as akin to fortunetelling, we think such a suggestion is at least premature.

The research and conclusions based on the initial surveys conducted by the FBI have led to useful, groundbreaking knowledge regarding offender typology. An example of such information is the distinction between organized and disorganized offenders.[5] Rather than accept the "status quo" of psychological profiling or dismiss the practice altogether, we would advocate for a continued investigation into current tenets and the development of new ones. For example, the organized–disorganized distinction should be explored empirically. Either way, the first crucial step is to look at psychological profiling through one's own (we hope, more skeptical) eye.

CASE REFERENCES

Commonwealth v. Hawkins, 534 Pa. 123; 626 A.2d 550; 1993 Pa. LEXIS 143 (1993).
Gannett v. State v. Pennell, 571 A.2d 735; 1990 Del. LEXIS 98 (1990).
Pennell v. State of Delaware, 602 A.2d 48; 1991 Del. LEXIS 441 (1991).
Penson v. State, 474 S.E.2d 104; 1996 Ga. App. LEXIS 796 (1996).
People v. Genrich, 928 P.2d 799; 1996 Colo. App. LEXIS 160 (1996).
State v. Haynes, Ohio App. LEXIS 3811 (1988).

---

[5] Crime scenes of organized offenders show planning and forethought, whereas a crime scene of a disorganized offender may suggest a more spur-of-the-moment or impulsive act. These distinctions can suggest additional information about offenders. For instance, an organized offender may have a more successful employment history.

CHAPTER 17

The Death Penalty

And he that killeth any man shall surely be put to death.
Breach for breach, eye for eye, tooth for tooth: as he hath
caused a blemish in a man, so shall it be done to him again.
—Leviticus 24:17, 20 (*The Bible*, King James version)

Excessive bail shall not be required, nor excessive fines
imposed, nor cruel and unusual punishments inflicted.
—Eighth Amendment to the U.S. Constitution

As the first quote demonstrates, the death penalty had its roots in
ancient law. Documentation of punishment by death dates back to the
18th century B.C. in the Code of Hammurabi, one of the earliest written
legal records. The second quote, authored by other historical (albeit
arguably less omniscient) authors, has been the source of legal challenge
to the death penalty in modern times. However, it is unlikely that the
founding fathers of America ever expected the death penalty to fall
under Eighth Amendment scrutiny when they ratified the Bill of Rights
on December 15, 1791.

DEATH PENALTY OPPOSITION

The movement to abolish the death penalty actually predates ratification
of the Constitution. Early Quakers and well-known authors such as Vol-
taire spoke out against government-sponsored execution. It was, however, Cesar Beccaria's seminal essay "On Crimes and Punishment" in
1767, that gave the movement a significant boost, culminating in the
abolition of the death penalty in several European countries (Schabas,

1997). Restrictions on the death penalty continued through the 1800s and into the early 1900s as states began to limit death-applicable crimes to treason and murder. Others, following the lead of Rhode Island and Wisconsin, abolished capital punishment altogether.

The 1950s and 1960s witnessed a dramatic decline in U.S. executions, mirroring widespread abolition of the death penalty in most European countries (Eisenberg, 2004). Throughout this period, the death penalty withstood challenges against its constitutionality. The 1960s did, however, see the first major refinement in death penalty trials on constitutional grounds.

Prior to 1968, prosecutors' practice of excluding any and all jurors who expressed reservations about the death penalty was practiced to varying degrees across jurisdictions. The U.S. Supreme Court significantly limited this practice in the 1968 case of *Witherspoon v. Illinois*, when it ruled that only jurors who make it clear that they would automatically vote against the death penalty could be properly excluded.

Prior to and throughout the 1960s, the death penalty survived constitutional challenges on a number of grounds. However, during the 1970s, advocates of death penalty abolition would find their most promising challenge in the Eighth Amendment (Eisenberg, 2004).

CONSTITUTIONAL INTERPRETATION
AND DEATH PENALTY REFORM

Verses in the Bible lend themselves to subjective interpretation. Indeed, passages discussing "an eye for an eye" are surrounded by instructions to stone murderous bulls to death and compensate for putting out a maidservants' eye. Also included is an instruction to put to death anyone who blasphemes the Lord's name, yet civilized society would clearly abhor any such suggestion today. Herein lie two problems in putting ancient law into practice: first, subjectively interpreting the passage; and second, adjusting any admonitions to coincide with the current standards of society.

Each of these difficulties has its contemporary counterpart in the application of the Eighth Amendment's protection from "cruel and unusual" punishment. Because the phrase is inherently subjective, courts need to interpret what "cruel and unusual" means, and what practices may violate such protections. These interpretations must also evolve to incorporate the current standards of the relevant society. The U.S. Supreme Court articulated this process in 1958, when it suggested that judges who need to interpret the Eighth Amendment be guided by "evolving standards of decency that mark the progress of a maturing society" (*Trop v. Dulles*). Not until the early 1970s was argument made to the U.S. Supreme Court that the current societal standards did not warrant continuation of capital punishment, despite the practice having withstood Eighth Amendment challenge up to that point. In 1972, the Court heard this argument in the combined cases of *Furman v. Georgia, Jackson v. Georgia*, and *Branch v. Texas*. The cases were considered together and have gone down in the annals of history, known only as *Furman v. Georgia*.

The Case of *Furman v. Georgia* (1972): Procedural Technicalities and Death Penalty Constitutionality

The cases of the three defendants in the *Furman* decision, Jackson, Furman, and Branch, are among the most important in American case law. Each defendant was African American. However, the other facts of the cases differ somewhat: Jackson and Branch were convicted of violent rapes (Branch's was against a 65-year-old woman), while Furman was convicted of murder during the commission of a robbery. By some accounts, Furman's murder even seemed accidental, because he had shot a pursuing homeowner through a closed door while tripping and falling. All three defendants were convicted of their crimes and sentenced to death. A common procedural technicality practiced at the time was that jurors did not formally explain any reasoning behind the sentence, nor were jurors told by the judge to consider anything specific. In any crime designated as a capital crime, jurors needed only to decide whether a sentence of death was appropriate for the defendant.

The cases were each appealed to the U.S. Supreme Court. Testimony provided to the Court showed a disproportionate number of ethnic minority members receiving the death penalty. Given this evidence of bias against minorities in criminal sentencing, the Court concluded that juries in the respective states were imposing the death penalty without sufficient legal guidance. Justice Stewart went so far as to describe the juries having done so "wantonly and freakishly." In a close 5 to 4 decision, the Court held that the death penalty was unconstitutional under such circumstances when judges or juries were allowed such unguided discretion in handing out sentences of death.

The Immediate Impact of *Furman v. Georgia*

Some of the wording in the *Furman* holdings suggests that the decision actually only applied to sentencing ethnic minority members to death.

Juries appeared to be quite conservative in sentencing white defendants to death. While the apparently less "wanton and freakish" capital sentencing of whites was a possible legal loophole that would allow it to continue, it was a loophole that was never tested.

The *Furman* decision had an enormous immediate impact on the U.S. legal system. None of the 40 states that had capital sentencing at the time could demonstrate more juror accountability than had Georgia and Texas in the *Furman* cases. As such, the ruling effectively disallowed the death penalty in all jurisdictions. Perhaps the most striking implication of *Furman* was that over 600 inmates on various death rows at the time had their death sentences commuted to life in prison.

While the *Furman* decision had this significant practical impact, it is commonly misrepresented in written accounts. *Furman* is frequently referred to as the decision of the U.S. Supreme Court that the death penalty was itself unconstitutional. However, such was clearly not the case. Rather, the *application* of the death penalty was found unconstitutional on the basis of what amounts to a legal technicality.[1]

Immediately following the decision, some states sought by various means to reform their statutes to conform to the *Furman* decision. While the states dared not try to carry out an execution (the Supreme Court would have disallowed it anyway), several continued to sentence criminals to death. One initial attempt by states, such as North Carolina, was to mandate the death penalty by law for some crimes, thus circumventing the problem of juries or judges "wantonly" and "freakishly" imposing the death penalty. But the Supreme Court ruled that this practice still violated the Eighth Amendment (*Woodson v. North Carolina*, 1976).

Meanwhile, states such as Texas, Georgia, and Florida sought to enact a system by which aggravating circumstances could "qualify" a criminal to receive the death penalty. In other words, while it was unconstitutional to require the death penalty for all who committed a capital offense (i.e., murderers), it could be imposed on some who committed their crime in a particularly heinous manner (i.e., a murder involving kidnapping and torture). In 1976, the U.S. Supreme Court

---

[1] We are interpreting the *Furman* ruling as resting on a legal technicality. Although jurors "wantonly and freakishly" imposing death sentences is certainly more than a technicality, this is not necessarily what happened. It may very well have been that the jurors in the respective cases had fine reasons for sentencing the defendants to death. There simply was no documentation of these reasons. In the eyes of the law, if it is not documented, it technically did not happen. Our "technicality" interpretation becomes more clear after the *Gregg* case below.

agreed to hear cases from Texas, Georgia, and Florida, in which the "aggravating circumstance" approach was challenged on the grounds that it still violated Eighth Amendment protections. The cases were argued to the Court on March 31, 1976, under the combined name of *Gregg v. Georgia*.

THE CASE OF *GREGG V. GEORGIA* (1976): THE IMPORTANCE OF AGGRAVATING CIRCUMSTANCES

On the afternoon of November 21, 1973, Troy Gregg and his 16-year-old traveling partner Floyd Allen were hitching their way north from Florida toward the Carolinas. Pulling over in a well-worn car to give the pair a ride were Fred Simmons and Bob Moore. Moore and Simmons were both drunk. At one point, the car broke down and Simmons purchased another car with some cash he had on hand. The four continued north. Even though the 13-year-old Pontiac did not cost much, Gregg and Allen had noticed Simmons paying for the car out of a large wad of cash. Just before crossing into Georgia, the men picked up another hitchhiker by the name of Dennis Weaver. Arriving in Atlanta at around 11 P.M., they stopped to let Weaver disembark. Continuing on, the four were later seen at a rest stop north of Atlanta. Farther north in Gwinnett County, the men stopped again, whereupon Simmons and Moore walked away from the car. While waiting for the two to return, Gregg told Allen that he intended to rob the others. Gregg then pulled a .25-caliber pistol from one of his pockets and steadied the pistol on the doorsill. When Simmons and Moore came back over an embankment, Gregg opened fire, hitting both men. To be sure that the job was finished, Gregg then left the car, running up to the wounded men as they lay in a ditch. Here, Gregg placed the gun to each man's head and pulled the trigger. After robbing the men of their valuables, Gregg returned to the car, in which he and Allen continued on their trip northward.

Reading of the shootings in the Atlanta newspaper 2 days later, fellow hitchhiker Dennis Weaver contacted the authorities and provided them with names and descriptions of Gregg and Allen and a description of the car. Knowing that the two were at least initially headed toward the Carolinas, police released an all points bulletin on the pair and their vehicle. The search was successful when the two were arrested in Ashville, North Carolina, the following afternoon. In the pair's nearby motel room, police found $107 in cash and two new stereos—the total take from the double murder. Police also found a .25-caliber pistol in

Gregg's pocket that would later be matched to the bullets found during the autopsies of Fred Simmons and Bob Moore.

Police promptly read Gregg and Allen their rights and placed them under arrest for murder. The following day, the two were en route back to Lawrenceville, Georgia, when the transporting officers stopped by the scene where the bodies were found. It was here that Allen provided police with the description of events. While Gregg initially concurred with Allen's statement, he later claimed in court that he had been attacked by Simmons and Moore, who were wielding a knife and pipe, respectively. Gregg claimed he had acted in self-defense.

Evidence at trial supported Allen's perspective, despite Gregg's testimony on his own behalf. While the judge instructed jurors that they could impose lesser crimes, the 12 Georgian citizens promptly found Gregg guilty of two counts of armed robbery and two counts of murder. In accordance with Georgia law at the time, Gregg then faced the same jury for a separate sentencing hearing. Neither Gregg's attorneys nor the prosecutor offered any additional evidence, although each offered lengthy arguments, respectively, against and for the death penalty. The Court instructed the jury to consider whether or not any of the following aggravating circumstances applied in the current case:

> One—That the offense of murder was committed while the offender was engaged in the commission of two other capital felonies.
>
> Two—That the offender committed the offense of murder for the purpose of receiving money and the automobile described in the indictment.
>
> Three—The offense of murder was outrageously and wantonly vile, horrible and inhuman, in that they [sic] involved the depravity of mind of the defendant. (*Gregg v. Georgia*, p. 11)

In accordance with the post-*Furman*, revised Georgia statute, the trial judge instructed jurors that they could not impose the death penalty unless they found beyond a reasonable doubt that at least one of the previously mentioned aggravators had occurred. The jury indeed found that the first two aggravators had occurred and recommended the sentence of death for each of the four counts. On appeal, the Georgia State Supreme Court found that the death sentences for the armed robbery were excessive compared to the crimes. Although this vacated two of the death sentences, Gregg was still to be executed for the two murders.

In accordance with the recent *Furman* ruling, which specifically found the previous Georgia statute to be unconstitutional, Gregg's attorneys appealed the two remaining death sentences to the U.S. Supreme

Court, which agreed to hear the case. Arguments were made in March 1976, just over 3 years after the murders of Fred Simmons and Bob Moore. At the time, the Supreme Court also had before it the Florida murder case of Charles Proffitt and the Texas murder case of Jerry Lane Jurek, each of which had resulted in death sentences for the accused. As was the case in the *Furman* decision, the three cases were ruled upon concurrently.

While the entire country, and perhaps the world, anxiously anticipated the ruling, Gregg, Proffitt, and Jurek awaited the decision from their respective death rows. To these three men, along with others imprisoned on death rows around the country, the case was significantly greater than a philosophical debate on the country's "evolving standards of decency." On July 2 of that year, the Court published its 7 to 2 ruling. As was earlier alluded to in the *Furman* ruling, here the death penalty itself was explicitly deemed constitutional. The Court felt that the lawmakers of Florida, Georgia, and Texas had adequately addressed the specific problems that the Court had cited with the capital punishment system only 4 years earlier. [2] In fact, the only dissenting opinions, offered by Justices Brennan and Marshall, expressed the view that the death penalty would always constitute a violation of the Eighth Amendment. The majority, citing post-*Furman* attempts by 35 states to reorganize their death penalty statutes, found that current political sentiment was clearly in favor of maintaining states' choice to impose capital punishment. Those states trying to keep the death penalty represented the "evolving standards of decency," at least for the majority of states (35 out of 50).

THE LEGACY OF *FURMAN* AND *GREGG*

The *Furman* decision spurred on widespread procedural reform that in turn resulted in the reinstatement of capital punishment by the *Gregg* decision. On January 17, 1977, five years to the day after the Supreme Court heard the arguments in the *Furman* case, Utah inmate Gary Gilmore's execution by firing squad brought the end to the moratorium on capital punishment. While providing only a temporary stay, the *Furman* decision sent the clear message that capital punishment was not

---

[2] An interesting question is: What would have happened to Gregg had his attorneys not appealed the case? The state of affairs at the time was that no death sentences were being carried out due to the *Furman* decision.

immune from constitutional challenge. In fact, in the same year as Gilmore's execution, the U.S. Supreme Court ruled state statutes under which rapists could be sentenced to death a violation of the "cruel and unusual" standard (*Coker v. Georgia*, 1977).

While most of Western society had effectively abolished the death penalty by the early 1980s, the response in the United States continues to be placing clearer limitations and restrictions on the practice. Limitations on the imposition of the death penalty on juvenile offenders and opinions regarding the execution of mentally retarded offenders are two scenarios on which the U.S. Supreme Court has now officially ruled (see Chapters 14 and 20, this volume). The Court also ruled that an inmate must be able to appreciate the fact that he or she is being put to death (this curious ruling is dealt with in Chapter 6, this volume). Rulings on each of these issues are interpreted as upholding the rights of the accused against infringement upon constitutional rights. However, the practice of juror death qualification, has been argued by many to jeopardize any fairness with which capital punishment is meted out.

DEATH-QUALIFIED JURIES: CURRENT STANDARDS AND PRACTICES

Under the Constitution, American citizens are legally allowed to entertain and express almost any thoughts or opinions they so desire. Such an opinion may, for instance, favor marijuana legalization. Suppose, though, that a citizen holding this belief were seated as a juror in a trial in which the defendant was charged with possession of marijuana. Were the juror to vote for acquittal on the basis that he or she did not believe the act was truly criminal, many would argue that this juror has failed to carry out the law. Such could also be the case if a juror were to vote against the imposition of the death penalty when a convicted criminal was clearly "eligible" for it. However, this practice, known as juror nullification, is a phenomenon that is protected by law. Once seated on a jury, individual jurors do not have to justify their individual opinions. To make jurors do so would make them more prone to public opinion or tampering (i.e., threats). But what about before they are seated on the jury? As discussed in Chapter 1, this volume, voir dire is a procedure by which potential jurors are excused by either side (i.e., prosecution or defense) prior to the start of the actual trial. In this manner each side seeks to remove potential jurors who may be particularly biased against its views (strikes for cause). Each side is usually also allowed a number of removals for which it has to provide no (or minimal) justification (peremptory strikes).

In attempting to compose the jury of members who would be able to enforce the law, including capital punishment, the voir dire procedure produces a jury that is "qualified" to impose the death penalty, known as a "death-qualified" jury (Eisenberg, 2004). As discussed earlier, it was in the area of jury death qualification that the U.S. Supreme Court first articulated a protection of the rights of the accused. In *Witherspoon v. Illinois* (1968), the Court stated that jurors could only be struck for cause if they make it clear that they would *automatically* vote against the death penalty. Thus, a prospective juror could still be included on the final jury despite having significant anti–death penalty views. The juror need only be able to fathom some instance in which he or she *might* be able to impose the death penalty. While this practice inevitably allowed some jurors on capital cases who would, practically speaking, never impose the death penalty, it protected the representation of such views on juries, allowing defendants to benefit from these sentiments. However, it also theoretically produces juries that are unable to enforce the law, which includes the full range of penalties, even death. Seldom are such protections of the accused maintained without challenge for long. This phenomenon was illustrated in 1985, in the case of *Wainwright v. Witt*.

The Case of *Wainwright v. Witt* (1985): Striking Jurors for Death Qualification

Johnny Paul Witt was born on January 13, 1943. He lived out a relatively unnoticed existence for the next 30 years. In late October 1973, his life was to take a turn that reads like a contemporary (and probably less eloquently written) excerpt from Richard Connell's "The Most Dangerous Game."

Johnny had been bow hunting near his home in central Florida with his 19-year-old friend Gary Tillman. The two were hunting near a trail that was frequently used by the public. The choice of location was neither accidental nor merely irresponsible. The carefully chosen location allowed the duo to engage in a most sinister pastime: stalking humans like prey. While they had not yet killed anyone, the two had discussed doing so many times.

Riding along the path on his bicycle that day was 11-year-old Jonathan Kushner. As he was riding, he was struck in the head with a star bit from a drill. The blow knocked him off of his bicycle, onto the ground beside the trail. At the other end of the drill bit had been Johnny Witt.

Together, he and Tillman gagged their small victim tightly and placed him in the trunk of the car.

During the trip to a more secluded area, the gag was ultimately too constricting and Jonathan Kushner died. Upon arriving at their designation, the two subjected Kushner's body to what the 11th Circuit Court of Appeals would later call "various acts of sexual perversion" (*Witt v. Wainwright*, 1983, p. 1). After digging a grave in which to bury the body, Witt leaned down and slit Kushner's abdomen so that it would not bloat. Unable to avoid pursuing investigators, Witt was arrested on the afternoon of November 5th. The prosecutor sought the death penalty. The death-qualified jury returned a guilty verdict and sentenced Johnny Paul Witt to die in the Florida electric chair.

On appeal, the case was almost remanded back to the trial court on the grounds that one of the state's psychiatrists failed to inform Witt that information from his competency assessment would be admissible in court. Such was a potential violation of Witt's Fifth Amendment right against self-incrimination. However, it was the death qualification during voir dire that became most important focus of the appeal. During jury selection, the prosecution had excluded potential jurors who expressed views opposing the death penalty. However, it appeared that some of the subtle opinions did not meet the *Witherspoon* criteria of suggesting that the excluded jurors would have *automatically* voted against a death sentence. In considering this assertion with regard to three excused jurors, the 11th Circuit Court of Appeals relied upon the answers of the venireperson who was the least clear in her convictions. The questioning of this potential juror, Ms. Colby, proceeded as follows:

> Mr. Plowman [prosecuting attorney]: Now, let me ask you a question, ma'am. Do you have any religious beliefs or personal beliefs against the death penalty?
>
> Ms. Colby: I am afraid personally but not—
>
> Mr. Plowman: Speak up, please.
>
> Ms. Colby: I am afraid of being a little personal, but definitely not religious.
>
> Mr. Plowman: Now, would that interfere with you sitting as a juror in this case?
>
> Ms. Colby: I am afraid it would.
>
> Mr. Plowman: You are afraid it would?
>
> Mr. Colby: Yes, sir.
>
> Mr. Plowman: Would it interfere with judging the guilt or innocence of the defendant in this case?

Ms. Colby: I think so.

Mr. Plowman: You think it would?

Ms. Colby: I think it would.

Mr. Plowman: Your Honor, I would move for cause at this point.

THE COURT: All right. Step down. (*Witt v. Wainwright*, 1983, pp. 11–12)

Ms. Colby and the other jurors expressing similar views were excluded. Citing *Witherspoon*, the defense argued that Ms. Colby and some of the other excluded jurors did not explain how their personal beliefs would affect their imposition of the death penalty. An explanation of the *Witherspoon* ruling had been eloquently stated by Justice Stewart in his majority opinion in 1968:

> If the State had excluded only those prospective jurors who stated in advance of trial that they would not even consider returning a verdict of death, it could argue that the resulting jury was simply "neutral" with respect to penalty. But when it swept from the jury all who expressed conscientious or religious scruples against capital punishment and all who opposed it in principle, the State crossed the line of neutrality. In its quest for a jury capable of imposing the death penalty, the State produced a jury uncommonly willing to condemn a man to die. (*Witherspoon v. Illinois*, 1968, pp. 9–10)

The Court of Appeals agreed with this argument and ruled that it applied in Witt's case. They remanded the *Witt* case back to the trial court. However, on review of the case in January 1985, the U.S. Supreme Court upheld the exclusion of the jurors. In doing so, rather than argue that the exclusion of Ms. Colby met the *Witherspoon* criteria, the Court very clearly delineated a new standard:

> The proper standard for determining when a prospective juror in a capital case may be excluded for cause because of his views on capital punishment is whether the juror's views would prevent or substantially impair the performance of his duties as a juror in accordance with his instructions and oath. (*Wainwright v. Witt*, 1985, p. 1)

More jurors could be excluded under this standard, because they need not express that they would automatically vote against a death sentence. This relaxation of the standard seems in direct opposition to the *Witherspoon* ruling. Indeed, Ms. Colby had hardly done more that express "conscientious...scruples against capital punishment," as was specifically discussed by Justice Stewart. Are we then to generalize the

1968 standards to conclude that the jury in the *Witt* trial was "uncommonly willing to condemn [him] to die," as Justice Stewart had warned? Perhaps the dissenting Justices Brennan and Marshall thought so, having characterized juries formed under the new standard as "poisoned against the defendant" (*Wainwright v. Witt*, 1985, p. 1). Nevertheless, the appeals process was effectively exhausted, and Johnny Paul Witt remained in his cell on Florida's death row.[3]

DEATH-QUALIFIED JURIES:
IGNORING SOCIAL SCIENCE RESEARCH

As discussed in the introductory section to this book, the legal system can vary significantly in decision-making tactics from the methods used by social science researchers (Sales & Shuman, 2005). Prior to the mid 1980s, social science researchers built up a wealth of research that concluded death-qualified jurors and juries were (among other things) more prone to convict and hand out harsher sentences than were non-death-qualified juries (Cowan, Thompson, & Ellsworth, 1984; Ellsworth, Bukaty, Cowan, & Thompson, 1984; Ellsworth & Fitzgerald, 1984; Thompson, Cowan, Ellsworth, & Harrington, 1984; Horowitz & Seguin, 1986; Neises & Dillehay, 1987). Results or preliminary results from studies such as these (and several studies predating these citations) were included in an amicus brief forwarded to the U.S. Supreme Court by the American Psychological Association for the 1986 case of *Lockhart v. McCree* (American Psychological Association, 1986), which stated that social science research to date had concluded that

> (a) death qualified juries are conviction prone, (b) the barring of excludable jury members creates unrepresentative juries, thereby implicating defendant's right to a jury composed from a fair cross-section of the community, (c) death qualification excludes a significantly large subset of the popula-

---

[3] While the term *death row* implies a single, specific place, such is frequently not the case. In the state of Florida, male death row inmates may be housed either at Florida State Prison in Starke or at Union Correctional Institution in Raiford. Females on death row are housed at the Broward Correctional Institution in Pembroke Pines. All executions in the state are carried out at the Florida State Prison in Starke. Prior to legislated allowance of lethal injection in 2000, all executions in Florida were carried out by electric chair, in a solid oak chair originally put into service in 1923. The electrical apparatus remains unchanged to this day. At the less risky end of the wire is an anonymous private citizen who is paid $150 per execution to press the button (Florida Department of Corrections website: www.dc.state.fl.us/.)

tion, (d) those excluded through death qualification share common attitudes on issues related to criminal justice, (e) death qualification results in under representation on juries of blacks and women, and (f) the data suggests that death qualification interferes with the proper functioning of the jury.

The APA strongly defended against the prosecution's position that flaws in the research precluded its admissibility as evidence. Despite what the APA characterized as "three decades" of research supporting these findings, the Supreme Court ultimately ruled in favor of maintaining jury death qualification. Citing what it considered to be flaws in the research, the Court ruled that even if the evidence supported the finding that death-qualified juries were more conviction prone, the practice of death qualification itself did not infringe upon any constitutional rights.

While not all social scientists agreed with APA's assertions (Rogers, 1992), yet another generation of researchers have gone on to replicate and extend the findings regarding the conviction proneness of death-qualified juries (Butler & Moran, 2002; Filkins, Smith, & Tindale, 1998; Goodman-Delahunty, Green, & Hsiao, 1998). While juror death qualification remains a practice today, it may once again fall prey to constitutional challenges in the face of increasing evidence of its biasing effects on juries.

LEGAL DARWINISM:
CURRENT CHALLENGES TO CAPITAL PUNISHMENT

The *Furman* decision indicates that the practice of capital punishment in the United States may one day fall by the evolutionary wayside as society's standards evolve. One would expect that in a post-9/11 era, favorable sentiment toward the death penalty would be easier to come by. Many Americans would have gladly sent Mohammad Atta to death had he not completed the act himself. Yet just when public opinion would seem to favor the practice the most, reform continues to take place in capital punishment case law. In 2002, the U.S. Supreme Court dealt a blow to death penalty proponents when it ruled in *Ring v. Arizona* (2002) that only juries could sentence defendants to death. Judges can no longer do so in states where juries convict and judges impose sentence. This case immediately remanded 150 death sentences in five states (Arizona, Idaho, Montana, Colorado, and Nebraska) and may effectively have the same impact in four others (Florida, Alabama, Indiana, and Delaware) whose death row populations total almost 630. In response, the Florida Supreme Court issued a stay of all executions in the state while the new ruling was considered. The stay came just 6 hours before the scheduled execution of convicted murderer Linroy Bottonson and less than 72 hours before fellow murderer Amos King was to be subjected to lethal injection. Just the week before, the Supreme Court finally ruled on the issue of executing mentally retarded criminals in the case of a Virginia man (described in detail in Chapter 14, this volume). In the same 2002 session, the Court also expanded an earlier ruling (*Simmons v. South Carolina*, 1994) in deciding that a jury must always be made aware that life without parole is an alternative to death in any case involving an offender about whom there are concerns about future dangerousness (*Kelly v. South Carolina*, 2002).

These reforms may seem to represent a shift away from the endorsement of capital punishment; quite the contrary may actually be the case. Whether one agrees with it or not, these reforms give the perception of making capital punishment in this country more "refined." Any such changes can only help to ease international tensions arising from the practice, and will quiet many moderates from protesting as they may have before.

Within this air of refinement, the U.S. Supreme Court continues to hand down rulings that severely limit protections for the accused. Even in the 2002 term that saw major limitations placed on capital punishment, the Court severely limited the right of those sentenced to death to challenge their cases on the basis of ineffective counsel (*Mickens v. Taylor*, 2002; *Bell v. Cone*, 2002). The Court expanded an already strict standard for proving ineffectiveness (*Strickland v. Washington*, 1984), including denying a case in which the defense attorney had a previous relationship with the murder victim of his current client (*Mickens*). In 2004, the U.S. Supreme Court denied retroactive application of both the *Ring* jury sentencing requirement (*Schriro v. Summerlin*, 2004) and an earlier ruling (*Mills v. Maryland*, 1988) that had increased the salience of mitigating factors in capital sentencing (*Beard v. Banks*, 2004). These decisions left intact a number of death sentences that would today be deemed unconstitutional. Yet the same Court ruled that both limited intellectual capacity and any history of being abused in childhood must be introduced as mitigating factors at sentencing (*Tennard v. Dretke*, 2004).

To be sure, the answer is not yet complete. Further clouding the picture is occasional misrepresentation of cases in the media. One instance of such misrepresentation came in 2004, in the case of *Nelson v. Campbell*. Here, the Court ruled that a death row inmate may sue on

---

BOX 17.1. Where Are They Now?

Not surprisingly, none of the three defendants named in the cases known as *Furman v. Georgia* were ever executed by their respective states. At the time of this writing, neither Furman nor Jackson is listed as being incarcerated by the Georgia Department of Corrections. Information regarding the present status of Texas offenders was unavailable. Somewhat less expected, however, are the fates of the three defendants named in the *Gregg v. Georgia* decision, the ones whose death sentences were upheld by the U.S. Supreme Court. Jerry Jurek's death sentence was reduced to life in prison by the State of Texas in 1982. The Florida Supreme Court vacated Charles Proffitt's sentence in 1987, after his attorneys successfully argued that the lone aggravating circumstance of burglary was insufficient to warrant the punishment of death (*Proffitt v. State*, 1987). Proffitt was resentenced to life in prison without the possibility of parole for 25 years but is not currently listed as an inmate in the Florida State Correctional system. Troy Gregg, the man whose name is synonymous with the Supreme Court's reinstatement of capital punishment, was never executed by the State of Georgia. He is not currently listed as a Georgia inmate.

Less fortunate was Johnny Paul Witt, whose case provides the precedent for current jury death-qualification procedures. Witt was executed by the State of Florida less than 2 months after the U.S. Supreme Court upheld the procedures that resulted in his sentencing. On March 6, 1985, Witt, sharing death row with the infamous Ted Bundy, became the twelfth inmate to be executed in the State of Florida since the reinstatement of capital punishment 9 years earlier. Witt's accomplice Gary Tillman, only 19 at the time of the murder of Jonathan Kushner, was sentenced to life in prison. He resides in a Florida state prison facility in Avon Park and is currently scheduled for release in November 2100 [*sic*].

---

civil grounds to keep a state from using a specific medical procedure to facilitate lethal injection.[4] The media inaccurately portrayed the ruling as stating that the medically routine practice was cruel and unusual. Nevertheless, neither legislators nor high court justices are yet ready to relegate capital punishment to vestigial status. Only time will tell if the death penalty will fall prey to evolving standards of decency, or if those same evolving standards will propagate the practice through generations to come.

---

[4] In *Nelson*, the death row inmate's veins were badly damaged from extensive intravenous drug use. Prison physicians would have to use what is known as a veinal cutdown procedure, in which the vein is accessed with a scalpel. Such a procedure is routine in medical settings when there is difficulty finding a vein for injection. Therefore, the practice would actually stand little chance of being deemed cruel and unusual because it is not even unusual.

CASE REFERENCES

Beard v. Banks, 124 S. Ct. 2504; 2004 U.S. LEXIS 4572 (2004).

Bell v. Cone, No. 01-400, 122 S. Ct. 1843 (2002).

Branch v. Texas, 447 S.W. 2d 932; 1969 Tex. Crim. App. LEXIS 882 (1969).

Coker v. Georgia, 433 U.S. 584 (1977).

Furman v. Georgia, 408 U.S. 238; 1972 U.S. LEXIS 169 (1972).

Gregg v. Georgia, 428 U.S. 153 (1976).

Jackson v. Georgia, 439 U.S. 1102, 409 U.S. 1102 (1972).

Kelly v. South Carolina, 534 U.S. 246 (2002).

Lockhart v. McCree, 106 S. Ct. 1758 (1986).

Mickens v. Taylor, 122 S. Ct. 1237 (2002).

Mills v. Maryland, 486 U.S. 367 (1988).

Nelson v. Campbell, 541 U.S. 637; 2004 U.S. LEXIS 3680 (2004).

Proffitt v. State, So. 2d 896; 1987 Fla. LEXIS 2049 (1987).

Ring v. Arizona, 536 U.S. 584; 122 S. Ct. 2428; 153 L. Ed.2d 556; 2002 U.S. LEXIS 4651 (2002).

Schriro v. Summerlin, 124 S. Ct. 2519; 2004 U.S. LEXIS 4574 (2004).

Simmons v. South Carolina, 512 U.S. 154 (1994).

Strickland v. Washington, 466 U.S. 668, 694 (1984).

Tennard v. Dretke, 124 S. Ct. 2562; 2004 U.S. LEXIS 4575 (2004).

Trop v. Dulles, 356 U.S. 86, 101 (1958).

Wainwright v. Witt, 469 U.S. 412; 1985 U.S. LEXIS 43 (1985).

Witherspoon v. Illinois, 391 U.S. 510 (1968).

Witt v. Wainwright, 1983 U.S. App. LEXIS 26616 (1983).

Woodson v. North Carolina, 428 U.S. 280 (1976).

CHAPTER 18

Sex Offenders

Community Notification
and Predator Commitment

The terms *sexual psychopath* and *sexual predator* can each conjure up sensational images of a terrified would-be victim fleeing across the movie screen from the murderer on their heels, or the sadistic kidnapper from our favorite novel. These terms certainly *do not* conjure up pictures of the person next door. What is surprising is that both *sexual psychopath* and *sexual predator* are actually legal terms, and interestingly, the former historically denoted an offender for whom an arguably more lenient civil commitment was recommended in lieu of imprisonment (Conroy, 2003). From Chapter 15, the reader should immediately realize that a discrepancy exists between that previous legal definition and the use of the *Psychopathy* label in current mental health literature.

Perhaps the fact that these terms have been retained by legislators in a such a sensational form reflects society's loathing of the people who fall into these categories. Society's concerns are to a large extent warranted. Sex offenders are among the most recidivism-prone offenders, and sex crimes can have a life-altering (if not life-ending) impact on every individual victim. Nobody can deny that there exists a serious problem.

REGISTRATION AND COMMUNITY NOTIFICATION LAWS

Adding to these problems is the fact that the terms *do* fail to conjure up pictures of the man next door. But even dangerous sex offenders give no outward visual signs of their dangerousness (Miller et al., 2005). How are we to know when to be wary of the man next door, either for ourselves or for our children? State legislatures and their constituents began to ask this question, and they arrived at an answer: Require released sex offenders to register their current address with law enforcement officials. What may be surprising about these types of registration law is that they actually began back in the 1930s (Conroy, 2003). These laws allowed law enforcement officials to keep track of sex offenders' whereabouts and have since been upheld in courts as being an appropriate balance between the privacy rights of the offender and the protection of society. What the laws did *not* do was inform the public at large.

In 1990, Washington State enacted a law that would prove to be the beginning of a trend toward vastly expanding this registration system. The Washington law required that information in the sex offender registry be made public. This step away from protecting offenders' privacy and toward protecting society spawned new debate about this balance of rights. Had the offenders not paid their debt to society? Was any violation of the offenders' rights not justified by further protecting society? Had the offenders not forfeited these rights when they committed their horrible crimes? However, there was not much outward discontent with these laws expressed in society. Needless to say, there is still not much empathy for sex offenders floating around. Furthermore, endorsement of these laws is a nice "line on the résumé" of any politician who wants to appear tough on crime.

The U.S. Congress got involved in 1994, when it passed the Jacob Wetterling[1] Crimes Against Children and Sexually Violent Offender Registration Act. Under this Act, states that *did not* have a registration law stood to lose 10% of their federal funding for jails and prisons (Conroy, 2003). However, just because the registration laws made it *possible* for members of the public to access the information, few people actually *did* access it. Sadly, as the first case soon demonstrates, this loophole only became evident in the aftermath of tragedy.

---

[1]In 1989, Jacob, an 11-year-old boy from St. Joseph, Minnesota, was abducted near his home at gunpoint. He is still missing. Jacob's parents started the Jacob Wetterling foundation (www.jwf.org) whose mission is protecting children from sexual exploitation and abduction.

The Case of *New Jersey v. Timmendequas* (1999): Spurring Community Notification Legislation

Seven-year-old Megan Kanka lived with her parents in Hamilton Township, New Jersey. Diagonally across the street lived 33-year-old Jesse Timmendequas. Timmendequas had already spent time in prison for the aggravated sexual assault of a young girl in 1980, and sexual assault and attempted aggravated assault in 1982. Neither the Kankas nor any of the other nearby families had any way of knowing about Timmendequas's history. Children regularly played freely around the neighborhood, as was Megan on the evening of July 29, 1994.

Megan's mother would later testify that she took a nap at around 5:30 P.M. With her mother sleeping, Megan left with the intention to visit a friend down the street. Timmendequas watched his little next-door neighbor walk by his home. He lured Megan into his house, asking her to come play with the puppy. Megan never made it to her friend's house.

Timmendequas drew her into his bedroom where he began to touch her. When Megan screamed and tried to escape, he strangled her with a belt until she lost consciousness. He had hit Megan's head on a piece of furniture during the struggle. To avoid getting bloodstains on the carpet, he placed a plastic bag over Megan's head. He then sexually assaulted her until he was interrupted by his roommate's return. Believing Megan to be dead, Timmendequas placed her body in a toy box and carried it downstairs. He drove to local Mercer County Park, where he again sexually assaulted Megan before dumping her in some tall weeds.

When Mrs. Kanka awoke, she could not find Megan. The family called the police when Megan did not return home. Officers arrived and joined neighbors in the search. Mrs. Kanka gave them a photograph of her daughter and a description of the clothing Megan was wearing. Timmendequas himself participated in the search, handing out fliers with Megan's picture. He told Megan's mother that he had seen Megan before dinner. But when interviewed by police, he told them that he had last seen Megan riding a bicycle at 2:30 in the afternoon. Only when police asked about the inconsistency did he mention Megan riding her bicycle in front of his home between 5:30 and 6:00 P.M. Timmendequas also gave conflicting statements concerning his whereabouts during the time surrounding Megan's disappearance. Shaking and perspiring, Timmendequas then said that he saw Megan with a friend while he was washing his boat between 5:00 and 5:30 P.M.

The next morning, detectives saw Timmendequas take his puppy out for a walk and bring out the garbage. The officers searched the garbage and found a rope with some knots tied in it. The rope appeared to have dried blood on it. Also in the trash was the waistband of a small pair of pants and a piece of material that matched the waistband. Mrs. Kanka later confirmed that the tattered clothing belonged to Megan.

Timmendequas was immediately arrested. At headquarters, he confessed to the murder and eventually to the sexual assault. He led the police directly to the partially clothed body. Megan's head was still covered with the plastic bag. After signing the official confession, Timmendequas told authorities he felt he had been "slipping for a while," and "getting those feelings for little girls . . . for a couple of weeks or a couple of months" (New Jersey v. Timmendequas, 1999, p. 2)

At trial, the prosecution sought the death penalty. Timmendequas offered two witnesses who presented evidence of mitigating circumstances in his background. A social worker testified that Timmendequas's mother was a promiscuous alcoholic who had 10 children by seven different men, and that his father was a violent drinker with a criminal history. Timmendequas was raised in poverty and was often cold, dirty, hungry, and without adequate medical care. His father had reportedly sexually abused him and his brother, and they both saw their father rape a 7-year-old girl. The father also tortured and killed Jesse's pets. Timmendequas's second expert, a psychologist, found that he suffered from pedophilia, borderline Mental Retardation, fetal alcohol effect, and Schizoid Personality Disorder. The psychologist expressed the opinion that at the time of the crime, Timmendequas was under "extreme emotional disturbance." Megan's death, said the psychologist, was caused by a reflexive response to the panic the defendant felt when the victim attempted to flee (New Jersey v. Timmendequas, 1999, p. 10).

The State presented a psychiatrist as a rebuttal witness, who testified that there was no evidence to support Timmendequas's claims of extreme emotional disturbance and diminished capacity. He said that defendant's IQ showed a borderline intelligence that did not prevent him from functioning or appreciating the nature of his conduct.

Timmendequas himself pleaded to the jury:

Okay. I am sorry for what I've done to Megan. I pray for her and her family every day. I have to live with this and what I've done for the rest of my life. I ask you to let me live so I, some day, I can understand and have an understanding why something like this could happen. Thanks. (New Jersey v. Timmendequas, 2001, p. 6)

On May 30, 1997, the jury found him guilty of purposeful murder, first-degree kidnapping, and four counts of aggravated sexual assault. Timmendequas was sentenced to death. The Supreme Court affirmed his convictions and death sentence on direct appeal.

The Legacy of Megan Kanka

While not erasing the tragedy of the murder, Megan Kanka's story provided the impetus for community notification legislation at the federal level. Under these laws, neighbors and community members are notified when a registered sex offender moves into their neighborhood. After their tragic loss, Megan's parents pushed for the enactment of such a law in a passionate attempt to deter and prevent similar crimes in the future. The family's initial success in getting a New Jersey State statute passed eventually culminated in the U.S. Congress, in 1996, amending the Wetterling Act to include community notification. As a testament to public and governmental support of such laws, note that it took less time to pass even the federal legislation (1996) than it did for Timmendequas to pass through the court system (1999).

Across jurisdictions, the community notification can range from offenders' zip codes being published to having fliers handed out in their neighborhood that include a color picture, description of the offense, and current address. In addition, information is commonly posted on a web page for all to see. Many states, due to budget concerns, are resorting to this latter practice as the sole means of notification. Forever, such laws will be informally known by the name given to the New Jersey statute: Megan's Law.

FUTURE DIRECTIONS IN COMMUNITY NOTIFICATION

A challenge levied by community notification law opponents is that publication of ex-offenders' otherwise private information constitutes cruel and unusual punishment. Was community notification not an additional punishment to what had been proscribed to them in a court of law? Furthermore, many released offenders had been convicted prior to the enactment of the notification laws. Was this additional punishment not an *ex post facto* violation? (See Box 18.1 for a discussion of *ex post facto*.) While there is undeniable logic in these concerns, there continues to be very little empathy for sex offenders' position. For instance, it looked as if the U.S. Supreme Court was going to avoid the situation when it

---

BOX 18.1. "From What Is Done Afterward"

Ex post facto is Latin for "from what is done afterward." Here, the reference is to making something illegal after it has already been done, and then arresting those who previously committed the act. For instance, a legislative body could make driving an SUV illegal and prevent anybody from driving an SUV. However, if it tried to make the law retroactive and arrest anyone who had previously driven an SUV, the law would be an *ex post facto* law. *Ex post facto* laws are explicitly prohibited by Article 1 Sections 9.3 (for the federal legislature) and 10.1 (for states) of the U.S. Constitution. Laws that merely increase the penalty for a crime after the crime has been committed have also been interpreted as violating the *ex post facto* prohibition. Sex offender registration and sexual predator laws have been challenged on these latter grounds as increasing the penalty for offenders who committed their crimes before the laws were enacted.

---

refused to hear a 2000 case in which a registered sex offender charged that the law violated various protected rights (*Cutshall v. Sundquist*, 2000). However, in 2003, the U.S. Supreme Court ruled on several direct challenges to community notification laws. In *Smith v. Doe* (2003), the Court ruled that Alaska's notification law did nothing to impinge upon the rights of the defendants, despite the fact that the defendants in question had even been *released* from prison 4 years prior to the registration law. The Court in *Smith* found that all the notification laws did was to make already public information more accessible to the public. As such, the procedure was civil rather than criminal in nature. Hence, *ex post facto*, double jeopardy, and various other challenges were not applicable. In a separate but similar case, the Court ruled that notification procedures were not subject to due process, nor did the notification need to be linked to the dangerousness of the offender (*Connecticut Department of Public Safety v. Doe*, 2003).

SEX OFFENDER RISK ASSESSMENTS

The Constitution does not require a sex offender to be particularly dangerous in order to be subject to community notification. However, many states have included risk assessments designed to assess dangerousness as part of their notification procedure. It is in the capacity of providing these assessments that many mental health professionals become involved in these cases.

Dangerousness and predictions of reoffense are discussed at length in Chapters 8 and 15, this volume. In addition to procedures assessing general recidivism or violence, procedures for specifically assessing the risk of an offender to commit a sex crime have proliferated in recent years. Predictors of general violent recidivism been studied specifically with sex offenders (Porter et al., 2000; Rice & Harris, 1997). Specific assessment instruments have been created to address sexual violence risk (Miller et al., 2005; Hanson & Thornton, 1999; Epperson, Kaul, & Hesselton, 1998; Quinsey, Rice, & Harris, 1995).

Jurisdictions that require risk assessments for released sex offenders use the information from the assessments in a variety of ways. Most commonly, the resulting risk level (typically high, moderate, or low) is included in the notification material that gets communicated to the public. In some states, the level of risk dictates the length of time after release that a sex offender must register as part of the notification system, or the type of community notification. For instance, a low-risk offender may just have his information posted on the state's sex offender web page, whereas a high-risk offender may have fliers with his picture and information hand-delivered to his neighbors by police.

What is unclear is the future of risk assessments as part of community notification procedures in the wake of the *Connecticut Department of Public Safety v. Doe* (2003) decision. As the reader might imagine, conducting a thorough risk assessment on every released sex offender takes an enormous amount of resources. While the information in the assessments is very useful, states may begin to rethink the practice, since the U.S. Supreme Court has deemed it not necessary. However, as we see next, the courts have viewed risk assessments differently with regard to another area of sex offender law: sexual predator commitment.

SEXUAL PREDATOR COMMITMENT LEGISLATION

Community notification laws have clearly filled a gap between the collection of information that *could* protect the public and the dissemination of that information *to* the public. Yet these laws do not address a question that many readers may have: Why was someone like Jessee Timmendequas let out at all? This is exactly the question addressed by sexual predator commitment legislation.

By conducting sex offender risk assessments, mental health professionals can identify the most dangerous offenders among all of those who are released. At least in hindsight, Jesse Timmendequas was one of these high-risk offenders. The legal terms *sexual predator* and *sexual psycho-path* are virtually synonymous designations of these most high-risk offenders. Thus, sexual predators are a specific subset of sex offenders.

Most sex offenders, as a result of being apprehended and impris-oned, at some point come under the care of medical and mental health staff. Were such a meeting to take place in a noncorrectional (i.e., private practice) setting, serious concern would arise about the dangerousness of the client and the potential duty to warn and protect the public and/or intended victim(s).[2] Mental health professionals are bound by ethical duty and law to follow up on any serious concern that the client poses a threat to others. Yet what happens when a dangerous, incarcerated client is paroled, or finishes his or her prison sentence? While the duty to warn intended victims is still followed through with some regularity, the duty to protect (i.e., to seek civil commitment of the offender) is addressed with less consistency. To do so represents a legally sticky situation, since the offender has already paid his or her debt to society by serving a prison term. Increasing any penalty further would be a constitutionally prohibited *ex post facto* punishment.

To address the need to protect the public from dangerous sex offenders, Washington State enacted specific legislation in 1989, under which the most dangerous sex offenders would be civilly committed. Many states followed suit. These laws have become known as sexual predator civil commitment (or simply sexual predator) laws. These laws clearly result in a further deprivation of freedom for committed sex offenders. Not surprisingly, offenders have challenged these laws as an unconstitutional violation of rights.

THE INALIENABLE RIGHTS OF THE SEXUAL PREDATOR

An important perspective to consider, at least from a legal standpoint, is that of the offender. The rights of accused and convicted individuals rank high among the hallmarks of a civilized society. Among the most relevant rights here are protections against being punished or tried twice for the same crime (double jeopardy), and against the *ex post facto* laws dis-cussed earlier. While the double jeopardy protection was written into

---

[2] Duty to warn and to protect is a much more complicated issue than presented here. The same holds true for civil commitment, an issue to which we turn below. Readers are referred to Chapters 5 and 8, this volume, for more complete discussions.

the U.S. Constitution in the Bill of Rights (Fifth Amendment), *ex post facto* was prohibited in the original body of the Constitution. Clearly, these protections run deep in our society. However, confining sexual predators after they have served their debt to society set forth by the original trial court, seems a form of double jeopardy. Furthermore, the retroactive nature of these laws brings up the possibility of *ex post facto* punishment.

What happens, then, when deep-rooted constitutional protections conflict directly with contemporary protections from dangerous sex offenders given to the public? In 1997, the U.S. Supreme Court addressed this issue in *Kansas v. Hendricks*.

The Case of *Kansas v. Hendricks* (1997): The Constitutionality of Sexual Predator Laws

Leroy Hendricks's horrific history of abusing children began in 1955, when he exposed himself to two young girls. Two years later, he was convicted of lewdness. In 1960, he molested two boys at a carnival. Two years after that, he was rearrested for sexually assaulting a 7-year-old girl. After being released from a psychiatric hospital in 1965, he assaulted two more children, performing oral sex on an 8-year-old girl and fondling an 11-year-old boy. After receiving parole 7 years later for those crimes, he began abusing his stepdaughter and stepson. The abuse lasted over a period of 4 years. Hendricks's deviant sexual activities occurred intermittently, with consequential periods of incarceration and confinement in mental institutions. Eventually, he was again arrested for the abuse of two 13-year-old boys. Hendricks was scheduled to be released to a halfway house in 1994, having served 10 years in prison for these latest crimes.

Instead of releasing him, Kansas sought to apply its newly enacted Sexual Violent Predator Act, which established a civil commitment procedure for

> . . . . any person who has been convicted or charged with a sexually violent offense and who suffers from a mental abnormality or personality disorder which makes the person likely to engage in the predatory acts of sexual violence.

Hendricks admitted to his crimes and acknowledged his pedophilia. He explained that upon getting "stressed out" he could not "control the urge" to molest children. He volunteered that the only sure way he would never abuse children in the future was "to die" (*Kansas v. Hendricks*, 1997, p. 4). Under these circumstances, it was determined that Hendricks would be civilly committed.

Despite admitting his compulsions, Hendricks appealed the commitment, claiming that the Sexual Violent Predator Act violated the various constitutional protections, among them the right to due process of law. As an additional point of contention, the U.S. Supreme Court had previously ruled in *Foucha v. Louisiana* (1992; discussed at length in Chapter 8, this volume) that a finding of mental illness was required to civilly commit someone, because the civil commitment had to be linked to treatment. But note the terminology *mental abnormality*, which the Kansas statute broadly defined as a "congenital or acquired condition" that predisposes someone to commit a sexually violent offense. In addition to the term *abnormality* seeming less stringent than *illness*, the definition is circular in that if one commits some of these offenses (sex crimes against children), then one essentially has the condition (pedophilia). The Kansas Court agreed with Hendricks and reversed the decision to civilly commit him. The Court ruled that the Act's definition of mental *abnormality* did not satisfy the U.S. Supreme Court's requirement of mental *illness*, as set forth in 1992 in *Foucha*.

Kansas appealed to the U.S. Supreme Court, which, in a 5 to 4 split decision actually supported the constitutionality of the Kansas Act. In fact, the Court was essentially unanimous in supporting the Kansas definition of *mental abnormality*. It was on a separate point that the Justices differed, but it was on this point that the case hinged, particularly with regard to constitutional protections against double jeopardy and *ex post facto*. Like they had before with community notification laws, the majority of the Justices ruled that the Kansas Sexually Violent Predator Act was really a civil rather than a criminal procedure. Double jeopardy did not apply, because the commitment was not a punishment (let alone a *second* punishment). Similarly, the nonpunitive nature of Hendricks's commitment meant that the law could not be interpreted as an *ex post facto* violation. The five-person majority emphasized that Kansas had specifically labeled the procedure as civil. Furthermore, any committed offender who was no longer considered dangerous would be released, just as in any other civil commitment. The dissenting Justices argued that the procedure effectively *was* criminal, because the law only applied to those who had committed a criminal act. Furthermore, there was no reference to treatment as a purpose of the statute.

Predator Commitment in the Wake of *Hendricks*

In 2002, the Supreme Court seemed to move in the direction of protecting sex offenders from civil commitment in *Kansas v. Crane*. Michael Crane was convicted of sexual assault for exposing himself to two store clerks and forcing one to perform oral sex on him. Psychological expert testimony documented diagnoses of exhibitionism and Antisocial Personality Disorder. Hallmarks of the latter diagnosis include impulsivity and failure to plan for the future. However, the expert also testified that Mr. Crane's mental diagnoses did not impair his self-control to the degree that he was unable to control his behavior. For the expert to assert otherwise would have been acknowledging a key component of insanity. Crane was convicted and served his sentence. However, instead of releasing him into the community, Kansas sought civil commitment under the same Sexual Violent Predator Act that the U.S. Supreme Court had upheld in the *Hendricks* decision.

Appealing the commitment to the U.S. Supreme Court, Crane's attorneys asserted that the psychological expert testimony documented Crane's ability to control his behavior. Thus, he was not dangerous and, by extension, was not appropriate for civil commitment. Interpreting *Hendricks*, the Court ruled that the Kansas Predator Act was constitutional so long as it required proof that the offender had a "serious difficulty" in controlling his or her behavior. The Act need not require an *absolute* lack of control. The Court elaborated that predators subject to civil commitment must be distinguished from the "dangerous but typical" sex offender. Thus, the presence of a mental diagnosis and "typical" dangerousness are not enough. While this ruling seems to give added protection to sex offenders, it is unclear that the Court's opinion will provide for any significant practical changes.[3] The sex offenders being singled out by predator laws are presumably ones for whom increased risk has already been established.

---

[3] Interestingly, the *Crane* decision may eventually have an impact on general civil commitment procedures, discussed at length in Chapter 8, this volume. Civil commitment of a noncriminal requires presence of a mental disorder and some form of dangerousness. *Crane* essentially adds a requirement of "serious difficulty" controlling behavior in order to civilly commit a sex offender. Should sex offenders be afforded an *extra* protection from commitment, or should this additional requirement be extended to nonoffenders? This issue will likely surface in future legal challenges.

FUTURE TRENDS IN PREDATOR AND NOTIFICATION LAWS

Ex post facto challenges to these laws will eventually end. Offenders who committed their crimes after the laws were enacted have no *ex post facto* claim. The release of offenders who committed their crimes before the laws were enacted will eventually taper off and stop.

Community notification and predator commitment laws both represent a clear preference for protecting the rights of victims over the rights of the accused in recent years. The U.S. Supreme Court further limited the rights of offenders specifically convicted of sex crimes in the 2002 case of *McKune v. Lile* (discussed at length in Chapter 12, this volume). Those familiar with historical trends in our legal system recognize that there is the potential for the pendulum to swing back in the direction of protecting the rights of the accused. The 2002 *Crane* decision is a step in this direction, albeit a gentle one. A firmer step came in 2003 when the U.S. Supreme Court ruled that a state (California, in this case) could not extend the statute of limitations[4] for sex crimes in order to arrest and convict offenders who had committed their crimes years ago (*Stogner v. California*, 2003).[5] However, there is reason to believe that notification and predator laws may actually be extended to include other types of offenders.

FROM WHOM ARE WE *NOT* PROTECTED?

Many criticisms exist about both notification and sexual predator laws. Some of these arguments conclude that these laws give the public a false sense of security. Predator laws only apply to the individuals deemed most dangerous by a risk assessment, and these assessments are not fail-proof. Released offenders are subject to notification statutes, but how

---

[4] A statute of limitations sets a limit on the length of time after commission of a crime that the offender can be charged. For instance, if the crime of rape has a 20-year statute of limitations, then the perpetrator cannot be arrested if more than 20 years have elapsed since the crime. Some crimes (i.e., murder) have an unlimited statute of limitations, so an offender may be arrested at any time.

[5] In *Stogner*, the Court denied California the ability to change the statute of limitations and subsequently arrest people for whom the previous statute of limitations had already expired. This was deemed an *ex post facto* violation. However, the Court ruled that the new statute of limitations was fine, so long as it only applied to crimes committed *after* it was set in place.

effective have these statutes proven in reality? Legislators have all too frequently mandated community notification to be carried out by various law enforcement agencies, without appropriating any funds for the added burden. In response, many law enforcement agencies have reduced the community notification to publication on a web page. Yet not everybody has ready Internet access, and not every potential victim with Internet access regularly checks the web page.

A further problem with poor funding for notification programs is that the laws create a new group of offenders. Released offenders who do not comply with the registration requirements by updating their home addresses are fugitives from justice. Police not only need to find out that the offenders have moved in the first place, but they also have to find the fugitives who are not where they are supposed to be. How big is this problem? In January 2004, the State of California admitted that it had lost track of over 33,000 sex offenders who were out of compliance with the registration law. Clearly, the notification system was not protecting anyone from these offenders.

Another interesting point to consider is that these laws apply only when there is a sexual component to the crime with which the offender was convicted. There is no parallel for those who commit nonsexual violent crimes. For example, under current laws, an 18-year-old man who has intercourse with his 15-year-old girlfriend of 2 years (and soon-to-be wife) would be subject to community notification and could be considered for civil commitment as a sexual predator. However, a sniper who randomly shoots six unsuspecting people in Virginia parking lots will at no time be considered under these notification or predator statutes. This arrangement begs the questions: Are sex offender statutes *really* about protection of the public? What is it specifically about sex offenders that makes society willing to condone these forays into constitutional "gray areas?" Perhaps the answer is simply that the sex offenders were addressed first. Perhaps similar laws that include nonsexual violent offenders are on the legal horizon.

The virtually unanimous endorsement of predator commitment and notification laws across jurisdictions and appellate levels makes a successful fundamental challenge to these laws seem unlikely. We agree that any significant changes are probably distant. As discussed earlier, an expansion of similar legislation to other types of violent offenders seems much more likely, although such an expansion could itself be the driving force behind any eventual pendulum swing back toward protecting the accused. The one thing that seems clear about the future of predator commitment and notification laws is that there *is* a future.

CASE REFERENCES

Connecticut Department of Public Safety v. Doe, 538 U.S. 1; 123 S. Ct. 1160; 155 L. Ed. 2d 98; 2003 U.S. LEXIS 1951; 71 U.S.L.W. 4158 (2003).

Cutshall v. Sundquist, 529 U.S. 1053; 120 S. Ct. 1554; 146 L. Ed. 2d 460; 2000 U.S. LEXIS 2391 (2000).

Foucha v. Louisiana, 504 U.S. 71; 1992 U.S. LEXIS 2703 (1992).

Kansas v. Crane, 534 U.S. 407; 122 S. Ct. 867; 151 L. Ed. 2d 856; 2002 U.S. LEXIS 493; 70 U.S.L.W. 4117 (2002).

Kansas v. Hendricks, 521 U.S. 346; 1997 U.S. LEXIS 3999 (1997).

McKune v. Lile, 536 U.S. 24; 122 S. Ct. 2017; 153 L. Ed. 2d 47; 2002 U.S. LEXIS 4206; 70 U.S.L.W. 4502 (2002).

New Jersey v. Timmendequas, 161 N.J. 515; 1999 N.J. LEXIS 1007 (1999).

New Jersey v. Timmendequas, 168 N.J. 20; 2001 N.J. LEXIS 24 (2001).

Smith v. Doe, 538 U.S. 1009; 123 S. Ct. 1925; 155 L. Ed. 2d 844; 2003 U.S. LEXIS 3409 (2003).

Stogner v. California, 539 U.S. 607; 123 S. Ct. 2446; 156 L. Ed. 2d 544 (2003).

PART VII

Juveniles in the Legal System

Juveniles in the legal system represents perhaps one of the most controversial and consistently evolving areas of law. We present this section last, not due to its relative importance, but because law, as it relates to juveniles, may entail many, if not all, of the dilemmas dealt with in the previous sections. Thus, an understanding of the previous sections will serve to underscore the complexity of juvenile law as we know it today.

Chapter 19 takes a broad look at law as it specifically affects children in our society. Chapter 20 explores the history and current legal status of the practice of imposing capital sentences upon criminals who were under the age of 18 when they committed their crimes. Chapters 21 and 22 explore child abuse and child custody, the two areas of primary legal system involvement for mental health professionals who work extensively with children and their families.

CHAPTER 19

Juvenile Law
and School Law

The first basis for a separate juvenile court evolved out of the *parens patriae*, or "state as parent" model. The juvenile system now more closely resembles the adversarial adult model. The first juvenile code was formulated in 1899, in Illinois. Prior to that, juveniles had come under the criminal code, with age taken into consideration as a variable effectively reducing the seriousness of an offense. The initial shift to a juvenile code was a shift from an adversarial to a nonadversarial model that was intended to come up with a plan for what is best for the child. This resulted in a number of specific changes in terminology. In juvenile proceedings (1) "petitions" were "taken out," rather than "charges" being "brought against"; (2) there were no "findings of guilt," only "allegations supported as true"; and (3) there was no "sentencing," only "recommendations for disposition."

There were also other changes. For instance, juvenile court records were not public; they were treated as "sealed." The proceedings against juveniles were much more informal than those in adult court. Also added was a new category of "status offense" (based on a behavior that was not illegal for adults), as opposed to a criminal offense. If convicted of any type of infraction for which they were to serve time, juveniles were to be kept separated from adult inmates. At least, that was the ideal; it was not always met in practice.

Over time, there was an increasing consensus that the juvenile system was not working as it was intended (i.e., that juveniles were not being rehabilitated as hoped, yet they were not being afforded the legal rights or due process accorded to adults). This consensus emerged through a series of U.S. Supreme Court cases.[1]

Kent v. U.S. (1966) was the first Supreme Court case to allude formally to due process for juvenile proceedings. The opinion was written by Judge Fortas shortly before he was forced off the Supreme Court for receiving money from suspicious sources. This decision provided the *Kent* criteria for deciding whether or not a juvenile should be tried as an adult—criteria still used to varying degrees today:

1. The seriousness of the alleged offense and the potential danger to the community
2. The degree of violence and premeditation against a person and the degree of injury
3. The quality of evidence
4. Whether others involved will be tried as adults
5. The sophistication, maturity, and intelligence of the juvenile
6. The defendant's history and prospects for rehabilitation

The following year, legal reform continued for juveniles who remained under juvenile court purview. In *In re Gault* (1967), Gerald Gault, then 15 years of age, was committed as a juvenile delinquent to a state institution at the end of what he and his mother thought was a simple hearing. He was charged with making obscene telephone calls. No witnesses appeared, and the only evidence was hearsay (generally inadmissible statements based on [at least] secondhand knowledge). The Supreme Court reversed and remanded, specifically placing the due process requirement for juveniles from *Kent* within the Fourteenth Amendment. For the first time, the Court had acknowledged that juveniles had their own protected right to due process before their rights could be limited. The *Gault* decision thus established for juveniles; (1) a requirement of notice of charges; (2) a right to an attorney; (3) a right to cross-examine and confront witnesses; and (4) a right to avoid self-incrimination. So the juvenile process was again becoming more adversarial, though this evo-

---

[1] For some additional, specific information on law, psychology, and children, the reader is referred to the special issue of *Law and Human Behavior* (1993).

lution to an adult-like process was mitigated by some of the cases that
followed.

For example, just 3 years after the *Gault* decision, in the case of
McKeiver v. Pennsylvania (1971), the U.S. Supreme Court held that a
juvenile had no right to a trial by jury. Individual states did, however,
retain the right to require a trial by jury for juveniles in their jurisdiction. However, other cases throughout the 1970s and into the mid-1980s
furthered the adversarial approach to juvenile prosecution. In *In re
Winship* (1970), the Supreme Court established that, just as in adult
criminal cases, "reasonable doubt" is the standard of proof where there
is a formal adjudication, and all elements of a charged offense must be
proved beyond a reasonable doubt. In *Breed v. Jones* (1975), the U.S.
Supreme Court held that if a court adjudicates a juvenile in a juvenile
court proceeding, it is then double jeopardy to try him as an adult. On
the other hand, in *Schall v. Martin* (1984), the Supreme Court held that
juveniles may be denied bail for their own protection, or to protect the
community. Finally, in the case of *New Jersey v. T.L.O.* (1985), the
Supreme Court put limits on a student's right to be free from unreasonable search and seizure (Fourth Amendment) by holding that teachers could
search a student's locker without a warrant, even if this was not for a suspected criminal offense, but only for a suspected violation of school rules.

There are other areas of ambivalence in juvenile cases because of
the confluence of the above trends.

1. Do juveniles have a right to an insanity defense? It is generally
   held that they do not, because there cannot really be a "criminal
   act" under the juvenile code.
2. Is plea bargaining available? It is not, at least formally, but, of
   course, it occurs informally in many situations.
3. What is the standard of proof for waiver to adult courts? It varies
   by state, from "clear and convincing" to "preponderance" to
   "substantial evidence."

The adjudication of juveniles for illegal acts is certainly the area in
which the removal of basic rights (i.e., to move about freely) is most
likely. Thus, the legal establishment and refinement of these rights are of
the utmost concern in a civilized society. However, it is not just in the
courtroom that juveniles stand to have their rights violated. Such is also
the case with regard to inpatient commitment and even (to a lesser
degree) to outpatient treatment.

INPATIENT AND OUTPATIENT
JUVENILE TREATMENT ISSUES

A primary legal issue in dealing with many childhood disorders is the right of a minor to refuse treatment. "Voluntary" admission of a minor to a hospital, for example, means only that the parents are acting voluntarily. For the minor, admission may not be voluntary. Should minors, by law or through ethical principle, have the power to object to their treatment when their parents have already consented? Generally, a minor's ability to refuse treatment has not been recognized by law. Problems can quickly arise, however, in determining how much review should be given to a parent's or guardian's consent to hospitalization and treatment.

Two landmark cases regarding civil commitment of juveniles were handed down by the Supreme Court in the late 1970s. In *Kremens v. Bartley* (1977), the Court heard a case concerning five mentally disordered youth, ages 13 to 18, who challenged the constitutionality of a 1966 Pennsylvania law governing commitment and voluntary admissions to state mental health institutions.[2] The decision can be interpreted as affording to those 14 years and older the same protections as adults in such proceedings. Later, in *Parham v. J. R. and J. L.* (1979), a minor alleged that he had been deprived of his liberty without procedural due process by laws permitting parents voluntarily to admit minors to mental hospitals. The Court's majority opinion held that parents should be allowed to maintain a substantial, if not dominant, role in making the decision, absent a finding of neglect or abuse, and without evidence to contradict the traditional presumption that the parents acted in the best interest of their child. The Court stated, "Most children, even in adolescence, simply are not able to make sound judgments concerning many decisions, including their need for medical care or treatment. Parents can and must make those judgments" (p. 602). However, it was further noted in *Parham* that the child's rights and the nature of the commitment decision are such that parent's consent does not always carry absolute and unreviewable discretion over whether to have a child institutionalized. But the Court did say that the review

---

[2] For some reason unknown to us, the Pennsylvania mental health system was the source of most of the landmark civil rights cases. Notably, most of the alleged civil rights violations were acknowledged by the courts. Much more on this is presented in Chapter 14.

need not be held by judicial or administrative boards, but could be held as an internal hospital matter. The Court also ruled that children can be granted access to emergency medical or psychological treatment without parental consent.

Regarding outpatient treatment, authorities should not burden minors with decisions they cannot make intelligently, or inadvertently deny to some the opportunity to make decisions in which they are fully competent (Grisso, 2002). The results of their work suggest the following:

1. No circumstances sanction independent consent by minors under age 11, given the developmental evidence of their diminished capacities.
2. Ages 11 to 14 appear to make up a transition period involving cognitive, developmental, and social expectations. Independent consent by these minors may be justified for limited purposes, especially when competence can be determined in individual cases.
3. There appears to be no psychological grounds why minors age 15 and above cannot give competent consent.
4. In some minors, diminished capacity to provide meaningful consent may sometimes present such risk to the psychological or physical welfare of the minor as to offer a compelling reason for denial of the right to consent in certain circumstances.

Generally, adolescents who are more disturbed psychologically are likely to be more impaired in their judgment (Novak & Pelaez, 2004). This diminished capacity should thus be factored into the consideration of whether or not they may give consent. In the California juvenile case of *In re Kevin F.* (1989), Kevin had discussed thoughts of harming non-specified people to his therapist. These discussions were later admitted as evidence against him at a hearing. Kevin's attorneys argued that the duty to warn and protect requirements set forth in *Tarasoff* (see Chapter 5, this volume) did not apply to Kevin as he had identified no specific victim. However, the appeals court concluded that Kevin's discussions with his therapist were properly admissible under the California Evidence Code, which stated:

> There is no privilege under this article if the psychotherapist has reasonable cause to believe that the patient is in such mental or emotional condition as to be dangerous to himself or to the person or property of another

and that disclosure of the communication is necessary to prevent the threatened danger.

In so ruling, the Court rejected Kevin's argument that *Tarasoff* precedents required a threat of harm to a readily identifiable victim. The Court also ruled that Kevin was not entitled to *Miranda* warnings[3] before talking to the therapist, because the right to that warning only applies to interrogation. Kevin's therapist had clearly not been interrogating him.

As we have demonstrated, landmark juvenile case law seems to arise wherever children come into contact with the system. Not surprisingly, since most children spend the majority of their time as juveniles in school, educational systems have also been the subject of their share of significant case law.

SCHOOL LAW AND SCHOOL PSYCHOLOGY

Case law affecting juveniles is not limited to criminal law. Quite the contrary, a significant amount of case law concerning the rights of minority-age children falls under what can be termed *school law*. Some of school law relates specifically to school psychology. As any mental health professional who works with troubled youth knows, a significant amount of energy can be spent advocating for the rights of these clients in educational settings. Surprisingly, some of this case law has had an impact upon the rights of all individuals. After all, it would be difficult for the Supreme Court to grant a basic right (i.e., to a free education) to juveniles without similarly guaranteeing it to adults. Less surprisingly, the historical development of school law included cases involving the most basic of human rights. In *Plessy v. Ferguson* (1896), the U.S. Supreme Court had endorsed the "separate but equal" justification for all laws involving racial segregation. Later, while holding an Oregon statute forbidding children to attend parochial school to be unconstitutional in *Pierce v. Society of Sisters* (1925), the Court affirmed "the liberty of parents and guardians to direct the upbringing and education" of their children (p. 1). Thus, the state of affairs into the 1950s was that children (through their parents) had a right to a free education, and this education

---

[3] The *Miranda* warnings are the familiar rights that police read to people upon arrest (i.e. "You have the right to remain silent"). See Chapter 3 for a detailed account of the landmark *Miranda v. Arizona* case.

could take place in racially segregated schools, so long as the facilities were equal. However, school law was to be at the forefront of the racial equality movement in the country.

While the following case dealt directly with segregation in public schools, it is well known as a case that had a much farther reaching impact. As it has become such a basic tenet of U.S. law (with as much household familiarity as any legal decision), some interesting details of the case have slipped into obscurity. Thus, it warrants some detailed examination.

THE CASE OF *BROWN V. BOARD OF EDUCATION* (1954): THE INEQUALITY OF "SEPARATE BUT EQUAL"

This landmark Supreme Court decision was actually based on a consolidation of four similar cases from Kansas, South Carolina, Virginia, and Delaware. While they were based on different facts and local conditions, they were considered together because of the common legal question being considered. In each of the four cases, African American children were denied admission to state public schools attended by white children. This racial segregation operated under state laws that permitted or required the practice. These laws had to that point protected been by the precedent of *Plessy v. Ferguson*. The schools for blacks and whites in each case had been or were being equalized in terms of buildings, curricula, qualifications and salaries of teachers, and other tangible conditions. The question before the Supreme Court was whether or not the segregation of black children and white children resulted in the children being deprived of the equal protection guaranteed by the Fourteenth Amendment. A related question was whether or not the "separate but equal" doctrine of *Plessy v. Ferguson* could be applied in the area of public education.

Brown v. Board: The Cases

In the namesake Kansas case, *Brown v. Board of Education*, the plaintiffs were elementary school-age African American children residing in Topeka. A class action suit was brought on their behalf to challenge the constitutionality of a Kansas statute that permitted (but, interestingly, did not require) separate school facilities for black and white students in cities with a population of 15,000 or more. The Topeka Board of Education had elected to establish segregated schools. The U.S. District Court for Kansas had found that segregation in public education had a detrimental effect on black children but denied the need for desegregation on the grounds that the black and white schools were equal with respect to buildings, transportation, curricula, and educational qualification of teachers.

In the South Carolina case *Briggs v. Elliot,* the plaintiffs were African American children in Clarendon County that were both elementary and high school age. They brought a class action suit to challenge the constitutionality of provisions in the state constitution and statutory code that *required* the segregation of black and white students in public schools. The U.S. District Court for the Eastern District of South Carolina found that the schools for blacks were inferior to the schools for whites and ordered the defendants to begin immediately to equalize the facilities. The Court, however, denied the plaintiffs admission to the white schools during the equalization.

In the Virginia case *Davis v. County School Board,* the plaintiffs were high-school-age African American children residing in Prince Edward County. They brought a class action suit in the U.S. District Court for the Eastern District of Virginia to challenge the constitutionality of provisions in the state constitution and statutory code that required black and white children to be segregated in the public schools. The court found the African American school to be inferior in physical building conditions, curricula, and transportation. The defendants were ordered to provide separate and equal curricula and transportation for the black and white children, to remove the inequities in physical building conditions, and to "proceed with all reasonable diligence." However, as in the South Carolina case, the Court denied the plaintiffs' admission to white schools during the equalization process.

In the Delaware case, *Gebbart v. Belton,* the plaintiffs were both elementary- and high-school-age African American children residing in New Castle County. They brought a class action suit in the Delaware Court of Chancery to challenge the constitutionality of provisions in the state constitution and statutory code that required black and white children in the public schools to be segregated. In this case, the Court ordered the school system to admit black children to the schools previously attended only by white children. The African American schools were found to be inferior with respect to teacher training, pupil-teacher ratio, extracurricular activities, physical building conditions, and time and distance involved in travel. This finding was essentially the same as in the other cases, but with a different remedy. Given the apparent inconsistency in rulings, the school system applied to the Supreme Court and was granted a hearing consolidated with the aforementioned cases.

Brown v. Board: The Ruling

In the first three cases, black children were challenging rulings that denied them admission to white-only public schools. In contrast, the Delaware school system was attempting to regain such segregation. In each case, students had at one point or another been denied admission to schools attended by white children under laws requiring or permitting "separate but equal" segregation. The Court ruled:

> Segregation of white and colored children in public schools has a detrimental effect upon the colored children. The impact is greater when it has the sanction of the law; for the policy of separating the races is usually interpreted as denoting the inferiority of the Negro group. A sense of inferiority affects the motivation of children to learn. Segregation with the sanction of the law, therefore, has a tendency to [retard] the educational and mental development of Negro children and to deprive them of some of the benefits they would receive in a racial[ly] integrated school system. (*Brown v. Board of Education*, p. 494)

While the Supreme Court did not rely on all of the social science research available at the time in reaching their decision, this passage reflects the Court's reliance on research conducted by African American psychologist Kenneth Clark. Also reflected is the Court's almost wholesale acceptance of Dr. Clark's findings. Because this ruling would go on to impact upon virtually every subsequent court ruling in the African American civil rights movement, the importance of Dr. Clark's impact upon U.S. law cannot be overstated. In 2002, the *Review of General Psychology* published their extensively researched list of the top psychologists of the 20th century. Dr. Clark's ranking: nowhere to be found. We heartily concur with the assertion by Tomes (2002) that "Kenneth Clark and his works...deserve better."

The Court also held that racial segregation in education violated the equal protection clause of the Fourteenth Amendment. They ruled that where the state has undertaken to provide education, it must be provided to all citizens equally regardless of race. The Supreme Court concluded that in the field of public education the doctrine of "separate but equal" was unacceptable. While this decision can be read as theoretically allowing separate but equal education, the Court held in no uncertain terms that to attempt to do so would be practically impossible. The Court stated:

> Segregation of white and Negro children in the public schools of a State solely on the basis of race, pursuant to state laws permitting or requiring such segregation, denies to Negro children the equal protection of the laws

guaranteed by the Fourteenth Amendment—even though the physical facilities and other "tangible" factors of white and Negro schools may be equal. (*Brown v. Board of Education*, p. 446)

The Fallout of the *Brown* Decision

The 1954 *Brown* decision effectively mandated a massive restructuring of many school districts. As the ruling had come at the level of the federal government, and since few (if any) of the school systems were operating with a budgetary surplus, the question arose as to who bore the responsibility for making the changes. In *Brown v. Board of Education II* (1955), the Supreme Court was asked to render a decision to answer this question. The initial *Brown* ruling had merely stated that racial discrimination in public education was unconstitutional. The Supreme Court, in *Brown v. Board of Education II*, explicitly mandated desegregation in previously segregated schools. The Court further held that school authorities have the primary responsibility for assessing and solving the problems, such as administration, transportation, revision of school districts, determination of admission, and revision of the local laws which implemented school segregation. The Court also required that the school authorities make a "prompt and reasonable" start toward full compliance with the decision, and the district courts were authorized to issue orders that would allow for admission of African-American students to public schools on a nondiscriminatory basis "with all deliberate speed."

While the *Brown* decision(s) would be heavily relied upon both for case law and legislative reform, the changes did not happen quickly. Ten years after the *Brown* decision, Congress finally stepped in and passed the Civil Rights Act of 1964 which provided for desegregation in all places of public accommodation. Racial discrimination in most places of private employment also became illegal as a result of this act.

The right to a free education was alluded to in the *Pierce* decision in 1925. Yet the landmark *Brown* case held no language that confirmed a constitutional right. The right to a free education was again addressed by the Court decades later in *San Antonio Independent School District v. Rodriguez* (1973), in which it held that citizens have no direct, fundamental right to an education under the U.S. Constitution. However, it was held that state governments have assumed the duties to educate, to tax for it, and to compel attendance under the Tenth Amendment. Thus, the right to an education is given to its citizens by the state as a property right. The right to an education was further refined by the courts in *Goss*

v. *Lopez* (1975). In *Goss*, the defendant was suspended from school without a hearing. Attorneys argued that this was a violation of the student's Fourteenth Amendment right to due process. The Supreme Court held that due process must include notice and the opportunity to be heard, but procedures need not be lengthy, elaborate, or complex, as in a formal hearing.

The Supreme Court had relied on social science research in forming its opinions in the *Brown* cases. At about the same time that the *Brown* rulings were forming the foundation of school law that was to follow, the emergence of a new subspecialty, school psychology, helped to set school law within a mental health framework.

SCHOOL PSYCHOLOGY

Most experts view school psychology as having emerged as an identifiable profession in the 1950s, primarily stimulated by the Thayer Conference, organized by the American Psychological Association in 1954. The profession has developed under the guidance of both the APA and the National Association of School Psychologists (NASP). NASP governs the National School Psychology Certification System. Those school psychologists who come from a training program that meets NASP standards, and who also pass NASP's national examination and meet continuing education requirements, may use NASP's term, *Nationally Accredited School Psychologist*, or N.A.S.P. A major difference between American Psychological Association and NASP standards is the former's emphasis on the doctorate as the standard for licensure–certification, while NASP is less stringent.

Case law regarding issues directly related to school psychology continued to develop throughout the 1970s. Even the definition of *education* was rewritten in light of the growing awareness of the need to be responsive to students with physical and mental challenges. In *Pennsylvania Association for Retarded Children v. Commonwealth of Pennsylvania* (1971), the U.S. Supreme Court redefined *education* in the legal context, broadening it beyond the "three R's" to include training toward self-sufficiency for children with disabilities. Pennsylvania was required to provide notice to parents before placing their children in special education classes and, in general, to provide a free program of education and training appropriate to a child's capacity for all school-age children.

The presence of a school psychologist has never been mandated by case law. However, in *Kelson v. City of Springfield* (1985), the Circuit

Court suggested that schools have some staff who have had training in suicide prevention. Jacob and Hartshorne (1991) later interpreted the consensus of the professional literature as saying that (1) each school must orient staff and have a planned response to suicidal students; (2) the designated trained staff member should be brought in when suicide potential emerges; (3) the student's parents should be informed, and the school should be prepared to appropriately refer the student; and (4) the school should be prepared to transport the student to the referral if a parent is uncooperative or unavailable.

CASE LAW REGARDING EDUCATIONAL TESTING AND ASSESSMENT

School psychologists are bound to professional and ethical standards and responsibilities much the same as any mental health professionals. There is one other notable exception to confidentiality for mental health professionals conducting assessments. A standard exception to client confidentiality (or perhaps in this case, the confidentiality of the school) continues to be the necessary reporting of any suspected child abuse. This exception was explicated with specific regard to school psychologists in *Pesce v. J. Sterling Morton High School District 201, Cook County, Illinois* (1987). The results of any assessments will be forwarded to a third party (i.e., the school) rather than being kept strictly confidential (between the mental health professional and the student–family). Thus, professional ethics dictate that this be discussed when obtaining informed consent from parents.

Testing and assessment continue to comprise a large component of the duties of school psychologists. However, dilemmas develop when the school, a public institution, delves into the psychological makeup of a student. After all, ethical and legal guidelines now dictate that psychological test results, particularly in raw form, are one of the most legally private types of documents. Such is especially the case with regard to information pertaining to alcohol and drug abuse and treatment. Not surprisingly, there is an evolutionary history in case law with regard to school testing.

The courts first established that there were privacy rights regarding educational testing. In *Merriken v. Cressman* (1973), a Federal District Court ruled that parents have a right to be free from invasion of family privacy by their child's school. In this case, a private consultant administered questionnaires designed to identify eighth graders at risk for drug abuse. The questionnaire assessed risk factors such as familial history of abuse. Of note is that the Court held that the privacy rights belonged to the parent, not to the child.

Such rights were strengthened by the Buckley Amendment or FERPA (Family Educational Rights and Privacy Act of 1974, a part of Public Law 93-380), under which schools would lose federal funding if they did not adhere to the pupil record-keeping procedures dictated by law. In 1978, this thrust was continued by the Hatch Amendment (part of Public Law 95-561), which amends the Elementary and Secondary Education Act of 1965. Under the Hatch Amendment, a student may not be required to submit to psychological or psychiatric examination, testing, or treatment as part of any federally funded program unless there is informed parental consent. Collecting certain types of information is expressly forbidden (e.g., embarrassing psychological data, criminal or sexual history, family income, and political [affiliation]) without such consent.

Interestingly, this "protection" of parents may have somewhat of a paradoxical effect, if it stifles the ability of school professionals to assess and intervene with students. An example of this phenomenon was evident in the first criminal conviction of parents, Susan and Anthony Provenzino, of St. Clair Shores, Michigan, on May 9, 1996. The Provenzinos were convicted for failure to control the behavior of their child. Arguably, had the school system had more freedom to assess and intervene, the problematic behavior might have been headed off sooner.

What about the flip side of the privacy issue, the protection of psychological tests? Opportunities for the abuse of the test information become much more likely if the test is released to the client (i.e., student or family) in "raw" form, that is, the actual scoring sheets, individual responses, and perhaps even the actual questions. While an important concern is that someone who is not qualified to interpret the data could attempt to do so, another concern is the protection of the test itself. For instance, it is not hard to imagine the devastating effect of having IQ test questions publicly known. Students would know what to expect and be able to prepare for the test, rendering the test useless. For this reason, test results are typically released in the form of a synthesized report, effectively disclosing the results of the test, while protecting the testing process. Professional ethics for psychologists strongly guard against the release of raw data, but courts of law have not always endorsed these protections. For example, though of limited precedent value, this District Court held that raw test data, in this case, Rorschach test responses, were part of "educational records" under FERPA, thus allowing access to the parents (*John K. and Mary K. v. Board of Education for School District #65, Cook County*, 1987).

Additional legal issues pertaining to psychological testing include the means by which results are applied to students, particularly across racial groups. Before this issue was raised with specific regard to educational testing, the U.S. Supreme Court declared its intent with regard to testing used in employment decisions. In *Griggs v. Duke Power* (1971), the Court held that the Civil Rights Act of 1964 prohibited an employer from requiring the passing of standardized intelligence tests as a condition of employment or as a requirement for job transfer when (1) these standards are not significantly related to successful performance of the job in question, and (2) these requirements serve to disqualify racial minorities at a significantly higher rate than white applicants. Also of great significance, the Court held that discrimination need not be intentional to be illegal. In holding that performance on a standardized test could be caused by something other than the employee's aptitude, the Court relied in part on a 1960 census, which showed that in North Carolina, while 34% of white males had completed high school, only 12% of black males had done so. Furthermore, a study by the Equal Employment Opportunity Commission (EEOC) found in one case that the use of a battery of tests, including the Wonderlic and Bennett tests used by Duke Power, resulted in 58% of whites passing the tests, as compared to only 6% of blacks. While the Court placed the burden of proof on the plaintiff (someone claiming discrimination on the basis of IQ testing must prove the discrimination; *Wards Cove Packing Company, Inc. v. Atonio*, 1989), the *Griggs* decision set a legal precedent that IQ testing could be racially biased.

In the session following the *Griggs* decision, the Court turned its attention specifically to the application of these principles in educational settings. In *Larry P. v. Riles* (1972), the center of the Court's decision was the use of IQ tests to place children in educable mentally retarded (EMR) classes. The plaintiffs in the case claimed that the IQ tests used in the placement of students into EMR classes funneled a disproportionately large number of minority students away from regular classrooms. This high rate of placement into special classrooms worked to the students' disadvantage. Considerable testimony was presented both in favor of and opposed to IQ testing. This Court ultimately found that the tests violated federal law and the Constitution, and permanently enjoined their use. It further required that any intelligence tests given for educational placement or selection must yield the same pattern of scores for different groups of students, yield approximately equal means for all standardization sample subgroups, and yield scores correlated with relevant criterion measures (i.e., a student receiving a low IQ score should also be getting poor grades). Essentially, the Court found that the tests were racially or culturally biased and that the differences between interracial group means on the tests had not been explained. Eight years later, a somewhat similar suit ended in a contrary conclusion to *Larry P. v. Riles*. A different court determined that standardized intelligence tests (used with other criteria) were not racially biased against minorities in the placement of students in special classes (*PASE v. Hannon*, 1980). In that case, the judge personally reviewed each question on standard intelligence tests and "determined" himself that very few of them were racially or culturally biased.

As may be immediately evident, both of these prior cases are problematic. While they provided a legal decision, their logic should seem flawed to someone familiar with the issues from a mental health perspective. In the *Larry P.* case, the court essentially required that IQ tests produce the same overall result for different racial groups. While there continues to be considerable debate on this issue (which is well beyond the scope of this text), "forcing" scores to be equivalent across racial groups can be very problematic. At the root of this problem is the possibility that there are actual differences in IQ scores across ethnic groups. While these differences are probably more attributable to socioeconomic status than to actual intelligence, the scores cannot simply be "fixed" to alleviate differences. In the *PASE* case, the judge intuitively decided whether specific test items were racially or culturally biased, a highly unreliable form of decision making. Both cases illustrate a serious lack of psychological sophistication in the judiciary. The question should not be whether they really measure some innate ability, but rather whether they adequately measure whatever they are being used to determine (e.g., classroom placement).

An interesting, and probably provocative, possibility is that the concerns about IQ tests favoring certain groups (i.e., white students) could in fact be argued in the reverse direction. It does not always benefit a child to receive a higher score on an IQ test (i.e., if the child could benefit from remedial services). While we have never heard such an argument made, it could be said that groups "favored" by the tests are disproportionately denied access to expensive remedial courses. After all, if a student truly needs special help, would it not be to his or her benefit to receive it if good help were available? At issue in this controversy may be the ability of a school system to afford special placement for a high number of students. What is a school's responsibility to provide such opportunities?

SPECIAL PLACEMENT: OBLIGATIONS FOR EDUCATION

The fact cannot be denied that placement in specialized classrooms can be relatively expensive, since instructors are typically required to have special training and usually work with a lower student:teacher ratio. Where does a school system's responsibility end with regard to providing for the education of students with special needs? Two more contemporary U.S. Supreme Court decisions provide the current answer to this question.

In the case of *Zobrest v. Catalina Foothills School District* (1993), the U.S. Supreme Court upheld a public school district's payment of a sign language interpreter for a deaf student in a parochial school. This was permitted even though it was clear that the religious aspects of the school were thoroughly mixed with the educational program. In earlier cases, the Court had rejected public payment of parochial schools' teachers or guidance counselors, so this ruling clearly applied to students with special needs. Justice White, now off the U.S. Supreme Court, provided the majority vote on this issue, so it is unclear how far this principle will be carried in future cases.

Where then does a public school system's responsibility end as far as providing specialized services? Under the Individuals with Disabilities Education Act, schools are required to provide any related services that a student may require in order to attend school within his or her district. If the needed services are available at another school *in the same district*, the student may be transported (at the school's expense) to the new facility. This requirement does not, however, extend to "medical services" that are ambiguously defined. Through the 1990s, school systems denied provision of special services for mental disorders (including behavioral disorders) that they deemed to fall under "medical." Finally, in *Cedar Rapids Community School District v. Garret F.* (1999), the school was required to provide and fund a full-time nurse to monitor a ventilator. The U.S. Supreme Court ruled that such support did not fall under the realm of "medical" support, which it defined very specifically as treatment requiring a physician. The impact of this ruling for mental health professionals should be readily apparent, because treatment by any nonpsychiatrist mental health professionals clearly falls outside of the exempted "medical" services. A little-realized (or at least little-utilized) implication for any mental health professional whose child client(s) may be struggling in school is that the school (not the parent) is responsible for paying 100% of the costs of any treatment that would help the student remain in school. An extreme (but very successful) example of the application of this law was implemented for a client of the second author of this volume who received one-to-one supervision by a trained caseworker during school hours, all at the expense of the school. A matter to which the court may have to attend in the near future may be applicability of this ruling to doctoral-level psychologists, particularly following the potential extension of prescription rights.

JUVENILE LAW: CLASSIC, CONTEMPORARY, AND BEYOND

Juvenile law in the United States arguably represents the extension of our most cherished civil rights to our most vulnerable citizens. In that way, the cases reviewed here represent successes for our legal system. However, understanding the legal issues that apply to juveniles (even those that also pertain to mental health) requires much more study. For this reason, the topics of the juvenile death penalty, child abuse, and child custody are each covered in their own chapters.

Nevertheless, the cases reviewed in this broad chapter should also hint at some future possibilities for juvenile law. While it is true that the systems for dealing with juveniles have historically continued to approximate those for dealing with adults, it is also true that the changes have generally represented significant protections of liberties for juveniles (at least, relevant to the state of the juvenile's rights before the rulings). However, at least with case law governing adult criminals, one typically expects vacillations away from the rights of the individual when they are in opposition to the rights of society. Such seems to be the case given the public perception that juvenile crime is on the rise, as is the severity of crimes committed by children. If we may draw any inference from the recent Washington, DC area sniper case, in which one of the defendants was 17 at the time of the shootings, the future looks less than bright for serious juvenile offenders. The choice of Virginia as the first jurisdiction to try the case was based upon one criterion: Virginia courts were the most likely to execute a 17-year-old.[4] Chapter 20, on the juvenile death penalty, provides a more in-depth analysis of the myriad issues pertinent to that topic.

---

[4] At the time of this writing, Lee Boyd Malvo, the 17-year-old sniper suspect, had received one sentence of life without parole. Jurors cited his youth as a mitigating factor in not sentencing him to death. Malvo still faces other charges for which jurors could impose the death penalty.

CASE REFERENCES

Breed v. Jones, 421 U.S. 519 (1975).

Brown v. Board of Education, 347 U.S. 483 (1954).

Brown v. Board of Education II, 349 U.S. 294; 75 S. Ct. 753; 99 L. Ed. 1083; 1955 U.S. LEXIS 734 (1955).

Cedar Rapids Community School District v. Garret F., 526 U.S. 66; 119 S. Ct. 992; 143 L. Ed. 2d 154; 1999 U.S. LEXIS 1709 (1999).

Goss v. Lopez, 419 U.S. 565 (1975).

Griggs v. Duke Power, 401 U.S. 424 (1971).

In re Gault, 387 U.S. 1 (1967).

In re Winship, 397 U.S. 358 (1970).

John K. and Mary K. v. Board of Education for School District #65, Cook County, 504 N.E.2d 797 (Ill. App. 1987).

Kelson v. City of Springfield, 767 F.2d 65 (9th Cir. 1985).

Kent v. U.S., 383 U.S. 541 (1966).

Kremens v. Bartley, 431 U.S. 119 (1977).

Larry P. v. Riles, 343 F. Supp. 1306 (N.D. Cal. 1972) (preliminary injunction), aff'd, 502 F.2d 963 (9th Cir. 1974), other proceedings, 495 F. Supp. 926 (N.D. Cal. 1979).

McKeiver v. Pennsylvania, 403 U.S. 528 (1971).

Merriken v. Cressman, 364 F. Supp. 913 (E.D. Pa. 1973).

New Jersey v. T.L.O., 469 U.S. 325 (1985).

Parham v. J. R. and J. L., 442 U.S. 584 (1979).

PASE v. Hannon, 506 F. Supp. 831 (N.D. Ill. 1980).

Pennsylvania Association for Retarded Children v. Commonwealth of Pennsylvania, 334 F. Supp. 1257 (1971).

Pesce v. J. Sterling Morton High School District 201, Cook County Illinois, 830 F.2d 789 (7th Cir. 1987).

Pierce v. Society of Sisters, 268 U.S. 510 (1925).

Plessy v. Ferguson, 163 U.S. 537; 16 S. Ct. 1138; 41 L. Ed. 256; 1896 U.S. LEXIS 3390 (1896).

San Antonio Independent School District v. Rodriguez, 411 U.S. 1 (1973).

Schall v. Martin, 467 U.S. 253 (1984).

Wards Cove Packing Company, Inc. v. Atonio, 490 U.S. 642 (1989) (superseded by statute).

Zobrest v. Catalina Foothills School District, 113 S. Ct. 2462 (1993).

CHAPTER 20

Capital Punishment of Juveniles

The execution of individuals who were under the age of 18 at the time they committed their crimes has never been commonplace in the United States. Such executions averaged about one per year in the 360 years since the since the first known North American court sentenced a juvenile to death in 1642, in Plymouth County, Massachusetts. The 1999 execution of Sean Sellers represented the first execution in over 40 years of a murderer who was only 16 at the time of his offense.

Despite the relatively low rate of juvenile executions, the recent increase in juvenile violence, as portrayed in the media and the public's outcry for strict punishment kept the issue current into the new millennium. Most states presently allow for the transfer of juvenile offenders to the adult court system. When a particular state's criteria are met, the juvenile may be "certified" to stand trial as an adult. Typically, the heinousness of the crime is the primary criterion. At present, 38 states and the federal court system endorse punishment by death for certain crimes. In early 2005, 22 of these jurisdictions allowed for execution of juvenile perpetrators, provided they were certified to stand trial in the adult system.

Imposing the death penalty on any offender involves issues related to mental competency, criminal responsibility, and the adult death penalty (see Chapters 6, 7, and 17, respectively, of this volume). Should the legal system condone punishment by death at all? If so, should a young age at commission of the crime imply decreased mental capacity to fully understand the criminality and wrongfulness of the act, limiting criminal responsibility? Should age be considered as a mitigating factor, or is the commission of a violent crime at a young age in fact an aggravating circumstance? Are juveniles competent to understand the gravity of proceedings in which they may be sentenced to death, and are they capable of being fully aware of the meaning of the punishment? Any of these questions represent areas under which the execution of a juvenile may violate the perpetrator's civil rights as spelled out in the Constitution and in subsequent amendments. The question is whether or not juvenile status at the time of the crime represents per se violation of one of these parameters. Or can it be that some juveniles have the capacity to fully appreciate all aspects of the case as well as an adult?

As we considered in Chapter 17, most arguments opposing the death penalty are based on the Eighth Amendment to the U.S. Constitution, which protects U.S. citizens against cruel and unusual punishment. Over the years, the U.S. Supreme Court has developed at least two concepts used in considering whether a punishment is "cruel and unusual." The first concept is that of disproportionality between the crime and the sentence. That is to say, if the punishment does not fit the crime, it may be deemed cruel and/or unusual. The second concept, and that which has been applied to the death penalty as pertaining to juveniles, is that of the "evolving standards of decency" of the society. This concept allows for the fact that the meaning of "cruel and unusual" may vary from generation to generation. The phrase stems from the 1958 U.S. Supreme Court decision in *Trop v. Dulles* (1957), in which it was suggested that future judges be guided by "evolving standards of decency that mark the progress of a maturing society" (p. 4) in considering the parameters of Eighth Amendment protection (Templeton, 2000).

What then is the age at which we as a society believe that the death penalty may be applied without violating constitutional rights? In consecutive terms in the late 1980s, the U. S. Supreme Court addressed this question head-on. The rulings from the 1988 case of *Thompson v. Oklahoma*, and the 1989 cases of *Stanford v. Kentucky* and *Wilkins v. Missouri* currently define the age limits of the death penalty in the United States.

THE CASE OF *THOMPSON V. OKLAHOMA* (1998): A MINIMUM AGE FOR CAPITAL PUNISHMENT

In January 1983, William Wayne Thompson was 5 weeks from his 16th birthday. At 15 years of age, he had a slender build and was 5´ 6″ tall.

William already had a history of previous arrests for violent crimes, including attempted burglary, two for assault and battery, and two for assault with a deadly weapon. His first arrest was for assault and battery at the age of 13. He had been in and out of several treatment programs offered by the Oklahoma Department of Human Services, none of which seemed to improve his behavior. William was close with his sister Vicki and his brother Anthony Mann, but there was trouble in the family. Vicki's husband Charles Keene was becoming increasingly abusive toward her. William's acceptance of the situation was about to come to an abrupt and violent end.

Late on the evening of January 22, 1983, William left his mother's home in the company of his brother and friends Bobby Glass and Richard Jones. On the way out, William explained to his girlfriend, "We're going to kill Charles." In the early morning hours of January 23, William and the others went to Charles Keene's home armed with a .45-caliber pistol. The four assailants abducted Keene from his home, beat him severely, and told him that he would eventually die that night. William himself kicked Keene in the head, getting Keene's hair on his boots. At some point during the prolonged assault, William and the others chased Keene to the home of Malcolm "Possum" Brown and his wife Myrtle. The Browns had just returned home from vacation and retired early. They were woken by a gunshot and pounding at their door, with Keene, terrified, begging, "Possum, let me in. They're going to kill me" (*Thompson v. State*, 1986, p. 3). William and the others caught up with Keene and beat him on the Browns' front porch, failing to notice Mr. Brown briefly watching from the doorway. During the fray, one of them yelled, "This is for the way you treated our sister" (p. 3). Mr. Brown would later testify at trial that Keene was unable to defend himself from the onslaught of kicks and punches thrown by three of the men, while a fourth, with the handgun, stood guard off to the side. While it had been too dark for him to identify any of the men, Brown had seen one of them hit Keene repeatedly with a long object, presumably a pipe or stick. After realizing that the Browns were in fact at home, the assailants dragged Charles Keene across the lawn to a waiting car and threw him into the trunk. Keene was never seen alive again.

William and one of the others drove the lifeless body of Charles Keene to the banks of the Washita River. It was here, a codefendant later testified, that William cut Keene's throat, abdomen, and chest "so the fish could eat his body." The assailants chained Keene's lifeless body to a concrete block and threw it into the river. Upon returning home, William was overheard telling his mother that Keene was dead and that his sister Vicki would not have to worry about him again. In the following weeks, the four friends were heard making various comments regarding the fate of the missing Keene.

Charles Keene's body was recovered from the Washita River on February 18, 1983, and examined by the Oklahoma Chief Medical Examiner. It was concluded that he had been severely beaten including the infliction of a broken leg. He had also suffered knife cuts to his throat, chest, and abdomen, and two gunshots from the .45. William was arrested along with his brother and the two friends. Each of the four would receive a separate trial.

Due to his significant involvement in this particularly heinous crime, William was certified to stand trial as an adult by the District Court of Grady County, Oklahoma. He was charged with first-degree murder, which carried the maximum penalty of death. The evidence against William was overwhelming. Material torn from his baseball cap linked him to the Brown residence, and his three coassailants testified against him. Perhaps most damning was testimony by William's own girl-friend that he had admitted to shooting Keene in the head and slashing his throat. In further condemnation, a psychologist testified at trial that William suffered from Antisocial Personality Disorder and would likely not benefit from treatment in the juvenile justice system, citing his history of failed attempts at rehabilitation. Given the weight of the evidence and the ferocity with which Keene had been beaten and killed, the jury unanimously decided upon a verdict and punishment. Despite his young age, William Wayne Thompson was guilty of the crime of murder in the first degree and should be sentenced to death. The judge agreed with the jury's recommendation, and William was sentenced to death. One by one, in separate trials, his three collaborators received the same fate.

The Appeal Process

The Court of Criminal Appeals of Oklahoma denied the initial appeal, citing the atrociousness of the crime, William Thompson's direct involvement in killing Keene, and the appropriateness with which he had been certified to stand trial as an adult. Thompson and his attorneys then appealed the case to the U.S. Supreme Court. The primary issue on appeal was the constitutionality of imposing the death penalty on a defendant who was only 15 years old (albeit 15 years, 10 months, and 3 weeks) at the time of the offense.

The case was argued before the Court on November 9, 1987. Seven months later, on June 29, the Court handed down a 5 to 3 (Justice Kennedy declined participation) decision that the State of Oklahoma had indeed violated the 15-year-old's constitutional Eighth Amendment protection against cruel and unusual punishment. Justice Stevens wrote the plurality decision (joined by Justices Brennan, Marshall, and Blackmun), which stated that the current standards of decency in the country were against capital punishment of juveniles. To support this finding, Justice Stevens cited the fact that the majority of states that specified a minimum age for execution did so at 16. Justice O'Connor concurred, citing her primary concern that a juvenile could not be constitutionally subjected to the death penalty under a state statute that did not place *any* restriction whatsoever on the age of defendants who may be tried as adults.[1] Justice Scalia, writing the dissent (joined by Chief Justice Rehnquist and Justice White) argued that the Oklahoma court *had* considered the ramifications of sentencing Thompson to death, because his young age was argued to the judge and jury as a mitigating factor throughout the trial.

The Legacy of *Thompson*

On June 29, 1988, the U.S. Supreme Court remanded the case back to the Oklahoma Court of Criminal Appeals, with an order to vacate William's death sentence, effectively doing the same for all death row inmates in the United States who were age 15 or younger at the time of their offenses. After the case of *Thompson v. Oklahoma*, 15-year-old offenders were protected from receiving the death penalty. Five and a half years after participating in the brutal beating and murder of Charles Keene, William left Oklahoma's death row, never to return.

This decision, however, left open the constitutional question of the death penalty for offenders who were 16 or 17 at the time of the crime. The U.S. Supreme Court would respond to this question the following year in the cases of *Stanford v. Kentucky* and *Wilkins v. Missouri*. These two separate cases reached the U.S. Supreme Court at the same time, and so were considered together under the combined name of *Stanford v. Kentucky* (1989).

---

[1]Justice O'Connor's statement implies that had the Oklahoma statute specified a minimum age less than 15, under which juveniles could not be sentenced to death, the Court might very well have reached a split decision.

THE 1989 CASES OF *STANFORD V. KENTUCKY* AND *WILKINS V. MISSOURI:* CAPITAL SENTENCING OF 16- AND 17-YEAR-OLDS

The Case of Kevin Stanford

Kevin Stanford lived in Louisville, Kentucky, 8 months shy of his 18th birthday in midwinter of 1981. Kevin already had a history of legal involvement, with charges including arson, burglary, sexual abuse, theft, and assault, leading to multiple placements in juvenile treatment facilities. In between institutional confinements, Kevin lived with various relatives. By this time, he was an experienced drug user, having started using at around age 13. Relatives were concerned about the negative impact that the drug use had on his personality, including his lack of appropriate social skills.

On the evening of January 7, 1981, Kevin Stanford and his friends David Buchanan and Troy Johnson were riding around in Johnson's car. The trio stopped at a Checker convenience store in Louisville's west end, intending to rob the place. Kevin and David exited the car, entering the store as Johnson kept lookout in the getaway car. Barbel Poore was working alone that night in the store. During the robbery that ensued, Ms. Poore was repeatedly raped. The three assailants kidnapped her and took her to a secluded area a short distance away. There, she was again raped before her captors shot her, once in the face and once in the back of the head. The three then returned to the store and stole 300 cartons of cigarettes and a minimal amount of cash. While Kevin Stanford later attempted to implicate one of his friends in the murder, evidence eventually showed that he himself was the triggerman.

After their arrests in mid-January, both Buchanan and Johnson implicated Kevin as the primary perpetrator. However, it was Stanford's own statements that ultimately proved to be the most damning evidence against him. Besides leaving physical evidence on the victim's body, Stanford, in a conversation with a correctional officer while awaiting trial, stated, "I had to shoot her; the bitch lived next to me and she would recognize me" (p. 7). The officer would later testify that Stanford discussed his role in the murder in a "laughing manner."

In considering a potential transfer to adult court, the Jefferson County Juvenile Court considered the likelihood that Stanford could benefit from treatment. Despite a finding by that Court that he *was* amenable to treatment, the state of Kentucky did not currently have a program in which Stanford could seek appropriate treatment. The case was therefore transferred to adult court, as was that of David Buchanan, who was 16 at the time of the crime. Stanford and Buchanan were to stand trial together as adults. Initially, prosecutors sought the death penalty for both individuals but later dropped it for Buchanan.

During the 2-week trial in August 1982, the overwhelming physical evidence and admissions made by each of the three robbers proved too much for the defense to surmount. The death-qualified jury found both defendants guilty and recommended the maximum sentence for each. On September 28, 1982, the judge announced that Kevin Stanford would be put to death by the Commonwealth of Kentucky for the murder of Barbel Poore. On appeal, his conviction and death sentence were affirmed by the Supreme Court of Kentucky.

The Case of Heath Wilkins

Five hundred miles west of where Kevin Stanford appealed his conviction from Kentucky's death row, 16-year-old Heath Wilkins had already embarked on his own criminal career in Kansas City, Missouri. Wilkins had served time in a juvenile detention center for, among other things, attempted murder of his mother at age 12.

In mid-July 1985, Wilkins and his friend Patrick Stevens began discussing plans to carry out their own convenience store robbery. The two later told their plan to a friend and to Wilkins's girlfriend. The four had been living on the street for the past few months and were running short on funds. The plan was to rob Linda's Liquors in north Kansas City. While finalizing the plans, Wilkins stated to the other three that he would kill anyone in the store, so as to leave absolutely no witnesses.

On the night of July 27, 1985, the four friends met at the North Kansas City Hospital. Wilkins and Stevens walked through the woods to the liquor store, while the other two went to procure a taxi to take after the robbery. Wilkins carried with him a recently sharpened butterfly knife, while Stevens carried a bag in which to stow their take. Arriving at a creek near the liquor store around 10:30 that night, the two watched and waited while customers filtered through. Wiping their shoes as they entered, the two carried out their well-thought-out plan to complete the robbery. Wilkins distracted the owner and lone attendant, Nancy Allen, while Stevens positioned himself to subdue her. As soon as Stevens grabbed Ms. Allen, Wilkins sprung behind the counter and stabbed her in the kidney area, inflicting what he later said he thought would be a fatal wound. Falling to the floor, Nancy

Allen lay bleeding on her back behind the counter. Stevens had difficulty opening the cash register. Hoping the robbers would get what they wanted and leave, Ms. Allen told the robbers how to open the register. Realizing that she was still alive, Wilkins stabbed her three more times in the chest. Allen continued pleading for her life, so Wilkins stabbed her four times in the neck. Medical testimony would later show that the 26-year-old mother of two was likely dead before the final wound was inflicted. The two assailants left the store with a total of $450 in cash and checks, and some liquor.

The four friends rendezvoused back at the hospital and carried out a mix of taxi and greyhound trips designed to confuse any pursuing authorities. Eventually, they went to a nearby lake park, where they planned to spend the rest of the summer in hiding. However, back in town, word got out that Wilkins and his friends were responsible for the robbery and brutal murder. Police soon found the four friends and arrested them 2 two weeks after Nancy Allen bled to death on the floor of her store.

Wilkins made a statement to the police detailing the commission of the crime and his role as executioner. He was promptly certified by the Missouri juvenile system to stand trial as an adult. The court cited the ferocity of the crime and the previous failure of the juvenile system's attempts at rehabilitation. During the trial, Wilkins objected to his attorney's initial plea of not guilty by reason of mental disease or defect (insanity). He requested, and was granted, the right to proceed without an attorney, following two independent psychological assessments establishing his competency to do so. Despite numerous admonitions by Judge Glennon McFarland as to the questionable judgment used in making the decision, Wilkins was allowed to plead guilty to all charges.

During the sentencing phase of the trial, with his ex-attorney standing by, as ordered by the court, both the prosecutor and Wilkins requested that the punishment be set at death by lethal injection. In explaining that he had indeed weighed the options of life without parole and death, Wilkins explained, "One I fear, the other one I don't" (p. 26).

After reviewing all of the aggravating circumstances of the robbery, Judge McFarland complied with both parties' requests and handed down a sentence of death. From death row, Wilkins objected to appellate briefs filed on his behalf. The Supreme Court of Missouri ordered another competency evaluation be conducted to determine Wilkins's ability to waive his right to appellate counsel. After deeming Wilkins competent during all stages of the first trial, the psychologist appointed by the State Supreme Court concluded that Wilkins suffered from a mental disorder that sufficiently impaired his decision-making ability and judgment so as to render him incompetent to waive his appellate rights. As such, an appeal was subsequently made to the Missouri Supreme Court on Wilkins's behalf, but the initial judgment was upheld.

Wilkins appealed to the U.S. Supreme Court, where his case was combined with a similar case of a 17-year-old who had committed a similar crime in Kentucky 4 years earlier. While Kevin Stanford and Heath Wilkins had never met, their lives were soon to convene in the highest court in the land. Both were to have the constitutionality of their death sentences challenged in the U.S. Supreme Court.

STANFORD AND WILKINS:
THE COMBINED U.S. SUPREME COURT APPEAL

Both cases were appealed on the grounds that imposition of the death penalty for convicted felons who were less than age 18 at the time of their crimes violated the Bill of Rights protection against cruel and unusual punishment. As in the *Thompson* case the previous year, the Court considered the evolving standards of decency in the country. The 5 to 4 majority (including Justices Scalia, White, O'Connor, Kennedy, and Chief Justice Rehnquist) upheld the death sentences. As in the *Thompson* case, they cited the fact that the majority of states specifying a minimum age for capital punishment set it at age 16. The dissent (including Justices Brennan, Marshall, Blackmun, and Stevens) argued that the majority had wrongly assumed that the states not setting an age limit were endorsing unlimited age for the death penalty. Nevertheless, the same court that granted William Thompson a reprieve from his death sentence the previous year ruled that Kevin Stanford and Heath Wilkins could be sentenced to death despite being juveniles at the time of their crimes. In this manner, the Supreme Court set the precedent that states may indeed sentence juveniles to death, provided they are at least 16 years of age at the commission of the crime.

THE LEGACY OF THOMPSON, STANFORD, AND WILKINS

These three cases set the precedent regarding age parameters for imposition of the death penalty in the United States into 2005. Up until that time, juveniles who committed capital crimes at age 16 or 17 could be

---

BOX 20.1. Where Are They Now?

William Wayne Thompson is currently serving his life sentence at the Joseph Harp Correctional Center in Lexington, Oklahoma, about 30 miles south of Oklahoma City. His brother Anthony Mann is currently listed as serving life without the possibility of parole at another medium-security facility 170 miles to the north. The fate of Bobby Glass and Richard Jones is less clear, because they are not listed as residing in any Oklahoma prison at this time, nor are they listed on Oklahoma's past execution list.

Through 2003, Kevin Stanford lived on death row at the Kentucky State Penitentiary in Eddyville, Kentucky. Amid much debate, Kevin Stanford's life hung in the balance between Governor Paul Patton, whose political career was waning following a Clintonesque sex scandal. Attorney General Ben Chandler staunchly advocated that the Governor let the rulings of "20 courts and 101 state and federal judges over the past 20 years" stand (Wolfson, 2003, p. 1). On December 8, 2003, Governor Patton commuted Kevin Stanford's death sentence, forever freeing him from his home on death row.

Three hundred and twenty miles to the east, David Buchanan is incarcerated at Eastern Kentucky Correctional Complex. Buchanan was denied parole in January 1989, and again in January 1999. His next date before the Kentucky parole board is scheduled for January 2007. Troy Johnson is not currently incarcerated in the state of Kentucky.

On final appeal in Missouri's Clay County Circuit Court in May 1999, Heath Wilkins was allowed to plead guilty to second-degree murder and armed robbery. While this verdict precluded imposition of the death penalty, Wilkins was sentenced to three life sentences, no doubt a strong message to any parole board. Now in his early 30s, he will most likely spend the rest of his days incarcerated in the Missouri prison system.

---

tried as adults and legally be given the death penalty. Recall, however, that each of these cases was decided on the basis of the *"evolving* standards of decency." Thus, changing standards may beget different rulings. On January 26, 2004, the U.S. Supreme Court agreed to revisit the juvenile death penalty in the Missouri case of *Roper v. Simmons* (2003). The Missouri Supreme Court vacated the death sentence of Christopher Simmons, who was 17 when he murdered Shirley Cook in 1993. The Court ruled that the standards of decency had evolved since the *Stanford* ruling, such that sentencing juveniles to death is no longer condoned. The U.S. Supreme Court heard the case on October 13, near the close of the 2004 session. The Court did not publish its opinion until March 2005. In the interim, it continued to grant stays of execution to offenders who were under 18 at the time of their crimes.

THE CASE OF *ROPER V. SIMMONS* (2005): ABOLISHING THE JUVENILE DEATH PENALTY

In September of 1993, Christopher Simmons, a white male, was only 7 months shy of his 18th birthday. At around that time, Simmons made known to friends that he wanted to murder someone. In chilling, callous terms, he described his plan to his friends Charles Benjamin (age 15) and John Tessmer (age 16). Simmons proposed that the three friends break into and rob a home, tie up a victim, and throw the victim off a bridge. Simmons encouraged his friends by assuring them that they could "get away with it" because they were minors (*Roper v. Simmons*, 2003, p. 22). The assertion may have seemed out of place coming from Simmons who had never been involved with the police before.

At about 2 A.M. on September 9, 1993, the three friends met for the purpose of carrying out the robbery. Deciding not to participate, Tessmer left before Simmons and Benjamin went to the home of Shirley Crook. Simmons and Mrs. Crook had previously been involved in a car accident with each other. Simmons reached through an open window and unlocked the back door. Inside, he turned on a hallway light, waking Mrs. Crook. When she called out, "Who's there?" Simmons entered her bedroom. By Simmons's own account, it was at this point that he decided to kill her.

Overpowering the much weaker Mrs. Crook in a struggle, Simmons and Benjamin bound her with duct tape, covering her eyes and mouth. The two then stole her minivan, loaded her inside, and drove to a nearby state park. At the park, Simmons and Benjamin reinforced Crook's bindings with more duct tape. They covered her head with a towel before walking her a short distance to a small bridge that crossed the Meramec River. Once on the bridge, Simmons and Benjamin wound electrical wire around Crook's wrists and wrapped duct tape around her face. They then threw Mrs. Crook from the bridge, drowning her in the waters below. Simmons had carried out his plan.

Returning home from an overnight trip the next day, Mrs. Crook's husband found his bedroom in disarray and immediately reported his wife missing. That same afternoon, fisherman recovered Mrs. Crook's body from the river. Meanwhile, Simmons had been bragging to friends and acquaintances that he had killed a woman while robbing her house "because the bitch seen my face" (*Roper v. Simmons*, 2003, p. 5). Police arrested Simmons at his high school the next day. At the police station in Fenton, Missouri, Simmons waived his right to have an attorney and agreed to perform a reenactment of the crime.

Simmons at Trial

The State of Missouri charged Simmons with burglary, kidnapping, and murder, and tried him as an adult. John Tessmer, saving himself from being charged, testified against Simmons during the trial. Tessmer laid out in detail how Simmons had carefully planned the murder before-hand. However, Tessmer was not to be the star witness. Simmons, him-self, took that honor when police played his videotaped confession and reenactment of the crime. The defense called no witnesses in the guilt phase, and the jury promptly returned a verdict of murder.

In cases eligible for capital sentencing, Missouri operates under a bifurcated system in which a separate penalty phase follows any finding of guilt. At the penalty phase, the State sought the death penalty. Among the aggravating factors, the prosecutor asserted that the murder was out-rageously and wantonly vile, horrible, and inhumane. As if the facts of the case were not enough to verify this assertion, Shirley Crook's hus-band, daughter, and two sisters testified to the jury about the impact that the loss had on their families.

Simmons's parents testified on his behalf, describing to jurors the close relationships they had formed with their son and the help that Simmons had provided in raising his siblings and caring for his grand-mother. The devastated parents pleaded for the jury's mercy.

Simmons's young age was a banner waived by both the prosecutor and defense attorney in their respective final arguments. Simmons's attorney argued that his client was not old enough to be held fully accountable as he wasn't even old enough to drink, serve on juries, or even see R-rated movies, because "the legislatures have wisely decided that individuals of a certain age aren't responsible enough" (*Roper v. Simmons*, 2003, p. 5). The prosecutor rebutted: "Age, he says. Think about age. Seventeen years old. Isn't that scary? Doesn't that scare you? Mitigating? Quite the contrary I submit. Quite the contrary" (p. 5).

The jury sided with the prosecutor and sentenced Simmons to death. His appeals to state and federal courts were rejected. However, in the 2002 case of *Atkins v. Virginia* (discussed at length in Chapter 14), the U.S. Supreme Court essentially held that mentally retarded offend-ers could not be sentenced to death due to diminished capacity to understand their crime and sentencing. To execute a murderer with Mental Retardation would constitute cruel and unusual punishment, prohibited by the Eighth Amendment of the Constitution, as well as a violation of the Fourteenth Amendment's due process guarantee. Simmons's attorney filed a new appeal on the basis that the reasoning in *Atkins* also applied to juveniles. The Missouri Supreme Court actually agreed that U.S. standards of decency had evolved such that the execution of juveniles could now be considered cruel and unusual. Prosecutors appealed to the U.S. Supreme Court, who agreed to hear the case.

Prosecutors' U.S. Supreme Court Appeal

Missouri prosecutors argued that their state supreme court was in violation of *Stanford v. Kentucky* (1989). A litany of amicus briefs were filed on Simmons's behalf from groups ranging from Nobel Peace Prize laureates to victim's rights groups to the American Medical and Psychiatric Associations. The American Psychological Association filed a brief, which concluded that "scientific evidence shows persons under 18 lack the ability to take moral responsibility for their decisions" (American Psychological Association, 2004, p. 18).

Citing the defense's arguments, the Court ruled 5 to 4 that imposing the death penalty on an offender who was younger than 18 at the time of the crime was indeed in violation of the cruel and unusual punishment and due process clauses in the Eighth and Fourteenth Amendments, respectively. The majority justified overturning *Stanford* on the basis that the standards of decency had evolved since 1989.

In his dissent, Justice Scalia specifically took aim at the brief from the American Psychological Association. He pointed out that a brief filed by the same organization in 1990 (American Psychological Association, 1990) supported juveniles' decision-making capacity for having abortions. He continued:

> The APA brief, citing psychology treatises and studies too numerous to list here, asserted: "By middle adolescence (age 14–15) young people develop abilities similar to adults in reasoning about moral dilemmas, understanding social rules and laws, [and] reasoning about interpersonal relationships and interpersonal problems." (p. 45)

Regardless of this apparent inconsistency, the slim majority ruling of the Court effectively abolished the juvenile death penalty. In doing so, the Court clearly referenced a belief that the evolving standards of decency in society *currently* forbade the practice. But were these really new sentiments? At least with respect to international sentiment, the answer is clearly, "no."

CAPITAL PUNISHMENT OF JUVENILES:
THE BROADER INTERNATIONAL PICTURE

The majority of U.S. jurisdictions that endorsed the death penalty did so for offenders as young as 16. However, the United States was one of only six countries that executed anyone for a juvenile offense during the 1990s, executing as many juveniles as executed in the other five countries combined. As of 2000, at least 144 countries expressly prohibited the execution of juveniles.

Any execution of juvenile offenders is actually in violation of several international civil rights treaties that have been either endorsed or even formally ratified by the United States. Such treaties date back to the fourth Geneva Convention, which was ratified by the U.S. following World War II. As another example, the International Covenant on Civil and Political Rights (ICCPR) clearly stipulates that the "sentence of death shall not be imposed from crimes committed by persons below eighteen years of age" (as cited in Templeton, 2000, p. 5). This particular provision is specifically deemed "nonderogable, even in times of public emergency" (p. 5) meaning that it may not be broken under any circumstances. However, in ratifying the Covenant in 1992, the U.S. Senate specifically stated, "The United States reserves the right, subject to its Constitutional constraints, to impose capital punishment on any person . . . including . . . persons below eighteen years of age" (p. 5). Additional international treaties that have been endorsed by the United States include similar exclusions of the capital punishment of juveniles, but the United States has to date declined formal ratification. In late 2003, the Inter-American Commission on Human Rights ruled that the United States was in violation of international law when an offender who was under 18 at the time of the crime was put to death. The Commission went so far as to rule that the U.S. government should compensate the deceased offender's family. The juvenile death penalty was never challenged in the U.S. Supreme Court on the grounds of violation of international law. The 2005 decision in *Roper v. Simmons* indicated that the standards of decency in the United States had finally evolved into accordance with decades of international law.

CASE REFERENCES

Roper v. Simmons, 538 U.S. 923; 123 S. Ct. 1582; 155 L. Ed. 2d 314; 2003 U.S. LEXIS 2213 (2003).
Roper v. Simmons, 125 S. Ct. 1183; 161 L. Ed. 2d 1; 2005 U.S. LEXIS 2200 (2005).

Stanford v. Kentucky, 492 U.S. 937 (1989).

Thompson v. Oklahoma, 487 U.S. 815 (1988).

Thompson v. State, 1986 OK CR 130; 724 P.2d 780; 1986 Okla. Crim. App. LEXIS 318 (1986).

Trop v. Dulles, 356 U.S. 86; 78 S. Ct. 590; 2 L. Ed. 2d 630; 1958 U.S. LEXIS 1284 (1957).

CHAPTER 21

Child Abuse

The physical and sexual abuse of children has been clearly documented throughout history and across cultures. Such abuse was frequently abhorred, but few preventive measures were traditionally taken. The first formal legal intervention in a child abuse case, in 1875, had to be prosecuted through animal protection laws and with the efforts of the Society for the Prevention of Cruelty to Animals (SPCA). All 50 states, partly spurred by the federal Child Abuse Prevention and Treatment Act (1984), have now established legal routes to identify and intervene in abusive families.

ISSUES IN DEFINING AND IDENTIFYING CHILD ABUSE

Varying laws across the states create complexity in legally defining child abuse and maltreatment. *Child abuse* is typically defined as physical abuse, sexual abuse, or neglect. However, some states also include emotional or psychological maltreatment. Further complicating the already varied legal definitions are the more specific subdivisions sometimes identified, such as sexual exploitation (child prostitution and pornography), medical neglect, and a failure to protect a child from witnessing domestic violence. A review of problems related to the multiple legal definitions for child maltreatment can be found in Reppucci and Fried (2000). For the purpose of this chapter, only child physical and sexual abuse are addressed.

Identifying and defining what is physical abuse is a complex task as well. In the vast majority of physical abuse cases, the first diagnostic cues are the actual physical signs. The commonly taught signs of physical abuse are the classic "four Bs," which consist of unexplained or unusual bruises, burns, bald spots, or bleeding. The problem here is that a great many children who are not being abused may evidence several of these physical signs. After all, many children, through accidents or normal play, sustain injuries that can mimic abuse symptoms. However, concern should be heightened if children or their caretakers provide explanations for physical signs of abuse that are inconsistent with their injuries. There are also behavioral indicators of physical abuse, which may include problems with schoolwork and peers, shrinking from physical contact, wearing clothes that seem more designed to cover the body than to keep one warm, and dissociative experiences.

There has been increasing attention to the sexual abuse of children (Edens, Buffington-Vollon, Keilen, Roskamp, & Anthony, 2005). Specific physical signs of sexual abuse are pain, rashes, itching or sores in the genital or anal areas, enuresis, encopresis, frequent urinary infections, or frequent vomiting. Behavioral symptoms of sexual abuse may include extreme secrecy, excessive bathing, indications of low self-worth, provocative or promiscuous sexual patterns, appearing more worldly than friends, or suddenly possessing money or merchandise that could have been used to bribe the child to keep quiet.

While additional behavioral indicators of both physical and sexual abuse can be identified, it is important to note that the presence of these traits is also common among nonabused children and should not be utilized in isolation to substantiate that abuse has occurred (Berliner, 1998; Fisher & Whiting, 1998; Kovera & Borgida, 1998; Lyon & Koehler, 1998). When evaluating whether behavioral characteristics such as age-inappropriate sexual acts are possible indicators of sexual abuse, it is imperative to be knowledgeable of the current normative data on the developmental research of children's sexuality. A more comprehensive review of the current literature on assessing for child abuse is beyond the scope of this chapter, but it can be found in Edens et al. (2005) and Kuehnle (2003).

Adding to the problem of assessing for child abuse is the method of recording the actual diagnoses. The text revision of the fourth edition of the *Diagnostic and Statistical Manual of Mental Disorders* (DSM-IV-TR) includes three categories relevant to child abuse: physical abuse of child (V61.21/995.54); sexual abuse of child (V61.21/995.53); and neglect of child (V61.21/995.52) (American Psychiatric Association, 2000). Yet even experienced frontline clinicians frequently fail to note that the V-codes listed are used when diagnosing the *perpetrator* of the abuse or neglect;

however, the latter 995.5 codes are utilized when the focus of attention is on the *child victim*. This common diagnostic error can lead to misidentification in, among other areas, research conducted on the prevalence of the diagnoses.

CHILD ABUSE AND CASE LAW

The idea of abused children meeting a common diagnosis was initially identified and addressed in the medical profession in the early 1950s. However, the first written acknowledgment of it was articulated in a landmark article over a decade later, in 1962, by Kempe, Silverman, Steele, Droegemueller, and Silver. This universal set of symptoms came to be referred to as the "battered child syndrome." The first clear legal identification of the battered child syndrome was established in the case of *People v. Jackson* (1971), where the court asserted that it had become an accepted medical "diagnosis." The *Jackson* court explained that the essence of this diagnosis was that a child's injuries were not inflicted by accidental means.

The formal legal acknowledgment of the battered child signified a step toward intervention by the system in cases of child abuse. But how did the system find out about the abuse in the first place? With diagnostic issues that are cloudy at best for even well-seasoned medical and mental health providers, legal professionals would surely struggle to make accurate identifications. Yet medical and mental health professionals were typically not in a position to hand out legal sanctions (to the offenders) or legal reprieves (to the victims). What rules, then, were to govern communication between the two professional groups? The following two court cases set the rules that currently apply.

THE CASE OF *LANDEROS V. FLOOD* (1976)[1]: MANDATED REPORTING OF SUSPECTED CHILD ABUSE

Gita Landeros was born on May 14, 1970, and spent the first year of her life being severerly abused by her mother. She received repeated, severe physical beatings at the hands of her mother and the mother's common-

---

[1] Except where specifically noted, information from this case was gathered from *Landeros v. Flood* (1976).

law husband Reyes. At 11 months of age, on April 26, 1971, Gita Landeros was taken to the San Jose Hospital by her mother and treated by Dr. A. J. Flood for a comminuted spiral fracture of her right tibia and fibula, which appeared to have been caused by a twisting force. This type of fracture indicates that the bones in the infant's right leg were "splintered or crushed into numerous pieces" (Webster's New International Dictionary (3rd ed., 1961 p. 457), as cited in *Landeros v Flood*, 1976). The physician noticed bruises all over her back, along with cuts and scrapes covering various other parts of her body. Even more significant was evidence of a skull fracture that was already in a stage of healing. Although the infant expressed fear and anxiety when approached, and the mother was unable to provide an explanation for her child's present injury, Gita Landeros was discharged from the hospital into her mother's custody without any further intervention. Gita returned home and was subjected to further physical abuse, which included "traumatic blows to her right eye and back, puncture wounds over her left lower leg and across her back, severe bites on her face, and second and third degree burns on her left hand" (p. 3).

On July 1, 1971, only a few months since she had last received medical treatment, Gita Landeros was taken to another hospital and treated by a different doctor, who immediately diagnosed battered child syndrome. This attending physician notified the local police and juvenile probation authorities, the appropriate procedures when a physician suspects abuse. At this time, Gita Landeros was finally removed from her abusive environment and placed into protective custody. After being hospitalized and undergoing surgery, she was placed in a foster home with foster parents who eventually adopted her.

Although the perpetrators were charged and convicted of the crime of child abuse, the child victim Gita Landeros was expected to suffer the probable loss of use or amputation of her left hand, along with enduring symptoms of mental distress that are often the result of abuse.

On behalf of Gita Landeros, her adopted parents brought forth civil charges of medical malpractice charges against Dr. A. J. Flood and the San Jose Hospitals and Health Center, Inc. The complaint alleged that the physician negligently failed to appropriately examine, diagnose, and treat her battered child syndrome, which should have included the procedure of taking X-rays and reporting the injuries to local law enforcement authorities or a juvenile probation department. While the initial trial court dismissed the charges, the Supreme Court of California later reversed this judgment in favor of Gita Landeros. This case generally established the basis for civil liability, essentially defining failure to diagnose battered child syndrome as malpractice, and specifically holding that there could be civil liability and damages awarded for failure to diagnose.

MANDATED REPORTING AND PROFESSIONAL ETHICS

All states currently mandate therapists to report cases of abuse, and many states require anyone aware of abuse to report it. Most states also require the reporting of any cases of "suspected" abuse (Herman, 2005). In most states, failure to report constitutes a misdemeanor, usually involving a fine and/or short jail term. Failure to report would also open the therapist to civil liabilities. Of course, such reporting breaks confidentiality, but state laws typically provide protection from civil suits when one breaks any ethical principles of confidentiality or any legal statutes regarding privileged communication. An excellent review of the issue of mandated reporting of child abuse is found in Kalichman (1993).

Therefore, mandated reporting of child abuse is fairly universally supported and *required* by both legal and ethical means. However, the *Landeros* decision does not represent the final word in case law on this matter. Thirteen years later, the U.S. Supreme Court would actually extend the duty to *report* to include a duty to *protect*, but with significant exceptions.

THE CASE OF *DESHANEY V. WINNEBAGO COUNTY* (1989)[2]: A DUTY TO PROTECT?

In 1979, Joshua DeShaney was born to Randy and Melody DeShaney in Wyoming. Shortly thereafter, in 1980, the DeShaney's were granted a divorce by a Wyoming court that also awarded custodial rights of Joshua to his father. His father moved him away to Neenah, Wisconsin, a city located in Winnebago County. Randy DeShaney married again; however, this second marriage also ended in divorce.

At the time of Randy DeShaney's divorce in January 1982, Joshua's stepmother alleged to the police that Randy DeShaney had previously hit his son Joshua so hard that marks were left on his body. The

---

[2] Except where specifically noted, information from this case was gathered from *DeShaney v. Winnebago County* (1989).

Winnebago County Department of Social Services (DSS) closed the case after interviewing Randy DeShaney, who denied the allegations.

In January 1983, Joshua DeShaney, covered with multiple bruises and abrasions, arrived at the local emergency room and was admitted to the hospital. Randy DeShaney's girlfriend Marie had brought Joshua to the hospital and had explained his injuries as the result of a physical attack by another child. The emergency room personnel suspected child abuse, and the Winnebego County DSS was immediately notified. A Wisconsin juvenile court order was then obtained that same day by DSS, and Joshua was placed in the temporary custody of the hospital. An impromptu "child protective team" was put together by the county a few days later to address Joshua's situation. The team consisted of a pediatrician, a psychologist, a police detective, a lawyer for the county, and several DSS caseworkers, including Ann Kemmeter and her superior, along with other hospital staff. It was determined by the team that Joshua could not be retained in the court's custody due to insufficient evidence of child abuse; therefore, he was returned to the custody of Randy DeShaney. The team, however, did make several recommendations, at that time intended to protect Joshua. Randy DeShaney had voluntarily signed a written agreement with DSS that he would comply with the team recommendations, which included enrolling Joshua in the Head Start program, receiving counseling services for himself from the Department, and telling his girlfriend Marie to move out of his home, because Randy had suggested that she might be perpetrating abuse against Joshua. Three weeks later, the Wisconsin juvenile court dismissed the child protection case that had been brought forth by DSS.

Only one month after the child protection case had been closed, DSS caseworker Ann Kemmeter was informed by emergency room personnel that Joshua had again received treatment for injuries of a suspicious nature. However, after consulting with the social worker from the hospital, she decided there was no evidence of child abuse to warrant any further action.

Ann Kemmeter later documented several suspicious injuries on Joshua's head during monthly visits she made to the DeShaney home for the next 6 months. In May, she observed a bump on Joshua's forehead, which, according to Randy DeShaney and Marie, he had gotten falling off a tricycle. During the month of July, the caseworker noted that Marie had not left the residence nor had Joshua been enrolled in the Head Start program as Randy DeShaney had promised in his previous agreement with DSS. In September, she was not even able to see Joshua, because he allegedly had been taken to the emergency room again, due to a scratched cornea. At her next home visit in October, Joshua had another bump on his head. One month later in November, she saw a scrape on Joshua's chin that appeared to be a burn mark caused by a cigarette. While Ann Kemmeter continued to note her suspicions that Joshua DeShaney might be a child victim of physical abuse perpetrated by someone in his own home, no action was taken by DSS to protect him. When DSS was notified by hospital personnel in late November 1983, that Joshua had again been treated at the emergency room for injuries including a cut forehead, bloody nose, swollen ear, and bruises on both shoulders that hospital personnel suspected to be caused by child abuse, DSS still did not respond.

During another home visit in January 1984, Ann Kemmeter's request to see Joshua was refused, because he was supposedly too sick and bedridden with the flu. On March 7, 1984, the caseworker unknowingly made her final visit to the DeShaney home. At this time, she learned that Joshua had passed out a few days earlier, without an explanation as to why. Ann Kemmeter neither saw nor asked to see Joshua on this date. One day later, 4-year-old Joshua DeShaney fell into a life-threatening coma after receiving a severe beating from Randy DeShaney. The treating physician who performed emergency brain surgery on Joshua discovered evidence of several previous traumatic head injuries, as well as other wounds and bruises all over his body, that had been inflicted over a long period of time. When Joshua's mother learned of the tragedy involving her son, DSS caseworker Ann Kemmeter informed her, "I just knew the phone would ring some day and Joshua would be dead" (*DeShaney v. Winnebago County*, 1989, p. 3). While Joshua did not die, his brain was so critically injured that it was half-destroyed, leaving Joshua so profoundly retarded that he would be forced to spend the rest of his life in an institution. Randy DeShaney was found guilty of child abuse and given a minimal sentence of 2 to 4 years.

Joshua DeShaney and his mother brought forth charges against Winnebago County, its DSS, and caseworker Ann Kemmeter and her supervisor for violating Joshua's Fourteenth Amendment rights by depriving him of his liberty without due process of law.

The question in this case was not whether the State had failed to protect Joshua, but whether it was to be held responsible for the consequences of its ultimate failure to protect him. The complaint alleged that Winnebago County DSS failed to *intervene* to protect Joshua against a risk of violence about which it knew or should have known. The District Court found that the failure of a State agency to provide protection from private violence to persons within its jurisdiction does not violate the due process clause. The Court of Appeals for the 7th Circuit affirmed this decision. The case was then appealed to the Supreme Court, which upheld previous rulings from lower courts that the State had no affirmative duty to protect Joshua.

While the court acknowledged that it had a duty to protect, it was found that the State was not liable for the injuries imposed on Joshua, because he was not actually in the custody of the State. The Court has acknowledged a duty to protect children not in the State's custody when it can be determined that a "special relationship" (i.e., prison inmates, psychiatric inpatients) exists between the State and the child.[3] Such was not the case with Joshua.

The DeShaney Court noted that Ann Kemmeter had acted with competence in accordance with her training. The Court also acknowledged that she was forced to walk a thin line in maintaining contact with the DeShaney family, because Joshua was not in State custody. Because the State knew that Joshua might be at risk for child abuse, the State therefore had a duty to protect him. However, in Joshua's case, the Court provided the rationale that because he was not in the custody of the State, the Court was not bound legally to protect him. This ruling leaves much to be desired when looking at State protection for children's rights.

A difficulty in interpreting the DeShaney case is that many have since construed this as a "failure to protect" case. Paradoxically, laws relevant to the ruling were actually created to protect individuals from State interference rather than to force the State to act. In the case of DeShaney, the State was found to have taken no action. Since the law did not mandate a duty to act (but merely requires that any action taken must be done so competently), the ruling favored the State in this particular case (Crosby-Currie & Repucci, 1999). Certainly, room for interpretation exists, and DeShaney should not be read as giving the State permission not to act in a particular case.

CHILDREN'S TESTIMONY IN ABUSE CASES

Other issues arise when trying to protect the rights of child who may at risk for abuse. These include the apparent suggestibility of children and

---

[3] Other cases that demonstrate a "special relationship between an individual and the state" can be found in Estelle v. Gamble (1976) and Youngberg v. Romeo (1982).

how this can impact their testimony in court proceedings (Herman, 2005). Suggestibility in legal proceedings involving children is an often-debated subject. However, it is known that a number of factors can cause a child (or adult, for that matter) to recall events incorrectly. Repetition, misinformation, and leading questions have all been shown to bias a child's memory at recall (Ceci, Ross, & Toglia, 1987). Repetitive questioning might lead the child to question whether his or her first answer had in fact been correct, and in so doing may cause the child to "recall" new information. Misinformation, information that comes after an event has occurred, can also sway an individual's memory. Leading questions used in the courtroom have been known to have an exceptionally profound impact on memory. The choice of words used by a skilled attorney can cause a witness to confuse events.

Cases that rely on memory, without other evidence to support the claim (i.e., medical evidence substantiating abuse), are quite tricky indeed. Numerous laboratory studies have demonstrated the fallibility of memory. In a hallmark study, Loftus (1993) utilized misleading and suggestive questioning to convince five subjects that they had each been lost in a shopping mall as a child. She concluded that it is possible to implant false memories, and that this can be done through repetition, suggestion, misinformation, and leading questions. Loftus coined the term *misinformation effect* to refer to the tendency of information received after an event has occurred to become integrated into an individual's memory. There is an extensive literature regarding the veracity of child testimony. See Chapter 2, this volume, for further discussion. For a much more thorough review of the research, the reader is referred to Kuehnle (2003) and Sparta (2003).

Not surprisingly, the accuracy of child testimony has been grappled with in the courts. The following case illustrates one such instance. In the case of *State v. Huss* (1993), the Supreme Court of Minnesota overturned a father's conviction for criminal sexual assault, stating that the child's sex abuse allegations against her father were improperly influenced by a highly suggestive book on sexual abuse.

THE CASE OF *STATE V. HUSS* (1993):
CHILD TESTIMONY AND SUGGESTIBILITY

Not long after divorcing her husband, Nancy Huss observed some behaviors in their 3-year-old daughter that would at least warrant some initial concern (i.e., increased rebellious and destructive behavior, trying to urinate standing up, using nicknames for body parts, and kissing on the lips). Ms. Huss also observed that her daughter came back from nonovernight visits wearing different clothes, and that the child's vaginal area was "bright red." No medical corroboration of abuse could be found, but Ms. Huss contacted a therapist. The therapist used play therapy, as well as several books on sex abuse. One book included a tape that referred to abuse events as "yucky secrets." From the library, Ms. Huss checked out the book and the companion tape, *Sometimes It's OK to Tell Secrets*, which she played for her daughter numerous times. After hearing the tape many times, the child told the mother that she had a "yucky secret," that her father, Robert Huss, had "put his fingers into her vagina and her butt" (p. 2). Ms. Huss told her daughter that she was proud of her, and that she had been very brave.

A week later, the child made a similar statement to the therapist, and several weeks later, the therapist reported this to the authorities. The father was arrested. At trial, the court summarized the child's testimony as follows:

> The child was on the stand for almost an hour before she made any accusation of abuse, and then she said both her mother and her father had touched her in a bad way. When she was asked repeatedly on direct examination whether she had any "yucky secrets," she answered in the negative....She also called a hug and a touch to her hair "bad touches." Although the child had not seen her father for approximately a year before trial, she testified that she had taken a shower at his house on the day she gave her testimony. The child was not able to identify [her father] in the courtroom. (p. 3)

Testifying for the defense were a family physician and two clinical psychologists. The physician testified that he had never seen any physical evidence of sexual abuse in his examinations of the child. The first psychologist testified that the child had made no disclosures of abuse to him. The second psychologist testified to the suggestive nature of the book and the tape, and to his belief that the therapist's notes revealed the use of "suggestive and repetitive techniques." He also testified that "the book might cause a child to make false statements about being abused" (p. 4) The use of the book indicates that the child may have "remembered" events that may have not occurred. Nevertheless, Mr. Huss was convicted, and the Minnesota Court of Appeals affirmed, basing their decision on the fact that the victim and other witnesses had testified that sexual abuse had occurred. However, this decision was appealed, and on October 1, 1993, the Minnesota Supreme Court reversed the decision, found the book in question "a highly suggestive book and...its repeated use by the child's mother and therapist, combined with the mother's belief that abuse had occurred, may have improperly influenced the child's report of events" (p. 3). Emphasizing that such use of this book was the key to its decision, the Court concluded: "In sum, the child's testimony was contradictory as to whether any abuse occurred at all, and was inconsistent with her prior statements and other verifiable facts. However, even given this contradictory testimony, we might not have been persuaded to reverse [the conviction] absent the repeated use of a highly suggestive book on sexual abuse" (p. 3).

CHILD ABUSE AND THE RIGHTS OF THE ACCUSED

As seen in *State v. Huss,* the frequent situation in cases of child abuse (and particularly so with child sexual abuse) is that the child and the perpetrator are the only two witnesses to the offense. All adult perpetrators who have been accused of such an offense have the right to confront their accuser in an adversarial setting. However, some of the protections are limited when the perpetrators are juveniles. For a more in-depth discussion of issues of juvenile law, refer to Chapter 19, this volume. Thus, any legal proceeding stemming from any allegations made by a child involves an adversarial proceeding in which the child is pitted against the alleged offender.

Defendants are all initially presumed innocent, and there are fundamental rights afforded to them. In child abuse cases, the primary defense concern is the defendant's right to confront his or her accuser. However, this right becomes complicated when the accuser is a minor.

THE RIGHT TO CONFRONT THE ACCUSER

The Sixth Amendment of the U.S. Constitution provides defendants with the right to confront their accusers in a court of law. Since the passing of the Bill of Rights in 1791, courts have dealt with defining the nature of the word *confront* in the passage. The general trend has been the staunch protection of a face-to-face meeting separated only by a table and the wall (if there is any) of the witness stand.

However, the age of multimedia has had an impact on this right. For instance, in *Edwards v. Logan* (1999) a Virginia judge upheld a ruling that had required a defendant to pay for his own transportation (in this case from New Mexico to Virginia) to physically confront his accuser, because he could otherwise testify via videoconference. However, that same year, in *U.S. v. Navarro* (1999), the 5th Circuit Appellate Court disallowed a sentencing hearing conducted via videoconferencing, because it would be too depersonalizing to the defendant. Many of the questions as to the impact that such proceedings may have on the trial process are empirical ones that could be borne out in social science research.

Rulings regarding some form of separation between a defendant and a child accuser have been mixed. In *Coy v. Iowa* (1988), the Supreme Court found that it violated the Sixth Amendment to allow a defendant to see the victim through a one-way screen (through which the victim could not see the defendant). Yet in *Maryland v. Craig* (1990), only 2 years later, the Supreme Court allowed the interrogation and cross-examination of the 6-year-old victim to take place over closed-circuit television. The Court held that this procedure was not in violation of the Sixth Amendment, since the State's interest in protecting children from emotional trauma overrides the defendant's Sixth Amendment right. Yet the trend toward protection of the child did not end there.

In *White v. Illinois* (1992), the Supreme Court extended the protection of the victim when it ruled that defendants charged with molesting children have no absolute right to confront their young accusers at trial. It was established that statements made by an alleged victim outside of court could be presented to a jury (previously regarded as inadmissible hearsay), even when the child is available to testify. Furthermore, different states may grant additional exceptions and allow limited hearsay evidence in order to shield child victims from harm. Many of the issues involved when a child reports abuse can further complicate legal proceedings. In the previous sections, we have seen that the right to confront an accuser, the custody of a child that has been abused, and the possible suggestibility of children can all have an impact on legal proceedings. However, other controversial issues in abuse merit closer examination.

"PREBIRTH ABUSE" AND OTHER CONTROVERSIAL ABUSE ISSUES

An interesting "abuse" issue concerns pregnant women when their behavior has been termed *prebirth abuse*. In July 1996, the South Carolina

Supreme Court upheld the prosecution in the 1992 case of Cornelia Whitner, who was sentenced to 8 years in prison for smoking crack cocaine while pregnant. Ms. Whitner served 19 months in prison before a lower court set her free by deciding that the State's child abuse laws did not apply to a fetus. However, the State Supreme Court reinstated the conviction. The 3 to 2 ruling was the first time a court at that level had approved such prosecutions. Top courts in Florida, Kentucky, Nevada, and Ohio have reached opposite conclusions in deciding similar cases.

Under the South Carolina ruling, pregnant women who use drugs can be punished by up to 10 years in prison on misdemeanor charges for abuse to a fetus. Illegally obtaining a third-trimester abortion would bring a penalty of 2 years in prison. The South Carolina Court said that a healthy, viable fetus could be considered a "child" or "person" under state law and should, as a result, be afforded legal protection.

The *child sexual abuse accommodation syndrome* (CSAAS), coined by Summit in 1983, is also a controversial issue (as cited in Meyer, 1995; Meyer & Weaver, 2006). It emphasizes that the victim's retraction of an accusation is evidence that the abuse actually occurred. In *State v. J.Q.* (1993), the New Jersey Supreme Court held that the CSAAS was a "nondiagnostic syndrome," and though it can help to explain traits often found in children who have been abused, it does not and cannot be used to establish child abuse. On August 29, 1996, the Kentucky Supreme Court reversed the conviction of a man found guilty of raping and sodomizing his 10-year-old niece, saying that a psychologist had been improperly allowed to attribute the child's recantation of her accusation to CSAAS. Some experimental evidence against CSAAS is provided by Bradley and Wood (1996), who examined the disclosure process in 234 sexual abuse cases validated by the child protective services in El Paso, Texas. Although this study's population is atypical (76% were Hispanic) and earlier studies provide some support for the CSAAS, this study found retraction in only 4% of the cases.

There have also been increasing reports of "Munchausen Syndrome by Proxy" (e.g., when a mother induces multiple hospitalizations in her child). It was first clearly conceptualized and named in 1977, by Meadow, a British pediatrician. In virtually all reports, usually single-case studies, the mother perpetrates the pattern. False reports of allergies, hematuria, and seizures are common, as are induced vomiting and/or diarrhea. Victims are of all ages, though age 4–5 appears to be the mode. On average, children are around age 3 when they first get sick, and not surprisingly, the mothers tend to be pathological liars. The pattern is often an overlay to actual or past illness, and there is evidence that the child victims may begin to participate in the deception as they get older. The mothers are preoccupied with medical terms and equipment, and may manifest Borderline Personality Disorder components. Often, they also initially present themselves as cooperative and then passively subvert or resist all interventions.

THE FUTURE OF CHILD ABUSE LAW

This chapter has illustrated some of the difficult legal and psychological elements in dealing with child abuse. A number of controversial debates arise in this subject, including the limits of the State to protect (*DeShaney v. Winnebago County*), the possibility of falsely recovered memories, the suggestible nature of children (*State v. Huss*), and "prebirth abuse" and other controversies.

It was shown in *DeShaney v. Winnebago County* that there are limits to the protection that the State has to provide to a child. The child who receives the most protection from the State is the one who is in the custody of the State. The child who may be at risk for abuse but is not in State custody could potentially fall through the cracks of our system in this way. State agencies are not responsible for children who fall through the cracks, and to make them financially responsible would tax their already tenuous ability to make do with available resources. This tragic dilemma should be addressed in the near future, for all children should be protected to the fullest extent possible, regardless of who has custody of them.

In *State v. Huss*, it was shown that a number of factors can cause a child to provide questionable testimony, such as suggestibility, misinformation, and leading questions. Indeed, the memory of all individuals is fallible, and children may be particularly prone to difficulty. The noted fallibility of memory, particularly in children, remains a difficult obstacle when a child accuses someone of abuse (Deffenbacker et al., 2004), and it is further complicated by the fact that a person accused has a right to confront his or her accuser in most cases. Having the accused in court could be an additional factor that causes the testimony of a child to waver, potentially rendering the testimony of the only witness invalid. All of these topics are controversial in some measure and merit considerable attention by both mental health and legal professionals.

CASE REFERENCES

Coy v. Iowa, 487 U.S. 1012 (1988).

De Shaney v. Winnebago County, 489 U.S. 189 (1989).

Edwards v. Logan, 38 F. Supp. 2d 463; 1999 U.S. Dist. LEXIS 3249 (1999).

Estelle v. Gamble, 429 U.S. 97; 97 S. Ct. 285 (1976).

Landeros v. Flood, 551 P.2d 389 (Calif. 1976).

Maryland v. Craig, 497 U.S. 836 (1990): on remand, *Craig v. Maryland*, 588 A.2d 328 (Md. 1991).

People v. Jackson, 95 Cal. Rptr. 919 (Calif. App. 1971).

State v. Huss, 506 N.W.2d 290 (1993).

State v. J.Q., 617 A.2d. 1196 (1993).

U.S. v. Navarro, 169 F.3d 228; 1999 U.S. App. LEXIS 3602 (1999).

White v. Illinois, 112 U.S. 736 (1992).

Youngberg v. Romeo, 457 U.S. 307; 1982 U.S. LEXIS 128 (1982).

CHAPTER 22

Child Custody

All parents, good and bad alike, are automatically afforded certain parental rights under the Fourteenth Amendment of the U.S. Constitution. Section 1 of the Fourteenth Amendment states in part, "nor shall any state deprive any person of life, liberty, or property, without due process of law." While the right to parent one's child is not directly expressed, such a right has been protected under the umbrella of "life, liberty," and initially even under "property." The most fundamental of parental rights is to maintain custody of one's child. Therefore, if the abilities of a living parent have been called into question, these rights must be terminated via due process, and a more appropriate placement for the child sought.

CUSTODY PROCEEDINGS

In child custody cases, courts try to answer the specific question: With whom should a child (or children) reside?[1] While the initiating event for such proceedings is frequently parental separation or divorce, such is not always the case. Alleged or substantiated abuse or neglect of a child by any person in the home may also precipitate custody proceedings. Custody cases may also ensue following the death of guardians, or the birth of a newborn whose parents are themselves juveniles, or when one or both parents may be incarcerated.

---

[1] Separate from but related to custody is the concept of visitation rights. Legal visitation rights spell out who has a legal right to visit with children, even though the children may not live with that person. Except where expressly noted, issues that apply to custody typically apply to visitation as well.

In most U.S. jurisdictions, termination of parental rights and subsequent placement decisions are now conducted as separate proceedings, each addressing the specific relevant issue. Currently, custody proceedings in the United States are fairly complex processes. Ideally, the abilities of each interested party have been assessed by mental health and child care professionals who testify to the court. The power to make the ultimate decision lies with the court. However, as with most areas of the law, this has not always been the process. As with most areas of juvenile law, legal precedent for current custody procedures is quite contemporary relative to the common law or constitutional foundations of most adult law.

LEGAL HISTORY OF CHILD CUSTODY

Recorded legal precedent for child custody dates back to Roman times, when ancient law dictated that only men could hold legal title to property. Under the doctrine of *parens potestas*, children were considered property; thus, they were "given" to the father in the case of a separation. Under this practice, no recognition was given to the needs of the children, however basic, and no consideration was given to the mother. This practice carried into English common law where it persisted long enough to transfer to early American law. However, even under the English system, this practice could be set aside when there was clear paternal misconduct or potential for harm to the child.

In the latter half of the 19th century, concern for the children's well-being in custody disputes grew. At the forefront of this movement was the increasing legal influence of the *parens patriae* (state as parent) doctrine. *Parens patriae*, grew from the acknowledgment that the government bore some responsibility to care for individuals who could not otherwise care for themselves. This included a responsibility to ensure that children were properly cared for following a change in custody. As such, judicial practices were gradually amended, and decisions began to favor considerations of the welfare of the children, over and above the property rights of any adults. Early on, however, the best welfare of the child was interpreted as the parent who could most likely maintain the child's material and sustenance needs. Thus, the system maintained an overwhelming favor toward fathers, then the primary financial providers. Thus was preserved the status quo, albeit under new rationale.

The paternal gender bias remained well through the first quarter of the 20th century. In the 1925 case of *Finlay v. Finlay*, the New York State

Supreme Court first officially articulated the view that custody decisions should reflect the "best interests of the child." Slowly but gradually, U.S. courts began to interpret this standard as incorporating interests beyond those of monetary support. As greater emphasis was placed on the emotional and developmental needs of children, a corresponding gender shift took place, favoring mothers as the best custodial choice. In *Tuter v. Tuter* (1938, as cited in Meyer, 1995), the Missouri State Court of Appeals articulated the "tender years doctrine," stating in a fit of eloquence:

> There is but a twilight zone between a mother's love and the atmosphere of heaven, and all things being equal, no child should be deprived of that maternal influence unless it be shown that there are special and extraordinary reasons for so doing.

This ruling effectively turned the prevailing sentiment that children should spend their "tender years" with mother into legal precedent. Throughout the remainder of the 20th century, fully 90% of all custody cases were decided in favor of the mother (Meyer, 1995).

CUSTODY AND THE NONTRADITIONAL FAMILY

So far, we have addressed custody decisions that are a choice between two biological parents. But might the label of "parent" be applied to someone other than the biological parents? What rules and standards apply in determining the best custody for a child who has been raised by another relative? What rights, if any, do the biological parents and the relatives respectively retain? The 1966 Iowa State Supreme Court case of *Painter v. Bannister* addresses some of these questions.

The Case of *Painter v. Bannister* (1966a, 1966b): Establishing the Concept of "Psychological Parent"

Harold W. Painter was born into an unstable California family in the mid-1930s. His parents divorced when he was only 2½ years old, whereupon he was placed in a foster home. This turned out to be a good placement for Harold. He continued into adulthood feeling as if his foster parents were his true family, despite maintaining contact with his biological parents. Curiously enough, similar sentiments would come to haunt him in the future.

Harold never developed strong academic interests, eventually flunking out of high school. While he was considered by those who knew him to be quite intelligent, even an attempt at trade school met with failure. When he was 17, Harold joined the Navy, another experience for which he did not develop much of a liking. He sought and received an honorable discharge and later completed requirements for a high school diploma. Continuing to live with his foster family, Harold went to college for 2½ years, eventually quitting in November 1955, for a job with a newspaper in Ephrata, Washington.

Harold soon grew weary of his job and moved on to work for a newspaper in Anchorage, Alaska, the following year. It was at this job that Harold met Jeanne Bannister. The two could not have come from more different backgrounds. Jeanne was a midwestern girl, born and raised in rural Iowa, near the town of Gilbert, 40 miles north of Des Moines. She went to Grinnell College, 2 short hours away from the safety of her parents' home. Her parents, Dwight and Margaret, were college educated. Her father working for Iowa State University while serving on the local school board and teaching Sunday school classes at the Gilbert Congregational Church. Each of Jeanne's three sisters held college degrees and were married to college graduates. The Gilberts were well respected in their community and lived in what was later described as a "well kept, roomy, and comfortable" home.

The two were married in April 1957, against the wishes of Jeanne's parents back in Iowa. While accounts varied, their marriage was described as being generally positive, with expected ups and downs. The couple gave birth to two children: first their son, Mark, and later a daughter. They lived on the West Coast and maintained ties back to Jeanne's parents in Iowa.

As a couple, the two had surmounted significant obstacles, but the marriage was not to last. The life of the family was forever tragically disrupted on December 6, 1962. While driving near the town of Pullman, Washington, Jeanne and her daughter were in a car accident. Neither survived.

Frivolous spending had left Harold without much of a financial cushion. Harold's employment history did not lend itself to supporting a child as a single father. His "liberal" attitudes had gotten him into trouble while employed at the University of Washington for supporting the American Civil Liberties Union (ACLU) in the school newspaper. His primary aspiration was to be a freelance writer and photographer. Though he had never demonstrated an ability to make a steady income through such means, he held on to his dream despite opportunities for stable jobs that would have provided more steady income for himself and his son.

Harold tried to procure various means of care for young Mark, who at the time was described as being poorly adjusted, showing instances of aggression toward smaller children and cruelty to animals, and having trouble distinguishing fact from fiction. Mark was unpopular with peers and seemed to have little concept of appropriate behavior and limits. After 7 months of unsuccessful attempts, Harold sought respite through Jeanne's parents. The Bannisters gladly went to California to pick up Mark, whereupon they took him back to their farm home in rural Iowa in the summer of 1963. Mark was 5 years old.

Back in California, Harold struggled to build a respectable life for himself and was gradually able to do so. Harold described his home near Berkeley as "very old and beat up and lovely." While the Court would later note the unkempt nature of the yard and the fact that the outside of the house was not painted, the house was indeed "inexpensively, but tastefully decorated." Harold remarried in November 1964. He maintained his practice of Zen Buddhism, while his new wife was Roman Catholic. She held an advanced degree in cinema design and was quite excited about Mark's return. By all accounts, the new Mrs. Painter would provide a positive influence on the household, and specifically on Mark.

Having made these preparations, Harold sent word to the Bannisters that he was ready for Mark, then 7 years old, to return. However, Jeanne's parents refused to let him come back and filed in an Iowa court for legal custody of their grandson.

During the first resulting trial, the Bannisters claimed that Harold was merely reneging on his initial agreement for Mark to stay with them permanently. They contended that Harold had effectively given Mark away. Harold hotly contested this assertion, claiming that he had always intended the stay to be temporary. In Harold's favor, the Court noted that Jeanne's will named Harold as her successor in Mark's care, unless he failed to provide for Mark. Furthermore, the Bannisters were already 60 years old. Ms. Bannister had written letters reporting difficulties they were having in caring for Mark, and the Court attributed these problems to their advanced age. In favor of the Bannisters, Court records indicated that Mark's behavior had improved "a great deal." In the 2 years he spent with his grandparents, he had managed to become generally popular with his classmates. Mark was now a well-disciplined and happy young boy, despite being prone to "more than normal anxiety."

The Bannisters also had a psychologist testify on their behalf. Dr.

Glen R. Hawks was head of the Department of Child Development at Iowa State University, where the Bannisters also worked. He had written many articles and a textbook on child development, and had served both as a White House consultant and consultant for the development of the Head Start program. In his testimony, Dr. Hawks was clear that he did not consider Harold Painter to be unfit as a father. He found "no evidence that psychiatric instability is involved" in Harold's choice of lifestyle. Despite describing Harold as a "romantic and somewhat of a dreamer," Dr. Hawks characterized the differences between Harold and the Bannisters as "divergent life patterns" that represented "alternative normal adaptations." However, the doctor placed significant weight on his opinion that Mark saw Mr. Bannister as a "father figure," psychologically trumping the importance of Harold's role as biological father. Dr. Hawks elaborated that removing Mark from the stable environment of the Bannister household would not be in Mark's best interests. Dr. Hawks stated, "I am appalled at the tremendous task Mr. Painter would have if Mark were to return to him because he has got to build the relationship from scratch." He further stated, "The chances are very high [Mark] will go wrong if he is returned to his father" (p. 5).

Harold's attorneys intimated that Dr. Hawks's and the Bannisters' mutual employment at the University was a dual relationship and potentially skewed the doctor's findings. They also criticized Dr. Hawks for not adequately assessing Harold or investigating his home. The original trial Court stated that it had given full consideration to the doctor's testimony but could not "accept it at full face value because of exaggerated statements and the witness' attitude on the stand" (p. 4). The initial judge did not give more specific descriptions. Despite the doctor's testimony and recommendation that Mark stay with the Bannisters, the initial trial judge awarded legal custody back to Harold. The Bannisters immediately appealed to the Iowa State Supreme Court, which ordered that Mark stay with the Bannisters through the appeal process.

While the State Supreme Court agreed that Mark's stay with the Bannisters was always intended to be temporary, it gave much more weight to Dr. Hawks's expert psychological testimony. The Court ruled that it could "find nothing in the written record to justify such a summary dismissal of the opinions of this eminent child psychologist" (p. 4). Dr. Hawks's conclusions are closely echoed in the State Supreme Court's predictions of Mark's future in each respective home. Mark's life with his father would provide him with "more freedom of conduct and thought with an opportunity to develop his individual talents. It would be more exciting and challenging in many respects, but romantic, impractical and unstable" (p. 2). The Court characterized Harold's lifestyle as financially irresponsible, "unconventional, arty, and Bohemian." In contrast, the Bannister home provided Mark with a "stable, conventional, middle-class, middlewestern background and an opportunity for a college education and profession, if he desires it. It provides a solid foundation and secure atmosphere" (p. 2). Despite this apparently biased review, the Court explicitly concurred that Harold's lifestyle was merely an alternative rather than a dysfunctional one. The Court even went so far as to state, "It is not our prerogative to determine custody upon our choice of two ways of life...and we will not do so" (p. 2). That being said, on February 8, 1966, the Iowa State Supreme Court arrived at the following conclusion:

> Mark has established a father–son relationship with Mr. Bannister, which he apparently had never had with his natural father. He is happy, well adjusted and progressing nicely in his development. We do not believe it is for Mark's best interest to take him out of this stable atmosphere in the face of warnings of dire consequences from an eminent child psychologist and send him to an uncertain future in his father's home. Regardless of our appreciation of the father's love for his child and his desire to have him with him, we do not believe we have the moral right to gamble with this child's future. He should be encouraged in every way possible to know his father. We are sure there are many ways in which Mr. Painter can enrich Mark's life. (p. 5)

Thus, Mark was to remain with the Bannisters. Evident in this decision is the heavy reliance on the expert testimony of Dr. Hawks despite little, if any, direct assessment of Harold Painter. Harold immediately set to preparing for an appeal to the U. S. Supreme Court. He obtained support on his behalf from the Methodist Church, the ACLU, and the Attorney General and Deputy Attorney General of the State of California. Despite his efforts, the U.S. Supreme Court declined to hear the case on November 14, 1966, without elaboration as to why, leaving the Iowa State Supreme Court ruling as the final word.

The Legacy of *Painter*

While the term was not directly expressed in the legal record, the Iowa State Supreme Court ruling in *Painter v. Bannister* established the concept of "psychological parent." The psychological parent is who a child "sees" as his or her parent, much as Harold Painter himself saw his foster parents. A child's psychological parent may not be the same as his or her biological parent. In the *Painter* case, the Court ruled that the psychological and biological parents were indeed different, and that it was in Mark's best interests to remain with his psychological parents. The Court in this case expressly stated that it did not base its decision on any type of moral comparison of lifestyles, but it is difficult to believe after reviewing the rulings that it was not influenced to some degree by such comparisons.

Of more contemporary relevance is the fact that the outcome of the case rested largely on the basis of psychological expert testimony provided without appropriate direct assessment of Mr. and Mrs. Painter and their household (Grisso & Vincent, 2005). We return to this issue later in the chapter.

FURTHER REFINEMENTS IN CHILD CUSTODY LAW

After the *Painter* decision, procedures for child custody considerations were further defined in 1971 by the Uniform Marriage and Divorce Act (UMD). While not officially adopted by Congress, the UMD has influenced several state statutes. The UMD suggests five factors that should be considered in custody decisions:

1. The wishes of the child's parent or parents.
2. The wishes of the child.
3. The interaction and interrelationship of the child with his or her parents, siblings, and any other person who may significantly affect the child's best interest.
4. The child's adjustment to his or her home, school, and community.
5. The mental and physical health of all individuals involved.

Despite the *Painter* ruling, this wording shows a slight bias toward the traditional (biological) definition of "parent." This bias also holds in the "reversion doctrine," which states that a child's custody will revert back to one (or both) of the biological parents, despite the fact that they may both be relatively poor custodians. While this may in any specific case be inconsistent with the "best interests of the child," it protects the constitutional rights of parents against being held to unreasonable standards.

PARENTAL RIGHTS AND THE LEGAL STANDARD OF PROOF

Prior to 1982, "preponderance of the evidence" was the legal standard by which all custody cases were decided in many jurisdictions. Legal precedent for this lies in civil law, in which one party merely has to prevail over the other by the slimmest of margins (51% for readers who are mathematically inclined). This was challenged that year in the case of *Santosky v. Kramer* on the grounds that a higher standard should be used when constitutional rights were at stake. While it would be difficult to apply a more stringent standard against opposing parties, as in a custody dispute (since the side with the best evidence should prevail), *Santosky v. Kramer* addressed the issue in terms of the initial termination of the parents' rights. It is to this case that we now turn.

The Case of *Santosky v. Kramer* (1982): Standard of Proof for Terminating Parental Rights

John and Annie Santosky were living in Ulster County, in southeastern New York State near Woodstock in the early 1970s. They had two children, Johnny and his older sister Tina. The family lived by meager means at best. A Family Court judge would later describe both John and Annie as being "unemployable" due to limited intelligence and emotional maturity (*In re Santosky*, 1977).

In November 1973, neighbors and local hospital staff reported to the Ulster County Department of Social Services (DSS) that the Santoskys' 2-year-old daughter Tina had suffered a broken left leg. The Santoskys had tried to treat the injury with a homemade splint. Reports also suggested that multiple other bruises and abrasions covering most of Tina's body were not accidental. The Commissioner of DSS (the Kramer referred to in the case name) initiated a neglect proceeding, and Tina was removed from the Santosky home. DSS briefly attempted to return Tina to the family, but she was again removed following continued reports of her mistreatment and concerns about John Santosky's physical abuse of his wife Annie. The following summer, hospital staff reported treating the Santoskys' infant son Johnny for malnutrition, blisters on his hands, multiple bruises and abrasions, and "multiple pin pricks on the back." Following another DSS proceeding, infant Johnny was placed in a foster home in September 1974. That same day, Annie gave birth to the couple's third child, Jed. While there was never any documented abuse of Jed, DSS decided that danger to his life or health was imminent. Three days after his birth, Jed was also removed from the Santosky home.

From the time Tina was initially removed, the Santoskys maintained contact with their children through the DSS. Over the following years, the couple gave birth to their fourth and fifth children, both boys. These youngest children continued to live at home. During a progress hearing in 1975, the Family Court judge criticized the DSS for not having an appropriately specified reunification plan for the children who had been removed. Such was required by state law. DSS developed a plan, and made diligent efforts to strengthen the relationship the Santoskys had with their three removed children. Through public assistance programs, DSS provided the Santoskys with various forms of parent and vocational training and counseling, costing the taxpayers over $15,000.

Despite John and Annie's continued contact with each of their removed children, and the presumably appropriate care of the two children who remained in the home, DSS sought termination of parental rights for the three oldest children in September 1976. The New York State statute governing such proceedings insisted that the judge take into account DSS efforts to rebuild the relationship between parents and children, as well as the parents' response to these efforts. Should the parents not respond to the best of their abilities, the children could be deemed "permanently neglected," and parental rights terminated.

To have rights terminated for permanent neglect, the State had to prove that the Santoskys had failed to "substantially plan for the future of their children." The legal standard of proof required was a mere "preponderance of the evidence." Thus, whichever side presented even a slightly better argument than the other would prevail. The DSS argued that the Santoskys' participation in the training and treatment that was provided to them was at best marginal. They had sporadically participated in some interventions, while completely disregarding other opportunities. The Santoskys' attorney countered that DSS had not seen fit to remove the youngest two children from the home. The judge ultimately found in favor of the Santoskys, ruling that while their response to the DSS efforts at reunification had been "nonresponsive, even hostile," the couple had been "at least superficially cooperative," suggesting the possibility of eventual change. This finding was affirmed on appeal to the New York State Supreme Court. For the time being, the Santoskys' rights were not terminated, but the children remained in the physical custody of the State.

By late 1978, Tina, Johnny, and Jed had spent the last 4 years in the custody of the State of New York, living in various foster homes and institutions. The DSS again petitioned for termination of parental rights in October of that year. The Santoskys' primary claim was that they had diligently maintained contact with each child. This time, the Family Court judge deemed the Santoskys' visits with their children "at best superficial and devoid of any real emotional content" (p. 6). The judge was now very disenchanted with the family's response to DSS efforts and found that the Santoskys were "incapable, even with public assistance, of planning for the future of their children" (p. 6). At the following dispositional hearing on April 10, 1979, John and Annie's parental rights were terminated in the best interests of their three oldest children, then ages 7, 5, and 4.

The Santoskys appealed to the New York Supreme Court, partly on the basis that the "preponderance of the evidence" standard required in the statute did not sufficiently protect their constitutional rights. On appeal, the State Supreme Court affirmed the termination, ruling that the "preponderance" standard was indeed "proper and constitutional." After over 4 years of court battles and intensive supervision by DSS, the Santoskys were now legally disconnected from any right to visit their children. DSS was now free to seek permanent placement and adoption for the children.

Since the case had been affirmed on appeal, it was considered closed in the eyes of the State of New York. However, the Santoskys appealed to the U.S. Supreme Court, again on the grounds that the "preponderance of the evidence" standard did not adequately protect their due process rights. The U.S. Supreme Court agreed to hear the case in November 1981. The Court was divided on whether it was even appropriate to comment on a Family Court case. Justice Rehnquist wrote, "This area has been left to the States from time immemorial, and not without good reason" (p. 16). Nevertheless, the U.S. Supreme Court's 5 to 4 opinion, written by Justice Blackmun, reversed the termination, stating that a requirement of at least "clear and convincing" evidence was necessary to protect the parents' constitutional rights.

Some of the logic that the U.S. Supreme Court applied in reaching the decision in this case is particularly relevant to child custody proceedings. It had already established that due process rights applied to parental right termination (*Lassiter v. Department of Social Services*, 1981), and that due process protection generally pitted the private interests against the State interests (*Mathews v. Eldridge*, 1976). But the New York Court's reliance on the "preponderance" standard only made sense if the rights of the parents were being pitted against the equal rights of the *children*. The Court reasoned that until rights were terminated, the parents' and children's interests were one and the same, thus favoring reunification. Furthermore, the Court ruled that even the State's "*parens patriae* interest favors preservation, not severance, of natural familial bonds," (p. 14) until the legal termination of parental rights. The Court elaborated, "Any *parens patriae* interest in *terminating* the natural parents' rights arises only at the dispositional phase, *after* the parents have been found unfit" (p. 14). Thus, in initial termination proceedings, all parties have an interest in keeping the family together, rendering a preponderance standard illogical.

Addressing the risk of an erroneous determination, the Court further referenced *Addington v. Texas* (1979; discussed in detail in Chapter 8, this volume) and ultimately concluded in the Santoskys' case that

> a standard of proof that allocates the risk of error nearly equally between an erroneous failure to terminate, which leaves the child in an uneasy status quo, and an erroneous termination, which unnecessarily destroys the natural family, does not reflect properly the relative severity of these two outcomes. (p. 3)

The decision terminating the Santoskys' parental rights was reversed, and the New York Court was ordered to reconsider the facts of the case under "at least" an intermediate standard of "clear and convincing evidence." It was expressly left as an option for States to apply a more stringent standard, such as "beyond a reasonable doubt."

The Santoskys returned to New York, where the State Supreme Court affirmed the termination under the more stringent standards (*In re John AA*, 1982). That Court also refused a new hearing, citing psychiatric testimony that one of the children had become "neurotic" due to Court delays, and at least one of the others was on the way to a similar problem. Thus ended the family's legal battle for Tina and Jed.

The last bit of legal record on the *Santosky* case speaks to how "legally permanent" termination may not always mean "psychologically permanent." In the summer of 1989, 15-year-old Johnny ran away from his adoptive parents, who had recently relinquished custody of Johnny back to the State of New York. By some means not detailed in the Court record, Johnny found his way back to his biological parents. John and Annie petitioned the State to reconsider Johnny's termination, but the termination was upheld by the State Supreme Court of New York on May 17, 1990.

The Legacy of *Santosky*

Following *Santosky*, there has been little change in precedent specifically for custodial rights. However, the related issue of visitation rights continues to evolve. More recently, the U.S. Supreme Court ruled in *Troxel v. Granville* (2000) that a Washington State statute allowing "any person" to seek visitation rights was unconstitutional. Even though, in this particular case, the "any person" was paternal grandparents, and even though the wording in the statute made clear reference to the "best interests of the child," the statute was deemed to violate the mother's Fourteenth Amendment right to parent her child. It is unclear how this case may impact upon custodial fathers, or even others (i.e., grandparents, adoptive parents) who have gained legal custody.

CUSTODY EVALUATIONS

Some reform is currently gathering steam in professional circles regarding the practice of custody evaluations by mental health professionals. There is currently wide disparity in the manner in which mental health professionals conduct assessments prior to offering an expert opinion to the court. For some professions, there are strict ethical mandates as to how a custody assessment must be conducted prior to offering an opinion. For instance, psychologists are required to be specially qualified (through special training or experience) to conduct custody assessments. Furthermore, psychological custody assessments should include contact with each child involved, and with each adult who is seeking custody. The rationale behind such strict restraint is awareness that to recommend removal of a child from the parent's custody is to recommend a deprivation of basic constitutional rights. Any such recommendation should only come after conducting as thorough an assessment as possible. Dr. Hawks, himself a psychologist, was accused of such an indiscretion in 1966, while testifying in the *Painter v. Bannister* case. At least by today's scientific and ethical standards, the decision in *Painter* may have been based largely on faulty expert testimony. However, despite current ethical constraints, even mental health practitioners working under psychology licensure do not always follow these procedures (Grisso & Vincent, 2005). In the face of pressure from attorneys, child protective services workers and even judges, clinicians still often fail to adequately assert their ethical limitations. Exacerbating this dilemma is the fact that some mental health professions do not yet have similar ethical restraints, leaving their practitioners with little guidance. A current movement is on in some states, where the respective psychology licensing boards are bringing charges of ethical misconduct against psychologists who offer an opinion after either a partial assessment or after no formal assessment at all (i.e., after serving as the child's therapist). This trend will most likely continue while the problem persists and may expand to other professions as they continue to develop their own sets of ethical standards.

FUTURE DIRECTIONS IN CHILD CUSTODY LAW

Scientific advances have provided their own impetus for legal reform in the area of child custody. In the mid-1960s, *Painter v. Bannister* (1966a, 1966b) brought us the concept of psychological parent. The 21st century brings us DNA as evidence in paternity and custody cases. Later, in Massachusetts, a man tried to absolve himself of child support responsibilities when a postdivorce DNA test showed that the little girl he thought was his daughter was actually not his biological child (Goodman, 2001). The State Supreme Court denied his request, stating in the decision, "No judgment can force him to continue to nurture his relationship with [her], or protect her from whatever assumptions she may have had about her father. But we can protect her financial security and other legal rights." The Court cited the fact that the girl "grew to know and to rely on him as her father," in effect stating that while he was not her biological parent, he was her "psychological parent." Other states have enacted laws trying to address this issue. In some states, financial responsibilities end after such evidence is found. South Dakota took this a step further and ruled that the mother must repay any child support already received. Still other states give men 2 years from the time of birth to request DNA testing and sever ties. No doubt, courts will be dealing with different variations on this theme and others for some time to come.

CASE REFERENCES

Addington v. Texas, 441 U.S. 418; 1979 U.S. LEXIS 93 (1979).
Finlay v. Finlay, 240 N.Y. 429; 148 N.E. 624 (1925).
In re John AA, 89 A.D.2d 738; 453 N.Y.S.2d 942 (1982).
In re Santosky, 89 Misc. 2d 730; 393 N.Y.S.2d 486 (1977).
Lassiter v. Department of Social Services, 452 U.S. 18 (1981).
Mathews v. Eldridge, 424 U.S. 319, 335 (1976).
Painter v. Bannister, 258 Iowa 1390; 140 N.W. 2d 152 (1966a).
Painter v. Bannister, 385 U.S. 949 (1966b).
Santosky v. Kramer, 455 U.S. 745 (1982).
Troxel v. Granville, 530 U.S. 57 (2000).
Tuter v. Tuter, 120 S.W.2d 203, 205 (Mo. App. 1938).

References

Abram, K. M., & Teplin, L. A. (1991). Co-occurring disorders among mentally ill jail detainees: Implications for public policy. *American Psychologist, 46,* 1036–1045.

Addington v. Texas, 441 U.S. 418; 1979 U.S. LEXIS 93 (1979).

Ake v. Oklahoma, 470 U.S. 68 (1985).

Albertsons v. Kirkingburg, 527 U.S. 555; 1999 U.S. LEXIS 4369 (1999).

Almonte v. New York Medical College, 851 F. Suppl. 34 (1994).

American Law Institute, *Model Penal Code 4.01* (Official Draft 1962).

American Psychiatric Association. (1968). *Diagnostic and statistical manual of mental disorders* (2nd ed.). Washington, DC: Author.

American Psychiatric Association. (1987). *Diagnostic and statistical manual of mental disorders* (3rd ed., rev.). Washington, DC: Author.

American Psychiatric Association. (1994). *Diagnostic and statistical manual of mental disorders* (4th ed.). Washington, DC: Author.

American Psychiatric Association. (2000). *Diagnostic and statistical manual of mental disorders* (4th ed., text rev.). Washington, DC: Author.

American Psychological Association. (1987). In the Supreme Court of the United States: *Lockhart v. McCree.* Amicus curiae brief for the American Psychological Association. *American Psychologist, 42,* 59–68.

American Psychological Association. (1990). *In the Supreme Court of the United States:* Hodgson v. Minnesota. *Amicus curiae brief for the American Psychological Association.* Washington, DC: Author.

American Psychological Association. (2004). *In the Supreme Court of the United States:* Roper v. Simmons. *Curiae brief for the American Psychological Association.* Washington, DC: Author.

Andrews, W. P., Meyer, R. G., & Berla, E. P. (1996). Development of the Lost Pleasure of Life Scale. *Law and Human Behavior, 20*(1), 99–111.

Arizona v. Fulminante, 499 U.S. 279; 1991 U.S. LEXIS 1854 (1991).

Atkins v. Commonwealth of Virginia, 260 Va. 375, 534 S.E.2d 312 (2000).

Atkins v. Virginia, 122 S. Ct. 2242; 2002 U.S. LEXIS 4648 (2002).

Austin v. Barker, 110 A.D. 510; 96 N.Y.S. 814; 1906 N.Y. App. Div. LEXIS 15 (1906).

Baehr v. Lewin, 852 P.2d 44 (1993).

Baker v. Wade, 774 F. 2d 1285 (1985).

Ballew v. Georgia, No. 76-761 (U.S. filed March 21, 1978).

Barber, T. X., & Glass, L. B. (1962). Significant factors in hypnotic behavior. *Journal of Abnormal and Social Psychology, 64*, 222–228.

Barefoot v. Estelle, 463 U.S. 880; 1983 U.S. LEXIS 110 (1983).

Bartol, C., & Bartol, A. (2004). *Forensic psychology*. Thousand Oaks, CA: Sage.

Batson v. Kentucky, No. 84-6263 (U. S. filed April 30, 1986).

Baxtrom v. Herold, 383 U.S. 107 (1966).

Beard v. Banks, 124 S. Ct. 2504; 2004 U.S. LEXIS 4572 (2004).

Bell v. Cone, No. 01-400, 122 S. Ct. 1843 (2002).

Bell v. Great Northern Railway Co., 12 S.W. 321 75 Tex. 50 (1890).

Bellah v. Greenson, 81 Cal. App. 3d 614; 1978 Cal. App. LEXIS 1607 (1978).

Berliner, L. (1998). The use of expert testimony in child sexual abuse cases. In S. J. Ceci & H. Hembrooke (Eds.), *Expert witnesses in child abuse cases: What can and should be said in court* (pp. 11–27). Washington, DC: American Psychological Association.

Bersoff, D., Glass, D., & Blain, N. (1994). Legal issues in the assessment and treatment of individuals with dual diagnoses. *Journal of Consulting and Clinical Psychology, 62*, 55–62.

BMW v. Gore, 517 U.S. 559 (1996).

Borawick v. Shay, 68 F.3d 597 (1995).

Bounds v. Smith, 430 U.S. 817; 97 S. Ct. 1491 (1977).

Bowers v. Hardwick, 478 U.S. 1039; 107 S. Ct. 29; 92 L. Ed. 2d 779; 1986 U.S. LEXIS 2828 (1986).

Boy Scouts of America v. Dale, 530 U.S. 640; 2000 U.S. LEXIS 4487 (2000).

Boyd, A., McLearen, A., Meyer, R., & Denney, J. (2006). *The assessment of deception*. Sarasota, FL: Professional Resource Press.

Bradley, A. R., & Wood, J. M. (1996). How do children tell?: The disclosure process in child sexual abuse. *Child Abuse and Neglect, 20*, 881–891.

Brady v. Hopper, 570 F. Supp. 1333; 1983 U.S. Dist. LEXIS 13755 (1983).

Branch v. Texas, 447 S.W. 2d 932; 1969 Tex. Crim. App. LEXIS 882 (1969).

Breed v. Jones, 421 U.S. 519 (1975).

Brown v. Board of Education, 347 U.S. 483 (1954).

Brown v. Board of Education II, 349 U.S. 294; 75 S. Ct. 753; 99 L. Ed. 1083; 1955 U.S. LEXIS 734 (1955).

Buchanan v. Kentucky, 483 U.S. 402 (1987).

Burch v. ACMHS, 840 F.2d 797; 1988 U.S. App LEXIS 3530 (1988).

Burch v. Louisiana, 441 U.S. 130 (1979).

Butler, B. M., & Moran, G. (2002). The role of death qualification in venirepersons' evaluations of aggravating and mitigating circumstances in capital trials. *Law and Human Behavior, 26*, 175–184.

Caces, M. F., & Stinson, F. S. (1991). Comparative alcohol-related mortality statistics in the United States by state, 1979–1985. *Alcohol Health and
Research World, 15*(2), 161–168.

Caesar v. Mountanos, 542 F.2d 1064; 1976 U.S. App. LEXIS 7171 (1976).

Calcedo-Barba, A. L., & Ordonez, A. C. (1994). Violence and paranoid schizophrenia. *International Journal of Law and Psychiatry, 17,* 253–263.

Campbell v. Sundquist, 926 S.W.2d 255 (1996).

Canterbury v. Spence, 464 F.2d 772 (D.C. Cir.), *cert. denied,* 409 U.S. 1064
(1972).

Ceci, S.J., Ross, D.F., & Toglia, M.P.,(1987). Suggestibility of children's memory:
Psycholegal implications [Electronic version]. *Journal of Experimental Psychology,* 116 38–49.

Cedar Rapids Community School District v. Garret F., 526 U.S. 66; 119 S. Ct.
992; 143 L. Ed. 2d 154; 1999 U.S. LEXIS 1709 (1999).

Chapman v. U.S., 500 U.S. 453 (1991).

Chen v. Superior Court, 54 Cal. App. 4th 168 (1997).

Christy Bros. Circus v. Turnage, 144 S.E. 680 38 Ga. App. 581 (1928).

Cleckley, H. (1982). *The mask of sanity* (6th ed.). St. Louis, MO: Mosby.

Coker v. Georgia, 433 U.S. 584 (1977).

Coleman v. Alabama, 399 U.S. 1; 1970 U.S. LEXIS 17 (1970).

Collins v. State, 52 Md. App. 186; 447 A.2d 1272; 1982 Md. App. LEXIS 317
(1981).

Colorado v. Connelly, 107 S. Ct. 115 (1986).

Commonwealth v. Hawkins, 534 Pa. 123; 626 A.2d 550; 1993 Pa. LEXIS 143
(1993).

Connecticut Department of Public Safety v. Doe, 538 U.S. 1; 123 S. Ct. 1160; 155
L. Ed. 2d 98; 2003 U.S. LEXIS 1951; 71 U.S.L.W. 4158 (2003).

Conroy, M. A. (2003). Evaluation of sexual predators. In A. M. Goldstein (Ed.),
Handbook of psychology: Forensic psychology (Vol. 11, pp. 463–484). New
York: Wiley.

Consolidated Rail Corp. v. Gottshall, 512 U.S. 532 (1994).

Cooke, D. J., & Michie, C. (2001). Refining the construct of psychopathy:
Towards a hierarchical model. *Psychological Assessment, 13*(2), 171–188.

Cooper Industries v. Leatherman Tool Group, 69 U.S.L.W. 4299 (2001).

Cooper v. Oklahoma, 517 U.S. 348; 1996 U.S. LEXIS 2649 (1996).

Cornell, D., Warren, J., Hawk, G., Stafford, E., Oram, G., & Pine, D. (1996). Psychopathy in instrumental and reactive violent offenders. *Journal of Consulting and Clinical Psychology, 64,* 783–790.

Cowan v. State, 112 S. Ct. 1371 (1994).

Cowan, C. L., Thompson, W. C., & Ellsworth, P. C. (1984). The effects of death
qualification on jurors' predisposition to convict and on the quality of
deliberation. *Law and Human Behavior, 8,* 53–79.

Coy v. Iowa, 487 U.S. 1012 (1988).

Crosby-Currie, C., & Reppucci, N.D. (1999). The missing child in child protection: The constitutional context of maltreatment from *Meyer* to *DeShaney*. *Law and Policy, 21*(2), 129–157.

Cutshall v. Sundquist, 529 U.S. 1053; 120 S. Ct. 1554; 146 L. Ed. 2d 460; 2000 U.S. LEXIS 2391 (2000).

Daubert v. Merrell Dow Pharmaceuticals, 113 S. Ct. 2786 (1993).

Daubert v. Merrell Dow Pharmaceuticals, Inc, 509 U.S. 579; 1993 U.S. LEXIS 4408 (1993).

Daw, J. (May 2002). A primer on privacy. *Monitor on Psychology, 33*.

Dean v. District of Columbia, 653 A. 2d 307 (1995).

Deffenbacker, K., Bornstein, B., Penrod, S., & McCorty, E. C. (2004). A meta-analytic review of the effects of high stress eyewitness memory. *Law and Human Behavior, 29*(1), 687–706.

DeLong v. DeLong, 1998 Mo. App. LEXIS 69 (1998).

De Shaney v. Winnebago County, 489 U.S. 189 (1989).

Dickerson v. U.S., 530 U.S. 428; 120 S. Ct. 2326; 147 L. Ed. 2d 405; 2000 U.S. LEXIS 4305 (2000).

DiClemente, C. C. (2003). *Addiction and change: How addictions develop and addicted people recover.* New York: Guilford Press.

Dillon v. Legg, 68 Cal. 2d 728 (1968).

Dinnerstein v. State, 486 F.2d 34; 1973 U.S. App. LEXIS 7497 (1973).

Donaldson v. O'Connor, 493 F.2d 507; 1974 U.S. App. LEXIS 8960 (1974).

Douglas, J., & Olshaker, M. (1995). *Mindhunter: Inside the FBI's Elite Serial Crime Unit.* New York: Scribner.

Drope v. Missouri, 420 U.S. 162 (1975).

Durham v. U.S., 214 F.2d 862 (D.C. Cir. 1954).

Durrant, R., & Thakker, J. (2003). *Substance use and abuse.* Thousand Oaks, CA: Sage.

Dusky v. U.S., 271 F.2d 385; 1959 U.S. App. LEXIS 3123 (1959).

Dusky v. U.S., 362 U.S. 402 (1960).

Dusky v. U.S., 295 F.2d 743; 1961 U.S. App. LEXIS 3290 (1961).

Easter v. District of Columbia, 124 U.S. App. D.C. 33; 361 F.2d 50 (1966).

Edens, J., Buffington-Vollon, J., Keilen, A., Roskamp, P., & Anthony, C. (2005). Predictions of future dangerousness in capital murder trials. *Law and Human Behavior, 29*(1), 55–86.

Edwards v. Logan, 38 F. Supp. 2d 463; 1999 U.S. Dist. LEXIS 3249 (1999).

Eisenberg, J. (2004). *Law, psychology, and death penalty legislation.* Sarasota, FL: Professional Resource Press.

Eisenmenger, M. (2002). Sexual orientation discrimination: Teachers as positive role models for tolerance. *Journal of Law and Education, 31*, 235–244.

Ekman, P. (1985). *Telling lies.* New York: Norton.

Ellsworth, P. C., Bukaty, R. M., Cowan, C. L., & Thompson, W. C. (1984). The death qualified jury and the defense of insanity. *Law and Human Behavior, 8*, 81–93.

Ellsworth, P. C., & Fitzgerald, R. (1984). Due process vs. crime control: Death qualifications and jury attitudes. *Law and Human Behavior, 8*, 31–51.

English, P., & Sales, B. (2005). *More than the law*. Washington DC: American Psychological Association.

Epperson, D. L., Kaul, J. D., & Hesselton, D. (1998, September). *Final report on the development of the MnSOST–R*. Paper presented at the Association for Treatment of Sexual Abusers, Vancouver, Canada.

Estelle v. Gamble, 429 U.S. 97; 97 S. Ct. 285 (1976).

Estelle v. Smith, 451 U.S. 454 (1981).

Evans v. Romer, 854 P.2d 1270; 1993 Colo. LEXIS 628 (1993).

Evans v. Romer, 882 P.2d 1335; 1994 Colo. LEXIS 779 (1994).

Ewing, C. P. (2003). Expert testimony: Law and practice. In A. M. Goldstein (Ed.), *Handbook of psychology: Forensic psychology* (pp. 55–66). New York: Wiley.

Faigman, D.L. (2003). The limits of the polygraph. *Issues in Science and Technology, 20*(1), 40–47.

Faretta v. California, 422 U.S. 806 (1975).

Farmer v. Brennan, 511 U.S. 825; 114 S. Ct. 1970 (1994).

Filkins, J. W., Smith, C. M., & Tindale, R. S. (1998). An evaluation of the biasing effects of death qualification: A meta–analytic/computer simulation approach. In R. Tindale & L. Heath (Eds.). *Theory and research on small groups: Social psychological applications to social issues* (Vol 4., pp. 153–157). New York: Plenum Press.

Finlay v. Finlay, 240 N.Y. 429; 148 N.E. 624 (1925).

Fisher, C. B., & Whiting, K. A. (1998). How valid are child sexual abuse validations. In S. J. Ceci & H. Hembrooke (Eds.), *Expert witnesses in child abuse cases: What can and should be said in court* (pp. 159–184). Washington, DC: American Psychological Association.

Ford v. Wainwright, 477 U.S. 399 (1986).

Forth, A. E., & Burke, H. C. (1998). Psychopathy in adolescence: Assessment, violence, and developmental precursors. In D. J. Cooke, A. E. Forth, & R. D. Hare (Eds.), *Psychopathy: Theory, research and implications for society* (pp. 205–229). Boston: Kluwer Academic.

Forth, A. E., Hart, S. D., & Hare, R. D. (1990). Assessment of psychopathy in male young offenders. *Psychological Assessment, 2*, 342–344.

Foster v. California, 394 U.S. 440; 1969 U.S. LEXIS 2050 (1969).

Foucha v. Louisiana, 504 U.S. 71; 1992 U.S. LEXIS 2703 (1992).

Frendak v. U.S., 408 A.2d 364; 1979 D.C. App. LEXIS 463 (1965).

Frye v. U.S., 295 F. 1013 (D.C. Cir. 1923).

Fulero, S. M. (2001, May). Recent cases focus on false confessions and expert testimony. *Monitor on Psychology, 32*, p. 20.

Fulmer, J. R. (2002). Dismissing the "immoral" teacher for conduct outside the workplace—do current laws protect the interests of both school authorities and teachers? *Journal of Law and Education, 31*, 271–289.

Funk v. Commonwealth, 379 S.E.2d 371 (Va. App. 1989).

Furman v. Georgia, 408 U.S. 238; 1972 U.S. LEXIS 169 (1972).

Gannett v. State v. Pennell, 571 A.2d 735; 1990 Del. LEXIS 98 (1990).

Garner v. Stone, 85 N.M. 716; 516 P.2d 687; 1973 N.M. LEXIS 1318 (1973).

Godinez v. Moran, 509 U.S. 389; 1993 U.S. LEXIS 4396 (1993).

Goodman, E. (2001, May 2). The "duped dads." *The Boston Globe*.

Goodman-Delahunty, J., Green, E., & Hsiao, W. (1998). Construing motive in videotape killings: The role of jurors' attitudes toward the death penalty. *Law and Human Behavior, 22*, 257–271.

Goss v. Lopez, 419 U.S. 565 (1975).

Grann, M., Langstrom, N, Tengstrom, A., & Kullgren, G. (1999). Psychopathy (PCL–R) predicts violent recidivism among criminal offenders with personality disorders in Sweden. *Law and Human Behavior, 23*, 205–217.

Greenberg, S. A. (2003). Personal injury examinations in torts for emotional distress. In A. Goldstein (Ed.), *Handbook of psychology: Forensic psychology* (pp. 233–257). New York: Wiley.

Greenberg, S., Meyer, R., & Shuman, D. (2005). Forensic psychiatric diagnosis unmasked. *Judicature, 88*(5), 210–215.

Gregg v. Georgia, 428 U.S. 153 (1976).

Griffin v. Coughlin, 88 N.Y.2d 674; 1996 N.Y. LEXIS 1522 (1996).

Griggs v. Duke Power, 401 U.S. 424 (1971).

Grisso, T. (2002). *Evaluating competencies: Forensic assessment and instruments* (2nd ed.). New York: Plenum Press.

Grisso, T., & Vincent, G. (2005). The empirical limits of forensic mental health. *Law and Human Behavior, 29*(1), 1–6.

Griswold v. Connecticut, 381 U.S. 479 (1965).

Grubin, D. (2002). The potential use of polygraphy in forensic psychiatry. *Criminal Behavior and Mental Health, 12*, S45–S53.

Halderman v. Pennhurst, 446 F. Supp. 1295; 1977 U.S. Dist. LEXIS 12200 (1977).

Hall, J. W. (1996). *Buzz cut*. New York: Dell.

Hall, G. C., & Hirschman, R. (1991). Toward a theory of sexual aggression: A quadrapartite model. *Journal of Consulting and Clinical Psychology, 59*, 662–669.

Hanson, R. K., & Thornton, D. (1999). *Static 99: Improving actuarial risk assessment for sex offenders* (User Report 99–02). Ottawa: Department of the Solicitor General of Canada.

Harding v. State, 5 Md. App. 230; 246 A.2d 302; 1968 Md. App. LEXIS 367 (1968/1969).

Hare, R. D. (1991). *The Hare Psychopathy Checklist—Revised*. Toronto: Multi–Health Systems.

Hare, R. D. (1993). *Without conscience: The disturbing world of the psychopaths among us*. New York: Guilford Press.

Hare, R. D. (1996a). Psychopathy: A clinical construct whose time has come. *Criminal Justice and Behavior, 23*, 25–54.

Hare, R. D. (1996b). Psychopathy and antisocial personality disorder: A case of diagnostic confusion. *Psychiatric Times, 13*, 39–40.

Hare, R. D. (2003). *The Hare Psychopathy Checklist—Revised* (2nd ed). Toronto: Multi–Health Systems.

Hare, R. D., Harpur, T. J., Hakstian, A. R., Forth, A. E., Hart, S. D., & Newman, J. P. (1990). The revised Psychopathy Checklist: Reliability and factor structure. *Psychological Assessment, 2,* 338–341.

Harmelin v. Michigan, 501 U.S. 957 (1991).

Harpur, T. J., Hakstian, A. R., & Hare, R. D. (1988). Factor structure of the Psychopathy Checklist. *Journal of Consulting and Clinical Psychology, 56*(5), 741–747.

Harris v. Forklift Systems, 114 S. Ct. 367 (1993).

Harris, G. T., Rice, M. E., & Cormier, C. A. (1991). Psychopathy and violent recidivism. *Law and Human Behavior, 14,* 625–637.

Hart, S. D., & Dempster, R. J. (1997). Impulsivity and psychopathy. In C. D. Webster & M. A. Jackson (Eds.), *Impulsivity: Theory, assessment, and treatment.* New York: Guilford Press.

Hart, S. D. & Hemphill, J. F. (2003). Forensic and clinical issues in the assessment of psychopathy. In A. M. Goldstein (Ed.), *Handbook of psychology: Forensic psychology* (pp. 87–107). New York: Wiley.

Hart, S. D., Kropp, P. R., & Hare, R. D. (1988). Performance of male psychopaths following conditional release from prison. *Journal of Consulting and Clinical Psychology, 56,* 227–232.

Harvard Law Review Association. (2002, May). *Harvard Law Review, 115,* 1838.

Hedlund v. Superior Court of Orange County, 34 Cal. 3d 695; 669 P.2d 41; 194 Cal. Rptr. 805; 1983 Cal. LEXIS 237 (1983).

Heilbrun, K., Marczyk, G., R., & DeMatteo, D. (2002). *Forensic mental health assessment.* New York: Oxford University Press.

Heller v. Doe, 113 S. Ct. 2637 (1993).

Hemphill, J. F., Hare, R. D., & Wong, S. (1998). Psychopathy and recidivism: A review. *Legal and Criminological Psychology, 3,* 139–170.

Herman, S. (2005). Improving decision making in forensic child sexual abuse violations. *Law and Human Behavior, 29*(1), 87–120.

Higgins v. McGrath, 98 F. Supp. 670 (D. Mo. 1951).

Hilgard, E. R., & Loftus, E. F. (1979). Effective interrogation of the eyewitness. *International Journal of Clinical Experimental Hypnosis, 27,* 342–357.

Holmes, R. M., & Holmes, S. T. (1996). *Profiling violent crimes: An investigative tool* (2nd ed). Thousand Oaks, CA: Sage.

Honda Motor Co. v. Oberg, 512 U.S. 415 (1994).

Honts, C., & Perry, M. (1992). Polygraph admissibility. *Law and Human Behavior, 16,* 357–379.

Horowitz, I. A., & Seguin, D. G. (1986). The effects of bifurcation and death qualification on assignment of penalty in capital crimes. *Journal of Applied Social Psychology, 16,* 165–185.

Illinois v. Knuckles, 165 Ill. 2d 125; 1995 Ill. LEXIS 80 (1995).

In re Gault, 387 U.S. 1 (1967).

In re John AA, 89 A.D.2d 738; 453 N.Y.S.2d 942 (1982).

In re Lifschutz, 2 Cal. 3d 415 P.2d 557; Cal. LEXIS 280 (1970).

In re M'Naughten, 8 Eng. Rep. 718 (1843).

In re Oakes, 8 Monthly Law Reporter (Mass. 1845).

In re Santosky, 89 Misc. 2d 730; 393 N.Y.S.2d 486 (1977).

In re Winship, 397 U.S. 358 (1970).

In re Zuniga, 714 F.2d 632; U.S. App. LEXIS 25231 (1983).

Ingram, S. (1998). Note: If the profile fits: Admitting criminal psychological profiles into evidence in criminal trials. *Washington University Journal of Urban and Contemporary Law, 54,* 239.

Insanity Defense Reform Act, 18 U.S.C. 17 (1988).

Jablonski v. United States, 712 F.2d 391; 1983 U.S. App. LEXIS 26766 (1983).

Jackson v. Georgia, 439 U.S. 1102, 409 U.S. 1102 (1972).

Jackson v. Indiana, 406 U.S. 715 (1972).

Jackson, R., Rogers, R., & Sewell, K. (2005). Forensic application of the Miller Forensic Assessment of Symptoms Test (MFAST). *Law and Human Behavior, 29*(3), 199–320.

Jacob, S., & Hartshorne, T. S. (1991). *Ethics and law for school psychologists.* Brandon VT: Clinical Psychology Publishing.

Jaffee v. Redmond, 518 U.S. 1; 1996 U.S. LEXIS 3879 (1996).

J.E.B. v. Alabama ex rel. T.B., 114 S. Ct. 1419 (1994).

Jenkins v. U.S., 307 F.2d 637 (1962).

John K. and Mary K. v. Board of Education for School District #65, Cook County, 504 N.E.2d 797 (Ill. App. 1987).

Jones v. Brooklyn Heights Railroad, 23 A.D. 141 48 N.Y.S. 914 (1897).

Jones v. U.S., 463 U.S. 354 (1983).

Jordan v. State, 124 Tenn. 81, 135 S.W. 327 (1911).

Kaimowitz v. State of Michigan, Civil Action No. 73-19434-AW (Cir. Ct. Wayne County, Mich. July 10, 1973) (1972), reprinted in A. Brooks. (1974). *Law, psychiatry and the mental health system.* New York: Little, Brown.

Kalichman, S. C. (1993). *Mandated reporting of suspected child abuse: Ethics, law, and policy.* Washington, DC: American Psychological Association.

Kansas v. Crane, 534 U.S. 407; 122 S. Ct. 867; 151 L. Ed. 2d 856; 2002 U.S. LEXIS 493; 70 U.S.L.W. 4117 (2002).

Kansas v. Hendricks, 521 U.S. 346; 1997 U.S. LEXIS 3999 (1997).

Kassin, S. (1997). The psychology of confession evidence. *American Psychologist, 52*(3), 221–223).

Katsh, M. E., & Rose, W. (2002). *Taking sides: Clashing views on legal issues* (10th ed.). Guilford, CT: McGraw–Hill.

Kelly v. South Carolina, 534 U.S. 246 (2002).

Kelson v. City of Springfield, 767 F.2d 65 (9th Cir. 1985).

Kempe, C., Silverman, F., Steele, B., Droegemueller, W., & Silver, H. (1962). The battered child syndrome. *Journal of American Medical Association, 181,* 17–24.

Kent v. U.S., 383 U.S. 541 (1966).

Kentucky v. Wasson, 842 S.W.2d 487; 1992 Ky. LEXIS 140 (1992).

Knecht v. Gilman, 488 F.2d 1136; 1973 U.S. App. LEXIS 6674 (1973).

Knight, S., & Meyer, R. (2006). Forensic hypnosis. In A. Goldstein (Ed.), *Advanced topics in forensic psychology*. New York: Wiley.

Kovera, M. B., & Borgida, E. (1998). Expert scientific testimony on child witnesses in the age of Daubert. In S. J. Ceci & H. Hembrooke (Eds.), *Expert witnesses in child abuse cases: What can and should be said in court* (pp. 11–27). Washington, DC: American Psychological Association.

Kovera, M. B., Dickinson, V. V., & Cutler, B. L. (2003). Voir dire and jury selection. In A. M. Goldstein (Ed.), *Handbook of psychology: Forensic psychology* (pp. 161–175). New York: Wiley.

Kremens v. Bartley, 431 U.S. 119 (1977).

Kressel, N. J., & Kressel, D. F. (2002). *Stack and sway: The new science of jury consulting*. Boulder, CO: Westview Press.

Kuehnle, K. (2003). Child sexual abuse evaluations. In A. M. Goldstein (Ed.), *Handbook of psychology: Forensic psychology*, (pp. 437–460). New York: Wiley.

Kumho Tire Co. v. Carmichael, 525 U.S. 959; 1999 U.S. LEXIS 6835 (1999).

Lake v. Cameron, 124 U.S. App. D.C. 264; 364 F.2d 657; 1966 U.S. App. LEXIS 6103 (1966).

Landeros v. Flood, 551 P.2d 389 (Calif. 1976).

Larry P. v. Riles, 343 F. Supp. 1306 (N.D. Cal. 1972) (preliminary injunction), aff'd, 502 F.2d 963 (9th Cir. 1974), other proceedings, 495 F. Supp. 926 (N.D. Cal. 1979).

Lassiter v. Department of Social Services, 452 U.S. 18 (1981).

Law and Human Behavior, 17(1). (1993). Special issue.

Lawrence v. Texas, 539 U.S. 558; 2003 U.S. LEXIS 5013 (2003).

Leedy v. Hartnett, 510 F. Supp. 1125; 1981 U.S. Dist. LEXIS 11444 (1981).

Levett, L. M., & Kovera, M. B. (2002). Psychologists battle over the general acceptance of eyewitness research, *Monitor on Psychology, 33*, 23.

Lewis v. Casey, 518 U.S. 343; 116 S. Ct. 2174 (1996).

Lewis v. Fletcher, 518 U.S. 343 (1996).

Link, B. C., & Stueve, A. (1994). Psychotic symptoms and the violent/illegal behavior of mental patients compared to community controls. In J. Monahan & H. J. Steadman (Eds.), *Violence and mental disorder: Developments in risk assessment* (pp. 137–160). Chicago: University of Chicago Press.

Lockhart v. McCree, 106 S. Ct. 1758 (1986).

Loftus, E.F. (1993). The reality of of repressed memories. *American Psychologist, 48*, 518–537.

Lyon, T. D., & Koehler, J. J. (1998). Where researchers fear to tread: Interpretive differences among testifying experts in child sexual abuse cases. In S. J. Ceci & H. Hembrooke (Eds.) *Expert witnesses in child abuse cases: What can and should be said in court* (pp. 249–263). Washington, DC: American Psychological Association.

Lyvers, M. (2000). "Loss of control" in alcoholism and drug addiction: A neuroscientific interpretation. *Experimental Clinical Psychpharmacology, 8*, 225–249.

Madduz, J. E., & Winstead, B. (2005). *Psychopathology*. Mahwah, NJ: Erlbaum.

Marquand, R. (1997). Do lie detectors lie?: Courts weigh the truth. *Christian Science Monitor, 89*(237).

Martinez v. California Court of Appeal, 531 U.S. 1054; 121 S. Ct. 661 (2000).

Maryland v. Craig, 497 U.S. 836 (1990); on remand, *Craig v. Maryland*, 588 A.2d 328 (Md. 1991).

Mathews v. Eldridge, 424 U.S. 319, 335 (1976).

McCarver v. North Carolina, 533 U.S. 975; 2001 U.S. LEXIS 5345 (2001).

McCullock v. H.B. Fuller Co., 61 F.3d 1038; 1995 U.S. App. LEXIS 20246 (1995).

McElhaney, J.E. (1987). *Trial notebook* (2nd ed.). Chicago: American Bar Association.

McIntosh v. Milano, 168 N.J. Super. 466; 1979 N.J. Super. LEXIS 798 (1979).

McKeiver v. Pennsylvania, 403 U.S. 528 (1971).

McKune v. Lile, 536 U.S. 24; 122 S. Ct. 2017; 153 L. Ed. 2d 47; 2002 U.S. LEXIS 4206; 70 U.S.L.W. 4502 (2002).

Medina v. California, 505 U.S. 437 (1992).

Meier v. Ross General Hospital, 69 Cal. 2d 420; Cal. LEXIS 251 (1968).

Meritor Savings Bank v. Vinson, 477 U.S. 57 (1986).

Merriken v. Cressman, 364 F. Supp. 913 (E.D. Pa. 1973).

Meyer, R. G. (1995). *Preparation for licensing and board certification examinations in psychology: The professional, legal, and ethical components* (2nd ed.). New York: Brunner/Mazel.

Meyer, R. (2006). *Case studies in abnormal behavior* (7th ed.). Boston: Allyn & Bacon.

Meyer, R., & Weaver, C. (2006). *The clinician's handbook* (5th ed.). Long Grove, IL: Waveland Press.

Mickens v. Taylor, 122 S. Ct. 1237 (2002).

Miller, H., Amenta, A., & Conroy, M. A. (2005). Sexually violent predator evaluations: Empirical evidence, strategies for professionals, and research directions. *Law and Human Behavior, 29*(1), 29–54.

Miller, N., & Chappel, J. N. (1991). The history of the disease concept. *Psychiatric Annals, 21*(4), 196–205.

Miller, R. D., & Stava, L. J. (1997). Hypnosis and dissimulation. In R. Rogers (Ed.), *Clinical assessment of malingering and deception* (2nd ed., pp. 282–300). New York: Guilford Press.

Miller, W. R., & Brown, S. A. (1997). Why pychologists should treat alcohol and drug problems. *American Psychologist, 52*(12), 1269–1279.

Miller-El v. Cockrell, 2003 U.S. LEXIS 1734; 537 U.S. 322 (2003).

Millon, T., Simonsen, E., & Birket–Smith, M. (1998). Historical conceptions of psychopathy in the United States and Europe. In T. Millon, E. Simonsen, M. Birket–Smith, & R. D. Davis (Eds.), *Psychopathy: Antisocial, criminal, and violent behavior* (pp. 3–31). New York: Guilford Press.

Mills v. Maryland, 486 U.S. 367 (1988).

Miranda v. Arizona, 384 U.S. 436 (1966).

Molien v. Kaiser Foundation Hospital, 27 Cal. 3d 916 (1980).

Molzof v. U.S., 911 F.2d 18 (7th Cir. 1991), ret'd, 112 S. Ct. 711 (1992).

Montana v. Egelhoff, 116 S. Ct., 64 L.W. 4500 (1996).

Moore, M. H., Petrie, C. V., & Braga, A. A. (2003). *The polygraph and lie detection*. Washington DC: National Academies Press.

Moran v. Warden, Nevada State Prison, 105 Nev. 1041; 810 P.2d 335; 1989 Nev. LEXIS 193 (1989).

Moran v. Whitley, 110 S. Ct. 207; 107 L. Ed. 2d 160; 1989 U.S. LEXIS 4580 (1989).

Morra v. State Board of Examiners of Psychologists, 212 Kan. 103; 1973 Kan. LEXIS 493 (1973).

Morris, N. (1986). *Insanity defense* (National Institute of Justice Crime File Study Guide). Washington, DC: U.S. Department of Justice, National Institute of Justice/Criminal Justice Reference Service.

Neil v. Biggers, 409 U.S. 188; 93 S. Ct. 375 (1972).

Neises, M. L., & Dillehay, R. C. (1987). Death qualification and conviction proneness: *Witt* and *Witherspoon* compared. *Behavioral Sciences and Law*, 5, 479–494.

Nelson v. Campbell, 541 U.S. 637; 2004 U.S. LEXIS 3680 (2004).

New Jersey v. Timmendequas, 161 N.J. 515; 1999 N.J. LEXIS 1007 (1999).

New Jersey v. Timmendequas, 168 N.J. 20; 2001 N.J. LEXIS 24 (2001).

New Jersey v. T.L.O., 469 U.S. 325 (1985).

Newcomb, M. D., Galaif, E. R., & Carmona, J. V. (2001). The drug crime nexus in a community sample of adults. *Psychology of Addictive Behaviors, 15*(3), 185–193.

Nichols v. Azteca Restaurant Enterprises Inc, 256 F.3d 864; 2001 U.S. App. LEXIS 15899 (2001).

Nietzel, M. T., McCarthy, D. M., & Kern, M. J. (1999). Juries: The current state of the empirical literature. In R. Roesch, S. D. Hart, & J. Ogloff (Eds.), *Psychology and law: The state of the discipline* (pp. 23–52). New York: Kluwer Academic/Plenum Press.

Novak, G., & Pelaez, M. (2004). *Child and adolescent development: A behavioral systems approach*. Thousand Oaks, CA: Sage.

O'Connor v. Donaldson, 422 U.S. 563 (1975).

Olmstead v. L.C., 527 U.S. 581; 119 S. Ct. 2176; 144 L. Ed. 2d 540; 1999 U.S. LEXIS 4368 (1999).

Olmstead v. L.C. by Zimring, 527 U.S. 581; 1999 U.S. LEXIS 4368 (1999).

Olmstead v. U.S., 227 U.S. 438 (1928).

Painter v. Bannister, 258 Iowa 1390; 140 N.W. 2d 152 (1966a).

Painter v. Bannister, 385 U.S. 949 (1966b).

Palsgraf v. Long Island Railroad, 248 N.Y. 339; 1928 LEXIS 1269 (1928).

Parham v. J. R. and J. L., 442 U.S. 584 (1979).

PASE v. Hannon, 506 F. Supp. 831 (N.D. Ill. 1980).

Pate v. Robinson, 383 U.S. 375 (1966).

Peel v. Attorney Registration and Disciplinary Commission, 496 U.S. 91; 110 S. Ct. 2281; 110 L. Ed. 2d 83; 1990 U.S. LEXIS 2909 (1990).

Pennell v. State of Delaware, 602 A.2d 48; 1991 Del. LEXIS 441 (1991).

Pennhurst v. Halderman, 451 U.S. 1; 1981 U.S. LEXIS 12 (1981).

Pennhurst v. Halderman, 465 U.S. 89; 1984 U.S. LEXIS 4 (1984).

Pennsylvania Association for Retarded Children v. Commonwealth of Pennsylvania, 334 F. Supp. 1257 (1971).

Pennsylvania v. Ritchie, 480 U.S. 39; 1987 U.S. LEXIS 558 (1987).

Penry v. Johnson, 2001 U.S. LEXIS 4309; 69 U.S.L.W. 4402 (2001).

Penry v. Lynaugh, 487 U.S. 164 (1988).

Penson v. State, 474 S.E.2d 104; 1996 Ga. App. LEXIS 796 (1996).

People v. Ebanks, 117 Cal. 652, 665 (1897).

People v. Genrich, 928 P.2d 799; 1996 Colo. App. LEXIS 160 (1996).

People v. Jackson, 95 Cal. Rptr. 919 (Calif. App. 1971).

People v. Leahy, 8 Cal. 4th 587; 1994 Cal. LEXIS 5373 (1994).

People v. LeGrand, Cal. App. Unpub. LEXIS 7994 (2002).

People v. Pierce, 40 Cal. Rptr. 2d 254 (1995).

People v. Shirley, 641 P.2d 775 (Calif. 1982).

Pesce v. J. Sterling Morton High School District 201, Cook County, Illinois, 830 F.2d 789 (7th Cir. 1987).

Pierce v. Society of Sisters, 268 U.S. 510 (1925).

Plessy v. Ferguson, 163 U.S. 537; 16 S. Ct. 1138; 41 L. Ed. 256; 1896 U.S. LEXIS 3390 (1896).

Porter, S., Fairweather, D., Drugge, J., Herve, H., Birt, A., & Boer, D. P. (2000). Profiles of psychopathy in incarcerated sexual offenders. *Criminal Justice and Behavior, 27*, 216–233.

Powell v. Texas, 492 U.S. 680 (1989).

Price Waterhouse v. Hopkins, 490 U.S. 228; 1989 U.S. LEXIS 2230 (1989).

Proffitt v. State, So. 2d 896; 1987 Fla. LEXIS 2049 (1987).

Quinsey, V. L., Rice, M. E., & Harris, G. T. (1995). Actuarial prediction of sexual recidivism. *Journal of Interpersonal Violence, 10*, 85–105.

R. v. Travers, 93 E.R. 793 (1726).

Ray, I. (1853). *A treatise on the medical jurisprudence of insanity* (3rd ed.). London: Brown Little.

Rennie v. Klein, 462 F. Supp. 1131; 1978 U.S. Dist. LEXIS 14441 (1978).

Reppucci, N. D., & Fried, C. S. (2000). Child abuse and the law. *University of Missouri at Kansas City Law Review, 69*.

Rice, M. E. (1997). Violent offender research and implications for the criminal justice system. *American Psychologist, 52*, 414–423.

Rice, M. E., & Harris, G. T. (1995). Psychopathy, schizophrenia, alcohol abuse, and violent recidivism. *International Journal of Law and Psychiatry, 18*, 333–342.

Rice, M. E., & Harris, G. T. (1997). Cross–validation and extension of the Violence Risk Appraisal Guide for child molesters and rapists. *Law and Human Behavior, 21,* 231–242.

Rice, M. E., Harris, G. T., & Cormier, C. A. (1992). An evaluation of a maximum security therapeutic community for psychopaths and other mentally disordered offenders. *Law and Human Behavior, 16,* 399–412.

Riggins v. Nevada, 112 S. Ct. 1810 (1992).

Riggins v. State, 107 Nev. 178; 808 P.2d 535; 1991 Nev. LEXIS 27 (1991).

Ring v. Arizona, 536 U.S. 584; 122 S. Ct. 2428; 153 L. Ed. 2d 556; 2002 U.S. LEXIS 4651 (2002).

Robinson v. California, 1962 U.S. LEXIS 850 (1962).

Rock v. Arkansas, 483 U.S. 44 (1987).

Rogers, E. (1992). On the alleged prosecution–proneness of death qualified jurors and juries. In P. Suedfeld & P. E. Tetlock (Eds.), *Psychology and social policy* (pp. 255–265). Washington, DC: Hemisphere.

Romeo v. Youngberg, 644 F.2d 147; 1980 U.S. App. LEXIS 11999 (1980).

Romeo v. Youngberg, 734 F.2d 7; 1984 U.S. App. LEXIS 23070 (1984).

Romer v. Evans, 517 U.S. 620; 1996 U.S. LEXIS 3245 (1996).

Roper v. Simmons, 538 U.S. 923; 123 S. Ct. 1582; 155 L. Ed. 2d 314; 2003 U.S. LEXIS 2213 (2003).

Roper v. Simmons, 125 S. Ct. 1183; 161 L. Ed. 2d 1; 2005 U.S LEXIS 2200 (2005).

Rouse v. Cameron, 373 F.2d 451 (D.C. Cir. 1966), later proceeding, 387 F.2d 241 (1967).

Roy v. Hartogs, 81 Misc. 2d 350; 1975 N.Y. Misc. LEXIS 2386 (1975).

Roy v. Hartogs, 85 Misc. 2d 891; 1976 N.Y. Misc. LEXIS 2080 (1976).

Sales, B., & Shuman, D. (2005). *Experts in court: Reconciling law, science, and professional knowledge.* Washington DC: American Psychological Association.

Salgo v. Leland Stanford Jr. Board of Trustees, 317 P.2d. 170 (1957).

San Antonio Independent School District v. Rodriguez, 411 U.S. 1 (1973).

Santosky v. Kramer, 455 U.S. 745 (1982).

Satterwhite v. Texas, 486 U.S. 249 (1988); but see *Perry v. Locke,* 488 U.S. 272 (1989).

Schabas, W. (1997). *The abolition of the death penalty in international law* (2nd ed.). New York: Cambridge University Press.

Schall v. Martin, 467 U.S. 253 (1984).

Schecter, H. (2003). *The serial killer files.* New York: Ballantine.

Schloendorf v. Society of New York Hospital, 211 N.Y. 125, 105 N.E. (N.Y. 1914).

Schriro v. Summerlin, 124 S. Ct. 2519; 2004 U.S. LEXIS 4574 (2004).

Sell vs. U.S., 539 U.S. 166; 123 S. Ct. 2174; 156 L. Ed. 2d 197; 2003 U.S. LEXIS 4594 (2003).

Serin, R. C. (1996). Violent recidivism in criminal psychopaths. *Law and Human Behavior, 20,* 207–217.

Serin, R. C., & Amos, N. L. (1995). The role of psychopathy in the assessment of dangerousness. *International Journal of Law and Psychiatry, 18*, 231–238.

Serin, R. C., Malcolm, P. B., Khanna, A., & Barbaree, H. E. (1994). Psychopathy and deviant sexual arousal in incarcerated sexual offenders. *Journal of Interpersonal Violence, 9*(1), 3–11.

Serin, R. C., Peters, R. D., & Barbaree, H. E. (1990). Predictors of psychopathy and release outcome in a criminal population. *Psychological Assessment, 2*, 419–422.

Shannon v. U.S., 114 S. Ct. (1994).

Shapiro, D. (1999). *Criminal responsibility evaluations: A manual for practice.* Sarasota, FL: Professional Resource Press.

Shor, R. E., & Orne, E. C. (1962). *Harvard Group Scale of Hypnotic Susceptibility.* Palo Alto, CA: Consulting Psychologists Press.

Simmons v. South Carolina, 512 U.S. 154 (1994).

Simmons v. U.S., 390 U.S. 377; 1968 U.S. LEXIS 2167 (1968).

Skinner v. Railway Labor Executives Association, 489 U.S. 602 (1989).

Slovenko, R. (2002). *Psychiatry in law/law in psychiatry.* New York: Brunner-Routlege.

Smith v. Doe, 538 U.S. 1009; 123 S. Ct. 1925; 155 L. Ed. 2d 844; 2003 U.S. LEXIS 3409 (2003).

Smith, S. R. (2002). The Supreme Court and psychologists: Trials amidst tribulation. *Bulletin of the American Academy of Forensic Psychology, 23*(1), 17–35.

Smith, S. R. (2003). The Supreme Court this term: Left, right . . . left, right, left. *Bulletin of the American Academy of Forensic Psychology, 24*, 1–21.

Smith, S. R., & Meyer, R. G. (1987). *Law, behavior, and mental health: Policy and practice.* New York: New York University Press.

Sparta, S. N. (2003). Assessment of childhood trauma. In A. M. Goldstein (Ed.), *Handbook of psychology: Forensic psychology* (pp. 209–231). New York: Wiley.

Spiegel, H., & Bridger, A. A. (1970). *Manual for hypnotic induction profile.* New York: Soni Medica.

Stanford v. Kentucky, 492 U.S. 937 (1989).

State v. Haynes, Ohio App. LEXIS 3811 (1988).

State v. Hurd, 432 A.2d 86 (N.J. 1981).

State v. Huss, 506 N.W.2d 290 (1993).

State v. J.Q., 617 A.2d. 1196 (1993).

State v. Mack, 292 N.W.2d 764 (Minn. 1980).

State v. O'Grady, 5 Ohio Dec. 654 (1896).

State v. Perry, 610 So. 2d 746, 1992 La. LEXIS 3170 (1992)

State v. Szemple, 135 N.J. 406; 1994 N.J. LEXIS 411 (1994).

State Farm Mutual Auto Insurance Co. v. Campbell, 123 S. Ct. 1513 (2003).

Steadman, H. J., Callahan, L. A., Robbins, P. C., & Morrissey, J. P. (1989). Maintenance of an insanity defense under Montana's "abolition" of the insanity defense. *American Journal of Psychiatry, 146*(3), 357–360.

Steadman, H. J., McGreevy, M. A. Morrissey, J. P., Callahan, L. A., Robbins, P. C., & Cirincione, C. (1993). *Before and after Hinckley: Evaluating insanity defense reform.* New York: Guilford Press.

Stogner v. California, 539 U.S. 607; 123 S. Ct. 2446; 156 L. Ed. 2d 544 (2003).

Stovall v. Denno, 388 U.S. 293; 1967 U.S. LEXIS 1087 (1967).

Strauder v. West Virginia, 100 U.S. 303; 1879 U.S. LEXIS 1830 (1880).

Strickland v. Washington, 466 U.S. 668, 694 (1984).

Substance Abuse and Mental Health Services Administration. (2002). *Substance abuse and mental health statistics.* Available from the U.S. Department of Health and Human Services SAMHSA website, www.drugabusestatistics. samhsa.gov/.

Sullivan, T., & Maiken, P. T. (1983). *Killer clown: The John Wayne Gacy murders.* New York: Winsor.

Sutton v. United Airlines, 1996 U.S. Dist. LEXIS 15106; 6 Am. Disabilities Cas. (BNA) 116 (1999).

Swain v. Alabama, 380 U.S. 202; 1965 U.S. LEXIS 1668 (1965).

Tarasoff v. the Regents of the University of California, 17 Cal. 3d 425; 551 P. 2d 334 (1976).

Taylor v. Illinois, 484 U.S. 400; 108 S. Ct. 646 (1988).

Templeton, E. (2000). Killing kids: The impact of *Domingues v. Nevada* on the juvenile death penalty as a violation of international law. *Boston College Law Review, 41,* 1175.

Tennard v. Dretke, 124 S. Ct. 2562; 2004 U.S. LEXIS 4575 (2004).

Thing v. Chusa, 48 Cal. 3d 644 (1989).

Thompson v. County of Alameda, 27 Cal. 3d 741; 1980 Cal. LEXIS 106 (1980).

Thompson v. National Railroad Passenger Corp., 44 U.S. 1035 (1980).

Thompson v. Oklahoma, 487 U.S. 815 (1988).

Thompson v. State, 1986 OK CR 130; 724 P.2d 780; 1986 Okla. Crim. App. LEXIS 318 (1986).

Thompson, W. C., Cowan, C. L., Ellsworth, P. C., & Harrington, J. C. (1984). Death penalty attitudes and conviction proneness: The translation of attitudes into verdicts. *Law and Human Behavior, 8,* 95–113.

Tomes, H. (2002, December). Recognizing Kenneth B. Clark's legacy. *Monitor on Psychology, 33,* 56.

Traynor v. Turnage, 485 U.S. 535 (1988).

Treasury Employees v. Von Raab, 489 U.S. 656 (1989).

Trop v. Dulles, 356 U.S. 86; 78 S. Ct. 590; 2 L. Ed. 2d 630; 1958 U.S. LEXIS 1284 (1957).

Trop v. Dulles, 356 U.S. 86, 101 (1958).

Troxel v. Granville, 530 U.S. 57 (2000).

Turvey, B. (2002). *Criminal profiling: An introduction to behavioral evidence analysis.* San Francisco: Academic Press.

Tuter v. Tuter, 120 S.W.2d 203, 205 (Mo. App. 1938).

TXO Products Corp. v. Alliance Resources, 509 U.S. 443 (1993).

University of Alabama v. Garrett, 531 U.S. 356 (2001).

University of Colorado v. Derdeyn,863 P.2d 929; 1993 Colo. LEXIS 887 (1993).

U.S. ex rel Edney v. Smith, 425 F. Supp. 1038 (E.D. N.Y. 1976).

U.S. v. Alvarez, 519 F.2d 1036 (3rd Cir. 1975).

U.S. v. Armstrong, 116 S. Ct. 1480, 64 L.W. 4305 (1996).

U.S. v. Brawner, 471 F.2d 969 (D.C. Cir. 1972).

U.S. v. Chandler, 393 F.2d 920; 1968 U.S. App. LEXIS 7445 (1968).

U.S. v. Currens, 290 F.2d 751; 1961 U.S. App. LEXIS 4649 (1961).

U.S. v. Galbreth, DC NM, Cr. No. 94–197 MV (1995).

U.S. v. Galbreth, 908 F. Supp. 877; 1995 U.S. Dist. LEXIS 20642 (1995).

U.S. v. Hall, 93 F.3d 1337, 1996 U.S. App. LEXIS 22173 (1996).

U.S. v. Navarro, 169 F.3d 228; 1999 U.S. App. LEXIS 3602 (1999).

U.S. v. Posado, 57 F.3d 428; 1995 U.S. App. LEXIS 15157 (1995).

U.S. v. Scheffer, 523 U.S. 303; 118 S. Ct. 1261; 140 L. Ed. 2d 413; 1998 U.S. LEXIS 2303 (1998).

U.S. v. Scholl, 528 U.S. 873; 1999 U.S. LEXIS 5825 (1999).

U.S. v. Sherlin, CA 6, No. 94–6111 (1995).

U.S. v. Sherlin, 67 F.3d 1208; 1995 U.S. App. LEXIS 29047 (1995).

U.S. v. Smith, 404 F.2d 720; 1968 U.S. App. LEXIS 4760 (1968).

U.S. v. Ursery, 518 U.S. 267; 116 S. Ct. 2135; 135 L. Ed. 2d 549; 1996 U.S. LEXIS 4256 (1996).

Vitek v. Jones, 445 U.S. 480; 1980 U.S. LEXIS 31 (1980).

Wade v. U.S., 426 F.2d 64; 1970 U.S. App. LEXIS 10089 (1970).

Wainwright v. Greenfield, 474 U.S. 284 (1986).

Wainwright v. Witt, 469 U.S. 412; 1985 U.S. LEXIS 43 (1985).

Wards Cove Packing Company, Inc. v. Atonio, 490 U.S. 642 (1989) (superseded by statute).

Washington v. Harper, 494 U.S. 210; 1990 U.S. LEXIS 1174 (1990).

Wechsler, D. (1997). *Wechsler Adult Intelligence Scale: Administration and scoring manual* (3rd ed.). New York: Psychological Corporation.

Wechsler, D. (2002). *Wechsler Preschool and Primary Scale of Intelligence: Administration and scoring manual* (3rd ed.). New York: Psychological Corporation.

Wechsler, D. (2003). *Wechsler Intelligence Scale for Children: Administration and scoring manual* (4th ed.). New York: Psychological Corporation.

Weisgram v. Marley, 528 U.S. 440; 2000 U.S. LEXIS 1011 (2000).

Weitzenhoffer, A. M., & Hilgard, E. R. (1959). *Stanford Hypnotic Susceptibility Scales, Forms A and B*. Palo Alto, CA: Consulting Psychologists Press.

Weitzenhoffer, A. M., & Hilgard, E. R. (1962). *Stanford Hypnotic Susceptibility Scale, Form C*. Palo Alto, CA: Consulting Psychologists Press.

Weitzenhoffer, A. M., & Hilgard, E. R. (1963). *The Stanford Profile Scales of Hypnotic Susceptibility: Forms I and II*. Palo Alto, CA: Consulting Psychologists Press.

Wells, G. L., & Loftus E. F. (2003). Eyewitness memory for people and events.

In A. M. Goldstein (Ed.), *Handbook of psychology: Forensic psychology* (pp. 149–160). New York: Wiley.

Whalem v. U.S., 120 U.S. App. D.C. 331; 346 F.2d 812; 1965 U.S. App. LEXIS 5807 (1965).

Wheeler v. U.S., 159 U.S. 526 (1895)

White v. Illinois, 112 U.S. 736 (1992).

Williams v. Florida, 399 U.S. 78; 90 S. Ct. 1893; 26 L. Ed. 2d 446; 1970 U.S. LEXIS 98 (1970).

Williamson, S. E., Hare, R. D., & Wong, S. (1987). Violence: Criminal psychopaths and their victims. *Canadian Journal of Behavioral Science, 19*, 454–462.

Wilson v. U.S., 391 F.2d 460 (D.C. Cir. 1968).

Witherspoon v. Illinois, 391 U.S. 510 (1968).

Witt v. Wainwright, 1983 U.S. App. LEXIS 26616 (1983).

Wolfson, A. (2003, November 26). Governor to spare Jefferson killer's life. *Louisville Courier Journal*, p. 1.

Woodson v. North Carolina, 428 U.S. 280 (1976).

Wyatt v. Stickney, 334 F. Supp. 1341 (M.D. Ala. 1971).

Young v. Slaughterford, 88 E.R. 1007 (1709).

Youngberg v. Romeo, 457 U.S. 307; 1982 U.S. LEXIS 128 (1982).

Youtsey v. U.S., 97 F.937 (6th Cir. 1899).

Zapf, P., & Roesch, R. (2005). An investigation of the construct of competence. *Law and Human Behavior, 29*(2), 229–252.

Zeisel, H., & Diamond, S. S. (1976). Jury selection in the Mitchell–Stans conspiracy trial. *American Bar Foundation Research Journal, 1*, 151–174.

Zinermon v. Burch, 494 U.S. 113 (1990).

Zipkin v. Freeman, 436 S.W.2d 753, 1968 Mo. LEXIS 739 (1968).

Zobrest v. Catalina Foothills School District, 113 S. Ct. 2462 (1993).

Index

Following a page number: "b" indicates a box; "f" indicates a figure; "n" indicates a note; "t" indicates a table.

Q

R